Interactive

PSYCHOLOGY

AN INTRODUCTORY WORKBOOK

Travis M. Heath • Michael Huxford

Kendall Hunt publishing company

Cover design by Lynn Allbright

Kendall Hunt
publishing company

www.kendallhunt.com
Send all inquiries to:
4050 Westmark Drive
Dubuque, IA 52004-1840

ISBN 978-0-7575-9001-6

Printed in the United States of America
10 9 8 7 6 5 4 3 2 1

CONTENTS

CHAPTER 1

DEFINING PSYCHOLOGY

A large part of understanding what psychology *is* is to seek an understanding of what it is *not*. It is similar with understanding illness. What is *abnormal* if not a departure from *normal*? To understand something we first have to set it apart from those things that it is not. Most of us do this without much effort or thought. After all, when most people, young or old, see a dog, they do not call it such by first saying, "that is *not* a cat"; however, this ability had to be developed.

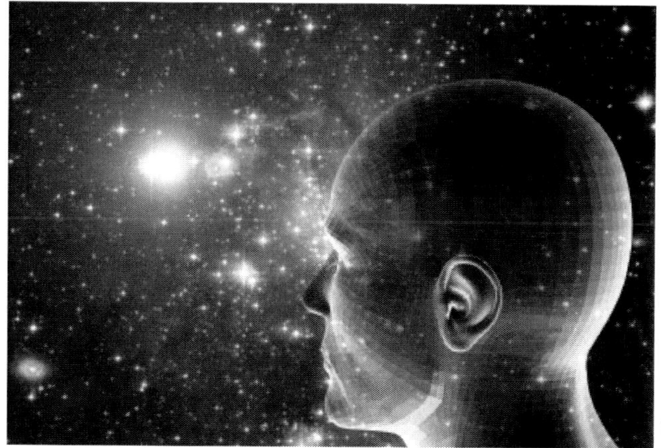

Before you start reading about psychology and using this book as a work guide, ask yourself some *should* questions:

1. What *should* psychology study?
2. Which areas of the human experience *should* be studied?
3. *Should* psychology study animal behavior and experience?
4. What methods *should* psychology use in its research?

Through your answers to these questions you will likely come upon your ideas of psychology *before* you took this class. As you progress in your study of psychology, reflect back on your answers to these questions.

ACTIVITY

Ask a family member, friend, or colleague a simple question, "In your mind, what is psychology?" Ask more people. Compare their responses. What do you notice about their answers? Are their answers similar to yours?

Psychology is the study of human behavior.
- The study of the human mind.
- Finding out why humans are the way they are.

© Fer Gregory, 2011. Used under license of Shutterstock, Inc.

PSYCHOLOGY AND PHILOSOPHY

The Greek philosopher Aristotle (384–322 BCE) thought deeply about ideas like dreaming, sensing the world, emotion, and memory. This was over 2000 years ago! Aristotle wrote extensively and debated with others about the nature of human experience and morality. Close to 1700 years later, René Descartes (1596–1650) introduced an idea that the mind and the body (brain) are separate and, in their interaction with each other, produce the sensations of the world, the dreams and the emotions that Aristotle devoted so much of his life thinking and writing about. Descartes' idea is called *dualism.*

© Panos Karapanagiotis, 2011. Used under license of Shutterstock, Inc.

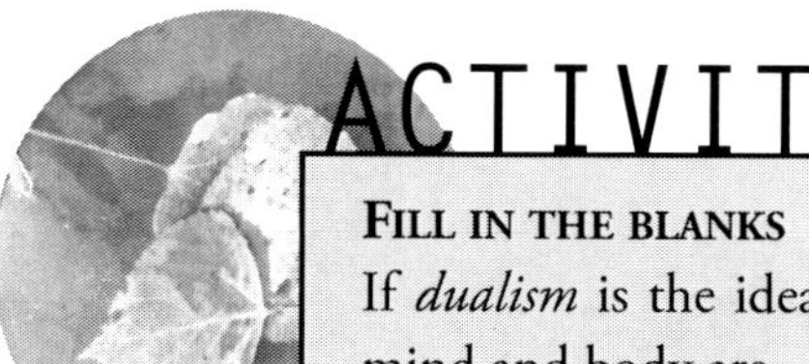

ACTIVITY

FILL IN THE BLANKS

If *dualism* is the idea that mind and body are *separate,* then ______________ is the idea that mind and body are ______________.

The heart is an organ that ______________.

The kidney is an ___________ that ______________.

The brain is an ___________ that ______________.

The mind is a/an ______________ that ______________.

Point to your mind. Is it possible to physically touch the mind? The brain is, of course, a fleshy organ that can be physically seen and studied. What exactly the mind is is another matter of debate spanning many centuries.

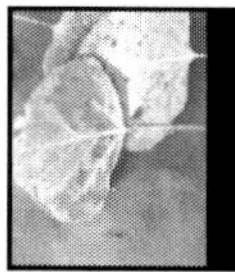

Should psychology devote its study more to the mind or more to the brain?

Philosophy and its philosophers laid much of the groundwork for many issues that psychology would later take on. The *nature–nurture* debate is one such issue. For centuries, philosophers deliberated about which is more important to the final product of the fully developed adult, the environment in which he or she developed, his or her childhood experiences and parent's involvement, or the inborn set of determined qualities?

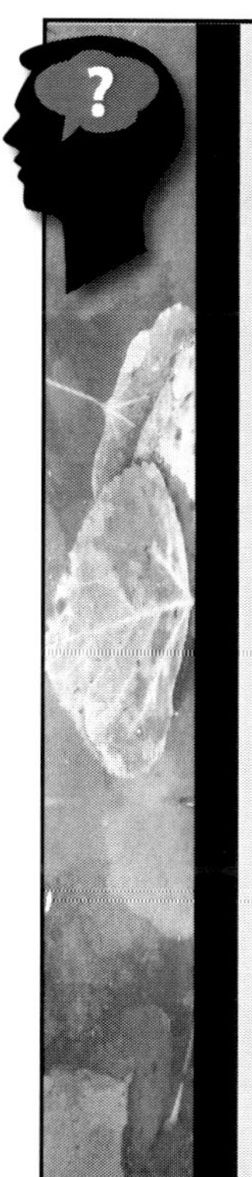

THINK ABOUT IT – Are you who you are today because of how your parents/caregivers taught you to be or because of your genetics and biological makeup?

© Monkey Business Images, 2011. Used under license of Shutterstock, Inc.

Think of a childhood activity you enjoyed doing with your parent. Did you enjoy this activity as a child because of your parent's *nurturance* or because you had a *natural* interest?

What activities do you enjoy as an adult that you think *could not* have been encouraged by your parents? (Because they came naturally to you?)

What activities do you enjoy now that you think *must have* been encouraged by your parents? (Would these activities likely be of no interest to you if they hadn't encouraged them?)

© Chepko Danil Vitalevich, 2011. Used under license of Shutterstock, Inc.

Likely the dilemma and conversation you've had around these questions mirror the debates of historical philosophy. Philosophy is limited to thought and logical processes in its efforts to understand the world. Around the time of Descartes, psychology emerged as a science. Standing on the shoulders of other sciences like biology and physiology, psychology began looking into the relationship that the brain had with behavior. What scientists in psychology discovered was that, in order to move beyond debate and to attempt to distinguish true from false, they had to employ different methods, the methods of science. These scientists became known as psychologists and they practice the scientific method.

ACTIVITY

René Descartes famously declared, *"Cogito Ergo Sum"* in what many say was his final conclusion for and only evidence of his own existence in the world. What is the translation of his famous pronouncement?

Curiosity is a sentiment all people have in some degree. To wonder about the nature of the world and about ourselves within such a world seems uniquely human. With this distinctiveness comes a motivating sense of speculation. This speculation gave birth to and continues to drive the scientific method. Philosophy, a field dedicated to thinking about thought and obtaining wisdom, is still alive and well today. However, from its relationship with science sprang the distinct field of psychology.

Arguably, psychology's emergency into the scientific world began in 1879 at the University of Leipzig, Germany. Two students and their professor, Wilhelm Wundt, were working to create an experimental device aimed at measuring the break in time between people's perception of a sound (a ball hitting a table) and their pressing of a button. Wundt and his students thought that the awareness of their thought about the ball's sound might take longer than actually hearing the noise itself. They were seeking the "atoms of the mind," or what they thought were the most basic of mental processes and the first psychology laboratory opened for operation.

Some Early Scientists in Psychology

- Wilhelm Wundt – father of psych
- Edward Titchener

- William James
- G. Stanley Hall
- John Watson
- Jean Piaget
- Carl Rogers
- Sigmund Freud
- Abraham Maslow

Even today psychology is the most infant of the recognized sciences. The pioneers in psychology were, of course, not psychologists in title as psychology was only slowly emerging in academic and scientific society. Wundt, though a philosopher, was also a physiologist. Charles Darwin, who proposed the theory of evolution and gave birth to evolutionary psychology, was a naturalist. Ivan Pavlov, who led the way for the study of how people learn and thus behave, was a Russian physiologist studying salivating patterns in dogs. Piaget, a Swiss biologist who got his start working with snails in Paris, pioneered a new scientific thought about the development of thinking in children. Freud, arguably the most recognized name in all of psychology was no psychologist at all but rather an Austrian physician curious about the motivations behind his patient's erratic behavior. Despite their training and work in a variety of different fields, history will likely remember these men all as psychologists.

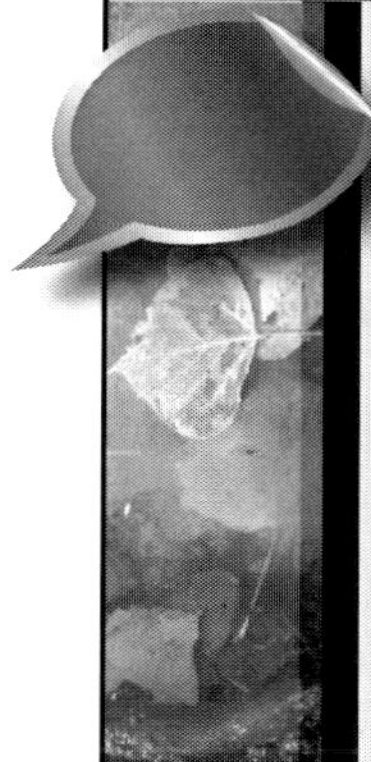

Discussion – Mary Calkins (1863–1930) completed all of the requirements for a Ph.D. in psychology at Harvard University, outscoring all the male students on exams. Harvard denied her the degree, offering her instead a degree from Radcliffe, a sister school for women only. Calkins refused and Margaret Floy Washburn at the age of 23 became the first woman to be awarded a Ph.D. in psychology (in 1894) from Cornell University, not Harvard. Calkins did, however, become the first woman president of the American Psychological Association.

What is the role of women in psychology today? How has it changed? Is the role of women in the field of psychology similar to their role in other fields? Different?

SCHOOLS OF THOUGHT IN PSYCHOLOGY

If your thought is that many issues that psychology investigates can be approached from many different angles and perspectives, then you are on the right track. Within psychological science lie different schools of thought. Each psychologist very likely has studied psychology, not from a fixed set of rules as one might find in a specific trade, but from a variety of theoretical approaches. Psychologists concentrate on problems from numerous different angles.

Psychodynamic

Sigmund Freud contributed a lot to modern psychology, in almost every school. However, he was no more influential in any field than in the realm of the psychodynamic. Also known as psychoanalytic, or the practice of psychoanalysis, this theory has its roots in the early days of psychology and attempts to conceptualize the role of unconscious influences on human behavior. In the mental health field, Freud and his students would often analyze patients' life stories as well as their dreams for a clue as to their behavior or problems. They would often find these clues in the patient's early life experiences and in the patterns of relationships throughout their lives, mainly their mothers. While these psychodynamic psychologists were concerned by the thoughts, emotions, and behaviors of people, their main focus was on the often-unconscious processes that motivated and informed these thoughts, feelings, and actions.

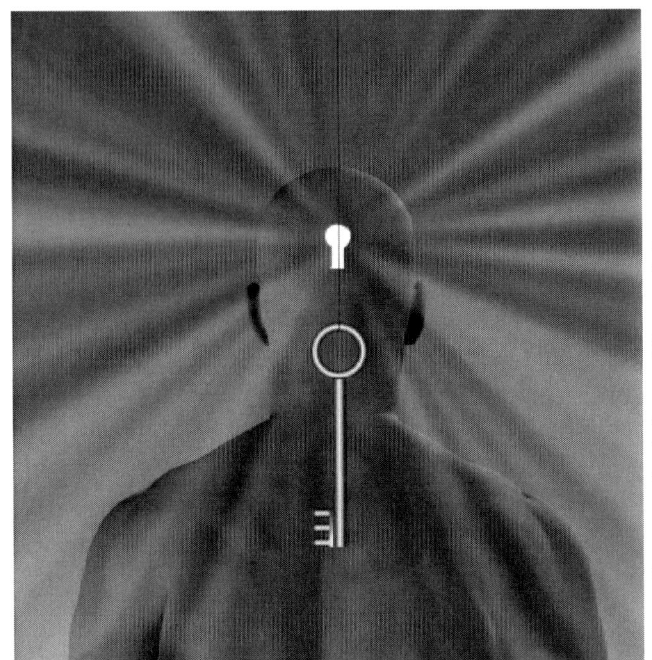

Behavioral

As a strong reaction to the subjective, difficult-to-research psychodynamic perspective, early behavioral psychologists insisted that psychology should focus primarily on the behaviors that we can see, observe, and actually record in a quantifiable manner. Behavioral psychologists focus their scientific lenses on theories of learning. They study how people and animals learn a variety of behaviors from a startle/fear response to a complex set of instructions. In the laboratory they conduct experiments to isolate the exact variables involved in the learning process of animals and try to make connections that will help animals and humans alike. In mental health or clinical work these behavioral psychologists concentrate on limiting or eliminating maladaptive behaviors.

Cognitive

As behavioral psychology reacted strongly against the subjective nature of the psychodynamic school of psychological thought, so did the cognitive psychologists react against the behavioral school's often-full denial of human mental processes. Where behavioral psychology looked only at the end product of a stimulus, the cognitive psychology movement emphasized the development of language and memory and the processes of problem solving. Using the newly invented computer as a model for human thought process, cognitive scientists began a transformation in psychology leading to models of sensation, perception, and intelligence still in use today. In research they look at the thresholds of sensing, memory, the development of thought, and intelligence. In mental health, cognitive psychologists have led the way in the development of developmental screening instruments for infants and children, measures of post-injury brain impairment, and diagnostic instruments for mental retardation and autism.

Biological/Evolutionary

At the core of the biological sciences is the idea that organisms change slowly and over time, a change that very often helps their species to survive. This perspective is called the evolutionary or the biological perspective. As you learned earlier, physiology and biology played a key role in the development of psychological science. Psychologists working from this perspective emphasize the role of physical processes when studying the behaviors and thoughts of humans and animals. They emphasize heavily the role of the brain as a physical organ, its structure, and relationship to the nervous system. The biological perspective has been key in understanding the impact of brain injuries (stroke, aneurysm, toxicity) on behavior as well as in the recent success in treatment of major mental illnesses like schizophrenia and depression. This approach places less emphasis on the social, behavioral, and emotional aspects of humans.

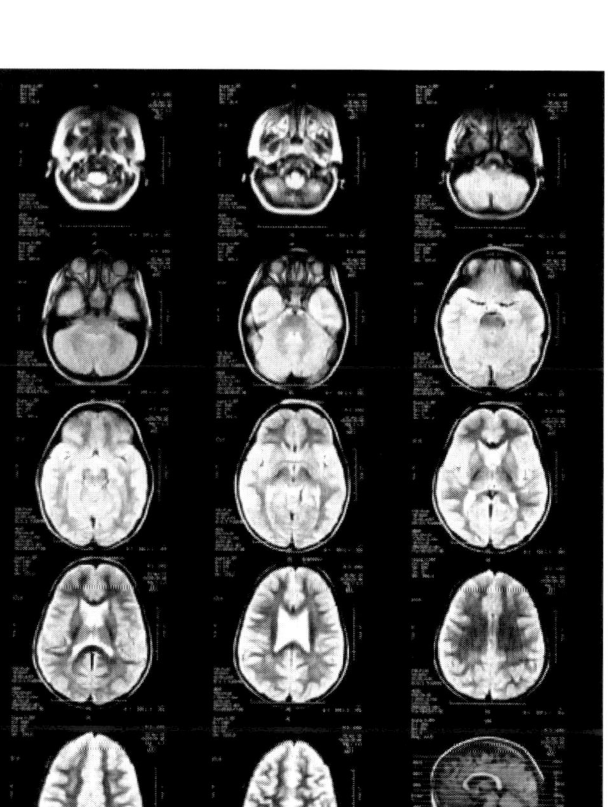

Humanistic

The humanistic perspective in psychology forwards the idea that people are motivated toward positive growth and seek out the best path toward this development. The groundwork for the humanistic perspective was mostly laid out by Carl Rogers and Abraham Maslow, and looks at the human as an ever-changing creature with basic and complex needs and at this human's life as a non-stop attempt to fulfill and maintain those needs. In mental health they look at the role of childhood abuse and neglect in the creation of personality and mental illness as well as ways to help people to realize their fullest potential. In research they attempt to understand what motivates people to think and behave in the ways they do.

© Jan Kremar, 2011. Used under license of Shutterstock. Inc.

Social and Cultural

Although all humans have very similar biological makeups (anatomy), needs (eat, drink, shelter), and characteristics of behavior (seeking happiness, formation of families), we all tend to do this in an assortment of often very different ways. *Culture* is a term that refers to the attitudes, values, and beliefs shared by groups of people and how they are passed down from one generation to the next (Matsumoto & Juang, 2008). Social psychologists look at this role that culture plays when assessing cognitive and behavioral phenomenon within different societies. Social psychologists study how the individual person relates to others within his or her social circles as well as with the larger social scene itself. In mental health and in research these psychologists look at the way people's thoughts, feelings, and behaviors are influenced by the actual, imagined, or implied presence of others.

© ARENA Creative, 2011. Used under license of Shutterstock, Inc.Inc.

ACTIVITY

Make a list of problems you think affect many people. This list may include issues like alcoholism, domestic violence, headaches, depression, gambling, or overeating. Now make a list how psychologists from the different schools described above would attempt an understanding of these issues (i.e., where they came from, how they developed, how they are maintained, how to cure).

ASKING QUESTIONS IN PSYCHOLOGY

Research Methods

Think back to a time when you were in a spirited disagreement with another person. Now, remember a time when the person you were in a disagreement with had statistics or a recent research study to bolster her argument and you did not. It can often stifle any further debate and leave you feeling defeated. After all, who can argue with statistics?

While studies backed by statistics as well as qualitative analysis are important tools at the disposal of psychologists and others conducting inquires about the world around us, it's important to understand these methods have limitations. The question isn't so much whether someone has research to support his position. Instead, the question is *how good* was the study? Moreover, the media or others in society can misrepresent even data from very well designed research studies to further a personal agenda.

It is not enough to simply have research to support an argument. After reading this section, it is hoped that you will be better able to evaluate the validity of research claims you are exposed to in the media and other areas of your everyday life instead of just passively accepting any formal study as absolute truth.

ACTIVITY

Before reading further in this section, write down some factors that you believe help distinguish a "good" study from one that is poorly done. We will come back and look at your answers after we have completed this section and see if they have changed.

Experimental Method

When you see the term "experimental method," there is one phrase you should recall immediately: *cause and effect.* In order for a researcher to establish that one variable *causes* a change in another, an experimental design must be used. This is the *only* method where a claim of causation can be made.

Four key components are needed in an experimental study. They include:

- *Independent Variable*: The variable in the experiment manipulated or controlled by the experimenter. In an experiment this is the factor that is supposed to cause the result.
- *Dependent Variable*: The variable in the experiment that is measured. In an experiment this is the factor that is going to be changed when something is added.
- *Experimental Group*: Group of people in the experiment who receive the active treatment.
- *Control Group*: Group of people in the experiment who do not receive the active treatment. Note: Members of this group can also receive what's called a placebo when appropriate. A placebo is a "fake" treatment, which often comes in the form of a sugar pill in drug research. Researchers use placebos because past research has shown that just the act of taking a pill, even without active ingredients, can make someone feel better (Price, Finniss, & Berndetti, 2008). In most forms of psychological research, it is difficult to use a true placebo.

In addition to the four key components listed above, there are also two other important considerations: sampling and random assignment. We will begin by discussing how we should go about selecting a *sample* for a research study.

Imagine if we wanted to have every student who attends the college take part in a study. Given the fact there are thousands of students on campus, it would be next to impossible for us to elicit the participation of each one. This means that we must select a *sample* from the entire population of college students. The way in which we go about selecting our sample is crucial.

One of our best options would involve trying to get a *representative sample.* Using this method, we would try to get a sample of students from the college that matches the entire college population across important demographic variables (e.g., age, gender, race, socioeconomic status). While this method of sampling sounds ideal, it is often difficult to achieve in real word practice.

If a representative sample cannot be achieved, we could opt for what is called a *random sample.* In this method, we choose a group of students from the college randomly as opposed to explicitly trying to match our sample to the population. Fortunately, when random sampling is done correctly, we often achieve a relatively representative and unbiased sample.

What we could not do is handpick participants that we suspect would confirm our hypothesis or already existing biases. Engaging in this sort of sample selection would be referred to as *sample bias.*

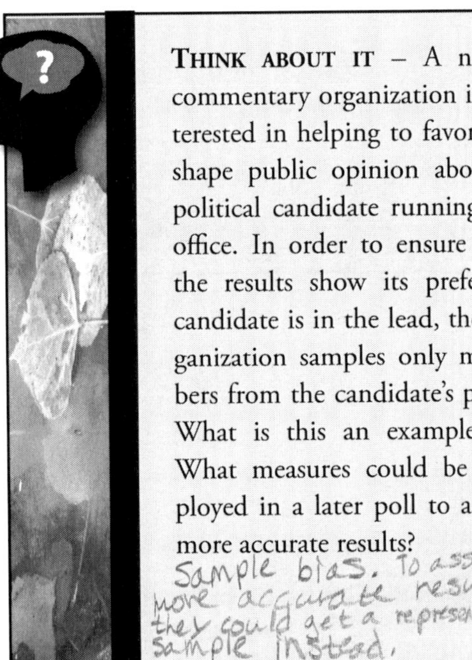

THINK ABOUT IT – A news/commentary organization is interested in helping to favorably shape public opinion about a political candidate running for office. In order to ensure that the results show its preferred candidate is in the lead, the organization samples only members from the candidate's party. What is this an example of? What measures could be employed in a later poll to assure more accurate results?

Sample bias. To assure more accurate results, they could get a representative sample instead.

Once we have selected a sample, we must now decide which participants are assigned to the *experimental group* (receives active treatment) and which are assigned to the *control group* (receives no treatment or placebo). To avoid potential bias, we must engage in a process called *random assignment.* What this means is that all of the participants selected for the study have an equal chance of being selected to the experimental or control groups. Random assignment can be accomplished by simply flipping a coin where heads means the person is assigned to the experimental group and tails results in assignment to the control group.

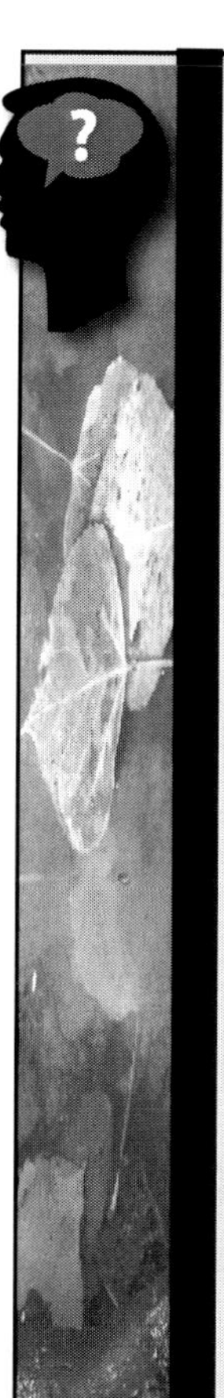

THINK ABOUT IT – To help ensure you understand the experimental method, consider the following example:

Dr. Johnson formulates a hypothesis that a specific violent videogame causes children to engage in acts of physical violence. He devises an experimental study to test his hypothesis. He begins by selecting a random sample of students from a local school for his experiment. He randomly assigns half of his participants to the experimental group where they will be exposed to the independent variable. In this study, the independent variable is the violent videogame. The other half of the participants are randomly assigned to the control group. Members of the control group are asked to play non-violent video games. Each group plays for 30 minutes. After they are done playing, children from both the experimental and control groups are exposed to a punching bag in the other room. The number of times the children hit the punching bag is recorded. The number of hits (acts of physical violence) is the dependent variable. When all of the participants have completed the study, Dr. Johnson compares the average number of hits in the experimental group to the control group.

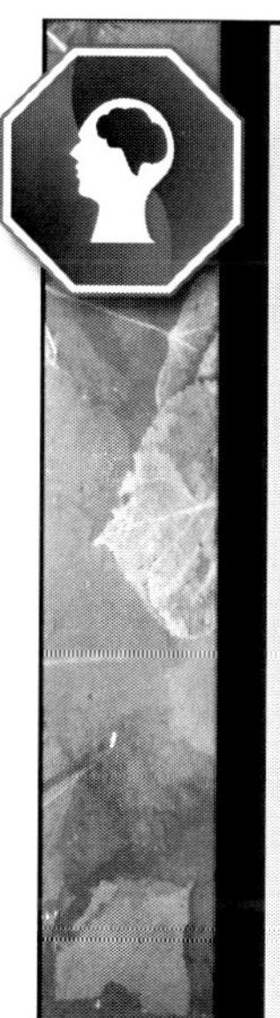

STOP AND THINK – Why is the violent videogame considered the independent variable in Dr. Johnson's study? Because violent videogames are the factors that are supposed to cause a result.

Why is the number of hits to the punching bag considered the dependent variable in Dr. Johnson's study? Because the number of hits to the punching bag is what is being measured in the experiment in order to record a change due to violent video games.

If there is no difference between the average number of hits to the punching bags by the children in the experimental group versus the children in the control group, what does this say about Dr. Johnson's hypothesis? His hypothesis is incorrect.

Since the experimental method is the only method that allows us to infer cause and effect, it is easy to wonder why we don't use the experimental method exclusively in our attempt to understand the world. In short, experimental research requires a large degree of control by the researcher. Many areas of study involving practical application of psychological principles do not lend themselves well to this kind of control.

For example, imagine that we were attempting to complete a true experimental study involving gender differences. Being good students of experimental design, we understand that we have to use random assignment. Okay, so we'll just randomly assign half of our participants to male and the other half to female. D'oh! We cannot randomly assign gender. Gender in this case would be referred to as a subject variable. Another example of a subject variable would be sexual orientation. These are variables that cannot be randomly assigned.

While experimental studies are a helpful tool in research, they are not the *only* tool. In fact, most applied psychological research is not experimental. In the space that follows, we will take a look a few other methods of inquiry often used in psychology.

Correlational Research

Correlational research is a way to understand the relationship between two variables. The researcher looks at two things that may or may not be related. If she wants to know how they are related, she can conduct this type of research. The clearest advantage of this type of research is that it allows us to better make predictions about one thing based on what we know about another.

Correlations can be either *positive* or *negative*. A positive relationship means that two or more variables move in the same direction. For example, as one variable increases, so does the other. Or, as one variable decreases, so does the other. A negative correlation means that two variables move in opposite directions. So as one variable increases, the other decreases.

Be careful! Just because two variables are related to each other does not necessarily mean that one causes the other. To demonstrate that one thing causes another we need to do an experiment. Correlational research is not an experiment.

ACTIVITY

Fill in the Blanks

Many of us use common-sense correlations all the time. Try the following:

The more hours I study for a test, the __higher__ my grade will be. (p)

The more alcoholic beverages Bob consumes, the __less__ able he will be to walk a straight line. (n)

The more education people have, the __more__ money they will likely make. (p)

Which of these are *negative* correlations and which are *positive*? How might the terms *negative* and *positive* be misleading to someone who hasn't studied this material?

Notice your responses don't likely imply that one *causes* the other. But, you may suspect that they do indeed have a causal relationship. Remember, correlation does not imply causation. How would you go about demonstrating that one of the examples above has a causal relationship?

Part of the reason that we do not assume that a relationship between two variables (a correlation) is a causal one is because other variables, variables we might not have thought of, are working to influence the relationship. For example, let's say that we want to test the basketball skills of everyone in class. I divide the class into two groups, one group is boys, the other group is girls. I have them play 10 games of basketball. The boys win all 10 games. I therefore conclude that boys have perfect basketball skills (a perfect ten!) and girls have no such skills at basketball (a goose egg zero!). What are the limitations of my conclusion? What might I do better in my next study? If you concluded that other variables, like strength and height, are at play rather than gender, you're on the right track.

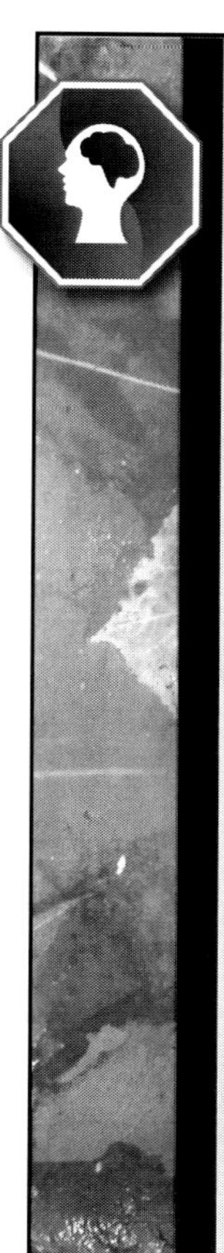

STOP AND THINK – Correlation Does Not Imply Causation

Give the following examples some thought:

The higher the rate of violent crime in Chicago, the higher the sales of ice cream cones.

The lower the sales of coffee, the higher the sales of swimsuits.

Would you conclude that that ice cream cone sales *cause* high crime rates or that by selling more coffee a company could decrease the sales of swimsuits at another?

No, there are other factors involved.

Try this one: A clock tower, every day at exactly noon, chimes just as another clock on the other side of town strikes noon. There is a perfect correlation but does the clock on one side of town *cause* the clock on the other side to chime? What evidence would a child need to be convinced that one does not *cause* the other?

They don't cause each other to chime. They chime at the same time because both chime at noon.

Or this one: Over the same period of time that the occurrences of smallpox disease diminished, there has been an increase in global warming. Therefore, global warming is caused by a lack of smallpox. False.

These seem like silly conclusions. But don't be too quick to judge. Many of us see causal relationships where there is merely a correlation. Many people believe that there is a causal relationship between a full moon and emergency department visits, prayer and healing, relaxation and fertility, pushing a button many times and the speed of an elevator, or childhood vaccines and autism. How many times have we uttered a phrase like, "the *only* time I forget a pencil is the day of the test" or "the *only* time I am late for work is the day my boss is early"?

What other variables might be at play in these examples? How would we go about figuring out if there was *actually* a causal relationship in any of them? What examples can you think of?

Descriptive Research

Descriptive research is used to observe and describe behavior. Psychologists using descriptive research methods are using methods like *naturalistic observation, case study research,* and *surveys.* These scientists study humans and animals and usually try to remain undetected. Studying humans and animals while remaining unidentified as a researcher allows psychologists to see behavior patterns that aren't likely to be apparent in a laboratory or experimental condition.

There are many advantages to descriptive research. One main advantage concerns *ethics.* Being ethical, or seeking to minimize any harm that could come to the people or animals involved, is a cornerstone of any scientific endeavor. Scientists often run into an ethical roadblock when they want to study the effects of negative or unethical behavior. For example, say that a psychologist wants to study aggressive behavior in children who were exposed to cocaine in utero. It would be unethical for the psychologist to expose unborn children to cocaine (to say nothing of their mothers!) and then study their behavior. But, it would be ethical to study children who had already been exposed. This method is called *naturalistic observation.*

Naturalistic observation can be used in any environment where patterns of behavior are in view. Chances are you have enjoyed an anonymous view of geese in a park, people in a mall, or children on a playground. What could you measure in each if you were a psychologist doing a study?

Another example of descriptive research is the *case study.* A case study is an in-depth look at a person or group of people. For example, say a psychologist wants to understand the effects that come from childhood sexual abuse or from the effects of nearby bomb explosions on the memories of women. They could not ethically set up an experiment to study such things, but they could do an in-depth study of those who have already experienced these terrible experiences.

Surveys are another popular way for scientists to study aspects of humans. A *survey* is a questionnaire or interview designed to look at the attitudes, behaviors, or opinions of people. Most of the time surveys include questions that are specifically designed to avoid bias and obtain the most accurate information possible. Most of the time these tests are pencil and paper and are mailed out to participants. This way, the researcher can gain a wide range of people in a variety of settings. Sometimes these surveys are administered in live interviews. Each approach has its advantages and disadvantages. For instance, a live interview may help the researcher to make the participant feel more comfortable and thus give more honest information, yet a mail survey could reach many more people in the same amount of time.

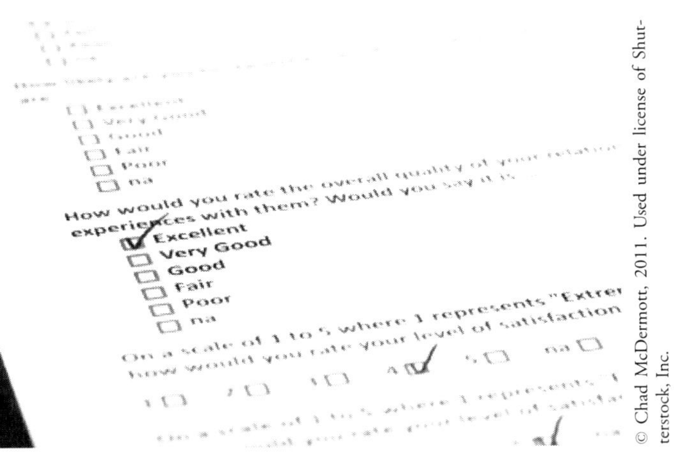

Bias is a problem that has plagued researchers since research itself began. It is especially poignant in survey research. The way a question is asked or phrased can encourage one participant while pushing another toward silence. The wording of questions can be confusing or offensive to participants and yield a less-than-honest answer, or the setting in which the questions are asked can yield different levels of comfort and thus different answers.

Consider the following examples: Say a researcher wants to understand the sexual behavior of high school students in order to design programs to decrease teen pregnancy. He creates a survey to be taken in a crowded classroom with only a few questions asking very specific questions about sexual history. It is likely that students will be less honest than if their confidentiality was guaranteed.

In another example, the wording of the question can bias the results: Say a researcher wants to understand people's opinions on two political candidates. She asks a question, *"Are you for the Republican candidate or are you for the candidate who favors the inclusion of socialist and communist ideas into our American democracy?"* How might this question yield inaccurate data?

Ask yourself – Think of one behavior of humans that has always fascinated you. Your thought might be something like, "I love going to professional sporting events. People tend to do __________________ and it is so interesting" or "the best time to watch people walking on campus is ________________." How would you go about studying this behavior? Would you prefer to do a case study or observe these people in a more naturalistic way? How would you design a survey to help you in this study?

Qualitative Research

All of the approaches to research we have discussed so far are quantitative approaches, in other words, approaches that take the experiences of people and try to understand them through statistics and numerical comparisons. Another approach to research that is being used more and more frequently in psychology is qualitative research. *Qualitative research* attempts to understand the complexity of human beings and/or human interactions without reducing these observations to numbers. Qualitative researchers often believe the essence of human experience is lost when one attempts to convert observations into numbers.

ACTIVITY

Fill in the Blanks

Quantitative research attempts to understand the world by turning experience into _______________.

Qualitative research attempts to understand the _______________ of human experiences and avoids turning these experiences into _______________.

Quantitative researchers strive to be objective or free from bias. Qualitative researchers, on the other hand, often believe that true objectivity is impossible to achieve. As such, they usually identify their own biases and openly acknowledge these biases throughout the research process. In addition, qualitative researchers often form more extensive and cooperative relationships with participants than quantitative researchers with the belief that the more the researcher understands the subjective experiences of the participants, the more the researcher will learn about the phenomena being studied.

Stop and think – Can a researcher simply put his or her biases and previous personal experience to the side and conduct a study that is 100 percent objective or free from bias? Defend your position.

Some of the specific methods used in qualitative research are similar to methods used in quantitative research. That is to say, the methods are not the only difference between these two types of research. Instead, it is the type of data collected. A description of a few of the most prominent qualitative methods will be discussed in the space that follows.

Interviews

One of the most common ways qualitative researchers gather data is via the spoken word of the participants. Interviews can, of course, take many forms and are not exclusive to qualitative work. We have already discussed quantitative survey research, which typically involves one kind of interview format. In qualitative research, interviews are often semi-structured and much more extensive. Qualitative researchers interview participants multiple times totaling many hours. The goal is to understand the participants through their descriptions of experience as opposed to asking a uniform set of questions and turning the experiences into numbers as we would in quantitative research.

Ethnography

While the popularity of qualitative research continues to grow in psychology, it has long been popular in fields that focus their study on societies and cultures such as anthropology. In fact, ethnography is one specific approach to qualitative inquiry that anthropologists have used for decades. Psychologists are discovering how this method, which involves the researcher immersing him- or herself in the environment of the participant, can benefit psychological understandings of the world. For anthropologists, ethnography often involves immersion in another culture. For psychologists, ethnography can involve immersion in a school, community center, hospital, or even a company. Becoming so actively involved as a participant in each of these environments allows the researcher to gather rich data from more of an insider's perspective and also provides a more complete understanding of context.

Case Study

Case studies, as discussed earlier in the chapter, can be quantitative or qualitative. A qualitative case study focuses on one case or a bounded unit of cases. The case on which the researcher is aiming her focus is usually a typical one and thus may be more reflective of the group as a whole. Sometimes, this focus is on a very atypical case, of interest because of its uniqueness. Qualitative researchers often spend months with the participant in a case study gathering data through observations, interviews, and accounts from people who surround the participant. The goal is to have a comprehensive understanding of that single participant's experience.

It is tempting to believe that a psychologist has to choose between qualitative and quantitative research. In truth, the approaches can often be used in tandem to help us gain a better understanding of the phenomena of interest.

Both approaches have strengths and weaknesses. Quantitative research is typically done with many more participants. This gives researchers the ability to generalize the results to a larger population in a way qualitative researchers cannot. On the other hand, qualitative research goes into more depth with each participant and can provide a much more detailed look at a participant's subjective understanding of the world. Good qualitative research can sometimes serve as the basis for the subsequent creation of a broader quantitative study or even provide the groundwork for a new working theory. The two can also be used together in a mixed methods design.

ACTIVITY

Now that you have been introduced to both qualitative and quantitative approaches to research, write down some factors that you believe help distinguish a good study from one that is poorly done.

Once you have finished your list, look back at the start of the Asking Questions in Psychology section of this chapter where you were asked to complete this same activity prior to being introduced to research methods in psychology. How have your answers changed? Why do you believe they have changed?

NATURE VS. NURTURE: REALLY A DEBATE?

Have you ever heard someone say something like, "He has his father's anger," or "She has her mother's intelligence"? We often make statements like these about relatives. Often there is an assumption that these similarities are genetic or passed on from one family member to the other. But how do we know these behaviors are not simply learned as a result of observing the behavior of relatives as opposed to being passed on through genetic codes? This is a complex question and one that is asked frequently in psychology (and will be a topic that surfaces throughout this book). It is often referred to as the "nature vs. nurture" debate, which is an attempt to determine whether personality traits, behaviors, and other forms of human expression come about as a result of the environment we are raised in (nurture) or as a result of genetic inheritance (nature).

As noted above, it is commonplace to refer to this as the nature vs. nurture debate. In reality, though, there is really not much of a debate. Almost everything is influenced to a certain degree by our genetics as well as the environment around us. Very rarely is something 100 percent genetic or environmental. For example, since I was adopted, I often joke that my parents had the best of both worlds when I was growing up because, when I was misbehaving they could blame it on the genetics of my birth parents and during my shining moments they could attribute it to the wonderful environment they helped create around me.

ACTIVITY

Fill in the Blanks

A trait that is passed on through genetics is often referred to in psychology as ______________, whereas one that is learned or fostered by the environment is referred to as ______________.

Researchers can attempt to separate the relative influence of heredity on various traits and see which of the two influences may be playing a bigger role with regard to a certain trait or characteristic. The best way to investigate this is through the use of identical twin studies. Since identical twins are a 100 percent genetic match, twin studies provide the most fertile ground for exploring genetic inheritance. In some instances, identical twins were separated very early in life and raised in totally different environments. This scenario is ideal for looking at nature and nurture influences since the 100 percent genetic match is present in identical twins, and the twins are raised in separate environments. Fraternal twins can also be used in such research, although the results are less convincing since fraternal twins, on average, share just 50 percent of their genetic makeup.

Obviously, examples of identical twins being raised in separate environments are rare. As such, other methods of separating genetics from environment are also used. Adoption studies, as I joked about in my personal experience earlier in this section, are another way of naturally creating an experiment where differences between genetic and environmental influences can be observed. Family studies can also be used if, for example, a certain trait is more common in first-degree relatives than it is in more distant relatives.

These studies give us what are called *heritability estimates.* These are mathematical computations that allow us to see the total amount of variance in a given trait that can be attributed to genetics. These estimates are done on groups of people, which means that the estimates may not apply directly to you. In other words, if you read on the Internet or see on a television news broadcast that heritability rates of intelligence are 30 percent (or 30 percent of the variance in intelligence can be attributed to genetics), you might be tempted to think that 30 percent of your intelligence was passed on to you by your ancestors and 70 percent was fostered by your environment. This would not necessarily be the case for you personally since these are simply heritability estimates or averages that were calculated on a large number of people.

Research is a vehicle by which psychologists seek to understand the world of complex behavior and mental processes. You have likely concluded that this process is multi-faceted and has many challenges. As you progress through this text and study the many subjects presented try to keep in mind some of the research approaches a psychologist may use to seek further understanding.

REFERENCES

Matsumoto, D., & Juang, L. (2008). *Culture and psychology* (4th ed.). Belmont, CA: Cengage.

Price, D. D., Finniss, D. G., & Benedetti, F. (2008). A comprehensive review of the placebo effect: Recent advances and current though. *Annual Review of Psychology, 59,* 565–590.

NAME ______________________________ DATE ____________________

WORKSHEET CHAPTER ONE

CHAPTER 2

THINKING AND INTELLIGENCE

"Cogito Ergo Sum"- Descartes

The human mind is perhaps the most amazing tool at our disposal. Our ability to think creatively and disparately allows us to create our own reality in ways other mammals simply cannot. In order to gain a true understanding of thinking, it is necessary to first draw a more complete distinction between the terms mind and brain (Note: We will discuss the brain in detail in Chapter 5).

Remember the difference between the brain and the mind as discussed in Chapter 1? The brain is the physical matter that resides inside of our craniums. Examples would be neurons, the amygdala, and all of the other physical structures that make up the organ we call the brain. The mind, on the other hand, is our own subjective experience or what we believe we know. Thoughts, feelings, and perceptions we have on a moment-to-moment basis are a product of the mind.

What happens in the brain affects the mind. Our sensory receptors take in stimuli that get perceived by the brain. The mind then makes meaning of this or helps the person gain a subjective understanding of the world. In other words, every person's brain might go through a process that is the same, or at least very similar, in gathering sensory information from the world. However, each person's mind has the potential to be unique, thus painting different subjective pictures of the data the brain processes.

One example of the power of the human mind can be traced back to the Wright brothers, Orville and Wilbur. The Wright brothers attended high school but neither received his diploma. Without any other formal schooling, the brothers went on to create the world's first motor-driven flying machine, later called an airplane. This was an accomplishment that many thought impossible. Moreover, the U.S. government showed no interest in the new technology for over two years. After all, how could a motor-driven flying machine be of any benefit to society? Over a century later, of course, we know the invention of the Wright brothers has fundamentally changed the way we live.

It was the *minds* of the Wright brothers that allowed them to create this never-before-seen and unfathomable piece of technology. Their ability to think in ways that defied convention and broke "rules" that people said could not be broken allowed them to see their vision through.

In this chapter, some common theories of thinking and intelligence will be examined. More importantly, you will be challenged to think in ways that may differ from the approaches you have been taught or conditioned to utilize. And who knows? Perhaps your mind will someday produce a revolutionary idea like the one the Wright brothers produced over a century ago.

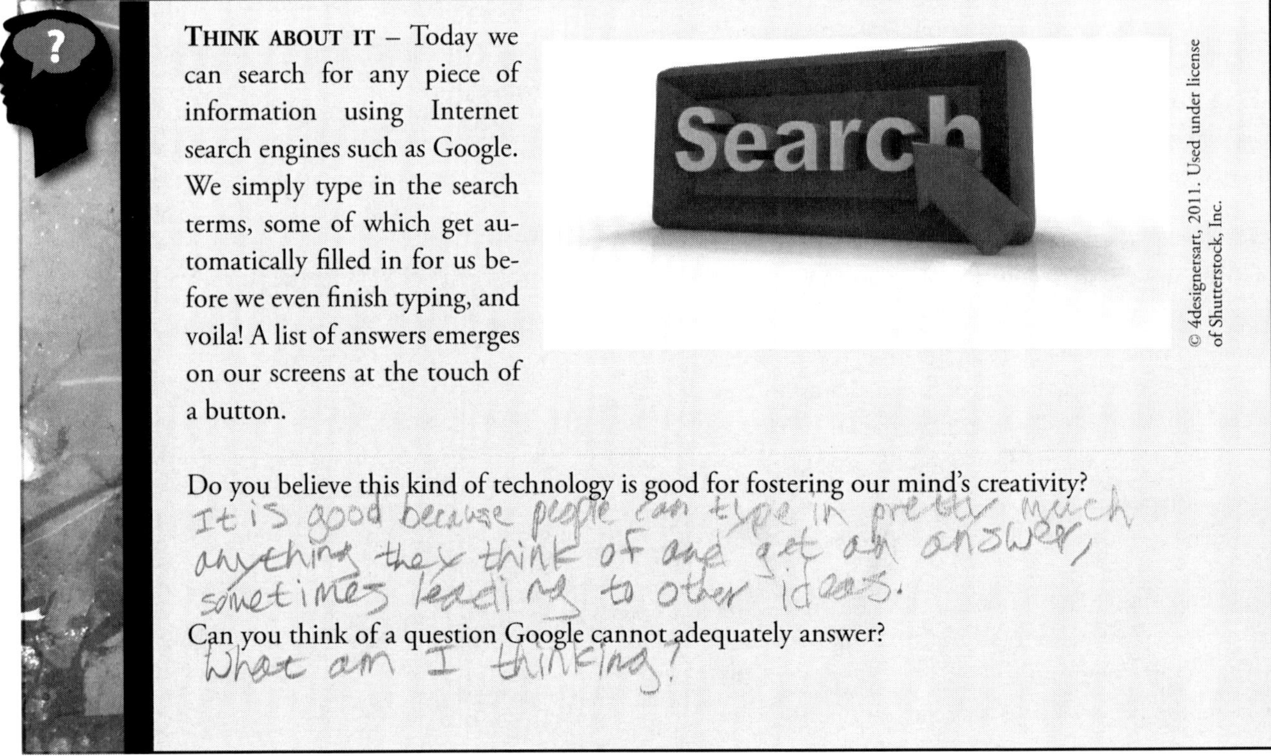

Think about it – Today we can search for any piece of information using Internet search engines such as Google. We simply type in the search terms, some of which get automatically filled in for us before we even finish typing, and voila! A list of answers emerges on our screens at the touch of a button.

Do you believe this kind of technology is good for fostering our mind's creativity?

It is good because people can type in pretty much anything they think of and get an answer, sometimes leading to other ideas.

Can you think of a question Google cannot adequately answer?

What am I thinking?

THE THREE STAGES OF PROBLEM SOLVING

1. *Thinking about the Problem:* In order to solve problems in our lives, we typically progress through three general stages. The first step most commonly involves thinking about the problem. We draw on existing information we have from past experiences as well as try to learn about new elements surrounding the problem we may not have been previously aware of. During this initial stage, we also formulate how we intend to go about solving the problem and may form hypotheses. We often define what our goals are and may break the problem solving sequence down into more manageable mini-goals.
2. *Attempting to Solve the Problem:* In the second stage we begin using strategies to attempt to solve the problem. There are many approaches we might use to try and solve any given problem, no matter how big or small the problem. Two strategies for problem solving that are commonly utilized by people include algorithms and heuristics.

An *algorithm* is a manualized approach to problem solving that involves following step-by-step instructions, which will eventually yield a correct answer. This is provided, of course, that the algorithm is followed correctly. Many of the basic math equations we first learned in elementary school are examples of algorithms (3 x 4 is really 3+3+3+3). The global positioning system (GPS) on your phone or in your car is based on an algorithm. In this case, a computer constructs a step-by-step path to ensure you arrive at your preferred destination.

The use of a *heuristic*—a rule that helps speed up the problem-solving process without guaranteeing a solution—is another common approach people use to try and solve problems. There are times when an exhaustive search for a solution is impractical or even impossible. In these situations, a heuristic can be helpful. While a heuristic does not guarantee one correct answer or solution, it can help limit the number of possible solutions.

ACTIVITY

You just moved to Los Angeles to attend college and are considering renting a new house with a few of your friends. You decide that it is impractical to look at all of the houses for rent in the greater Los Angeles area. Thus, you limit your search to four specific neighborhoods that are near the college you will be attending. Are you and your friends using an algorithm or a heuristic to attempt to solve this problem? Explain your answer in the space below:

A heuristic because this method speeds up the problem-solving process but does not guarantee a solution.

3. *Assessment and Evaluation:* After going through the problem-solving process, it is important to evaluate the quality of the solution obtained. A very simple heuristic such as trial-and-error requires frequent reassessment and evaluation after each trial. Moreover, while we may come up with a solution that solves a problem, it is important to remember that there are often multiple solutions to any problem. We may have found a workable solution and still attempt to go back through the problem-solving steps to refine or develop an even better solution.

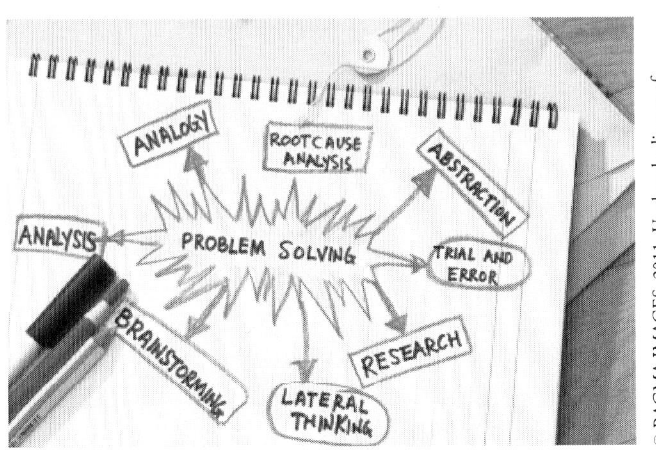

CREATIVE THINKING

How often have you been told by a teacher, parent, or mentor to "critically think" about something? The first time I heard this term, I imagined myself sitting down with a furrowed brow and clenched fists with sweat trickling down my forehead trying to think harder than I had ever thought before. Of course, to be able to truly engage in critical and creative thought requires more than just sheer effort and will power. While the people who ask you to engage is this exercise almost always mean well, what they usually fail to do is teach you the skills necessary to engage in such a process. In this section of the chapter, we will attempt to describe some specific processes that can help encourage critical and creative thought and also some roadblocks that can stifle novel ways of thinking.

Creativity can be defined many different ways. In this book, we define *creativity* as thinking in inventive ways such that it yields novel and useful outcomes. We often think of creative people as people who engage in the arts (e.g., painting, acting, dancing). However, this is a rather limited view of what makes one creative. Creativity permeates almost any profession or activity but is sometimes not defined as such. In other words, an electrician can demonstrate just as much creativity in his or her profession as a painter.

Sternberg and Lubart (1996) created investment theory, which states that creative people "buy low and sell high" in the world of ideas much the way a good stock broker would on Wall Street. That is to say, creative people support ideas that are not popular at the moment but have great potential. When these ideas gain prominence, creative people "sell high" and find another currently unpopular or obscure but potentially favorable idea to stand in support of.

THINK ABOUT IT – Do you think of yourself as a creative person? Why or why not? Many people are quick to answer no to this question without realizing ways in which their own personal creativity manifests. I think I have the potential to be creative.

Take a careful look at how we defined creativity. In what ways have you engaged in inventive thinking such that it resulted in novel and useful outcomes? Think of an example and write it below: I used my shelf that once held my childhood dolls as a shelf for all of my dvds.

Divergent and Convergent Thinking

Divergent thinking is a method that involves exploring many possible solutions in an effort to generate novel or creative ideas. This kind of thinking is often spontaneous and imaginative and is used to help measure a person's level of creativity. One example can be found in the activity that follows.

ACTIVITY

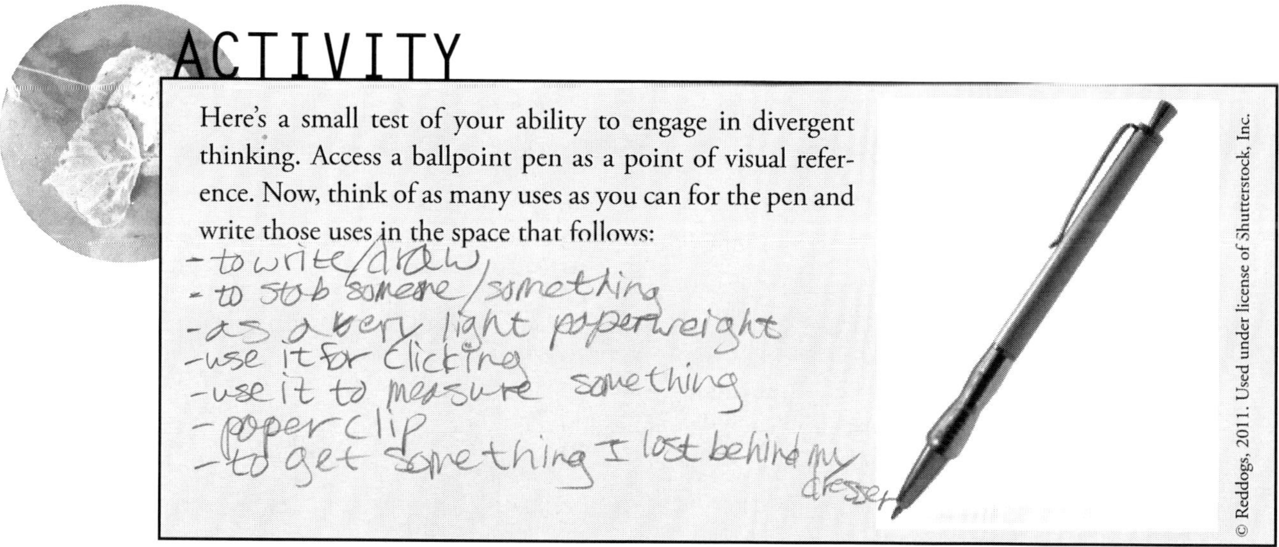

Here's a small test of your ability to engage in divergent thinking. Access a ballpoint pen as a point of visual reference. Now, think of as many uses as you can for the pen and write those uses in the space that follows:

- to write/draw,
- to stab someone/something
- as a very light paperweight
- use it for clicking
- use it to measure something
- paperclip
- to get something I lost behind my dresser

If you were able to generate a large number of potential solutions and found the last activity to be relatively easy and enjoyable, chances are you enjoy being a divergent thinker.

Convergent thinking is the ability to identify the one correct answer to a question. Using an algorithm, as discussed earlier, is a type of convergent thinking. Questions that require convergent thinking often do not require significant creativity to solve. Most standardized tests administered in school settings and tests of intelligence emphasize convergent thinking.

Both convergent and divergent thinking are important. In fact, some of the world's best thinkers are capable of doing both. When a modern engineer is creating a bridge across a ravine, convergent thinking helps ensure the specifications are accurate. A single correct answer is necessary in this situation to help ensure our safety when we drive across the bridge. However, the idea of bridging a gap with bamboo or wood from trees to create a shortcut to walk on as early humans did when the first bridges were serendipitously constructed was actually more of a divergent idea that required a great deal of creativity.

Three Important Factors in Creative Thinking

Creative thinking can sometimes be abstract and thus hard to define. That said, three common factors tend to emerge when examining the process of creative thought.

1. *Flexibility:* The ability to approach solving problems in many different ways. Creative individuals are able to transition quite easily from one problem-solving approach to another and do not cling rigidly to strategies that have been successful in the past.
2. *Fluency:* The ability to think of many possible solutions or outcomes. The higher the number of potential solutions generated, the greater the chance the problem will be solved or an unexpected creative outcome will result.
3. *Originality:* The ability to generate unique approaches to solving problems or unique solutions to problems.

Six Resources of Creative People

One question you might be asking is what makes a person creative? Are people just born creative (nature) or does the environment they are raised in (nurture) foster a sense of creativity? As is often the case in psychology, it is likely some combination of both.

Remember investment theory (Sternberg & Lubart, 1996) as noted earlier in the chapter, which discussed how creative people tended to "buy low and sell high" in the world of ideas? These same researchers discovered six interrelated resources that creative people tend to share.

1. *Intellectual Skills:* A high enough level of intelligence to be able to see problems in diverse ways and employ innovative problem solving strategies.
2. *Knowledge:* A person must have at least a working knowledge of the field in which he or she is attempting to solve a problem. Having insufficient knowledge will hinder a person's ability to solve a problem. However, having too much knowledge such that a person rigidly adheres to the way things are currently being done in the field can adversely impact creative thinking, too. So the key is to have sufficient knowledge but to avoid clinging too tightly to previously existing knowledge such that it prevents one from seeing problems in a new light.
3. *Thinking Style:* The preference to think in new ways and the ability to recognize which ideas or questions are worth pursuing.
4. *Personality:* Creative people tend to share certain personality characteristics, such as a high tolerance for ambiguity (no clear cut right or wrong answers), a high level of persistence, a willingness to engage in calculated risks and support unpopular opinions, and a high level of self-efficacy (a belief that one is capable).
5. *Motivation:* Internal or self-motivation to investigate curious phenomena in the world as opposed to more external motivation from potential rewards.
6. *Environment:* An external environment that is supportive of creative ideas and the process of creative thinking.

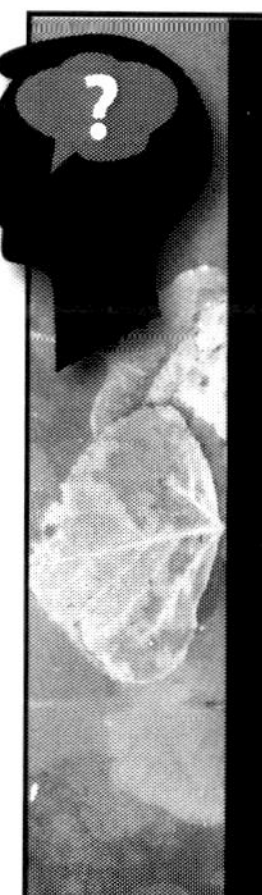

THINK ABOUT IT – Look at the list of the six resources of creative people. Which areas do you believe are strengths of yours? Which areas do you believe you have room for improvement and why? Elaborate in the space below:

WHAT KEEPS US FROM SOLVING PROBLEMS CREATIVELY?

Growing up, we were often taught by others how to think. To a certain extent it is necessary and helpful for children to be given some kind of structure or organization to assist them with problem solving. As we get older, though, this same structure can stifle creative thought and the space for possibility. In the text that follows we will discuss some potential roadblocks that often hamper our mind from reaching its optimal level of creativity when solving problems.

1. *Mental Sets*

ACTIVITY

Can you connect all nine dots using just four lines without lifting your pencil from the paper?

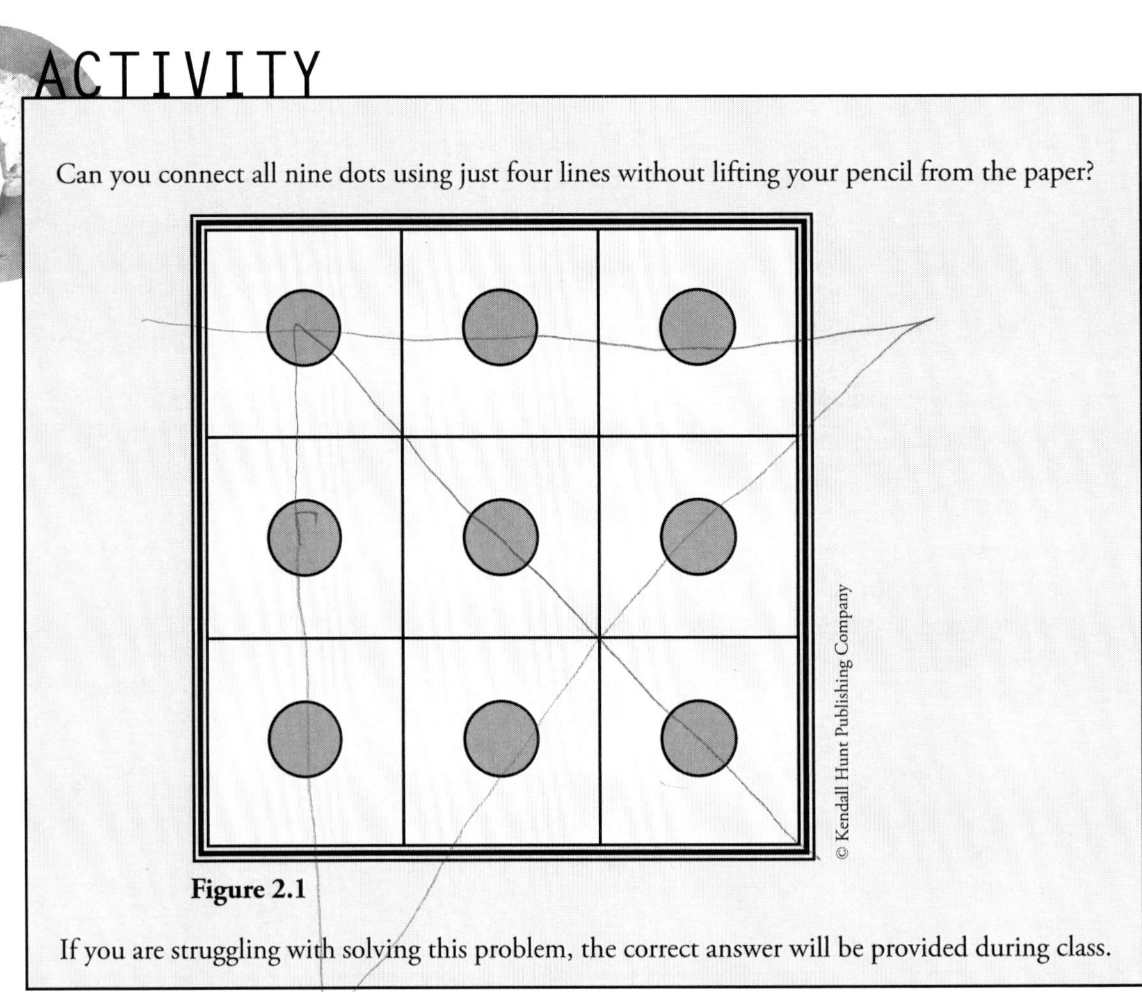

© Kendall Hunt Publishing Company

Figure 2.1

If you are struggling with solving this problem, the correct answer will be provided during class.

As you have now discovered, one must actually "think outside the box" to correctly complete the aforementioned activity. Chances are, most of you struggled to solve this problem. One major reason why was because you believed you had to stay inside the lines. We are taught from an early age not to violate this rule, but to solve the above activity, violation of this rule is a prerequisite.

Of course, there are times when staying inside the lines is advantageous. One such example is when we are commuting to campus. Certainly, we are happy the people on the other side of the yellow line of the road we are driving on understand the rules and stay inside their lane. However, when trying to solve more complex problems, it can be helpful to break free from conventional strategies, or strategies that have worked in the past.

When we continue to try and use problem-solving strategies that have worked in the past, this is described as a *mental set.* Human beings often have a tendency to stay within their mental sets, especially if they are not conscious of this tendency and unaware of ways to break free from it.

2. *Availability Heuristic*

Availability heuristic is a phenomenon first identified by Amos Tversky and Daniel Kahneman (1974, 1993) in which people predict the likelihood of a future event based on how readily accessible examples of that event are in memory. Another way of thinking about this concept it to say that if you can recall it from memory, it must be important. This can be seen in people using anecdotes and generalizing those experiences to entire populations.

ACTIVITY

A friend offers you a cigarette. You explain to your friend that you do not smoke because of the potential negative impact it has been demonstrated to have on your health. Your friend argues quite convincingly that she knows cigarette smoking is not bad for people because her grandmother smoked a pack a day and lived to be 103 years old.

Explain to your friend how she is ignoring relevant information and engaging in the use of the availability heuristic.

She is just using an example to make a generalization that you could live to be 103 even if you smoke.

The 24-hour news cycle we are exposed to currently in Western culture gives us an opportunity to see the availability heuristic at work and even fuels its impact. We know people often rate violent, sensational, and vivid causes of death covered in great detail in various news media (e.g., death by shark attacks or being struck by lightning) as being much more likely to occur than they actually are.

One specific example occurred after the attacks of September 11, 2001 when people overestimated their chances of being a victim of terrorism. More specifically, 20 percent of people sampled said they believed they had a chance of being hurt in a terrorist attack over the course of the next year (Lerner et al., 2003). If we step back and look at the data, we realize that our chances of actually being a victim of terrorism are miniscule. However, the vivid and extensive media coverage made people overestimate their chances of being a victim of terrorism, which is a classic example of availability heuristic.

3. *Confirmation Bias*

Remember in Chapter 1 when we discussed the importance of being able to distinguish the difference between good research studies and studies that were poorly executed? Unfortunately, many people do not engage in this exercise. Instead, they simply search for studies that support a position they already hold or are passionate about. People have a tendency to seek out information that supports their already existing beliefs and biases and ignore information that may contradict those beliefs and biases. This tendency is called *confirmation bias.* This kind of bias is seen frequently in very emotionally charged political or philosophical debates.

ACTIVITY

Increasing research is emerging with regard to the cause of homosexuality. While the precise cause is still uncertain, many scientists are finding that biology, genetics, and prenatal hormones play an important role (this data will be discussed later in Chapter 10).

If someone refuses to acknowledge this emerging research and instead holds to personal beliefs that homosexuality is a behavior one chooses to engage in with no biological and genetic influences, explain how he is engaging in confirmation bias in the space below:

He tries to seek out info. that support his already existing beliefs and biases & ignore info. that may contradict those beliefs & biases.

4. *Functional Fixedness*

Most of us have a cognitive bias toward using an object or device to complete the task it was designed to complete (or at least the task we were taught it was designed to complete). This bias is called *functional fixedness.*

Most objects or devices we use in our everyday lives were designed to complete a certain task or a small number of tasks. In reality, though, most of these objects can be used in many different ways. Take a hammer, for example. We have been taught that a hammer is used to insert nails into a piece of wood. While a hammer is certainly effective at accomplishing such a task, if we begin to think more creatively, we can likely come up with many more uses for a hammer (as we did with a ballpoint pen earlier in the chapter). One simple example is a hammer being used as a paperweight. While the hammer wasn't designed for this reason, its weight and size makes it a very effective paperweight in many instances.

ACTIVITY

Imagine that you are in an unfamiliar hotel room and wake up in the middle of the night and have to use the restroom. You reach for light switch but it will not turn on. You take a quick glance at the clock near the bed and notice that it is not on. You come to the conclusion the power must have gone out. Nevertheless, you still have to use the bathroom and your luggage is scattered all over the floor, which is a potential hazard in the dark. With the light switch no longer being an option due to the power outage, you remember your smart phone is sitting on the nightstand next to the bed. You push the button of the smart phone so the backlit LED illuminates. The light emitted from the phone functions as a flashlight and leads you to and from the bathroom safely.

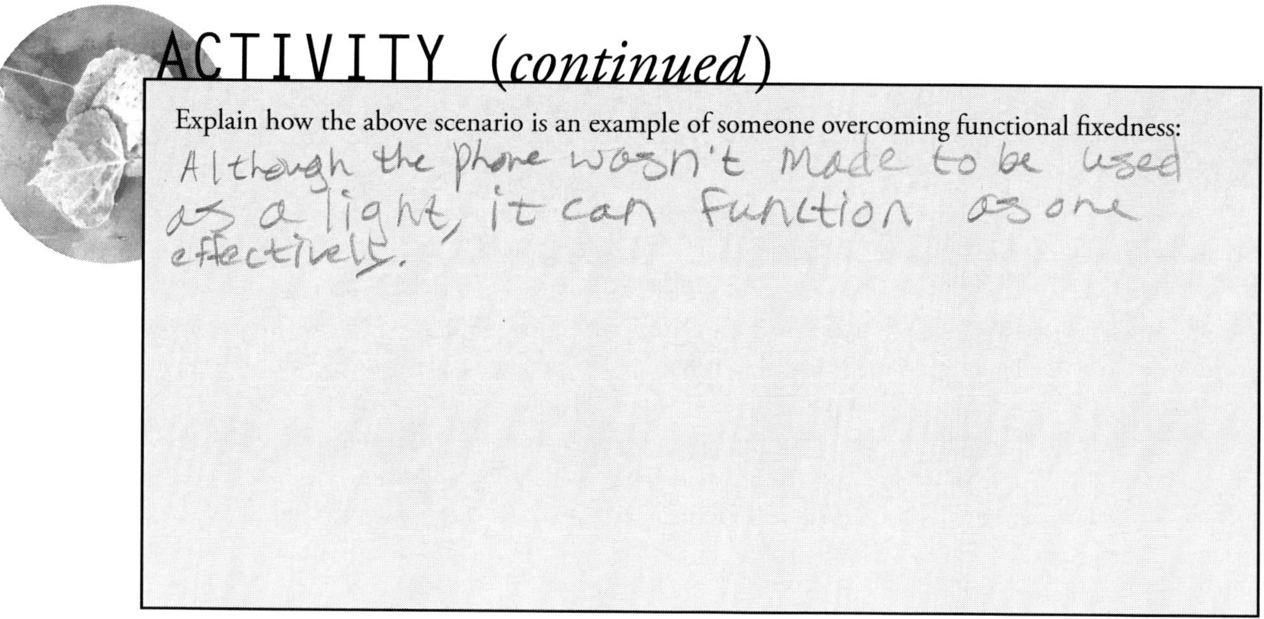

ACTIVITY (*continued*)

Explain how the above scenario is an example of someone overcoming functional fixedness:

Although the phone wasn't made to be used as a light, it can function as one effectively.

INTELLIGENCE

How do you know if someone is intelligent or not? Sounds like a simple question, right? After reading it, though, some of you may have very quickly formulated some other questions in your minds. One such question is often: Are you talking about "books smarts" or common sense? For example, you may have crossed paths with a professor who has a Ph.D. with complete mastery in her chosen area of study who cannot figure out how to complete a simple three-step process to connect a projector to a computer to show the class slides of important topic areas of a chapter she is currently teaching. Conversely, you may have encountered people who have incredible "street smarts" and are great at interacting with people in the world, but really struggle in the academic world of written papers and standardized tests.

Think about it – So which person is smarter? The person with a Ph.D. and academic mastery of a topic area or a person with superior street smarts and people skills who struggles on standard academic tests? Why do you believe this to be true?

In short, intelligence is a hypothetical and abstract concept. In other words, one cannot simply draw your blood and tell you how intelligent you are. This makes it hard to formulate a consensus definition of intelligence that all psychologists are completely comfortable with. It should also be noted that intelligence is a largely Western construct. In fact, in a number of other languages there is not a word that directly translates to intelligence. For our purposes we will borrow a definition from David Wechsler (1977), a well-known psychologist who created prominent intelligence tests still used today. He defined *intelligence* as "the global capacity to think rationally, act purposefully, and deal effectively with the environment." While this definition is not above scrutiny, it is broad enough that it represents many modern theories of intelligence.

History of Intelligence Measurement

Remember that intelligence is a hypothetical and abstract concept. What this means is that it is not particularly easy to measure. Moreover, decades worth of debate continues as to whether intelligence is composed of a single general ability or multiple abilities.

Charles Spearman (1923), a British psychologist, was the first to formulate a single ability theory of intelligence that he called *general intelligence* or *(g)*. He came to this conclusion after observing correlations between high scores on a number of different tests of mental ability. He believed that *g* was a measure of all of all of our intellectual abilities including: problem-solving abilities, general cognition, our ability to engage in rational thinking and use reason, and so on. Spearman's work served as a catalyst for the standardized intelligence tests that are used today.

Other researchers, such as L.L. Thurstone (1938) and J.P. Guilford (1967), argued that intelligence was composed of many different factors as opposed to the single ability model advanced by Spearman. Thurstone believed there were seven primary factors, while Guilford later hypothesized there were at many as 120 different factors. These ideas laid the foundation for more modern theories of multiple intelligences, which we will discuss in more detail later in this chapter.

While Thurstone was arguing for expanding the number of factors that comprise intelligence, Raymond Cattell (1971) contended that Spearman's single ability *(g)* could be divided into two subtypes: fluid intelligence and crystallized intelligence. Cattell defined *fluid intelligence* as innate intelligence including memory, reasoning, and information processing, without including the specific effects of learning or experience. He also indicated that fluid intelligence was susceptible to decline as people grew older. Cattell defined *crystallized intelligence* as knowledge or skills obtained through education and experience. In other words, crystallized intelligence measures what has been learned and tends to increase as we get older.

ACTIVITY

Fill in the Blanks

Charles Spearman created a ___single___ ability theory of intelligence, which he called ___general intelligence___.

J.P. Guilford believed there were as many as ______________ different factors involved in the structure of intelligence.

Cattell defined innate intelligence separate from the effects of formal education or life experience as ________________ intelligence.

Cattell defined skills or knowledge gained through education and other life experiences as ________________ intelligence.

Modern Intelligence Measures

The term IQ (intelligence quotient) is probably one you have heard before. It is often wrongfully assumed that IQ and intelligence are synonymous terms. In truth, IQ is a man-made construction that attempts to quantify intelligence. How accurate those attempts have been in the past and continue to be currently is still a subject of much debate. Most IQ tests do not have strong predictive validity beyond that of predicting future school and occupational success. In other words, modern intelligence tests are reasonably good at predicting what grades a student will earn in the future, but not so good at predicting other aspects of a broader definition of intelligence Nevertheless, intelligence measures are still used frequently by school systems, college admissions committees, and employers as important selection criteria As such, it is important we investigate and gain a basic understanding of a couple of the most frequently used intelligence tests.

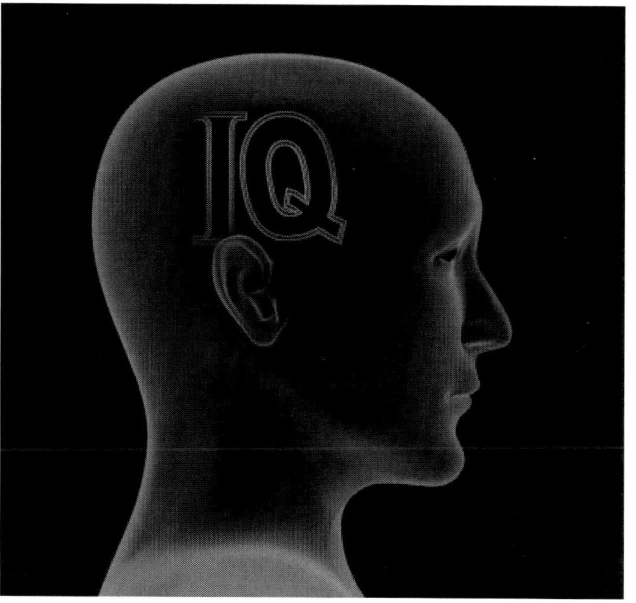

Technically, most modern intelligence tests no longer calculate a true IQ score. Instead, the scores are calculated by comparing a single person's performance to a normative data set (the average score of a large number of people of similar age who have taken the same test). These are called deviation IQ scores because they measure how far the score of the person taking the test deviates from the average score for a person their age (see the bell curve figure 2.2 from the Stanford-Binet Intelligence Scale below for a normal distribution of scores). It is worth noting that despite the fact true IQ scores as they were first devised are no longer calculated, the terms IQ and IQ tests persist as quick ways of referencing intelligence measures and the outcomes of such measures. You will notice on the graph below that an average IQ score is 100 and that 68 percent of people have an IQ that falls between 85 and 115.

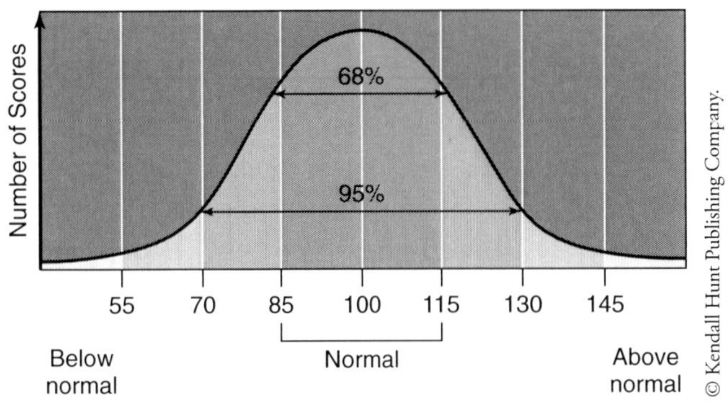

Figure 2.2

Wechsler Intelligence Scale

The most common intelligence scales used by psychologists today are the Wechsler Intelligence Scales. Currently, there are three different Wechsler scales, each devoted to a certain age group: the Wechsler Adult Intelligence Scale–4th Edition (WAIS-IV), the Wechsler Intelligence Scale for Children–4th Edition (WISC-IV), and the Wechsler Preschool and Primary Scale of Intelligence–3rd Edition (WPPSI-III). These allow different age groups to be tested in developmentally appropriate ways as opposed to simply testing every age group the same way. An advantage of the Wechsler scales is that in addition to yielding an overall intelligence score, separate scores for sub-areas, such as performance and verbal scores, are calculated. This allows non-English speakers to still take the performance sub-tests when language barriers may prevent them from taking the verbal sub-tests. The performance score consists of tasks such as arranging blocks in certain designs as quickly as possible, placing pictures in order to tell a story, and completing pictures with missing parts. Verbal tasks include reading comprehension, general knowledge questions, and similarities (e.g., in what ways are a pen and a pencil alike?).

Stanford-Binet Intelligence Scale

The Stanford-Binet was one of the first formal intelligence tests and was originally developed in France by psychologist Alfred Binet. Stanford psychologist Lewis Terman revised the test in the United States in 1916. Several revisions have happened since that time, and it is currently in its fifth edition. A total of 4,800 participants based on the 2000 U.S. Census were used to help create the normative sample for the fifth edition. The test can be used for children as young as age 2 all the way through adulthood.

What Makes a Good Intelligence Test

As you read about intelligence tests, you might have found yourself asking the question: How do I know the test is a good one? Chances are, you have found yourself surfing the Internet and had a pop-up emerge on your screen that said something like: "See how smart you are" or "Test your IQ!" What makes these tests on the Internet different from the Wechsler scales or the Stanford-Binet? We will discuss some of the essential differences in the space that follows.

You probably recall reading the term normative data or norms in the previous section. *Norms* are average scores from a group of people who have taken the test prior to the test being released for public consumption and are required prior to the release of psychological intelligence tests. Norms are necessary to serve as a point of comparison for every person who takes the test in the future, and norms must be established for every age group being tested. Norms help us establish what an average score on any given test is as well as scores that might be considered above or below average. Remember the term representative sample as discussed in Chapter 1? Norms for tests are established not by measuring a random group of people, but instead, by measuring a sample of people that is representative of the people who will be taking the intelligence test in the future.

ACTIVITY

Imagine that as a class we created a new adult intelligence test. Since we are familiar with the importance of establishing norms, we obtain a representative sample of adults from the United States. Several years later, another class decides to broaden the scope of the test and begins administering it in countries other than the United States without first establishing norms for these countries. They notice that people from other countries are scoring lower than people from the United States and conclude that people in the United States are smarter than people from other countries.

What is wrong with this conclusion and why? Explain in the space below:

This conclusion is not measured fairly because they didn't establish norms for the testing in other countries.

In addition to norms, intelligence tests must all possess uniformity. In other words, the test must be administered the same way every time for every participant who completes it. If a test has established norms and is administered the same every time, it is considered to be a *standardized test.* The Wechsler scales and the Stanford-Binet are both standardized intelligence tests, whereas the tests you have encountered on the Internet are almost certainly not.

In addition to standardization, psychological intelligence tests must also demonstrate reliability and validity.

Reliability refers to a test's ability to reproduce similar results over time. In other words, if you take an intelligence test today and again at a later date, your scores should be similar. Reliability on an intelligence test is often measured by using the test-retest method, which involves giving the person the same test on two different occasions. The split-half method is also sometimes used, which is when a test is split into two equal parts (often odd- and even-numbered questions) and the degree of consistency between the two parts is examined.

Validity is the degree to which a test measures what is says it is trying to measure. This is often determined by a test's ability to predict another variable of interest, which is called criterion-related validity. For example, we know intelligence tests are generally good at predicting a person's future performance in school as measured by letter grade achieved. The test is considered valid since it is proficient at predicting a person's behavior in a different specific situation.

ACTIVITY

FILL IN THE BLANKS

validity_____ is a term used to describe a test's ability to measure what it purports to measure.

You take the same intelligence test at two different intervals separated by six months and receive exactly the same score. This means the test likely has high reliability_____.

Nature vs. Nurture and Intelligence

Remember the nature vs. nurture "controversy" or "debate" we discussed in Chapter 1? Never has this debate been more contentious than when it comes to intelligence. The fundamental question is, do we genetically inherit our level of intelligence or is it fostered and molded as a result of our upbringing and the environment around us? As is the case with most any question looking at both genetic and environmental factors, it is likely some of both.

The Minnesota Study of Twins (Bouchard, 1999; Bouchard et al., 1998; Johnson et al., 2007) is the most comprehensive twins study to date. The study started in 1979, lasted for over two decades, and looked at identical twins raised in separate homes after being separated early in life. As noted in Chapter 1, this provided the researchers with a unique opportunity to try and separate genetic and environmental influences. IQ scores were one of the variables examined in this study. The results showed that genetics played a substantial role in IQ scores with concordance rates of 86 percent for identical twins reared together and 75 percent for identical twins raised apart (see Figure 2.3).

While the Minnesota Study of Twins leaves little doubt that genetics influence intelligence to a certain degree, people have argued that the findings do not completely remove environmental influences from genetics. First, the

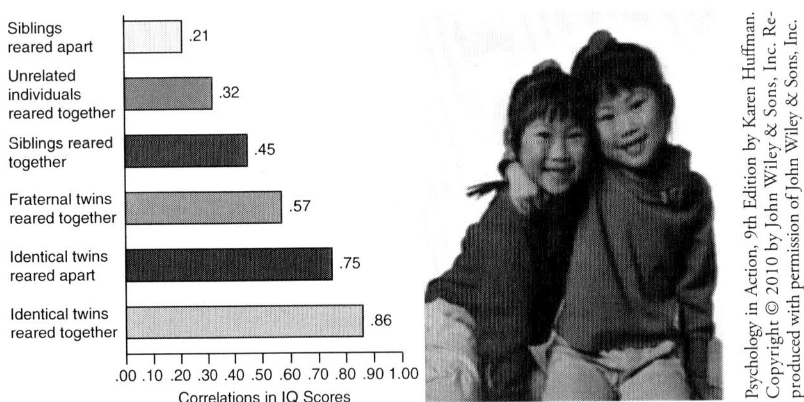

Figure 2.3

twins were together in the womb for nine months, which means they shared the same prenatal environment for a substantial period of time. Also, some of the twins stayed together longer than others before being separated and others were reunited before the study started. Finally, adoption agencies look for similar characteristics in potential adoptive families. This means that the environments the children were raised in were not random and may have been more similar than they were different.

Criticisms of Intelligence Measures

In a book written in 1994 entitled *The Bell Curve: Intelligence and Class Structure in American Life* authors Richard J. Herrnstein and Charles Murray tried to make the argument that African Americans score lower on IQ measures because of their "genetic heritage." This claim was rejected by mainstream psychology and really caused the psychological community to grapple with what differences among groups in IQ scores really mean and also whether IQ scores truly represent the entire scope of intelligence.

One criticism of intelligence tests is that they may contain forms of bias, which therefore means they are not true predictors of intelligence or ability for every person. African Americans, as well as other minority groups, are sometimes underrepresented in normative samples, and tests are often geared more toward Caucasians, which could adversely affect performance of underrepresented groups. Socioeconomic status (SES) is another variable that can lead to bias, since many intelligence tests have been normed on middle- and upper-class individuals. Moreover, children from minority groups are more likely to grow up in lower SES conditions, which can consistently limit their access to resources that help prepare children to perform better on standardized tests like those that measure intelligence. Certainly, students whose primary language is not used in the education system they are a part of are also at a disadvantage (Rutter, 2007; Sternberg, 2007; Sternberg & Grigorenko, 2008).

One of the biggest threats to the performance of minority groups on tests of intelligence is aptly named stereotype threat. *Stereotype threat* is when the threat of a negative stereotype adversely impacts a member of the stereotyped groups performance on a given task even if the member of the stereotyped group believes that stereotype to be untrue. This decrease in performance occurs because members of a stereotyped group may develop anxiety or self-doubt when asked to complete a task in which the stereotype is present out of fear they may fulfill the negative stereotype of the group in which they are a part.

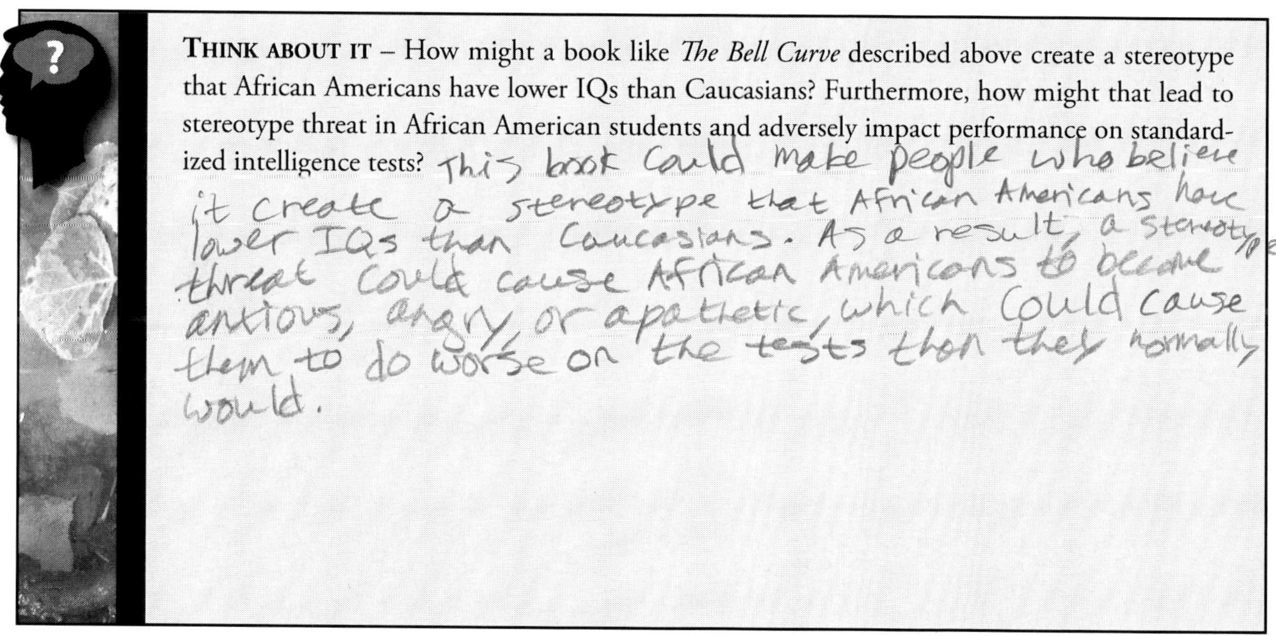

Think about it – How might a book like *The Bell Curve* described above create a stereotype that African Americans have lower IQs than Caucasians? Furthermore, how might that lead to stereotype threat in African American students and adversely impact performance on standardized intelligence tests?

STEREOTYPE THREAT IN ACTION

Steele and Aronson (1995) recruited both African American and Caucasian students from Stanford University to complete a test that was designed to measure general intellectual ability. The questions were similar to questions you might find on the Graduate Record Exam or GRE, which is a test that is required prior to admission to most graduate schools in psychology and other fields of study. One group of participants was given a test that was called a "performance exam." On this exam, Caucasian students performed better than African American students However, when the very same test was given but was called a "laboratory task" instead of a performance task, the differences in scores between African American and Caucasian students disappeared.

Why do think this was the case?

Because of the stereotype created by The Bell Curve, which states that African Americans don't perform as well on certain tests, this caused a stereotype threat. When the test is labeled "performance exam", they worry about how they will perform.

As noted previously in the chapter, intelligence is a hypothetical and abstract concept. As such, it is difficult to measure. Some psychologists question whether current intelligence tests really measure intelligence in its totality since the predictive validity of such tests is rather limited beyond, to a certain degree, predicting school and occupational success. Are we really measuring all aspects of intelligence or just a person's ability to perform well on standardized tests and obtain career positions afforded higher status in Western culture?

Lewis Terman completed an experiment that started in 1921 in which he identified and followed the progress of 1500 children with IQ scores of at least 140. Terman found high intelligence scores to be correlated with both academic and occupational success. However, not every child was successful across every domain in life. Some of these students had relationship problems, struggled with addiction, and even committed suicide at a rate near the national average (Leslie, 2000). In other words, people who score high on intelligence tests struggle with the same problems as those with average IQs. Moreover, IQ is not a great predictor of success in many endeavors beyond the classroom and the workplace.

Theories of Multiple Intelligences

As a result of the rather limited scope of prediction afforded by traditional intelligence tests, some psychologists have started expanding how psychology conceptualizes intelligence. What about abilities like music or athletic talent? How about the ability to form and maintain meaningful relationships or to read your own emotions or the emotions of someone else? Questions like these led to the formulation of the theory of multiple intelligences. Subsequent research has shown that traditional intelligence tests fail to accurately measure many of the abilities present in theories of multiple intelligences (Gardner, 2002; Naglieri & Ronning, 2000; Sternberg, 2009).

Howard Gardner and Robert Sternberg pioneered two of the most widely recognized models of multiple intelligences. Gardner (2002, 2008) has advocated for a model of intelligence that provides a profile of strengths and weaknesses across a number of different abilities (see figure 2.4). It is believed this unique profile impacts the way someone thinks about the world, solves problems, and learns new information. Gardner's work has been used effectively to help match people to career choices that maximize their unique ability and intelligence profiles.

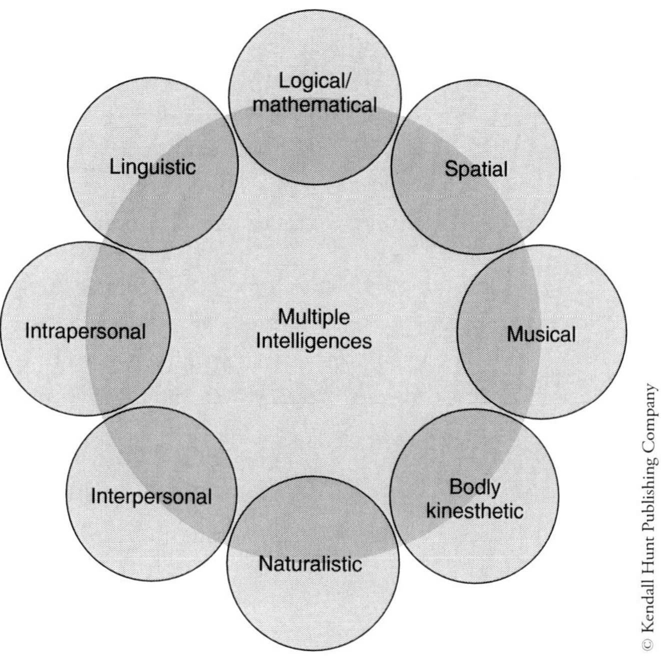

Figure 2.4

Sternberg (1985, 2007, 2009) also believes in multiple intelligences but set up his model a bit differently. His model is often referred to as the triarchic theory of intelligence (see figure 2.5). Think of it as a triangle with a learned component of intelligence on each of the three points. The three components consist of analytic intelligence, creative intelligence, and practical intelligence. Sternberg continues to be a proponent of looking at the process of creative thinking and problem solving as opposed to just the outcome. He believes in trying to measure intelligence in more real-world contexts rather than through the use of more detached forms of standardized testing. It is also worth noting that Sternberg coined the term *successful intelligence*, which describes a person's ability to choose and adapt to environments that will maximize his or her chances of successfully completing a goal.

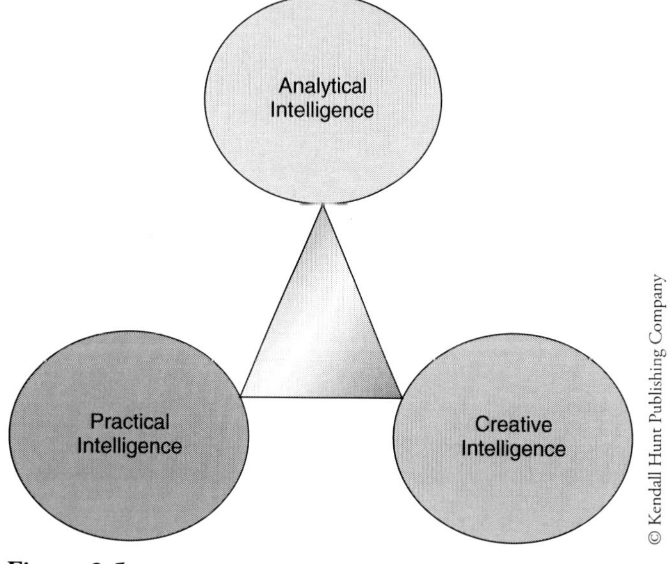

Figure 2.5

Emotional Intelligence (EI)

Daniel Goleman (1995, 2000) proposed an additional type of intelligence he called emotional intelligence (EI). He believes that people with high EI are able to recognize and label their own emotions as well as having a generally accurate sense for the emotions others are feeling along with ability to demonstrate empathy for another's plight. High EI lends itself well to forming successful and meaningful relationships with others. Goleman has suggested that people with a modest IQ but a high EI often have more successful all-around lives when compared to people with high IQs. Skills such as self-regulation, empathy, recognizing and behaving appropriately in various social contexts, appropriate charisma and humor, and self-awareness are crucial in finding success in not just school and the workplace but also in interactions with others. Goleman believes these skills are often ignored or neglected in traditional intelligence tests. Furthermore, he believes that EI can be developed in people by encouraging them to be able to identify and label emotions as well as learning how those emotions are related to actions they may be taking in the world. Goleman indicates that EI training programs should coincide with elementary education and could help decrease future violent and criminal acts such as assault and domestic violence.

EI remains somewhat controversial in the field of intelligence. One of the most common criticisms is that elements of EI are hard to quantify and measure (Mayer, Roberts, & Barsade, 2008). This is certainly an area of study that is still in progress, and more research will be done in the future that will likely help us understand more about not only Goleman's theory, but also about the ways emotions interact with intelligence and predict our ability to successfully navigate the world around us.

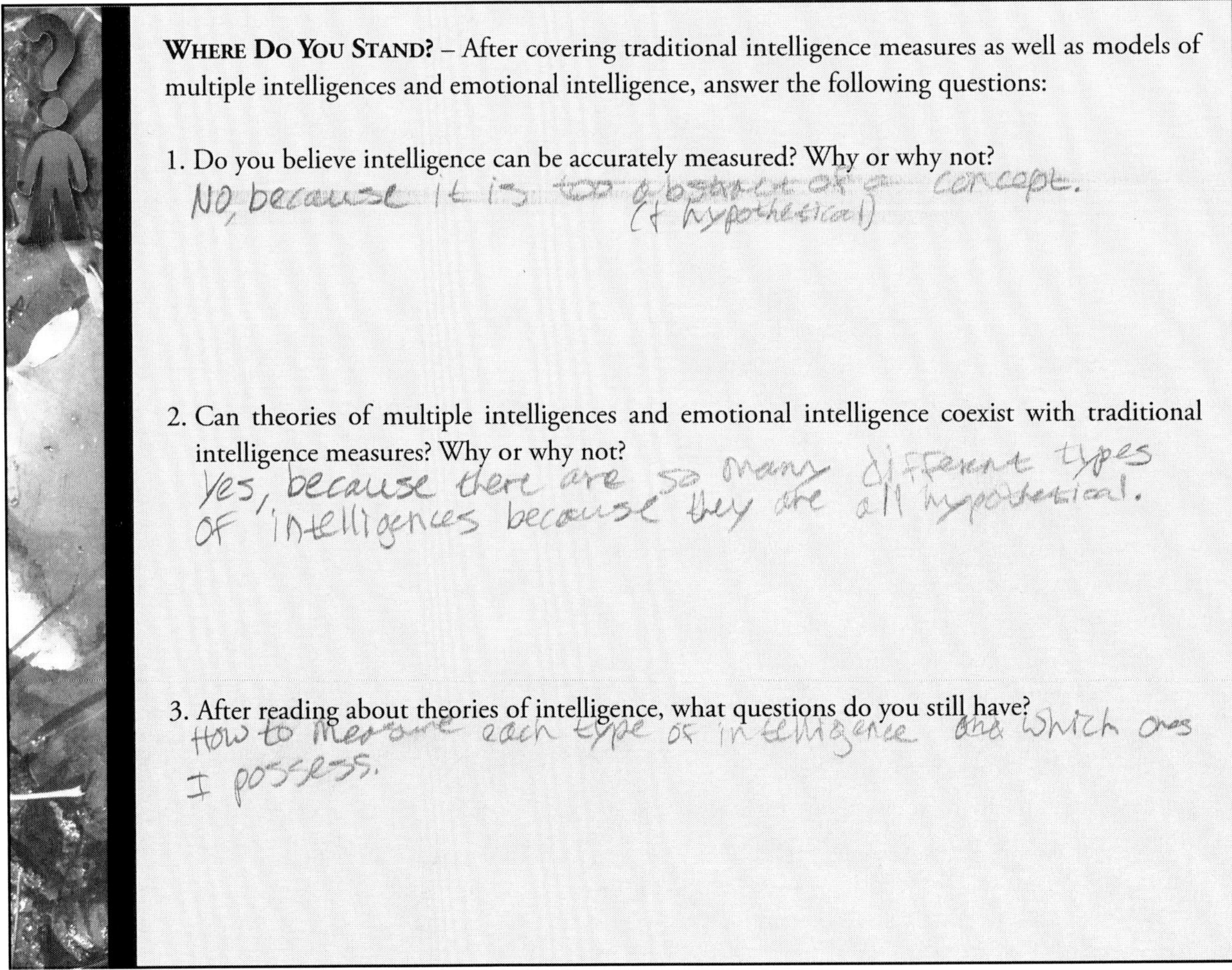

Where Do You Stand? – After covering traditional intelligence measures as well as models of multiple intelligences and emotional intelligence, answer the following questions:

1. Do you believe intelligence can be accurately measured? Why or why not?

   No, because it is too abstract of a concept. (+ hypothetical)

2. Can theories of multiple intelligences and emotional intelligence coexist with traditional intelligence measures? Why or why not?

   Yes, because there are so many different types of intelligences because they are all hypothetical.

3. After reading about theories of intelligence, what questions do you still have?

   How to measure each type of intelligence and which ones I possess.

REFERENCES

Bouchard, T. J., (1999). The search for intelligence. *Science, 284,* 922–923.

Bouchard, T. J., McGue, M., Hur, Y., & Horn, J. M. (1998). A genetic and environmental analysis of the California Psychological Inventory using adult twins reared apart and together. *European Journal of Personality, 12,* 307–320.

Cattell, R. (1971). *Abilities: Their structure, growth, and action.* Boston: Houghton Mifflin.

Gardner, H. (2002). The pursuit of excellence through education. In M. Ferrari (Ed.), *Learning from extraordinary minds.* Mahwah, NJ: Erlbaum.

Gardner, H. (2008). Who owns intelligence? In M. H. Immordino-Yang (Ed.), *Jossey-Bass Education Team. The Jossey Bass reader on the brain and learning* (pp. 120–132). San Francisco: Jossey-Bass.

Goleman, D. (1995). *Emotional intelligence: Why it can matter more than IQ.* New York: Bantam.

Goleman, D. (2000). *Working with emotional intelligence.* New York: Bantam Doubleday.

Guilford, J. P. (1967). *The nature of human intelligence.* New York: McGraw Hill.

Herrnstein, R. J., & Murray, C. (1994). *The bell curve: Intelligence and class structure in American life.* New York: Free Press.

Johnson, W., Bouchard, T. J., McGue, M., Segal, N. L., Tellegen, A., Keyes, M., & Gottesman, I. I. (2007). Genetic and environmental influences on the Verbal-Perceptual-Image Rotation (VPR) model of the structure of mental abilities in the Minnesota study of twins reared apart. *Intelligence, 35,* 542–562.

Lerner, J. S., Gonzalez, R. M., Small, D. A., & Fischhoff, B. (2003). Effects of fear and anger on perceived risks of terrorism: A national field experiment. *Psychological Science, 14,* 144–150.

Leslie, M. (2000, July/August). The vexing legacy of Lewis Terman. *Stanford Magazine.* [Online]. Available: www.standfordalumni.org/news/magazine/2000/julaug/articles/terman.html

Mayer, J. D., Roberts, R. D., & Barsade, S. G. (2008). Human abilities: Emotional intelligence. *Annual Review of Psychology, 59,* 507–536.

Naglieri, J. A., & Ronning, M. E. (2000). Comparison of White, African American, Hispanic, and Asian children on the Naglieri Nonverbal Ability Test. *Psychological Assessment, 12(3),* 328–334.

Rutter, M. (2007). Gene-environment interdependence. *Developmental Science, 10,* 12–18.

Spearman, C. (1923). *The nature of "intelligence" and the principles of cognition.* London: Macmillan.

Steele, C. M., & Aronson, J. (1995). Stereotype threat and the intellectual test performance of African Americans. *Journal of Personality and Social Psychology, 69,* 797–811.

Sternberg, R. J. (1985). *Beyond IQ: A triarchic theory of human intelligence.* New York: Cambridge University Press.

Sternberg, R. J. (2007). Developing successful intelligence in all children: A potential solution to underachievement in ethnic minority children. In M. C. Wang & R. D. Taylor (Eds.), *Closing the achievement gap.* Philadelphia: Laboratory for Student Success at Temple University.

Sternberg, R. J. (2009). *Cognitive psychology* (5th ed.). Belmont, CA: Wadsworth.

Sternberg, R. J., & Grigorenko, E. L. (2008). Ability testing across cultures. In L. Suzuki (Ed.), *Handbook of multicultural assessment* (3rd ed.). New York: Jossey-Bass.

Sternberg, R. J., & Lubart, T. I. (1996). Investing in creativity. *American Psychologist 51* (7), 677–688.

Thurstone, L. L. (1938). *Primary mental abilities.* Chicago: University of Chicago Press.

Tversky, A., & Kahneman, D. (1974). Judgment under uncertainty: Heuristics and biases. *Science, 185,* 1124–1131.

Tversky, A., & Kahneman, D. (1993). Probabilistic reasoning. In A. I. Goldman (Ed.), *Readings in philosophy and cognitive science.* Cambridge, MA: The MIT Press.

Wechsler, D. (1977). *Manual for the Wechsler Intelligence Scale for Children* (Rev.). New York: Psychological Corporation.

NAME ______________________________ DATE ____________________

WORKSHEET CHAPTER TWO

CHAPTER 3

LEARNING

What is it to learn? Is it to practice a behavior and later demonstrate that you can remember how to do it? Is it to memorize a lengthy speech or a poem or a mathematical formula and later produce it without aid? A computer anticipating its opponent's chess move after 10 games? A child acquiring the ability to speak?

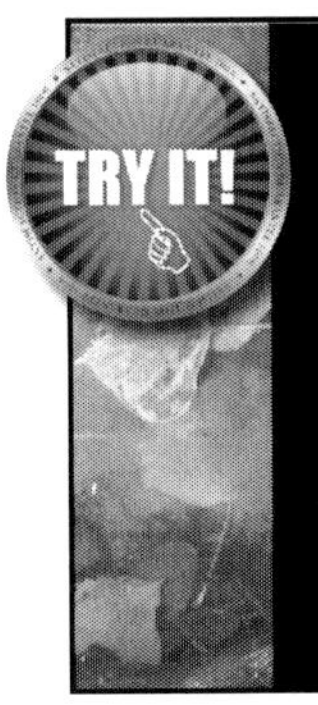

Try It – Ask a family member to give you as brief a definition of learning. Ask a friend or a fellow student. What do you notice about all their answers? Likely they are talking about different types of learning. How would you group these different answers? What types of learning are there?

How do *you* learn?

Scientists often turn to studying the behavior of animals to begin to piece together the complexity of the human learning process. Again, the **nature vs. nurture** dilemma is in play. When attempting to understand animal and human behavior, scientists are always trying to answer the question, Where did this behavior come from?

For example, when a wild Canadian goose is first born, its genetic blueprint gives it all the information it needs to fly south for the winter. To find food, these wild geese also fly in a large group. This group forms the shape of a "V," thus cutting wind resistance as well as decreasing the amount of effort each goose has to produce, allowing the group to fly lengthier distances. To study this phenomenon is, in a way, to attempt to understand if these birds learn this flying behavior or if they were born with it.

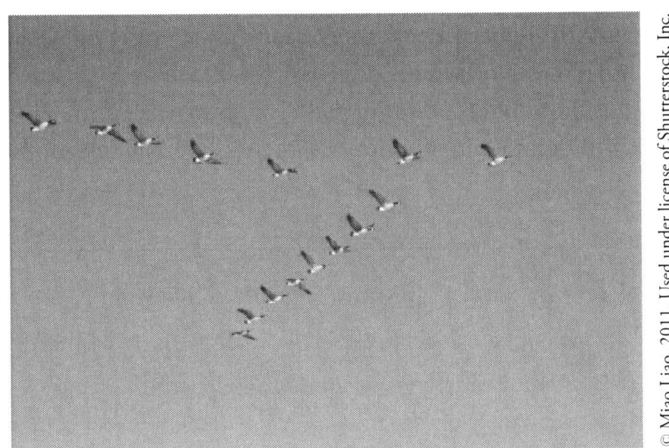

Many animals follow a built-in plan and behave in ways that demonstrate an inborn instinct outside of direct learning. For instance, Tinbergen (1951) showed that when young turkeys saw a silhouette model portrayed to look like a bird of prey they ran for cover. However, when the model was moved in the other direction, which portrayed it like a goose, the chicks didn't react at all.

What is clear is that these young birds did not "learn" to fly south for food or run for cover in the presence of a predator but rather were born with this behavior or what scientists call *instinct.*

Try It – Psychologists who study animal behaviors are called *comparative psychologists.* If you have a pet or live near a park where you can readily observe animals behaving, take a notepad and jot down every behavior you observe an animal perform, no matter how minimal. What patterns do you see? What are your guesses for why the animal behaves in this way?

TYPES OF LEARNING

As you have likely guessed, there are many ways to learn something. People are capable of learning a simple or complex behavior like tying a knot or throwing a ball. They are also capable of learning simple or complex sets of knowledge like the sum of 2+2 or directions to the movie theater across town. Rather than focusing on *what* people are capable of learning, we will focus this chapter, like many behavioral psychologists, on *how* people learn. We will study *classical conditioning* that involves an organism learning that different events occur together. We will learn about *operant conditioning* that involves behavior as a result of reinforcement or punishment. Finally, we will seek to understand *observational learning,* where an organism observes and imitates another's behavior.

Classical Conditioning

Russian psychologist Ivan Pavlov stumbled upon the most famous study of classical conditioning. Pavlov was initially engaged in a totally unrelated inquiry that looked at how saliva impacted digestion via a tube that was connected to the dog's salivary glands. It was actually one of Pavlov's students who noticed the dog salivated prior to feeding time at just the smell of the food or sight of the feeding bowl without the food actually being presented. This small observation shifted the course of Pavlov's study and his career, and when it was brought to his attention, he came to the conclusion that since the involuntary reflex of salivation happened prior to presentation of the food, this could not be an inborn process. Instead, it happened as a result of learning.

Intrigued by this accidental discovery, Pavlov and his associates conducted a series of experiments that involved creating a tone by hitting a tuning fork just before the dog would consume its food. After doing this every time before feeding for several days, the dog began drooling *before* the food was presented. This kind of learning later became known as classical conditioning.

Classical conditioning is a type of learning that occurs when a neutral stimulus (NS) and unconditioned stimulus (UCS) are repeatedly paired together and eventually cause a conditioned response (CR).

There are five crucial terms to be aware of in classical conditioning:

1. Neutral Stimulus (NS): a stimulus that does not induce a response of interest prior to conditioning.
2. Unconditioned Stimulus (UCS): a stimulus that produces a response without the need for prior learning.
3. Unconditioned Response (UCR): a response to a stimulus that is reflexive or unlearned and is naturally brought about by an unconditioned stimulus.
4. Conditioned Stimulus (CS): the once-neutral stimulus that through repeated pairings with the unconditioned stimulus acquires the capacity to bring about a response that was once only reflexive.
5. Conditioned Response (CR): a learned response to a conditioned stimulus.

Pavlov's study began with an unconditioned stimulus (UCS), which was food, and an unconditioned response (UCR), which was dog the salivating or drooling. It is important to note here that the UCR, which is salivation, is inborn or reflexive prior to conditioning. That is, dogs naturally salivate in the presence of food. However, a dog does not naturally salivate to the sound of a tone and thus must learn this association.

Pavlov's revolutionary discovery was introducing a neutral stimulus, which in this case was a tuning fork that he struck to create a tone. What Pavlov did before every feeding was strike the tuning fork to create a noise (NS) right before he presented the dog with the food (UCS). In other words, Pavlov repeatedly paired the NS and the UCS, or the tone and the food. After pairing the tone with the food several times, Pavlov noticed the dog would start salivating at just the sound of the tone without presentation of the food. At this point, the neutral stimulus (NS), which was the tone, became a conditioned stimulus (CS) and produced a conditioned response (CR). In other words, after conditioning Pavlov simply created a tone with the tuning fork (CS) and the dog salivated without the presence of any food (CR). (See Figure 3.1)

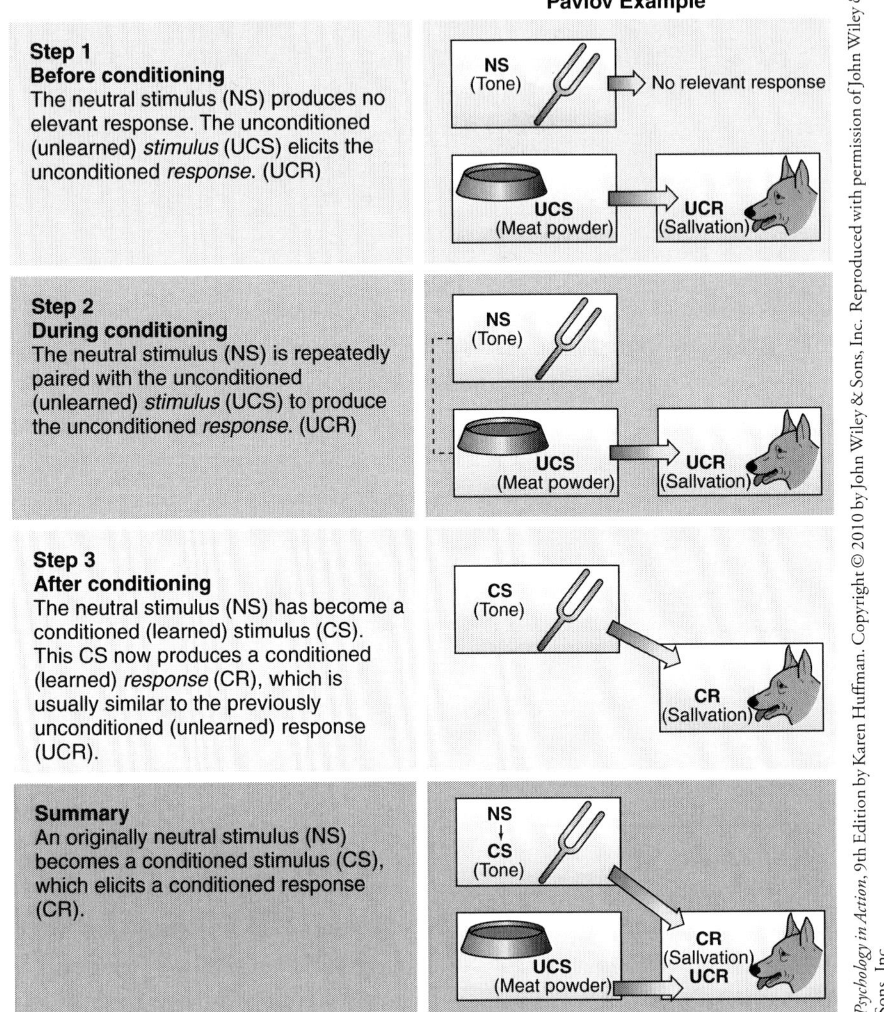

Figure 3.1

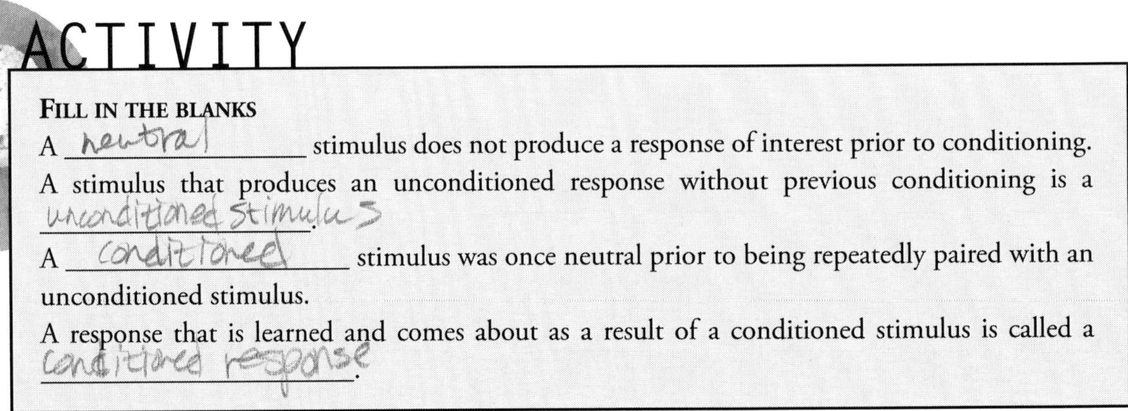

ACTIVITY

Fill in the Blanks

A ___neutral___ stimulus does not produce a response of interest prior to conditioning.

A stimulus that produces an unconditioned response without previous conditioning is a ___unconditioned stimulus___.

A ___conditioned___ stimulus was once neutral prior to being repeatedly paired with an unconditioned stimulus.

A response that is learned and comes about as a result of a conditioned stimulus is called a ___conditioned response___.

Classical conditioning might seem confusing at first, but most people can think of an example in their own life. Remember, classical conditioning occurs when a stimulus (like the sound of a bell) not normally associated with a response (like drooling) is paired with another stimulus (the smell of food) that is associated with the response (drooling).

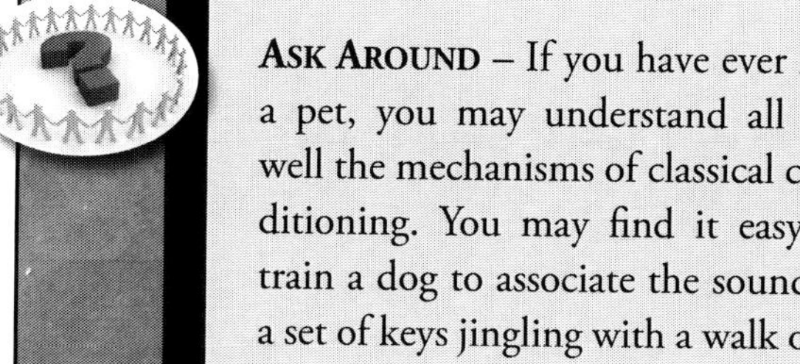

Ask Around – If you have ever had a pet, you may understand all too well the mechanisms of classical conditioning. You may find it easy to train a dog to associate the sound of a set of keys jingling with a walk outside or the sound of your footsteps with a forthcoming treat.

How about an example with the *human* animal? It is likely that if two stimuli were once paired (like the taste of tequila with the feeling of sickness), the stimulus (tequila) can, at even a much later date, elicit the same feeling (sick).

What examples of classical conditioning can you think of?

A song that once meant nothing to you, paired with a sad memory, can make you feel sad even at a later date.

Classical Conditioning and the Conditioned Emotional Response (CER)

Some of you may be asking, "What do drooling dogs have to do with me?" It is important to understand, though, that classical conditioning can be used in ways that are remarkably relevant to your life. For example, emotions and attitudes can also be shaped using classical conditioning.

Behaviorist John B. Watson and his research assistant Rosalie Rayner (1920) specifically investigated whether fear could be classically conditioned in a child in a controversial study in which he attempted to create fear of a white rat in a child. The child in the study is often referred to as "Little Albert." Albert was a healthy and well-adjusted 11-month-old child at the start of the study. The inquiry began with Albert's being introduced to a white rat.

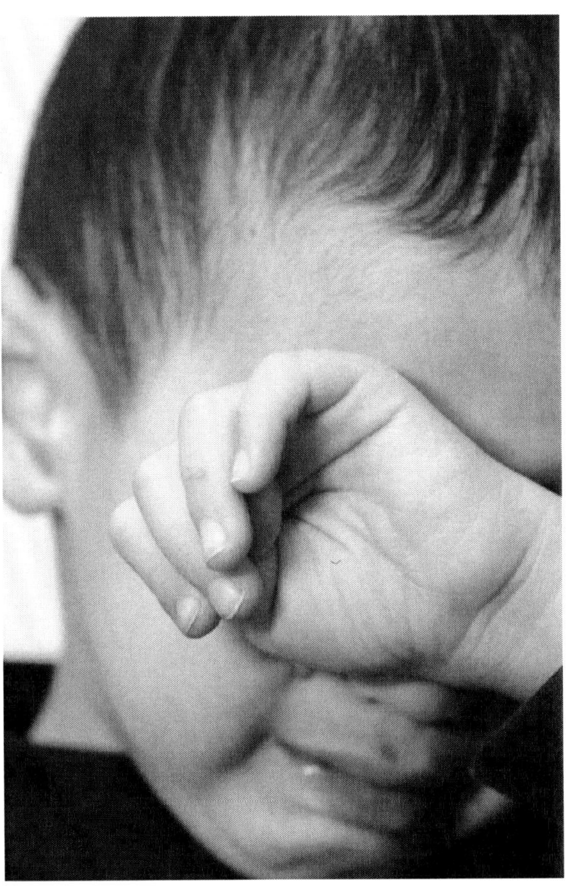

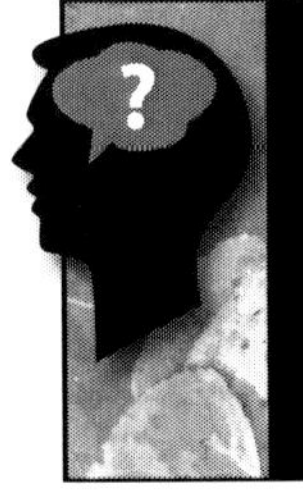

THINK ABOUT IT – Are children born afraid of things like rats or spiders? While it is tempting to believe this since many people are not particularly infatuated with these creatures, we actually learn or are conditioned to fear these animals. As such, how do you think Little Albert initially responded to the rat the first time he was introduced to it? Yep, you guessed it. He was actually curious and reached out to play with the rat.

In Watson's study he first presented Albert with the white rat (NS). When Albert began to interact with the rat Watson would initiate a loud noise (UCS) created by using a hammer to hit a steel bar. The loud noise was an unconditioned stimulus because children have a startle response and are naturally afraid of loud noises. The loud noise created the (UCR), which was fear.

NS= white rat

UCS = loud noise

UCR = fear

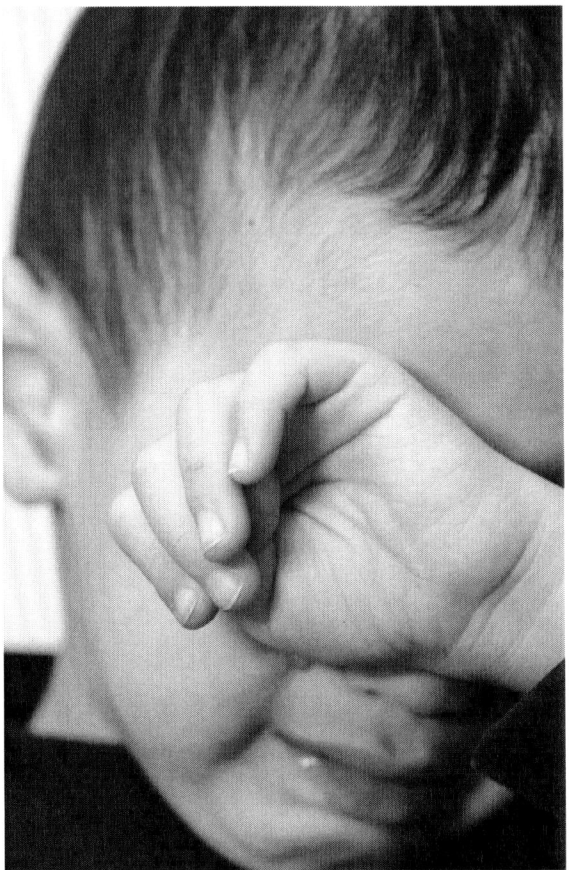

© ZouZou, 2011. Used under license of Shutterstock, Inc.

After repeatedly pairing the white rat with the loud noise, the rat became a conditioned stimulus, which caused a conditioned response of fear.

CS = white rat

© Maslov Dmitry, 2011. Used under license of Shutterstock, Inc.

CR = fear

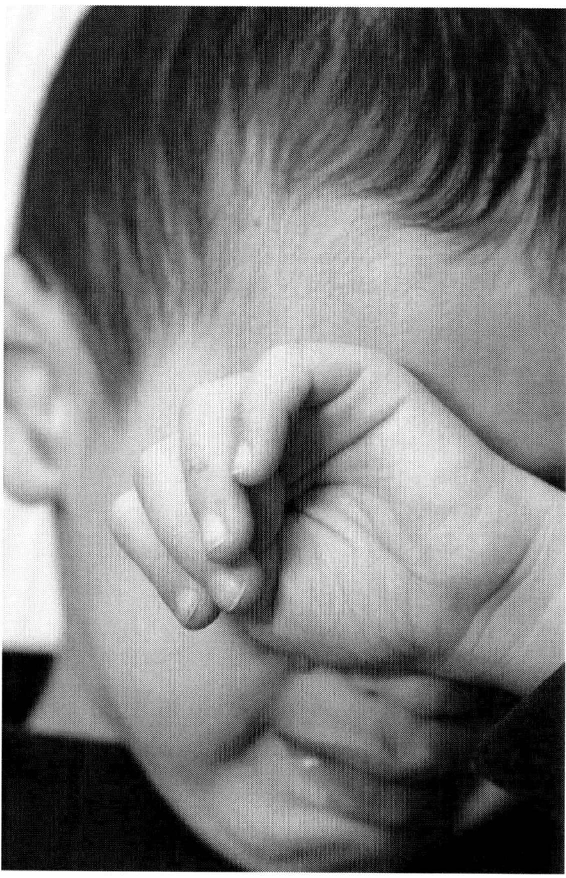

It actually took only seven trials before the white rat became a conditioned stimulus, meaning that the rat alone without the presence of the loud noise caused Albert to be fearful. This form of classical conditioning is often referred to as the conditioned emotional response (CER), since it specifically involves creating an emotional response to a stimulus that was once neutral.

ACTIVITY

Psychologists have an ethical obligation to protect participants in psychological research. That said, what ethical problems do you believe were present in Watson's study and why?

Watson has been often criticized for failing to "extinguish" or remove the fear of white rats in Little Albert after the study. And even if he had, the study might still have created long-term negative consequences for Albert. One such consequence could have involved Albert's being fearful of other animals or objects that resemble white rats.

Stimulus generalization occurs when a stimulus similar to the original conditioned stimulus (CS) elicits the conditioned response (CR). When only the original CS elicits the CR this is referred to as *stimulus discrimination.*

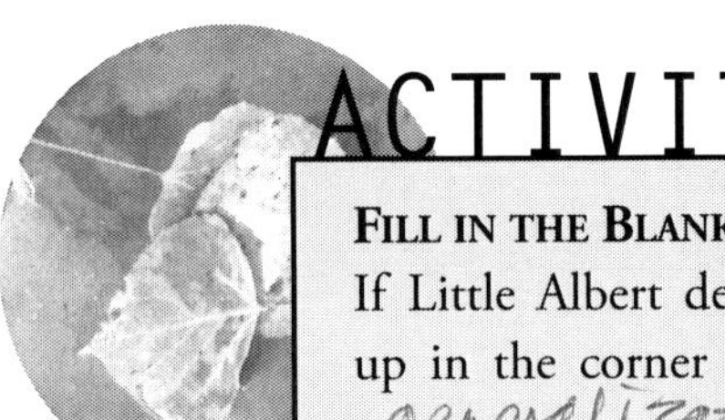

ACTIVITY

FILL IN THE BLANKS

If Little Albert demonstrated fear around white bunnies and even white T-shirts crumpled up in the corner of the room after Watson's study, this would be an example of stimulus generalization.

Classical Conditioning and Attitudes

In addition to the examples we have already discussed, classical conditioning can also have very large social implications and even help foster forms of potentially destructive prejudice.

CLASSICAL CONDITIONING IN ACTION – A mother holds a covert, or unspoken, prejudice toward members of a certain racial group. Twice daily she walks down the street with her 3-year-old daughter who does not yet hold any racial prejudice. Over the next several months her mother gets anxious, pulls her child closer to her, and crosses the street every time a member of the disliked group passes her and her daughter. Through this process, the child becomes conditioned to be fearful and therefore prejudiced of the same racial group as her mother.

How is this an example of classical conditioning? Remember to review the definitions of the five key terms of classical conditioning.

Prior to conditioning of the child, the neutral stimulus was the member of the disliked group, since the child had no natural negative or fearful reactions toward members of this group. The unconditioned stimulus was the mother's anxious and negative reaction when she encountered members of the disliked group, which caused the unconditioned response in the child of being anxious and upset.

NS = member of disliked group
UCS = mother's anxious and negative reactions
UCR = child's reaction of being anxious and fearful

During conditioning, the neutral stimulus (the member of the disliked group) was repeatedly paired with the unconditioned stimulus (the parent's anxious reaction). This caused the once-neutral stimulus to become a conditioned stimulus. In other words, the child learned that every time she saw a member of the racial group her mother disliked, she too should feel anxious and fearful.

CS = member of the disliked group
CR = child's reaction of being anxious and fearful

The end result is that a child who had no racial prejudice has now learned or been conditioned to be prejudiced toward a certain group. Notice how this could happen even if the mother said verbally that she did not hold any racial prejudices. Just her actions around members of the disliked group and the child's natural responses to her mother's anxiety and fear would be enough to condition the child's fear.

Operant Conditioning

E.L. Thorndike (1874–1949) was an early researcher in the psychology of learning. The principle of operant conditioning was not yet coined, and it was clear the road to such discoveries was being paved by another set of principles set forth by Thorndike and his colleagues.

Like other prominent behaviorists, Thorndike studied learning in animals, mainly cats. The learning of associations between stimulus and response fascinated him. A hungry cat was confined in a box with food as an incentive for escape. A number of devices including rings, panels, and levers were rigged in the box but only one would trigger the door for the cat's escape.

In studying these cats, Thorndike concluded that animals do not use abilities such as reason or logic but rather trial and error. He called this the *law of effect*, meaning that behaviors followed by a satisfying event were strengthened and thus occurred more often and, in repeated circumstances, more quickly. Conversely, behaviors that are followed by an annoying or frustrating event were decreased and eventually occurred very little or not at all.

B.F. Skinner (1904–1990) is arguably the most influential psychologist in history. Like Thorndike, this Harvard psychologist worked with animals in boxes, now often referred to as a Skinner box, to better understand the principles of learning that guided their behavior. This experimental chamber was designed to control as many environmental variables as possible, variables like temperature, light, and feeding/water schedule. The most popular types of these boxes contained a lever that would, when pressed, release pellets of food. In addition, they had floors comprised of metal so that an electric shock could be applied to the animal. As you may have concluded, Skinner studied how animals learn through very strictly controlling how and when reinforcements (food pellets) and punishments (electric shock) where administered.

Both Thorndike and Skinner laid the foundation for what we now call operant conditioning.

Operant conditioning is a type of learning where the behavior of an individual or organism is shaped by consequences. One important difference between operant and classical conditioning is that behavior shaped in operant conditioning is voluntary, unlike the salivation of Pavlov's dogs in the presence of food or the fear of Little Albert when a loud noise occurred. It is also important to understand what is meant by the word *consequences*. Many people tend to hold a parentified view of the word and think of consequences as being negative in much the way a parent might tell a child, "There will be consequences for that young man!" However, consequences can come in the form of reinforcement or punishment.

Reinforcement is the introduction or removal of a stimulus designed to strengthen a behavior, thus making it more likely to occur in the future. Thus, a reinforcing stimulus can take many forms and is often called a reward. *Punishment* is the introduction or removal of a stimulus designed to weaken a behavior, thus making it less likely to occur in the future.

Two types of reinforcement are commonly identified: positive and negative. Positive reinforcement occurs when a stimulus is added to help strengthen a behavior, making it more likely to occur in the future. Negative reinforcement is the removal of an undesirable stimulus that strengthens a behavior and makes it more likely to occur again in the future.

ACTIVITY

Positive and Negative Reinforcement

You enter your car and start the ignition. Before backing out of your driveway, an annoying sound ensues: "Bing! Bing! Bing!" To stop this intolerable racket, you buckle your seatbelt at which point the sound stops. This is an example of what kind of reinforcement? Explain your answer.

Negative because if you buckle up, you can take away an undesirable stimulus.

A basketball player runs a play the way her coach wants her to. When she returns to the sideline, her coach praises her and gives her a fist bump. This is an example of what kind of reinforcement? Explain your answer.

positive because if she does something right she gains praise.

As you might have already been thinking, the stimulus chosen to reinforce a behavior is crucial. Imagine for a moment that you are trying to positively reinforce good behavior of a child in the classroom. When the child behaves as you want him to, you give him a chocolate bar. This should positively reinforce his behavior, right? Well, that

assumption would prove to be true only if the child likes chocolate. What if the child happens to be allergic to chocolate and it makes him sick? Or, what if he just does not like the taste? For reinforcement to be most effective, the stimulus chosen as the reinforcer must be meaningful and desirable to the person being reinforced.

There are two general categories of reinforcers referred to as primary and secondary. *Primary reinforcers* are stimuli that satisfy some kind of biological need. Some examples include: food, water, and touch.

Secondary reinforcers are stimuli that we learn to value and do not serve a biological need such as money, toys, and praise.

© Yuri Arcurs, 2011. Used under license of Shutterstock, Inc.

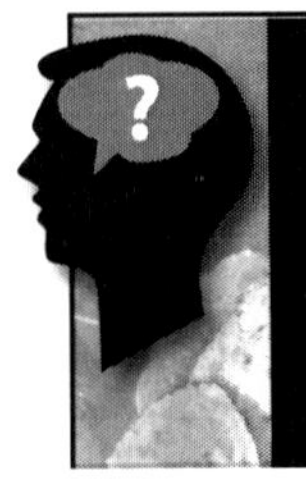

Think about it – What stimulus makes you more likely to perform a task? Does a paycheck cause you to work more diligently on a project? What reinforcers cause you to continue to come to a college course? If you wanted to teach a small child to not play in the busy city street, what would you do?

Just as there are positive and negative forms of reinforcement, there are also positive and negative forms of punishment. Positive punishment is the introduction of a stimulus that weakens a behavior, thus making it less likely to occur again in the future. Negative punishment is the removal of a stimulus such that it makes a behavior less likely to occur in the future.

ACTIVITY

Positive and Negative Punishment

A child at the dinner table throws a piece of corn on the floor and chuckles. The child's father spanks the child. This is an example of what kind of punishment? Explain your answer. positive because if the kid does something wrong, you add a punishment.

© Zurijeta, 2011. Used under license of Shutterstock, Inc.

ACTIVITY (*continued*)

Last month a teenager went over her limit for both text messaging and phone minutes on her smart phone. Her parents are incredulous and take away both her smart phone and her car keys for the next month. This is an example of what kind of punishment? Explain your answer. Negative punishment because they take something away as a consequence.

© Elena Elisseeva, 2011. Used under license of Shutterstock, Inc.

A common mistake that is made when learning about operant conditioning is to confuse the terms negative reinforcement and punishment. These are not the same! Remember, negative reinforcement is seeking to *strengthen* a behavior through the removal of an undesirable stimulus, whereas the goal of punishment is to *weaken* a behavior.

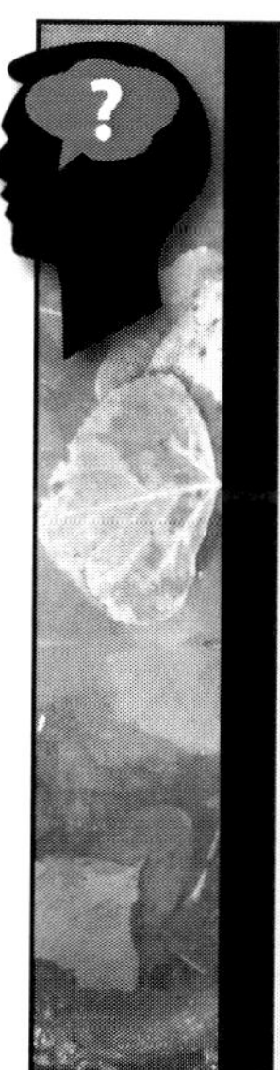

Think about it –
Negative Reinforcement vs. Punishment

Imagine your teacher said you could avoid the final exam by attending every class and getting an A on your midterm exam. Would this strengthen your attendance and study time by removing a stimulus (final exam)? If so, it is a negative reinforcement. Yes.

© Vixit, 2011. Used under license of Shutterstock, Inc.

(*continued*)

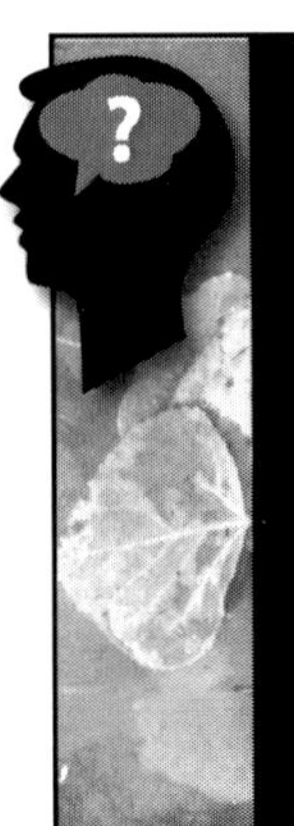

Think about it (*continued*)
Now, imagine your teacher docks you one letter grade for being late to class. Is this a negative reinforcement designed to increase a behavior (attendance) or a punishment designed to decrease a behavior (tardiness)? A negative punishment.

Remember! When thinking about the types of reinforcement, positive means the addition of a stimulus and negative means the subtraction of a stimulus. Positive and negative should not be thought of as good or bad in types of reinforcement. Whether positive or negative, each seeks to strengthen (reinforce) the behavior.

Operant conditioning can sound easy when you read about it in a book or sketch out a plan on paper. However, it is often much more complex in practice. For example, many parents find themselves waiting until a behavior occurs that they do not like and then punishing that behavior as opposed to identifying behaviors they want to see more of and reinforcing those behaviors. Moreover, sometimes a parent is attempting to punish a child but is actually reinforcing him or her.

This occurred with a family who was attempting to utilize the negative punishment of timeout with their son. When he would engage in a behavior they did not like, they would remove him from where he was playing and place him in timeout. Sounds good so far, right? The problem was they were putting him in timeout in his father's office in their home where he would spin around on a big leather chair, play with his dad's hourglass, look at his father's screen saver on his computer screen, and so much more. While their intention was to punish him, they were actually positively reinforcing his behavior!

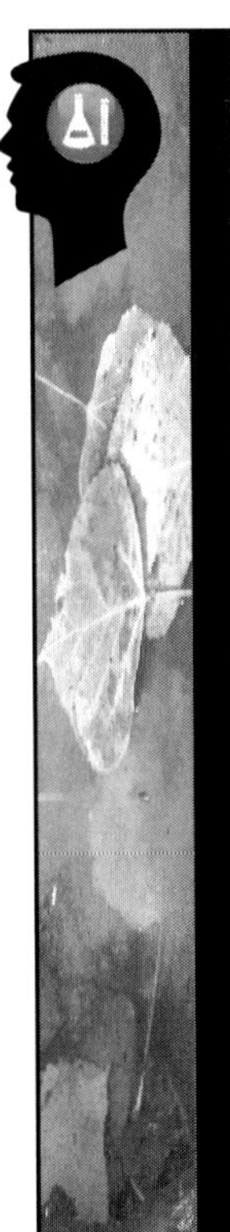

Thought Experiment – You see your beloved pet dog across the street digging a hole in the neighbor's prized rose garden. You scream, "Rover! Come here!" He immediately hears your command and having learned to obey it comes running toward you. Though you are trying to be patient, your frustration is so heated that when Rover arrives at your feet you immediately smack him on the nose and begin scolding.

Think in terms of what you have learned about operant conditioning. What behaviors have been shaped in this exchange? How have they been shaped? Were there reinforcers? Punishments?

Though you may have been trying to decrease Rover's digging in the neighbor's flowers by adding a punishment, you perhaps have unwittingly decreased the likelihood (punished) of another behavior, Rover's approaching when you call.

As human beings, we do not exist in a vacuum. What this means is that any form of punishment can have long-lasting implications, especially on children. In particular, aggressive forms of punishment can lead to future increased aggressiveness in the child (Anderson, Buckley, & Carnagey, 2008), learned helplessness (Bargai, Ben-Shakhar, & Shalev, 2007), and passive aggressive behavior. Some of these consequences can be carried with the child into adulthood ways of interacting with others.

This is not meant to imply that punishment is bad and should not be utilized. Instead, it is just a cautionary note that while operant conditioning can alter behavior, it can also have psychological consequences that were not initially intended.

Terms

Here are some terms in classical and operant conditioning that will be helpful to remember as you continue your studying.

- Acquisition: A term in classical conditioning referring to the development of conditioned responses. As pairings are made over and over again between the conditioned (sound of a bell) and unconditioned stimulus (food), the conditioned responses (salivation) will become stronger.
- Extinction: In classical conditioning, it is the weakening and eventual disappearance of the CR (salivation) in response to the CS (bell). This takes place by continually presenting the CS (bell) without the US (food). The animal eventually learns there is no association between the CS (bell) and the US (food). In operant conditioning, extinction refers to the loss of the response that was once learned. This happens when the reinforcers characteristically used to strengthen the behavior are no longer provided.
- Generalization: A term in classical conditioning referring to the shift of a response learned to one stimulus to a similar stimulus. For example, if a dog learns to associate the sound of a bell with a food, he may respond in a similar way (salivation) to the sound of something similar to a bell or a different-toned bell. This response is usually not as strong as the one to the original stimulus.
- Discrimination: A term in classical conditioning referring to the process by which an organism distinguishes between two or more stimuli. For example, if the sound of a bell (CS) is presented with the food (US) but only at a specific tone and another bell with a different tone (also a CS) is presented without the food (US) the dog may learn that, though there are two similar stimuli, only one is associated with the food and thus will only respond (salivate) to the tone associated with food.
- Spontaneous Recovery: Refers to the reemergence of a CR (salivation) that has become extinct. Spontaneous recovery tends to yield less intense responses than previously established. This is often called resurgence in operant conditioning.
- Reinforcement: In operant conditioning refers to the strengthening of a behavior.
- Positive reinforcement: The presentation of a stimulus that functions to strengthen the frequency of the targeted behavior. For instance, to effectively get a dog to sit when commanded to do so, a tasty treat presented as a reward for sitting when commanded will reinforce the behavior in the future.
- Punishment: The presentation or removal of a stimulus that functions to weaken or eliminate the frequency of a targeted behavior.
- Negative reinforcement: The removal of a stimulus that seeks to strengthen the frequency of the target behavior. For example, a rat receiving an electric shock learns that by pressing a lever, it can stop the shock; if it doesn't press the lever, the shock will continue. Its behavior (lever pressing) is reinforced by the removal of a stimulus (shock).

Observational Learning

Although operant and classically conditioned responses can tell us a large part of how humans and other animals learn, there are still yet other ways to learn and these ways of learning don't necessarily require any direct experience. Can you guess what they might be?

Higher-ordered species, usually those with the most active and largest brains like humans and monkeys, very clearly learn without any direct experience, that is without having been rewarded/punished (operant conditioning) or having their behavior paired with other stimuli (classical conditioning). These animals are capable of learning by merely watching another animal. This type of learning is called *observational learning.*

Think about it – Imagine that you're driving a powerful car on a desolate, open highway. Ahead of you is a clear road, and you feel the rush that comes with a high velocity. You crest a hill at top speed and see a highway patrol vehicle parked at the bottom of it. What is your next move? That is, what is your *behavior?*

Ask yourself, what *shaped* this behavior? Perhaps you have had a speeding ticket in the past (a stimulus added to decrease your behavior; punishment). However, it is quite possible that you have never had a speeding ticket nor have had your speeding behavior reinforced or punished in any direct way. Nevertheless, you *know* to slow down. Have you observed people being pulled over? On television? Perhaps you have watched as your parent or friend slowed down in the presence of a highway patrol car.

What other examples can you think of? A child watching his brother step on a spider or playing with a toy? How do you know to not lean on a hot stove?

The process by which an organism observes and imitates a behavior is called **modeling**. The psychologist Albert Bandura pioneered research looking into modeling and observational learning and made some most interesting discoveries (Bandura, Ross, & Ross, 1961). He believed that human behavior is acquired more through observing others than through direct experience with the consequences of behaviors and that reinforcement is not essential for effective learning to occur.

In his famous experiment, Bandura set a child to work on a drawing. An adult in the room, previously performing a mundane task, suddenly gets up and for approximately 10 minutes kicks, throws, and hits a large inflated doll, called the Bobo doll, all the while yelling aggressive statements like "Hit him! Kick him!" After watching this outburst, the child is taken to another room filled with enticing toys and shortly after, in order to frustrate the child, told that he cannot play with them. Now the child is taken to another room filled with toys and, you guessed it, a Bobo doll. What do you suppose the child does? How does the child behave?

As you may have suspected, children who were exposed to the adult and the outburst were much more likely to hit and kick the doll than those who were not exposed to the aggressive adult even when all the other variables (frustration) were controlled. What was especially striking was the extent to which the children imitated the adults. For example, one specific act of aggression the adults were instructed to engage in involved pinning the Bobo doll on the ground on all fours while hitting and punching the doll with a series of alternating punches. The children who watched the adults engage in this behavior mimicked the behavior almost exactly. So it was not as though the children were just randomly striking the Bobo doll, but rather, hitting the doll in the very same ways they observed the adults hitting the doll.

While it may seem like common sense that people look at the behaviors of others and use this behavior to modify their own, Bandura was the first to offer scientific evidence to support this claim. His results had a ripple effect suggesting both positive and negative observational learning. These are often referred to as *prosocial* and *antisocial* effects.

Ask Around – Can you think of examples of behavior that children learn by observing others that can be considered positive or helpful? Can you think of antisocial effects?

There have been many suggestions that violence and sex in the media impact behavior, especially the behavior of children. There are also media that seek to promote social change and healthy behaviors. Can you think of examples of each? How are their methods similar? Different?

To encourage children to read, it is clear that parents should read themselves and to the child. To increase the chances that children will do their homework, parents should actively engage in the homework themselves. Models of behavior are most effective when the actions and the commands are congruent. That is, the words match the actions. Parents who do not want their children to smoke cigarettes but continue to smoke themselves will likely have trouble achieving their objective. The old "do as I say and not as I do" method of parenting is rife with flaws due to the power of observational learning.

ACTIVITY

Imagine the following scenario. You are waiting in line at the checkout counter of your favorite grocer. You notice a parent struggling with two young children who are fighting with one another. You watch the parent slap one of the children sternly on the shoulder and exclaim, "No! We don't hit! Don't hit your brother."

Think back to what you learned about operant conditioning. Did punishment or reinforcement take place. What behavior was being shaped? Now think to what you know about observational learning. What did the two children observe? Certainly they observed the parent's words, "No We don't hit!" but they also observed the parent's behavior.

It is important to think about these situations from many points of view. Think of this from a learning perspective incorporating all you have learned about operant conditioning, classical conditioning, and observational learning. Discuss your observations in the space below:

This is positive punishment because the parent adds a slap as a punishment. The kid may learn from this through modeling & continue to hit people because he observed his parent doing it.

It is clear humans learn through observation, as evidenced by Bandura's pioneering work along with the work of many others who followed in his footsteps. Perhaps less clear is how animals learn through observation. Many non-human animals have been shown to exhibit new behaviors through observational learning. This learning may be as simple as learning the location of a food source or as complex as learning a chain of actions that lead to a reward. Apes and chimpanzees learn different survival skills by watching others of their species (Brosnan & deWaal, 2004), and even an octopus can learn to select an object over another from merely watching another perform this same action (Fiorito & Scotto, 1992).

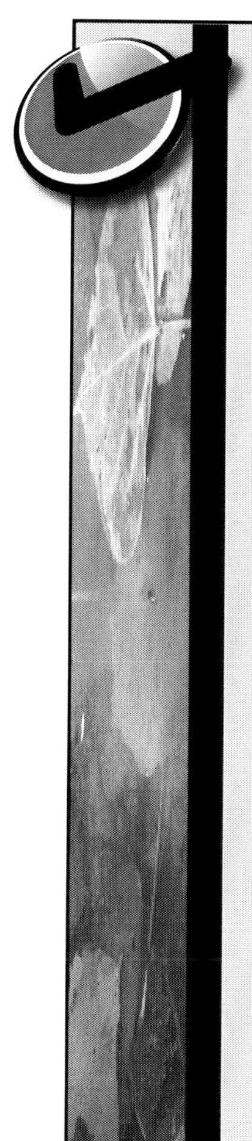

Review – What type of learning is illustrated in these examples?

John and his wife Candy move to a new city where she has found a great job. While she works full time, John spends his days learning the new city. Two months later, when Candy suggests meeting for lunch at a downtown restaurant, John knows right away where to go and needs no direction. Learning?

Observational learning.

13-year-old Megan rarely did her homework. Her father began giving her tickets to the movie and allowing more free time with friends for every week she finished all her homework. Megan now completes her homework regularly. Learning?

positive reinforcement - operant conditioning

John's abusive stepmother cooked tuna casserole three times per week for many years of his childhood. Now, as an adult John flinches every time he smells cooking fish. Learning?

Stimulus generalization

When Harry's older brother gave him a toy gun, he at once pointed it and began to make shooting noises. Learning?

Observational learning

REFERENCES

Anderson, C. A., Buckley, K. E., & Carnegey, N. L. (2008). Creating your own hostile environment: A laboratory examination of trait aggressiveness and the violence escalation cycle. *Personality and Social Psychology Bulletin, 34,* 462–473.

Bandura, A., Ross, D., & Ross, S. (1961). Transmission of aggression through imitation of aggressive models. *Journal of Abnormal & Social Psychology, 63,* 575–582.

Bargai, N., Ben-Shakar, G., & Shalev, A. Y. (2007). Posttraumatic stress disorder and depression in battered women: The mediating role of learned helplessness. *Journal of Family Violence, 22*(5), 267–275.

Brosnan, S. F., & de Waal, F. B. (2004). Socially learning preferences for differentially rewarded tokens in the brown capuchin monkey (Cebus appella). *Journal of Comparative Psychology, 118,* 133–139.

Fiorito, G., & Scotto, P. (1992). Observational learning in Octopus vulgaris. *Science, 256*(5056), 545–547.

Tinbergen, N. (1951). *The study of instinct.* Oxford: Clarendon.

Watson, J. B., & Rayner, R. (1920). Conditioned emotional reactions. *Journal of Experimental Psychology, 3,* 1–14.

NAME ______________________________ DATE ____________________

WORKSHEET CHAPTER THREE

CHAPTER 4
SENSATION AND PERCEPTION

"We see things not as they are but as we are."
Immanuel Kant

What if I told you that your eyes really do not see the words you are reading right now? What if I took it a step further and told you all your eyes see are actually rays of light? In truth, if we only had eyes and the sensory receptors located in our eyes, you would have never learned to perceive the words you are reading right now as words. It is not until the sensory impulse is passed on from the eyes to the brain that you actually perceive the light rays emitted from the page you are reading as a meaningful pattern we call words.

In this chapter, we will explore the major sensory receptor sites and the areas of the brain that help us perceive the world in a meaningful way.

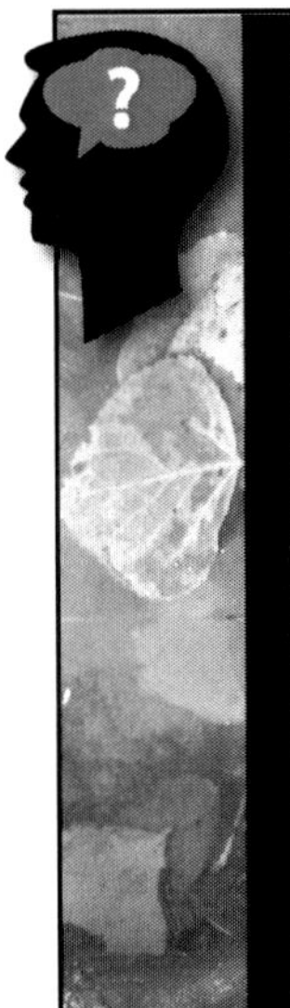

THINK ABOUT IT – Is perception always reality? In other words, is what our brain perceives always accurate and does it give us the true nature of reality? Write your answer below:

Perception is not always reality because everyone could interpret sensory information differently and it may not always reflect reality.

Note: You will be asked the same question after we finish covering sensation and perception and we will see if your answer has changed.

SENSATION AND PERCEPTION

The process of *sensation* involves detecting outside stimuli via specialized sensory receptor sites located in various sense organs (i.e., eyes, ears, skin, tongue) and then sending that raw sensory information from the receptor sites to the brain. The message is sent in the form of a neural impulse. Once that message is received by the brain, perception occurs. *Perception* is the process of interpreting the raw sensory information initially processed by the sensory receptors into meaningful patterns.

Sometimes the process of sensation and perception starts from the bottom-up as we just described. That is, raw sensory data are sent up to the brain where meaning is made of the information. However, there is also a form of processing called top-down. This happens when high-level cognitive processes initiate the process.

Recall the first paragraph of this chapter in which the ability to perceive letters and words was discussed. When we first learned to read, we engaged in bottom-up processing, learning that ink on paper in certain patterns form what are called letters, which we learned are imperative to our structure of language. As we continued to become more sophisticated in our language structure over many years of schooling, we learned to perceive words as a whole, and later, words joined together in meaningful patterns within a sentence rather than perceiving each single letter. It is simply more efficient when reading. This is a more sophisticated process and is referred to as top-down processing.

A Closer Look at Sensation

In this section we will cover the sensory receptor sites for each of our major sense organs. Before we do this, though, we need to understand in a little more detail how our sensory receptors gather data from the outside world and how those data are sent on to the brain.

The first step in the process involves *detection,* meaning our sensory receptors must detect the external stimulus. Once the stimulus is detected, it needs to be sent to the brain where meaning can be made of it. This process is called *transduction* and is jumpstarted by the energy from the stimulus converted by the receptor into a neural impulse. Finally, *coding* takes place that allows the brain to know what kind of sensory information is being sent (e.g., visual, auditory, touch). Coding helps determine what pathway to use to assure the information arrives in the correct area of the brain (specific areas of the brain important for perception will be described later in the chapter).

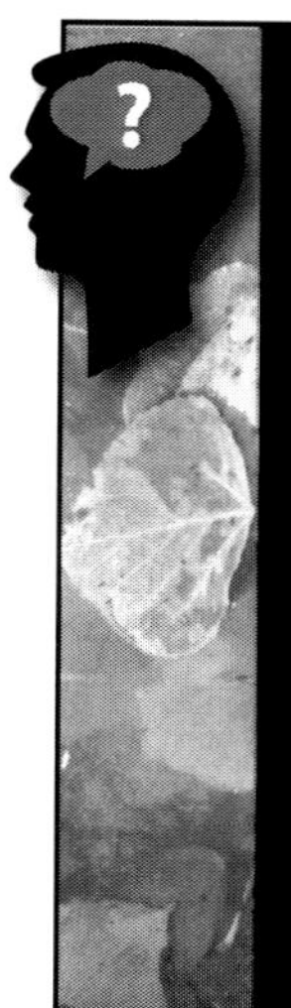

Think about it – The process of transduction and coding actually helps limit the amount of outside stimuli sent to the brain. In addition, the process of sensory reduction helps to further reduce and prioritize what sensory messages will get sent to the brain.

© marekuliasz, 2011. Used under license of Shutterstock, Inc.

Why is this important? What would it be like if every piece of sensory information in the world around us was sent to the brain?

This is important because if we perceived every single piece of sensory info, I don't think we would be able to focus on anything.

Sensory Adaptation

The town where I went to college is notorious for its awful smell. This smell is generated by a local meat processing plant as well as manure from nearby farms. During certain times of the year and with the right amount of wind, the smell can be overwhelming. When people first move to the town or visit from out of town, the smell is especially noticeable.

© dundanim, 2011. Used under license of Shutterstock, Inc.

Over time, though, a funny thing happened to me: I started to notice the smell less and less. In fact, after just two years living in the town, a friend came to visit me from out of state. As she was leaving my condo and heading for her car, she said with an excruciating look on her face: "What's that awful smell?" I sniffed around and could not smell a thing.

Why was it that my friend was dry heaving on her way to the car, and I could not smell anything out of the ordinary? The answer is sensory adaptation. *Sensory adaptation* occurs when our sensitivity to a stimulus decreases after prolonged and constant exposure. Our receptors actually get fatigued and stop firing as quickly as they once did. Since I lived around the smell every day, the sensory receptors in my nose adapted to the smell. As for my friend, the smell was new to her and thus much more intense.

Some senses adapt faster than others, with touch and smell being the quickest to adapt. The receptors for our eyes, for example, never completely adapt. If they did, we could not stare at a stimulus that remains constant without it eventually disappearing from our line of sight. From an evolutionary perspective, there are also some senses that we do not adapt to as well because doing so could compromise our survival. Heat and pain are just two examples.

Think about it – As you prepare to get dressed and come to class, you place shoes on your feet. When you first put on your shoes, you feel their presence since just moments earlier they were not touching your skin. However, you do not feel your shoes all day the same way you feel them when you first put them on. In fact, if your shoes are comfortable, you rarely notice you have them on the rest of the day. Why is this?

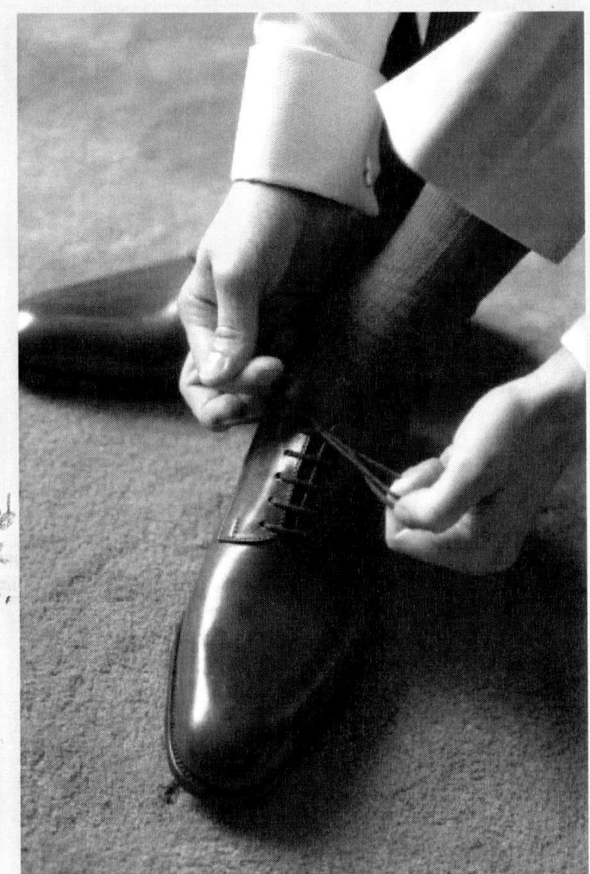

Atlaspix, 2011. Used under license of Shutterstock, Inc.

After class, you hop in your car to drive home. You hook your MP3 player up to your car and begin jamming to some of your favorite music. As you hit the open road, you crank up the volume on your radio even higher to make sure you can hear it over the increased road noise. As you pull into your neighborhood, you continue to jam at the same decibel level until you pull into your driveway. You turn the car off and go inside without turning the radio off or giving the decibel level of the MP3 player in your car a second thought. The next day when you start your car for the first time the music is playing at the same level you left it at the previous evening. However, it is so loud in the morning that you jump out of your seat before quickly reaching to turn it down. You wonder to yourself why it seemed so loud this morning after it was so perfect the previous evening. Explain how this is possible.

© Vlue, 2011. Used under license of Shutterstock, Inc.

A Tour of Our Major Sensory Receptors and Perception in the Brain

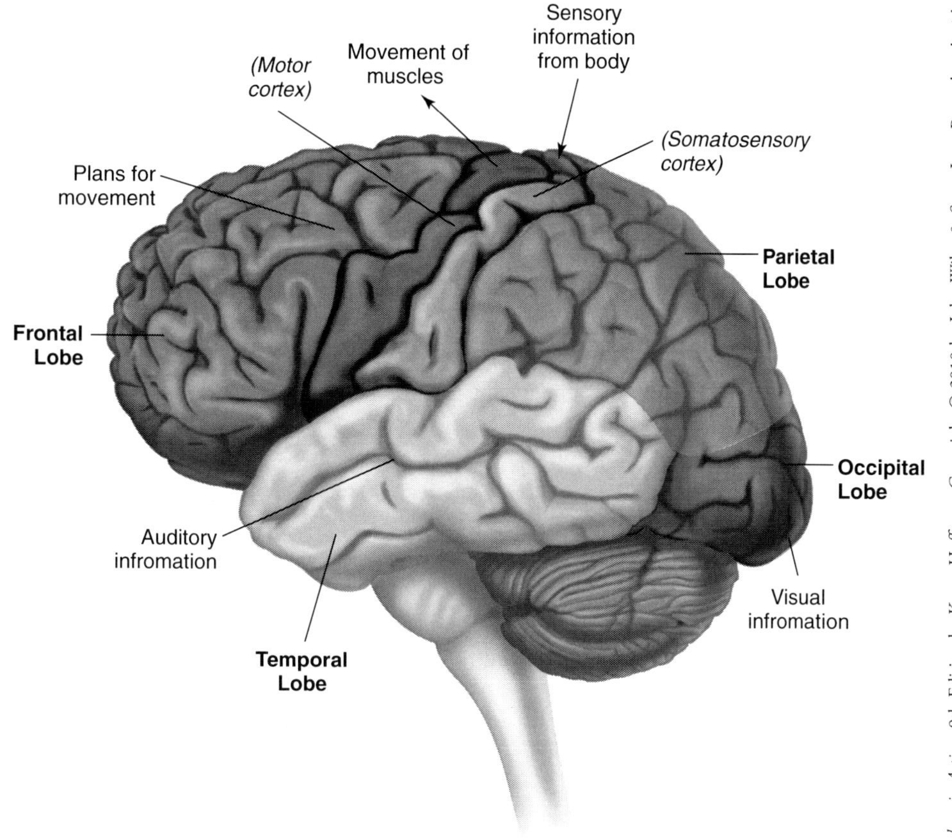

Figure 4.1

Vision

As mentioned at the start of the chapter, the process of making meaning out of visual stimuli first involves taking in outside light rays. At the level of the eye, we do not actually see a copy of the shapes or objects in the outside world. This does not happen until a neural impulse is sent from the eyeball to the brain.

Light rays enter the eye through the cornea, travel through the iris (responsible for color) and the lens (focuses light rays), and finish at the cornea. In the cornea the receptor sites for vision can be found. These are called rods and cones. *Rods* are concentrated on the outside edges of the retina and are responsible for detecting shades of gray, peripheral vision, and vision in dark or poorly lit

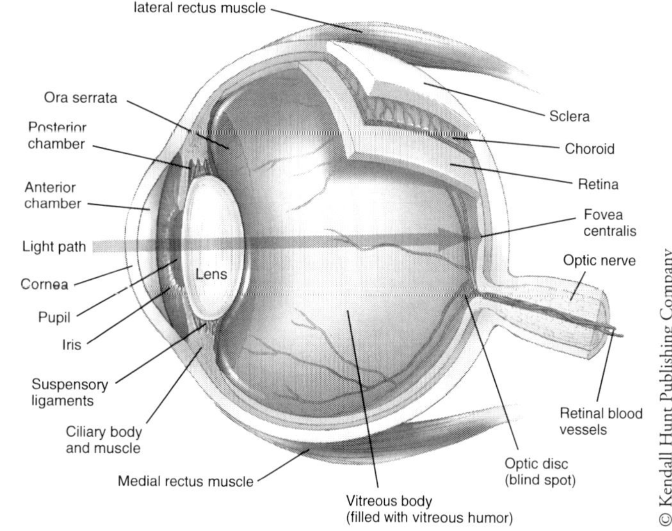

Figure 4.2

conditions. *Cones* are located in the center of the retina and are responsible for our ability to detect color, finer details, and our ability to see in well lit or bright conditions (See Figure 4.2).

After the light waves are processed by the rods and cones, the energy is converted into a neural impulse. This impulse or message is sent to the brain via the optic nerve. It is not until the impulse reaches the occipital lobe in the brain that we actually perceive light rays as something meaningful in our world.

Audition

The process of hearing also starts with the ability of our sensory receptors to receive waves from the outside world. In the case of hearing, though, these waves take the form of sound waves. More specifically, sound happens as a result of pressure from sound waves in the ear. Waves that have higher peaks and relatively low valleys produce louder sounds. Waves that have lower peaks and valleys produce sounds interpreted as softer.

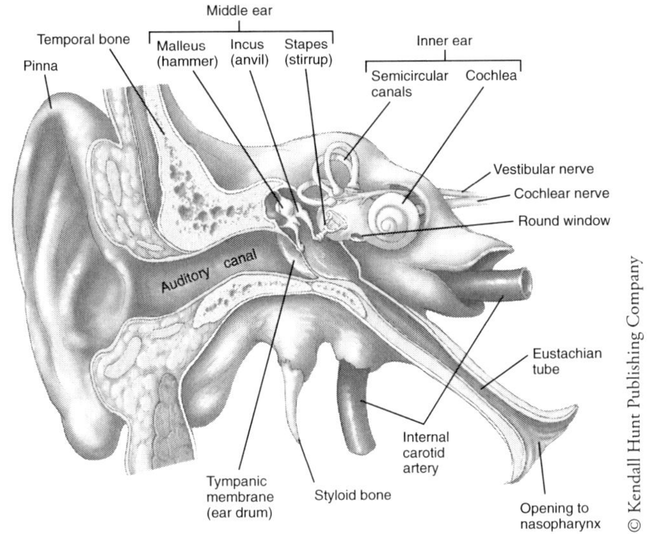

Figure 4.3

The sensory receptors for sound are located in a structure in the inner ear called the *cochlea.* Within the cochlea (See Figure 4.3) lie many tiny hair cells on the basilar membrane. These hair cells move in different ways as a result of sound waves and serve as the sensory receptors for audition. After the sound waves are received by the hair cells in the cochlea, a neural impulse is sent to the auditory cortex of the temporal lobe in the brain. Here, sound is perceived and assembled into meaningful patterns.

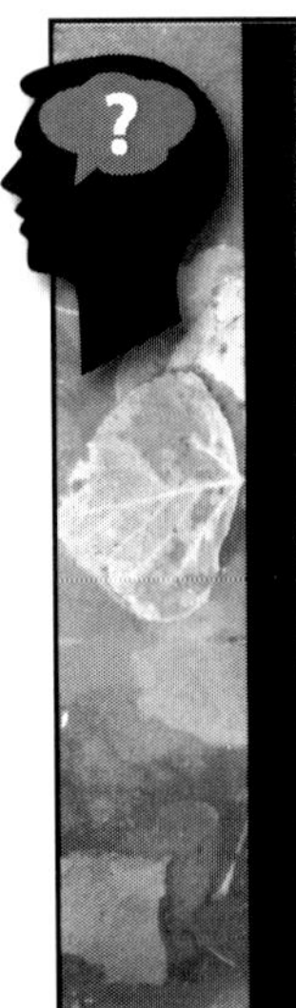

THINK ABOUT IT – Take a look around campus and you will likely notice many people with headphones on. This has become more and more common in the last decade with the creation of the MP3 player, giving us the ability to take an entire music library with us on one device. While this piece of technology certainly has its advantages, what do you suppose might be some of the disadvantages in terms of potential damage it might cause our sensory receptor sites for hearing?

It can do damage to the sensory receptors in the cochlea.

Sound is measured in decibels. As the decibel level increases, so does the chance prolonged exposure will do damage to our hearing. As a general rule, prolonged exposure to any sound over 85 decibels can cause permanent hearing damage. Exposure to a sound over 120 decibels can do damage much more quickly.

(*continued*)

THINK ABOUT IT *(continued)*

Do you know that most state-of-the-art MP3 players can reach 120 decibels? This means that an MP3 player turned up high but not all the way can still exceed 85 decibels. Moreover, "earbud" headphones that sit deeper in the ear can further amplify the sound.

How loud is your MP3 player?

Probably too loud.

Jose AS Reyes, 2011. Used under license of Shutterstock, Inc.

Olfaction

Our sense of smell, or olfaction, begins with molecules in the air reaching the olfactory epithelium in the nose. The *olfactory epithelium* is where our sensory receptors for smell are located. When air molecules make contact and bind with these tiny receptors, a neural impulse is generated. The impulse moves through the olfactory bulb where specific smells are coded and on to the through the temporal lobe and then the limbic system. The temporal lobe is responsible for most of the smells we perceive on a day-to-day basis. The limbic system is the emotional center of our brain and is also responsible for important aspects of memory, which explains why smells can trigger very intense memories.

Our ability to smell is a more important sense than some people realize. For example, do you notice how you often smell something you are not sure about eating before you put it in your mouth? While not a perfect solution, smelling something before consuming it can serve as a protective mechanism to avoid eating something that might be potentially dangerous to the body.

ACTIVITY

A man is standing in the line at the grocery story looking at the tabloids, candy, and other impulse buys as he waits to checkout. After standing in line for about 30 seconds, a woman walks up behind him in line. She is wearing a particular perfume that the man's "first love" used to wear over a decade ago in high school. All of a sudden, the man experiences a flood of internal emotions and memories about his first love. He's euphoric, jealous, and angry all at the same time.

Using what you've learned about the process of olfaction, explain what in the brain is likely causing this man's strong reaction to the perfume of the woman standing behind him in line.

The limbic system.

Gustation

Taste, or gustation, involves five major taste sensations: salty, sweet, bitter, sour, and umami (which means delicious). Umami involves a separate taste receptor than the first four taste sensations designed to detect glutamate, which is often found in meat. Receptors for taste are located on the tongue, where they receive information from food and liquid molecules. Most of these receptors reside inside of the little bumps on the tongue called papillae (See Figure 4.4), but there are a limited number of receptors located in the back of the mouth in the palate.

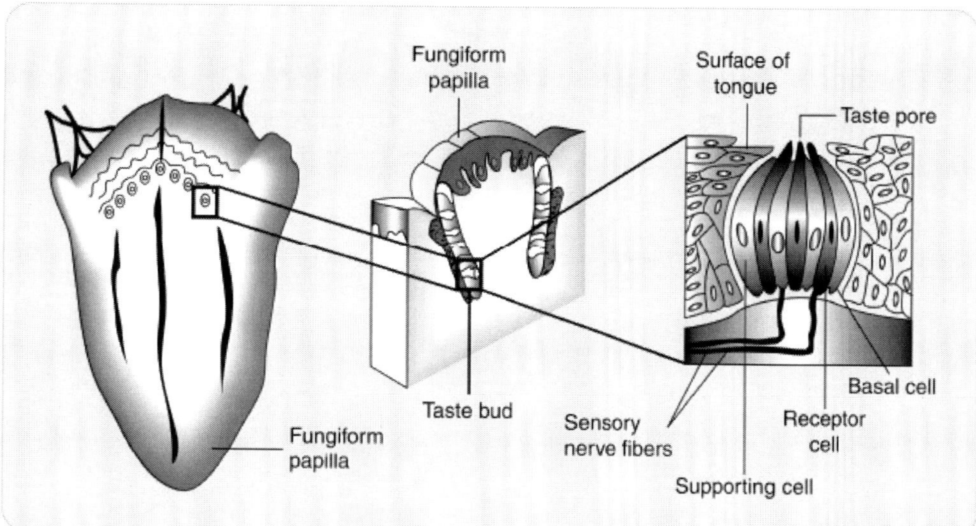

From *Science Majors Laboratory II* by Department of Biology, East Tennessee State University. © 2009 by Kendall Hunt Publishing Company. Reprinted by permission.

Figure 4.4

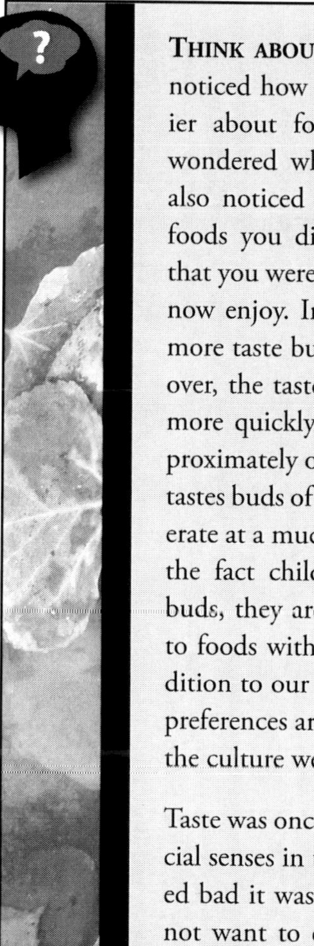

Sergey Andrianov, 2011. Used under license of Shutterstock, Inc.

Think about it – Have you ever noticed how some people are pickier about foods than others and wondered why? Perhaps you have also noticed that there are certain foods you did not like as a child that you were surprised to learn you now enjoy. In short, children have more taste buds than adults. Moreover, the taste buds of children die more quickly and are replaced approximately once a week. When the tastes buds of adults die, they regenerate at a much slower pace. Due to the fact children have more taste buds, they are often more sensitive to foods with intense tastes. In addition to our taste buds, some taste preferences are learned as a result of the culture we are a part of.

Taste was once one of our most crucial senses in that if something tasted bad it was a sign that we might not want to eat it, thus serving as a protective mechanism necessary for survival. In the Western world today, taste is more of a luxury.

Touch

Our skin serves as one of the most important and also most complex sensory systems. Not only does it register touch, or pressure, but it also registers temperature and pain. Our skin has many layers and our receptors for touch, temperature, and pain can be found at various depths. For touch, many of the receptors are concentrated on the fingers, which makes sense given that we often use our fingers to explore touch sensations. Touch receptors are also to a lesser degree concentrated in the face, legs, and back.

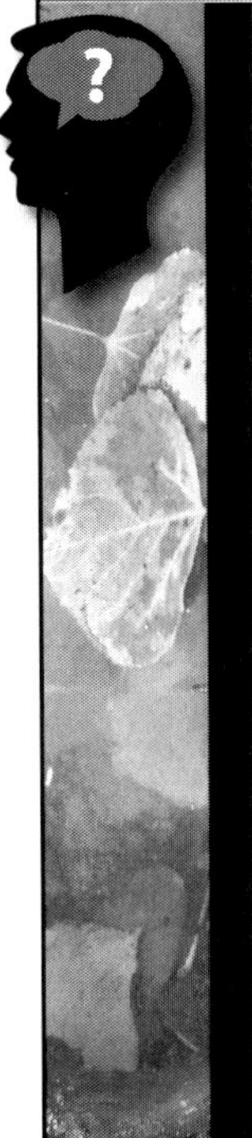

THINK ABOUT IT – Third-degree burns are considered more serious than first and second degree burns because third degree burns are deeper and destroy more layers of skin. However, third degree burns, while more damaging, are almost always less painful. Can you explain why this is?

Epidermis
Dermis
Hypodermis

First-degree burn

Second-degree burn

Third-degree burn

Blamb, 2011. Used under license of Shutterstock, Inc.

When third-degree burns are severe enough, they can destroy nerve endings. These nerve endings are responsible for sending pain messages to the brain. So while these burns are more severe in terms of the damage they do to the skin, the ability to feel pain will not exist if the nerve endings are destroyed. In contrast, crucial nerve endings are not destroyed in first- and second-degree burns, which can explain why second-degree burns are often more painful than third-degree burns.

Vestibular Sense

Have you ever experienced sea or motion sickness? You might be surprised to learn that the origin of this uncomfortable state of being is actually the inner ear. Semicircular canals in the inner ear give the brain important information about balance. Near the end of the canals reside the vestibular sacs. Inside of these sacs there are tiny hair cells that bend and move in accordance with the movement of the head. In other words, as our head moves and turns, so do the hair receptors and fluid inside the vestibular sacs. A neural impulse is carried from the semicircular canals and vestibular sacs to the brain, which communicates important information about balance and body orientation, especially with regard to the position of the head. Unexpected or random

wavebreakmedia ltd, 2011. Used under license of Shutterstock, Inc.

movement (like the movement one might experience on a boat) can cause the vestibular sense to become disrupted, causing symptoms often associated with motion sickness such as nausea, light-headedness, and dizziness.

Kinesthesia

When we think of the major senses, kinesthesia is not a word that is often mentioned. However, the information provided by our kinesthetic receptors is truly invaluable. While our vestibular sense provides information about balance, our kinesthetic receptors provide equally important information about out bodily position and movement. The specific receptors are found inside of tendons, muscles, and joints. Important information such as where our limbs are with respect to the rest of our body and whether muscles are contracted or relaxed is registered with every movement and a neural impulse is sent to the brain.

ACTIVITY

Imagine that you have just finished working out and all of a sudden your kinesthetic receptors stopped functioning. As you begin stretching, now without functioning kinesthetic receptors, what potential risks do you now face when stretching that you would not have had your kinesthetic receptors remained in working order?

You could break a bone or badly injure yourself.

ACTIVITY

What do your perceive?

Look at the above figure for the next two minutes and write down as many meaningful figures within the picture as you can find:

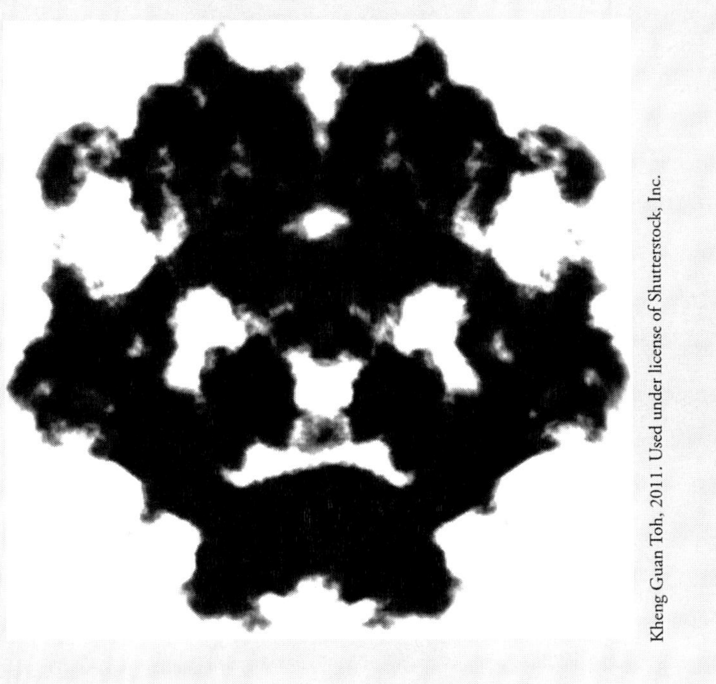

Kheng Guan Toh, 2011. Used under license of Shutterstock, Inc.

Now that you have finished, compare the list of what you saw to the list of the people near you. What similarities and differences are there?

Chances are, in the previous activity your list of what you saw in the figure did not completely match the list of the people sitting around you. Why is this? Shouldn't everyone *perceive* the figure the same way since everyone in the class was looking at the same figure? While there is some consistency in the general strategies our brains use to organize sensory information, there are differences in the ways people organize or perceive ambiguous (or random) stimuli.

ACTIVITY

More fun with perception

Look at Figure 4.5 and indicate whether you believe the vertical or horizontal line is longer.

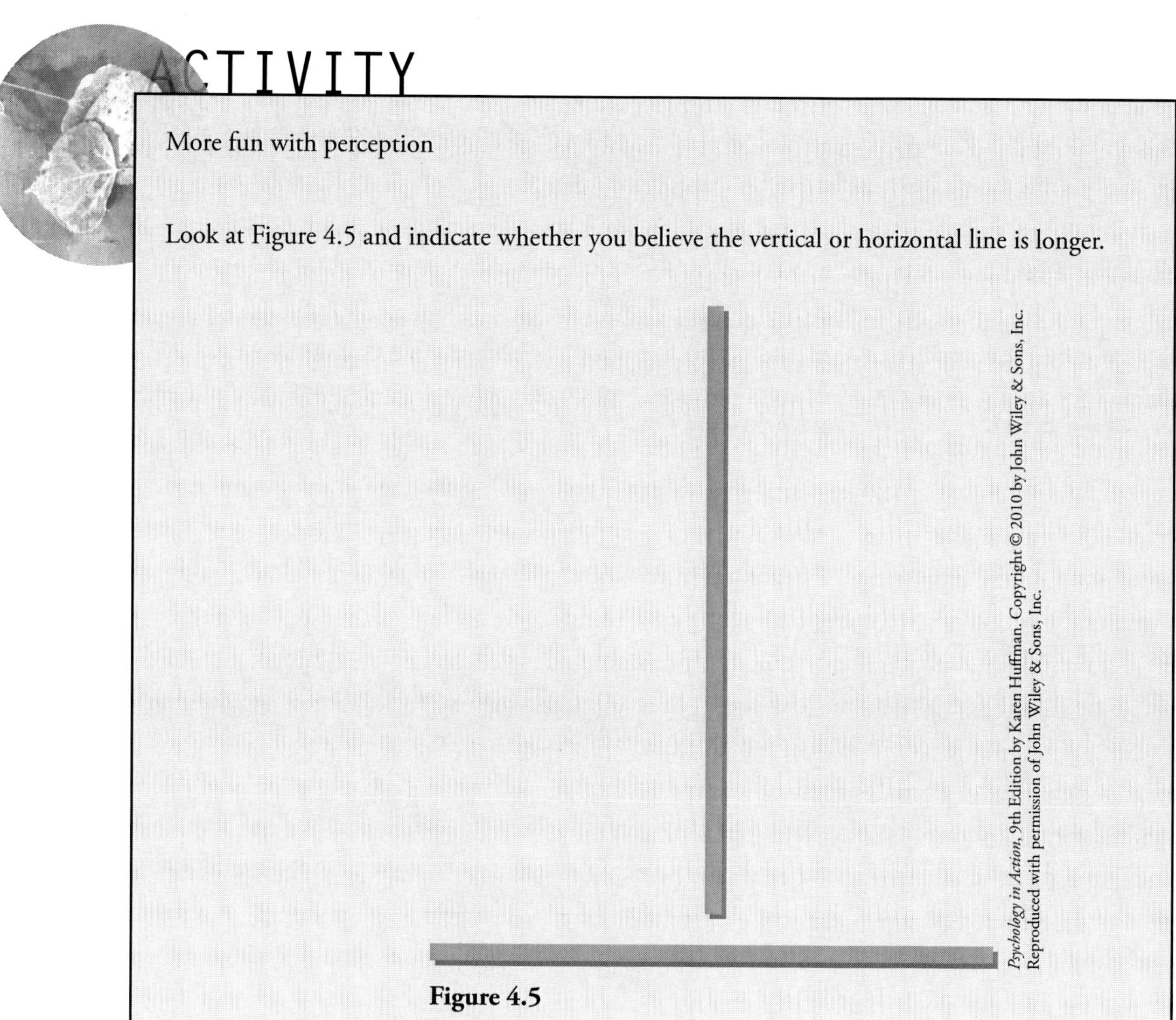

Figure 4.5

Most people who were reared in a more Western culture perceive the vertical line as being longer due to the fact that we are regularly exposed to long, straight lines in the world around us (think of roads and skyscrapers as just two examples). In reality, both lines are actually the same size. Note: If you don't believe this, get out a ruler and measure for yourself.

Some of you have undoubtedly been exposed to this illusion previously. While you may have learned the correct answer is that both lines are the same size, this doesn't mean you actually perceive this to be the case. In other words, just because you learned to answer the question correctly doesn't mean you've changed the way your brain actually perceives the length of the lines.

Illusions like the one we have just played with, while fun, are actually much more. They provide us with the opportunity to study how perception occurs in the brain. Furthermore, they raise the important question: Is what we perceive always reality? As the line illusion shows, the answer to the aforementioned question is no.

How Does Our Brain Select What Information to Perceive?

Just as our sensory systems are bombarded with external stimuli and must decide what messages to attend to or prioritize, our brain must do the same with perception. There are a number of tools our brain uses to help simplify this process.

Feature Detectors

Our brain has highly specialized neurons concentrated in certain areas that are designed to select and respond to specific sensory information. We have feature detectors that respond to certain angles, shapes, and even specific kinds of movement. For example, we have feature detectors in our occipital and temporal lobes that are responsible for helping us perceive and recognize the faces of others.

ACTIVITY

Stop whatever you are doing! For the next 60 seconds pay attention to everything around you and attempt to gather data using as many of your senses as possible. After the 60 seconds are complete, write down everything you noticed happening around you. Try and write something down from each of your major senses (vision, hearing, smell, taste, skin sensations, etc).

Now that you have completed your list, think about the following questions:

Is there anything on your list that you were not previously aware of before you completed this activity?

What would be the consequences if your brain attempted to perceive everything that was happening at any given time? How would this impact your ability to focus on a certain task such as reading this book or listening to a class lecture?

Selective Attention

As you just found out in the activity above, our brains are able to screen information and discriminate between important information and that which is less important. This is called selective attention. If our brains did not possess the ability to do this, our lives would be chaotic, and it would be very hard to focus on any one important activity.

iQoncept, 2011. Used under license of Shutterstock, Inc.

Habituation

Have you ever purchased a new videogame or perhaps a new smart phone and noticed how much fun it is at first? Right from the moment you open it and smell the packaging, your brain registers the fact that this is a new experience. There is an excitement to learning the new controls and features. Of course, anyone who has experienced the feeling of tinkering with a new gadget also understands this feeling does not last forever. Over time, we become used to the new technology and it loses its sense of novelty. This process is called habituation. *Habituation* can be defined as the brain's tendency to ignore stimuli in the environment that remain relatively constant. In other words, our brains like new experiences and attempt to avoid boredom.

Diego Cervo, 2011. Used under license of Shutterstock, Inc.

Gestalt Principles of Grouping and Organization

After the process of selecting what stimuli to attend to, our brains then attempt to organize the information into meaningful patterns. One of the primary ways our brains accomplish this is through a method known as the Gestalt principles of grouping. Without these principles for organization, our perceptual worlds would be chaotic and confusing. What follows is a look at some of the basic Gestalt principles.

Figure Ground

Remember this card from earlier in the chapter? Chances are that most of you see this as a white card with black ink on it. Why is this? Why don't you see it as a black card with white ink? The answer is the Gestalt principle of figure-ground. The figure (black ink) is always seen as being closer than the ground (white background).

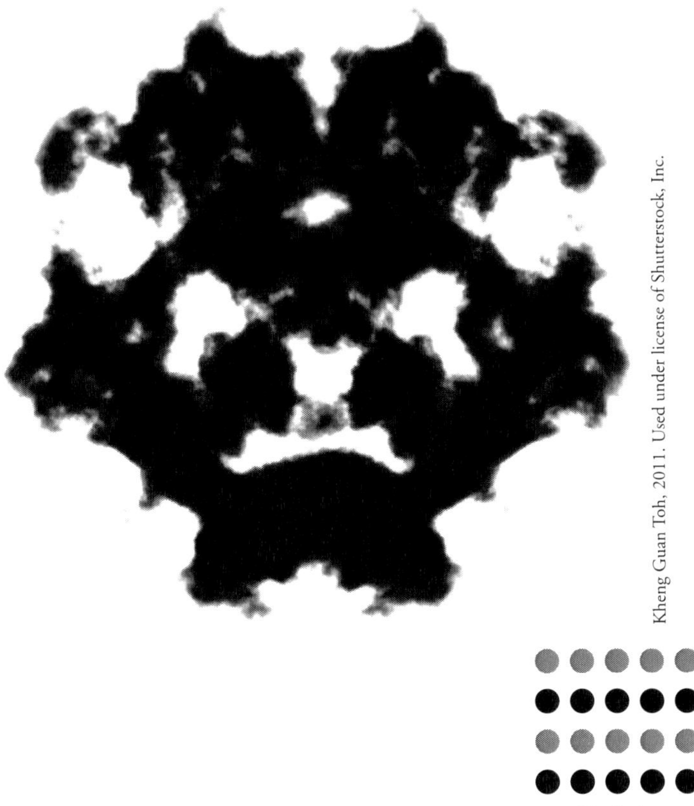

Similarity

Look at Figure 4.6. How do you group the dots together? Most people group the first horizontal line together because all of the dots are gray. They do the same thing for the third line with the gray dots and the second and fourth lines with the black dots. We group similar objects together, in this case by color. This concept is called similarity.

Figure 4.6

Proximity

How do you group the vertical lines together in Figure 4.7? Most people have a tendency to see three pairs of vertical lines. But why don't we just see six vertical lines? The answer is because of the how close the lines are to one another. We tend to group the first two lines together because of their proximity to one another. We do the same thing with the third and fourth lines and also the fifth and sixth lines. This is the Gestalt concept of proximity.

Figure 4.7

Closure

What shapes do you see in Figure 4.8? If you grew up in a Western culture, you probably answered circle and square without even giving it a second thought. Take a closer look, though? Are those really true examples of a circle and a square? You will almost certainly notice upon closer inspection that both shapes are not complete. Even so, our brain closes in the shapes to form meaningful patterns we are already familiar with. This is an example of the Gestalt principle of closure.

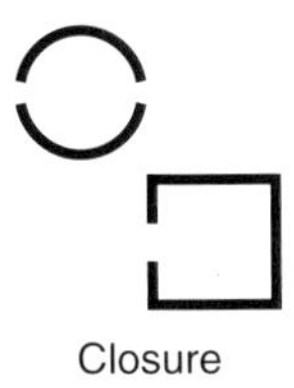

Figure 4.8

Continuity

Our brains have a tendency to perceive things as belonging together if they form a continuous and meaningful pattern. In Figure 4.9, we see an "X" and group each line of the "X" as a continuous pattern even though geometrically they are not continuous. This is the Gestalt concept of continuity.

Continuity

Figure 4.9

Perceptual Constancy and Depth Perception

Imagine that you are looking at a herd of elk on a hillside. You focus in on a single elk. Now imagine that as you walk closer to the animal, you perceive it as getting bigger. In order to avoid this, you would literally have re-evaluate the size of the elk relative to your position with each step. Fortunately, this is not a perceptual exercise we have to engage in. Instead, our brain perceives the environment as constant despite changes in sensory input. This is called perceptual constancy.

There are three types of perceptual constancy: size, shape, and brightness. The previous example with the elk is an example of *size constancy,* which means we perceive the size as constant no matter how close or far away we move from the object.

Shape constancy refers to our ability to perceive the shape of an object as unchanging regardless of what angle we see it from. Imagine that you have a penny in front of you and you start out looking at the front of coin. If you move it a quarter turn, you still perceive it as a penny. If you move it another quarter turn and see just the edge of the penny, you still see it as a penny thanks to shape constancy.

Imagine that you have purchased a nice pair of light brown shoes. You admire them as you walk throughout campus on a sunny day. As you walk inside for your class, all of a sudden you notice these once light brown shoes become darker. Obviously, you understand that your shoes do not actually change colors. Instead, you know the light around the shoes changes. This happens as a result of *brightness constancy.* Without brightness constancy we would constantly be reinterpreting colors in different lights and would believe our clothes were actually changing colors.

Along with size constancy, *depth perception* provides us with important information that allows us to see the world around us in three dimensions. While we can also estimate the distance of objects from using senses such as hearing and even smell, we rely on sight more than any other sense for estimating how far away a stimulus is from us.

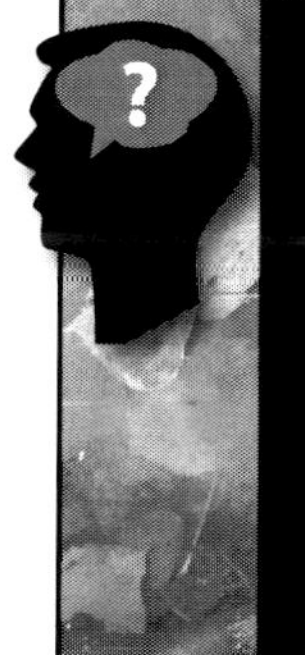

THINK ABOUT IT – Is depth perception inborn or learned?

In research, often referred to as the *visual cliff,* done by Gibson and Walk (1960) and Witherington et al. (2005), it was demonstrated that babies would hesitate when they reached a perceived cliff. For the safety of the babies, the cliff was actually an illusion created by a mirror. Nevertheless, the babies hesitated. What information does this give us with regard to the ability of infants to perceive depth and whether it is a learned behavior?

It is probably an inborn ability.

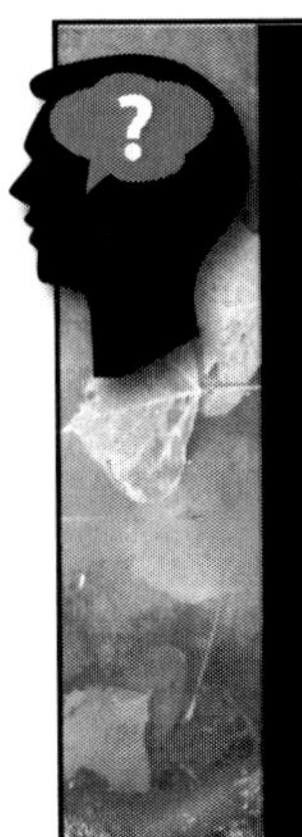

THINK ABOUT IT . . . AGAIN – Remember the question you were asked at the beginning of this chapter: Is perception always reality? In other words, is what our brain perceives always accurate and does it give us the true nature of reality? Our brains can usually accurately perceive things, but sometimes people perceive things differently than others.

After completing this chapter has your answer to this question changed? If so, how? If not, why? Not really because perception does not always reflect reality, but it usually does.

REFERENCES

Gibson, E. J., & Walk, R. D. (1960). The visual cliff. *Scientific American, 202*(2), 67–71.

Witherington, D. C., Campos, J. J., Anderson, D. I., Lejeune, L., & Seah, E. (2005). Avoidance of heights on the visual cliff in newly walking infants, *Infancy, 7*, 285–298.

NAME ______________________________ DATE ____________________

WORKSHEET CHAPTER FOUR

CHAPTER 5

THE BRAIN AND BIOPSYCHOLOGY

Imagine yourself in the landscape of the popular film *The Matrix* where you exist in a world created by another and communicated to your brain without your knowledge. How would you "figure this out"? How would you learn what is "real" vs. "created"? Imagine that your brain is kept alive outside your body, floating in a vat of brainy liquid straight from a science fiction film. If your brain is alive, are *you* still in there?

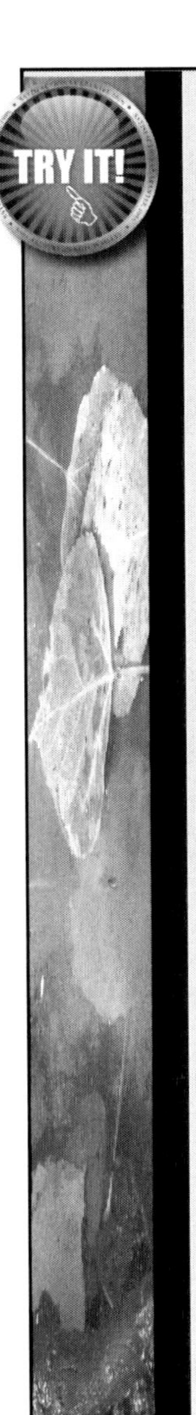

Try It – What is the brain? What is the mind?
Point to your mind. Point to your brain. Ask others to do the same. Draw a picture of a brain. Now draw a picture of a mind.

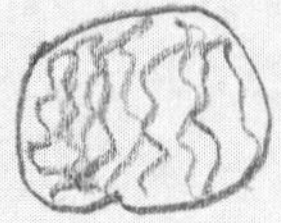

Ask now, what is the difference between the brain and the mind? *You are now using your brain to understand your brain.* How might this frustrate philosophers and scientists alike?

The fact that the brain + mind are different can cause confusion.

How does the concept of *mind* separate from *brain* help humans to understand this conundrum?

We can think of them separately.

Like the problem faced by Neo in *The Matrix,* how can we *know* that we really exist?

We can't really know for sure.

Who was René Descartes? What did he say about the nature of existence? How was his struggle similar to Neo's?

A philosopher who was not sure that what he perceived was real. Neither of them could really tell what was real + what was fake.

It seems that the mind is a creation of the brain and is, essentially, a product of a brain's function.The brain itself is made up of millions of synapses and billions of neurotransmitter molecules. It is an organ combining biological, chemical, and electrical processes, all of which we seem to call the mind. The complexities of the relationship between the mind and the brain are staggering. Psychology, in a large field of chemists, biologists, and neurologists, has a unique role to play in understanding where and how these mind and brain functions relate to each other.

The brain is a three-pound, highly complex organ with integrated systems of communications and complexities that continue to astonish and baffle the most brilliant scientists. Over the last 10 years we have learned more about the brain than at any other point in human history. However, scientific consensus is that we still have much more to learn about the brain than we already know.

Biopsychology is a branch of psychology that examines how the brain, specifically through its use and regulation of neurotransmitters, influences how an organism thinks, feels, and behaves. Biopsychologists, in their study of how biological developments interrelate with behavior, thoughts, and emotions, rely heavily on an understanding of anatomy and physiology, specifically the *nervous system* and the *endocrine system.* These two systems are the body's main communication network.

THE NERVOUS SYSTEM

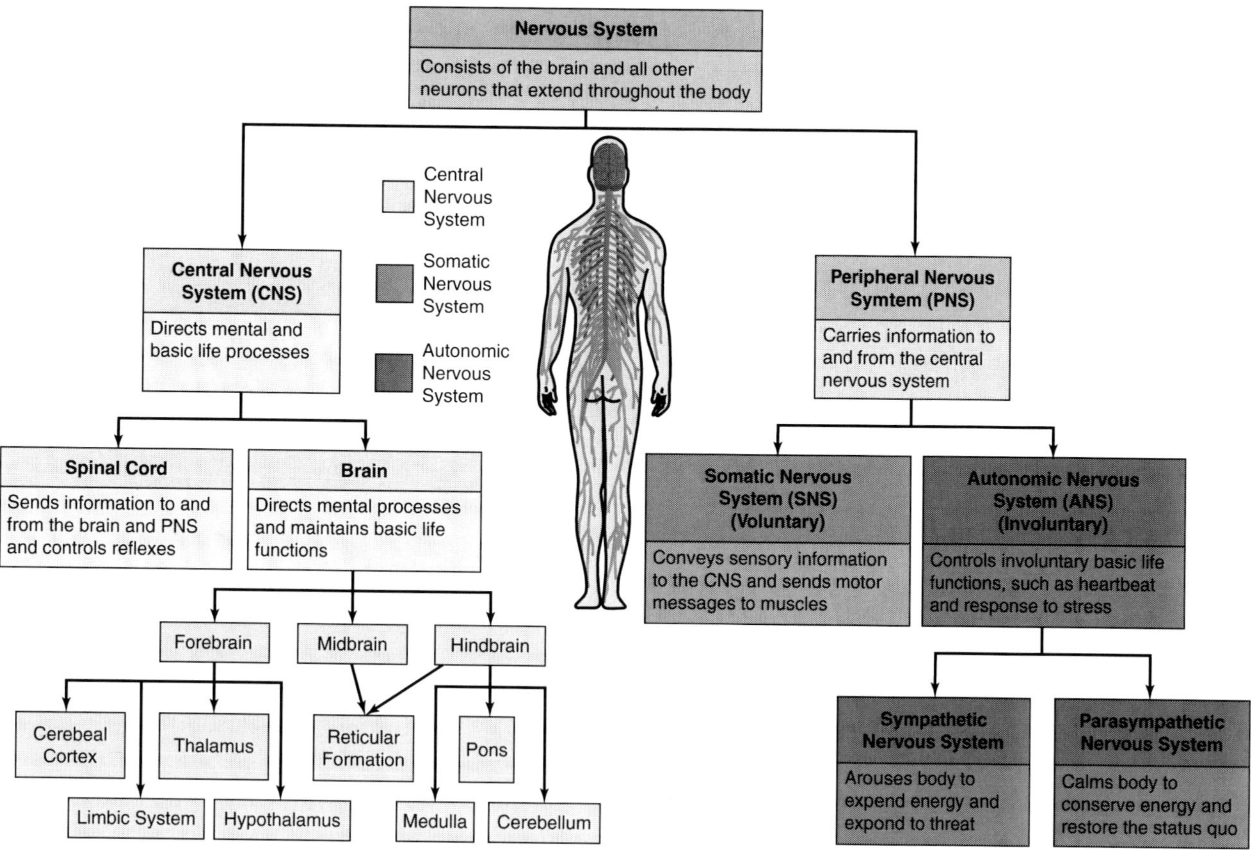

Figure 5.1

Before we begin to explore the brain in more depth, it is important to understand the larger system the brain is a part of which is called the nervous system. Figure 5.1 can be helpful in identifying and remembering the various parts of the nervous system.

The nervous system has two major parts, the *central nervous system (CNS),* which is composed of the brain and the spinal cord, and the *peripheral nervous system (PNS),* which contains all parts of the nervous system outside of the brain and spinal cord that extend to the outermost parts of your body, even to your skin. These two major parts of the nervous system have various subsystems. The peripheral nervous system is composed of two parts, the *somatic nervous system,* which regulates the actions of skeletal muscles, and the *autonomic nervous system,* which controls automatic processes. That these processes are automatic means we do not necessarily need to think about them for them to happen. These processes include blood pressure, heartbeat, and breathing.

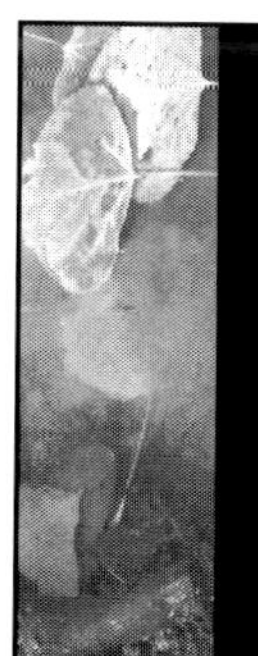

The Brain and Thinking

Your brain is a vastly complex organ and mainly thought of as a "thinking" organ. The brain's job is to think. But, "think" might not capture the entire picture of the brain's function.

What actions require you to think about them before doing them? Which actions require practiced thought? Think of playing a game of chess or checkers. One can improve his or her skills in this game with practice . . . but practice doing what? Thinking?

(continued)

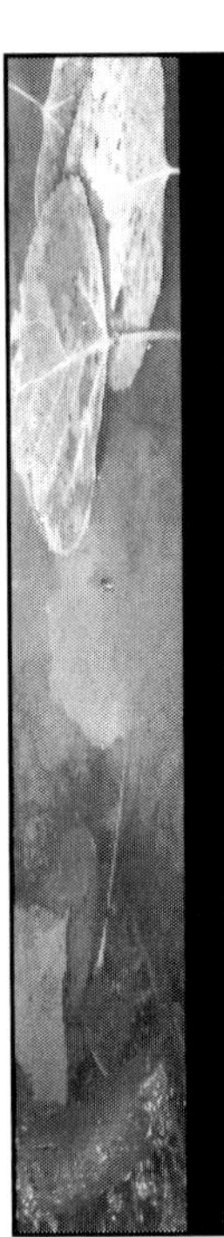

The Brain and Thinking (*continued*)
Think back to a time when you forgot to think. Puzzling, huh? What would happen if you forgot to breathe? Forgot to keep your heart beating? Forgot to keep your blood pressure or blood sugar in a healthy range? These seem like silly examples; however, they are examples of what your brain does. If the word "thinking" does not fit to describe this brain function, what other term could we use?

The *autonomic nervous system* is subdivided into two other systems called the *sympathetic nervous system* and *parasympathetic nervous system.* Remember, the autonomic nervous system controls involuntary functions such as blood pressure, heart rate, and breathing. The sympathetic nervous system is responsible for providing arousal to the body so it can adequately respond to a possible threat. It can be thought of as the body's fight-or-flight mechanism. The parasympathetic nervous system calms the body and helps it return to homeostasis or its baseline state.

ACTIVITY

You are driving home at 11 pm on a Friday night on a highway that is largely empty. The speed limit is 65 mph, but you are trying to make good time and are going 75 mph. As you cruise along, your headlights catch the red and blue lights of a police car by the side of the road about 100 yards ahead of you with all of its lights turned off in an obvious speed trap. The moment your headlights connect with the lights on top of the police car, you immediately hit your breaks and slow down to 60 mph before passing the speed trap. You notice that your heart is beating faster, your breathing has increased, and you have even started sweating.

These symptoms are signs that which subsystem of the autonomic nervous system has been activated? Why? Sympathetic because it aroused the body to expend energy + respond to the threat (fight/flight).

Let's break down the activity you just completed in even more detail. When you saw the police car, your brain (part of the CNS) initiated a message that you should step on the brake. That message was sent down the spinal cord (also part of the CNS) to the somatic nervous system (part of the PNS that controls voluntary actions). The somatic nervous system assured that the message was sent down to the muscles in your leg and that you were physically able to step on the break. At the same time, your autonomic nervous system (part of the PNS that controls involuntary actions) was activated as a result of the stress of seeing the police car.

The nervous system is made up of two basic types of cells. These cells are *neurons,* which are the functional communication system of the brain, and glial cells, which provide nutrients and insulation to the neurons. It is essential for neurons in our body to be able to communicate with other neurons. Without this, we would not survive. Most scientists believe each of us have somewhere in the neighborhood of 100 billion neurons.

There are three types of neurons. The motor neurons, or efferent neurons, send information to control the muscles of the human body. The sensory neurons, or afferent neurons, receive information from the senses (sight, touch, smell, hearing, or taste). Finally, the interneuron or the associative neuron provides the basic linkage and communication between other neurons in the brain. While no two neurons are exactly identical, typically each neuron contains five major parts: the *dendrites,* the *cell body,* the *axon,*the *myelin sheath,* and the *axon terminals.*

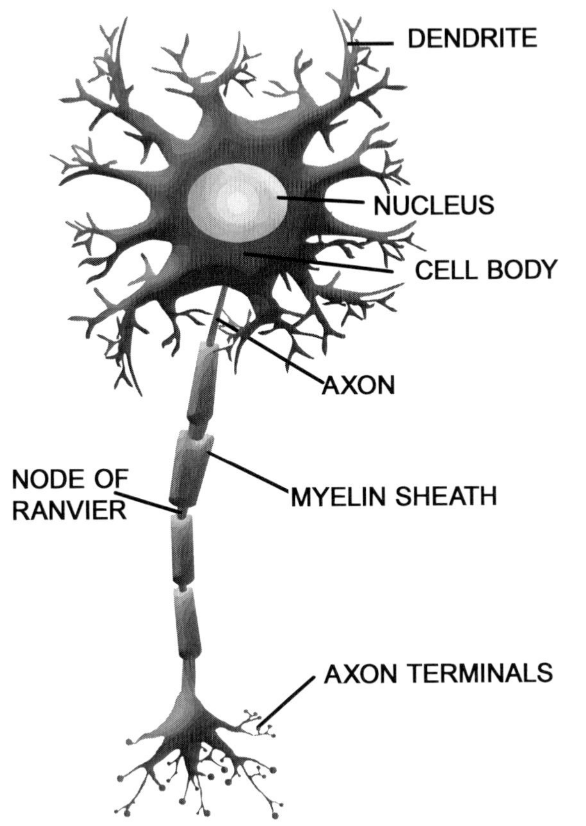

The dendrites are structures that look like little tree branches that receive information in the form of a chemical impulse from other neurons. It can be helpful to think of the dendrites as the ears of the neurons, since these structures are responsible for *receiving* the information from other neurons. Once the message is received by the dendrites, the information is passed on to the cell body. If there is enough stimulation, the cell body will send the message on to the axon. The cell body is also responsible for the basic life support functions of the neuron. The axon is a long tube-like structure that carries the message away from the cell body and toward the terminal buttons. The resting potential of the axon is −70 millivolts. When a strong enough signal is received and the axon reaches −62 millivolts, an *action potential* is triggered. When this happens, sodium ions from outside the axon flow into the axon, and potassium ions rush out. This creates an effect similar to when a gun fires and shoots the message through the axon. An action potential is also like a gun in that it either fires or it does not. There is no in between. After the action potential fires, the cell cannot fire again for a short time while it returns to its resting potential of −70 millivolts.

On the outside of some axons there is a fatty tissue called myelin sheath. This tissue works as a sort of slip-and-slide to help speed up the message as well as serving a protective function. Deterioration of the myelin sheath plays a major role in the disease multiple sclerosis (MS). Once the action potential fires, the neural message is sent through the axon (aided by the myelin sheath) and arrives at the terminal buttons. If the dendrites are the ears of the neuron, the terminal buttons serve as the mouth since the buttons *send* the message across the synaptic gap to the next neuron.

ACTIVITY

Without looking back in your book, label the major parts of the neuron below.

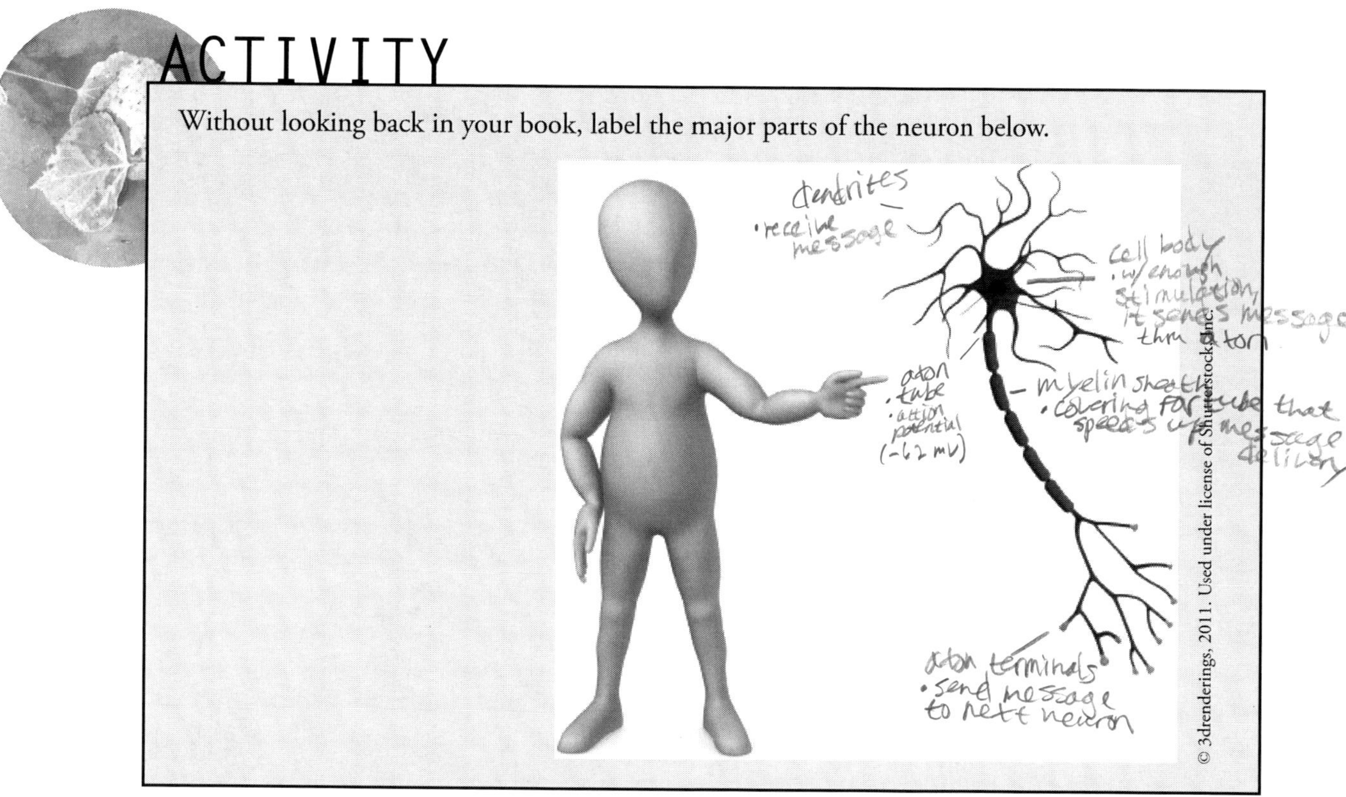

Although neurons are the basic building blocks of the brain's communication system, they do not necessarily perform such communication directly. That is, they do not necessarily come into direct contact with one another. Rather, they communicate between themselves across a space called the *synaptic gap.* This transmission occurs when the action potential triggers the release of a small amount of chemicals. These chemicals travel the synaptic gap and bind with receptor sites on the dendrites of the receiving neuron. The chemicals are called *neurotransmitters* and are the chemical component in the brain's vastly complex structure of communication.

There are many different kinds of neurotransmitters, and many have overlapping functions. Some of the most important and their effects are listed below.

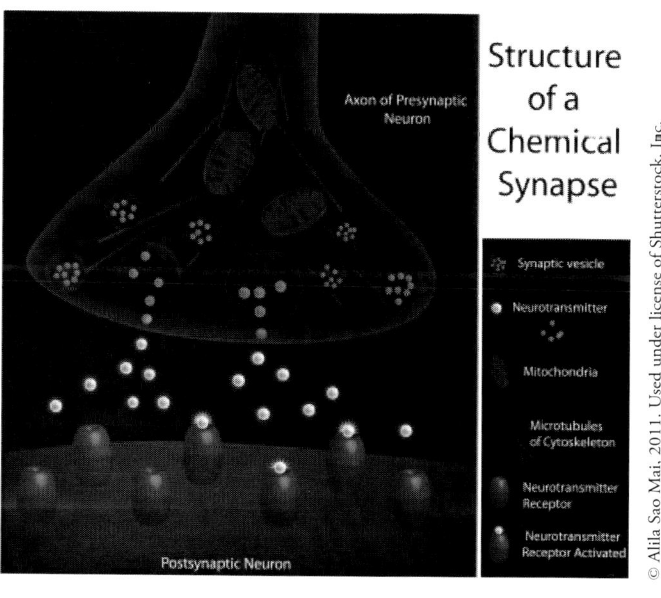

Dopamine: Emotion, mood, pleasure, addiction, attention, memory, learning, and movement. Too much dopamine is correlated with schizophrenia, whereas not enough dopamine is believed to play a role in Parkinson's disease.

Seratonin: Sleep, mood, arousal, body temperature, pain, and impulse control. Low levels of seratonin are believed to play a role in mood disorders such as depression.

Acetylcholine: Memory, learning, sleep, REM sleep, emotion, and muscle function. Neuroscientists believe acetylcholine may play a role in dementia, the most common form of which is Alzheimer's disease.

GABA (gamma aminobutyric acid): Inhibitory function in the central nervous system. Some anti-anxiety and panic medications such as Valium increase the effect of GABA.

Endorphins: Act as the body's natural painkiller. Also play a role in hunger, sex, and learning.

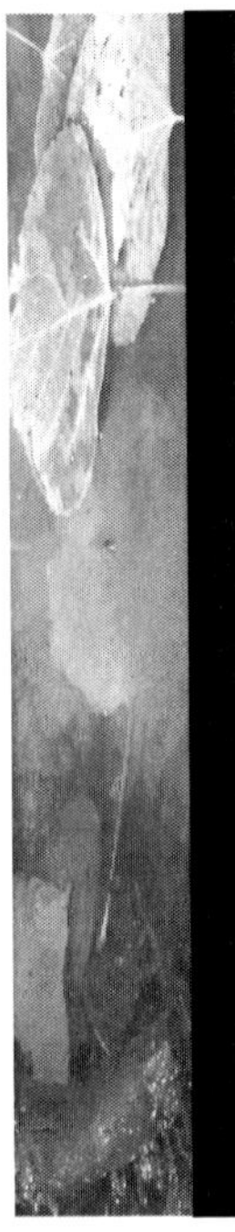

Study Tip – It can be helpful to think of neurotransmitters as keys and the dendrite receptor sites they bind to as locks. Imagine if you were to take the key to your room and stick it in the lock of your next-door neighbor's room. The door would not open, right? Well, the same thing would happen if dopamine were to attempt and bind with a serotonin receptor site. The key has to match the lock. This is often referred to as the lock-and-key analogy.

PARTS OF THE BRAIN

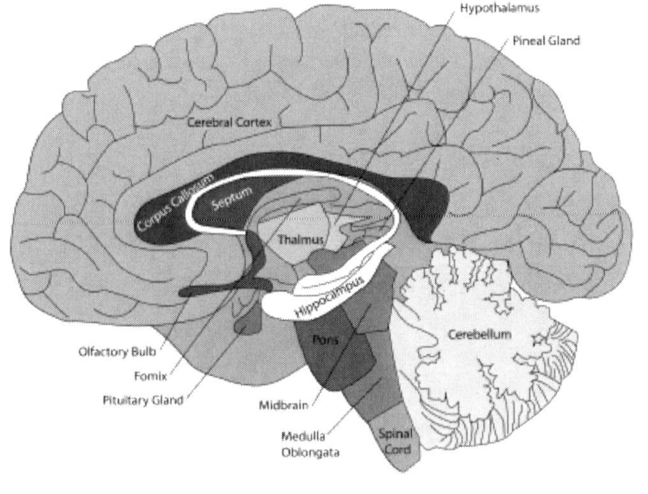

The brain is thought of as an organ consisting of three main parts, each divided into other specific parts. These three main parts are the *forebrain,* the *midbrain,* and the *hindbrain.*

A large chunk of the forebrain is occupied by the *cerebral cortex.* It is a large thin area that makes up much of what we think of as the wrinkled, grooved, and folded surface of the brain. The cerebral cortex is largely involved in what we know as higher brain functions, like intelligence and consciousness. The sphere-shaped cerebral cortex is formed into two halves connected by a grouping of axons called the corpus callosum. These two halves are often referred to as the right and left brain.

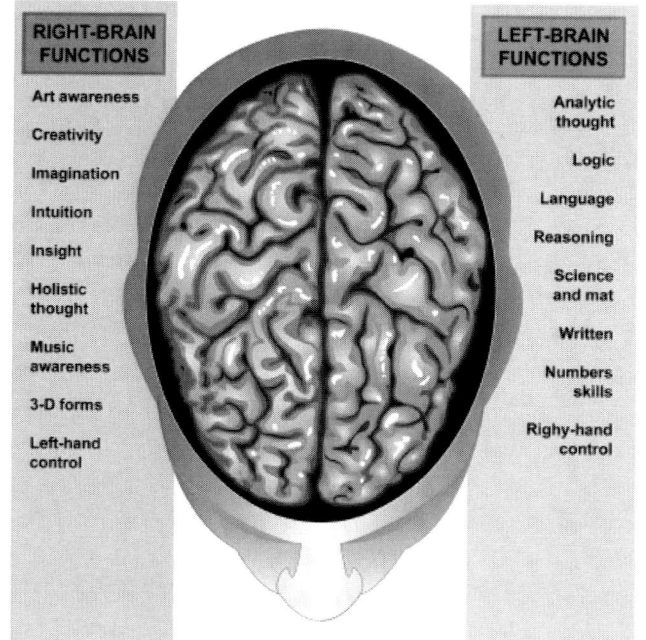

While there continues to be discussion, debate, and research into the complexities of the right and left brain functions, it has been hypothesized that the left half of the brain (or hemisphere) serves as the seat of language, logic, and analytic abilities, while the right hemisphere controls depth perception, spatial relation, and creative impulses. Keep in mind that the brain is a tremendously complex organ and that while some people perhaps thought of as "right-brained" can been seen as more creative or better with emotional expression, a healthy brain contains these two halves not separately but as a highly interconnected system. In fact, it seems that there is no clear evidence at all that the right brain, or right hemisphere, is any more creative than the left (Gazzaniga, 2005).

It is important to remember that the brain does not exist in a vacuum. In other words, the brain is interconnected and works together. While we will discuss the basic functions of the brain in the space that follows, it is important to understand that the different functions work together.

For example, we know the cerebellum plays an important role in movement. Thus, it might be assumed that a great dancer has a well-developed cerebellum. However, that only tells a part of the story. Think about how a dancer learns a new routine. She must first be able to listen to and integrate the instructions from a teacher. This involves the frontal lobes of the cerebral cortex. No matter what the potential of the individual's cerebellum, the information about the new routine will be useless to the dancer without the ability to understand and integrate the instructions from the teacher using the frontal lobes. In this case, the frontal lobes and the cerebellum must *work together*.

The Good, the Bad, and the Ugly

Ask some friends, family, and colleagues about the functions of the brain. Ask them to talk about all they *know* about the brain. Sometimes what emerges are commonly held false stereotypes, or myths, about the brain. Can you think of any?

One falsely held belief is that humans use only 10 percent of their brain.

The Good: Many motivational speakers, coaches, or counselors may tell you that you're using only 10 percent of your brain. While these people are misinformed, they may have the best intentions behind their ideas, like pushing you to achieve more than your potential.

The Bad: While many people, well intentioned and other, may operate under the belief that humans use only 10 percent of their brain, learning that it is not so can often be under painful circumstances and perhaps give false hope. Consider that you or a loved one has a massive stroke (a sudden interruption of blood flow to the brain), leading to 10 percent of the brain being damaged and beyond restoration. This is a painful imaginary exercise and likely not a scenario that any person, believing the 10 percent myth or not, would believe would leave little to no mark on the functioning of the affected person's brain. If it was true that 90 percent of the brain is not being used, then damage to any of this 90 percent would result in no functional impairment. It is clear that damage, even slight and small, to any part of the brain has a consequence (Beyerstein, 1999).

The Ugly: Often people, knowing better or not, will use the idea of the 10 percent brain usage to exploit others. Promising enhanced "energy," psychic powers, better intelligence, and/or "unlocking hidden potential," these charlatans often use the myth of 10 percent to sell a product or worse.

Can you think of specific examples for any of the Good, the Bad, and the Ugly?

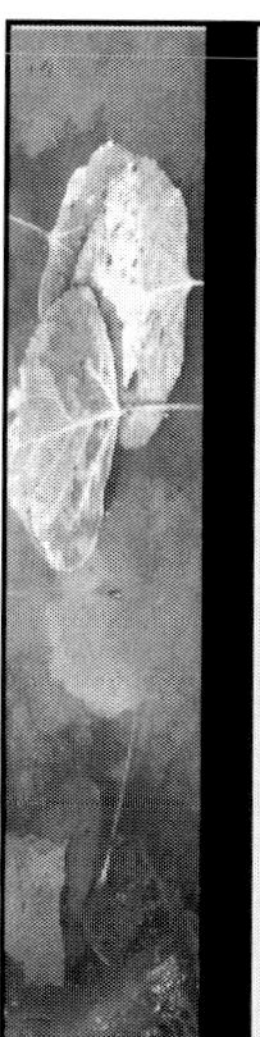

The Good, the Bad, and the Ugly (*continued*)

Can you think of other myths about the brain? Discuss the following.

- That a full moon has an effect on the brain and thus on behavior, often leading to increased aggressive, homicidal, or suicidal behavior.
- That we grow more intelligent as we age.
- That we can detect a liar by studying brain waves.
- A bigger brain is a better brain.
- Men's and women's brains are "hard wired" differently and these differences cause them to think differently.
- Playing classical music to a baby will increase brain development.

What do you think? Myths or truth? How will you find out?

Cerebral Cortex

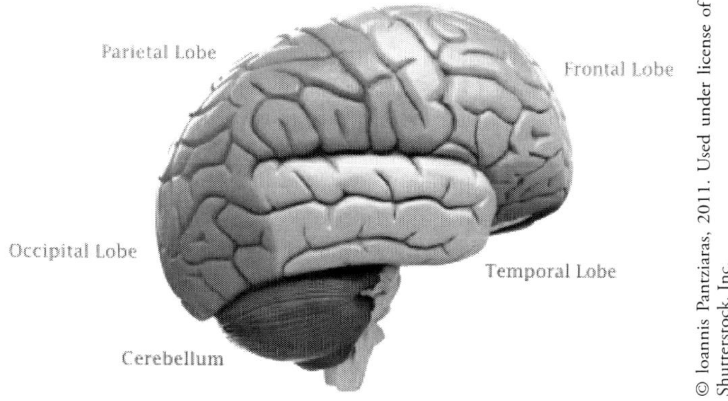

- Frontal lobes: involved in the planning and initiation of behavior and the control of emotion and personality.
- Temporal lobes: important in hearing, memory, and language.
- Occipital lobes: important to vision.
- Parietal lobe: important to the body's tactile sense or touch.

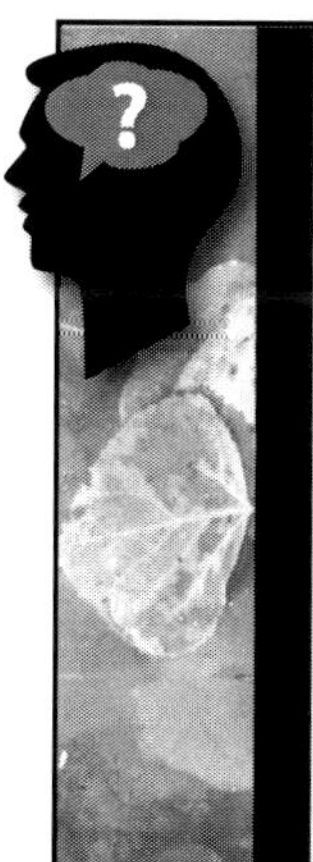

Think about it – The prefrontal cortex of our frontal lobes was the last part of the human brain to evolve. This is the part of the brain that makes us uniquely human. It gives us the ability to plan ahead in a way other animals cannot. While this ability is fantastic, it also carries with it the potential to cause a great deal of angst.

Have you ever been experiencing a day without a care in the world and then all of a sudden you ran out of things to do and just started thinking (or perhaps catastrophizing) about the future? The more you ponder the future, the grimmer it begins to look. Within 20 minutes, you are nearly in tears and have convinced yourself that you are a complete failure, your significant other

(*continued*)

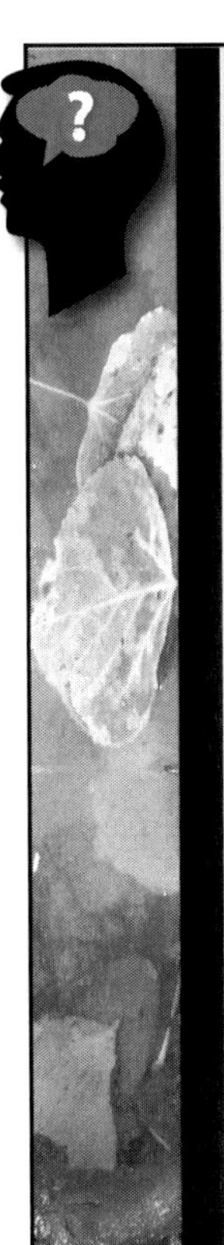

Think about it *(continued)*

© Eugenio Marongiu, 2011. Used under license of Shutterstock, Inc.

is going to leave you, and there is no hope of living the life you have always wanted. Remember, nothing changed from earlier in the day except the fact that you simply started thinking.

In short, the frontal lobes and our ability to plan ahead in such vivid detail is remarkable, but it's also something that gives us the ability to create anxiety about the future simply through the process of thinking in a way other animals cannot.

Limbic System

- Thalamus: located near the center of the organ and important in the processing of the senses of sight, hearing, and touch. Almost all sensory and motor information is processed through the thalamus.
- Hypothalamus: located near the lower central surface of the organ and important in the expression of emotions and drive states that aid in survival such as hunger, thirst, aggression, fear, and sexual arousal. It also regulates the autonomic nervous system, increasing and decreasing both heart rate and blood pressure. This "balance" of the body's functions is called *homeostasis.*
- Hippocampus: located in the temporal lobe and important in the ability to form new memories. The process of *neurogenesis* (the development of new neurons) takes place in the hippocampus.
- Amygdala: located at the base of the temporal lobe and important in emotional responses including fear and anger. It is also involved with the emotional content of processing and structuring new memories (Phelps, 2006).

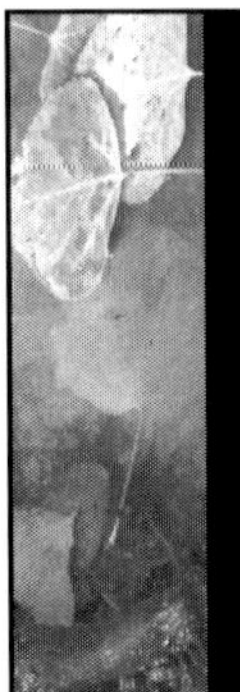

Critical Thinking
PTSD and the Amygdala

Posttraumatic Stress Disorder is a serious anxiety disorder that can develop in response to a trauma such as combat, natural disasters, serious accidents, or violent personal assaults. It is indeed a challenging puzzle for physicians and psychologists attempting to help those who suffer from PTSD.

(continued)

Critical Thinking *(continued)*

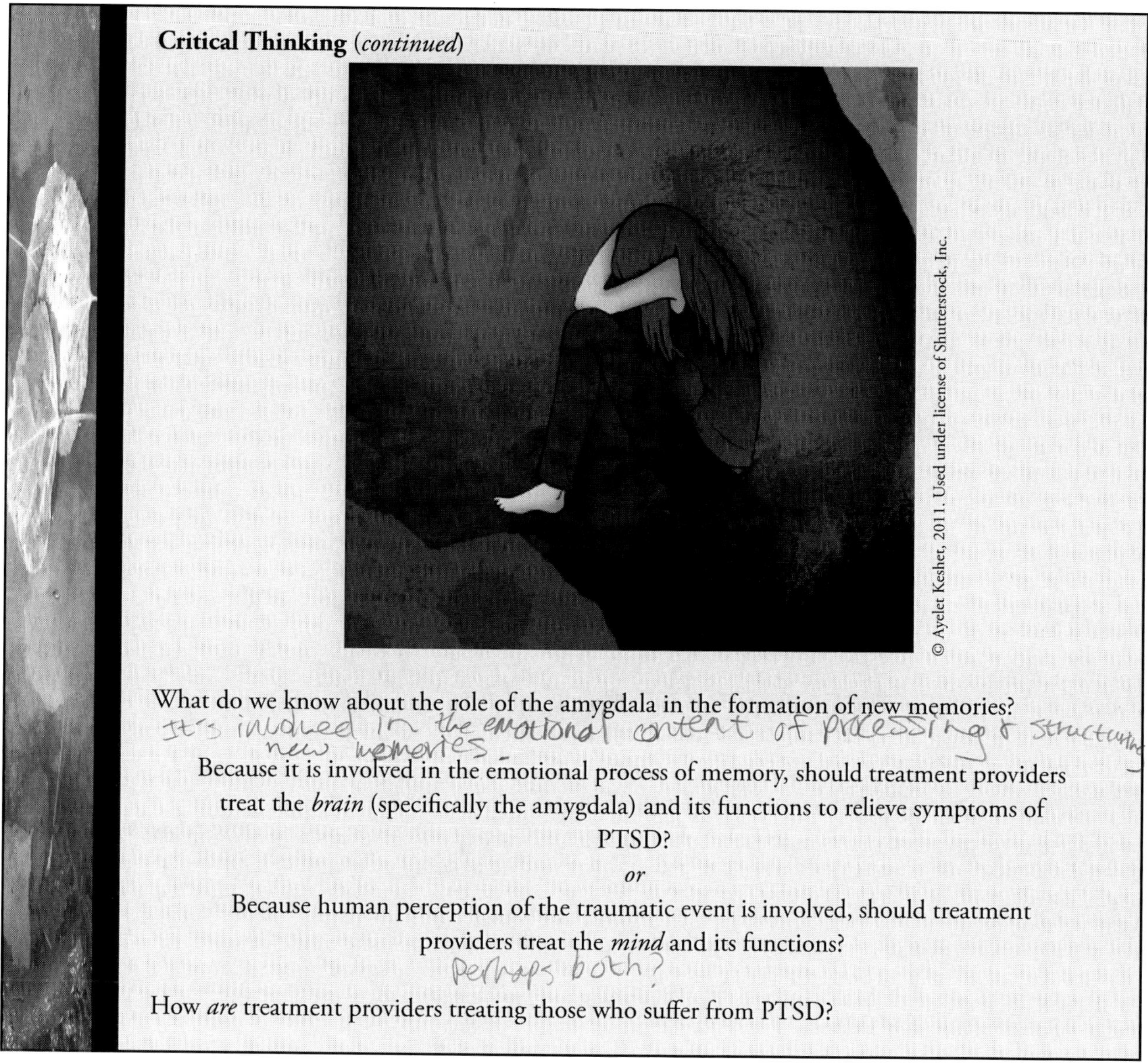

What do we know about the role of the amygdala in the formation of new memories?

Because it is involved in the emotional process of memory, should treatment providers treat the *brain* (specifically the amygdala) and its functions to relieve symptoms of PTSD?

or

Because human perception of the traumatic event is involved, should treatment providers treat the *mind* and its functions?

How *are* treatment providers treating those who suffer from PTSD?

The hindbrain is a region at the base of the brain that connects it to the spinal cord. It is made up of the *pons,* the *cerebellum,* the *reticular formation,* and the *medulla.* Sensory and motor information cross over pathways in the hindbrain to regions nearer the front of the brain. This sensory information from the body crosses from the side of the body stimulated to the opposite side of the brain. Similarly, motor messages from one side of the brain cross over and are experienced on the opposite side of the body. This is called *contralateral organization.* So, if you touch a hot burner with your left hand the right side of your brain will "light up" or be stimulated and vice versa. Also, when a patient has a stroke or other damage to one side of their brain, the opposite side of the body is affected in its motor ability.

Hindbrain

- Pons: important in the coordination of movements on each side of the body. The pons is located in the hindbrain and connects the medulla to both sides of the cerebellum.
- Cerebellum: located behind the pons and important in the control of balance, muscles, and coordinated motor movements.
- Reticular formation: located in the medulla and important in sustained attention, arousal, and sleep cycles.

- Medulla: located in the hindbrain and important in the regulation of vital functions of the body like heart rate, blood pressure, and breathing.
- Spinal cord: the downward extension of the brain made up of cell bodies and synapses and contains regions of sensory cells that carry signals toward the brain as well as motor cells that carry signals to the muscles of the body.

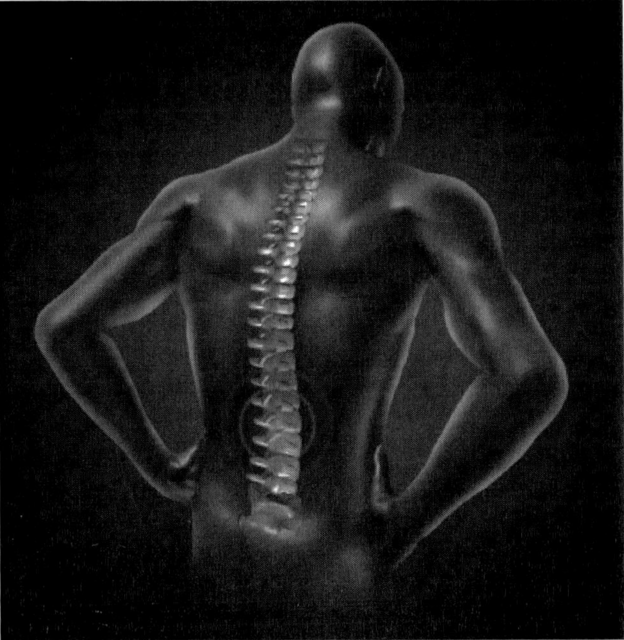

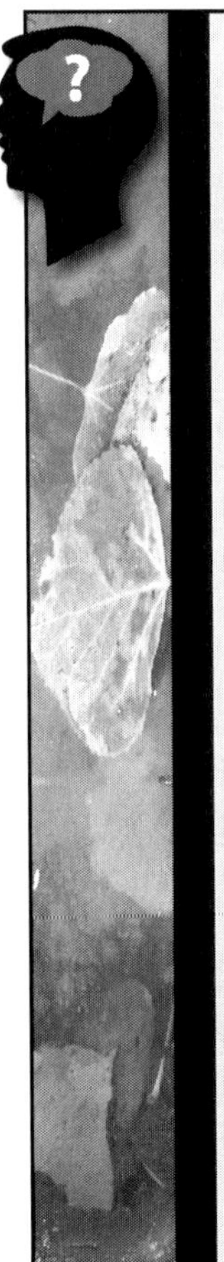

Think about it – In 1848, a railroad worker named Phineas Gage was pounding three-foot metal rods into the tracks. In what has become a famous case study in the study of brain-based behavior, one of the spikes was blown back at Phineas Gage. The spike traveled through the front of his face and brain, damaging his frontal lobes. Gage was knocked backwards and staggered to regain his footing. Amazingly, he was able to walk to the local physician and receive care.

Why didn't this injury kill Gage? A major missile injury to the brain stem (a part of the brain supporting vital life functions such as breathing and heart rate) would have resulted in instant death.

Given what you've learned about the brain in this chapter and what part of Gage's brain was injured, how do you predict this injury may have impacted him?

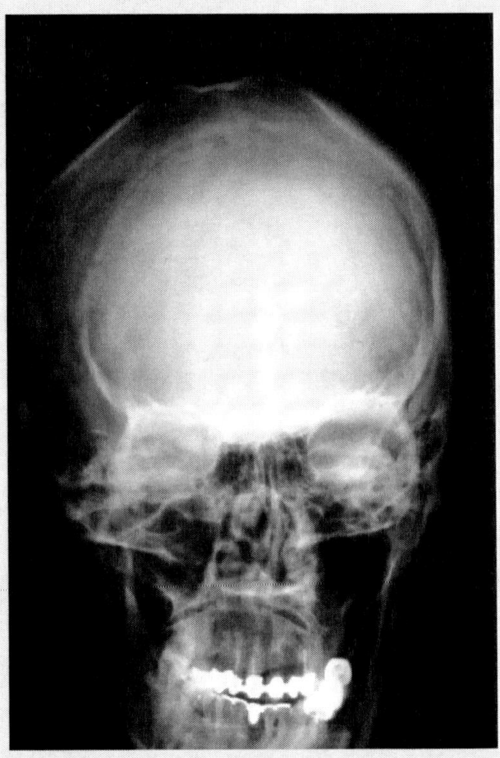

THE ENDOCRINE SYSTEM

The *endocrine system* is a system of glands that control many of the body's biological functions mainly by releasing (secreting) small quantities of chemical substances called *hormones* directly into the bloodstream. These hormones travel around in the bloodstream until they find a receptor on an organ or tissue at which time they act to regulate physical processes such as metabolism, growth, digestion, blood pressure, sexual functions like reproduction, and emotional response. The endocrine glands are made up of the pituitary, thyroid, adrenal, pineal, pancreas, and gonads.

- Pituitary gland: located in the brain under the hypothalamus and works with it to stimulate other glands into activity. For this reason it is often referred to as the "master gland."
- Thyroid gland: located in the neck below the vocal cords and important in the regulation of the metabolic (chemical changes necessary for growth) rate of the body.

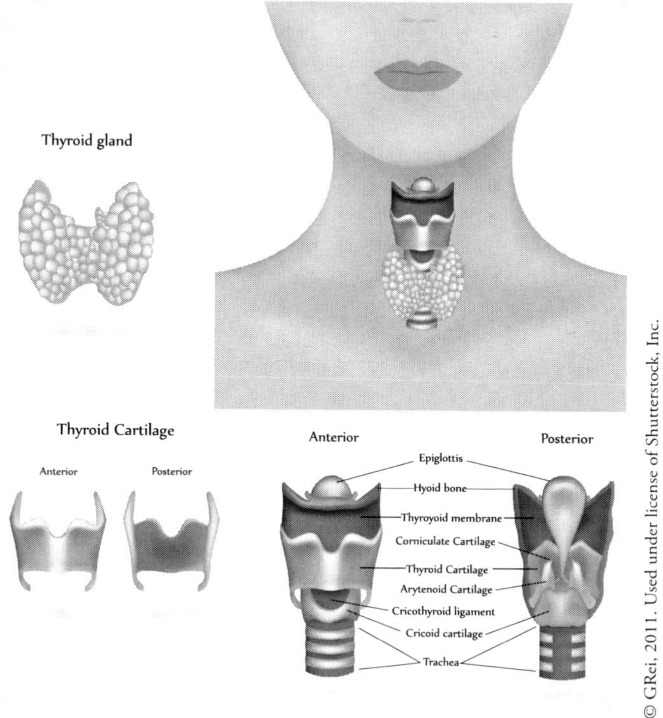

- Adrenal glands: a pair of glands near the kidneys that produce adrenaline (epinephrine), which activates the body during stressful/alarming states.
- Pineal gland: located in the brain and helps to regulate sleep functions.
- Pancreas: located in the abdomen behind the stomach and important in blood sugar and insulin regulation as well as hunger response.
- Gonads: testes in men/ovaries in women that are responsible for the development of secondary sex characteristics and reproductive functions.

Critical Thinking – Phrenology

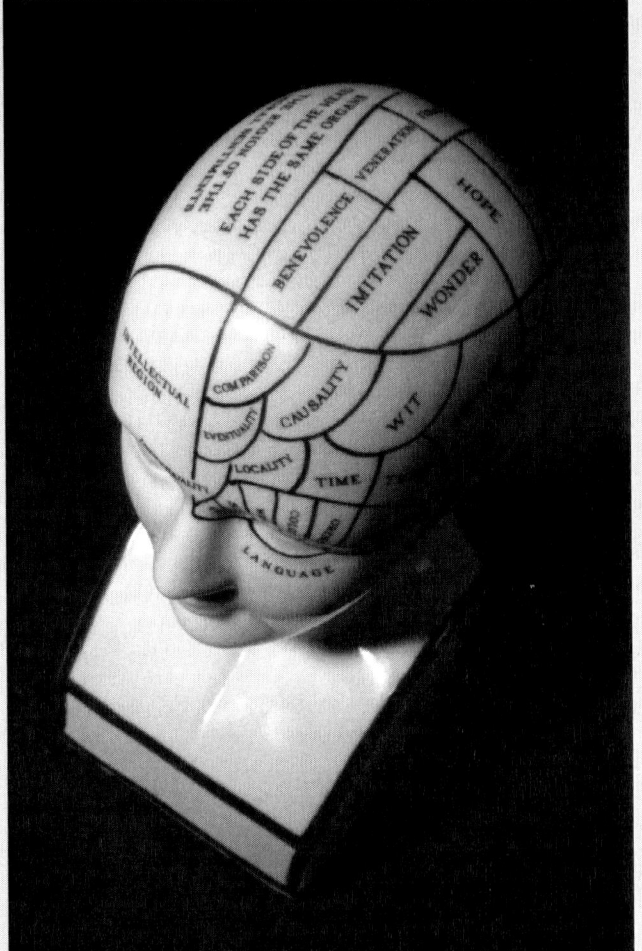

Can you tell the difference in the personalities of your friends or family by simply looking at the differences in their craniums? Do people with small bumps on the base of their heads have a propensity for the sciences? Are people with larger foreheads more intelligent? These may seem like silly questions; however, in the early 1800s, Franz Gall, a physician in Germany, put forth the idea that analysis of the human skull, specifically of over 25 "organs," could lead to predictions about individual tendencies, behaviors, and even aptitudes.

Like any *pseudoscience* (a pursuit resembling science but based on misleading and untrue assumptions), Gall's work was criticized for lacking evidence. It was at this time in the early-to-mid 1800s that he took his ideas out of the halls of science and into the public sphere. He established a society in the United States in Philadelphia in 1822 and gave numerous lectures as well as live examinations of people's craniums.

(*continued*)

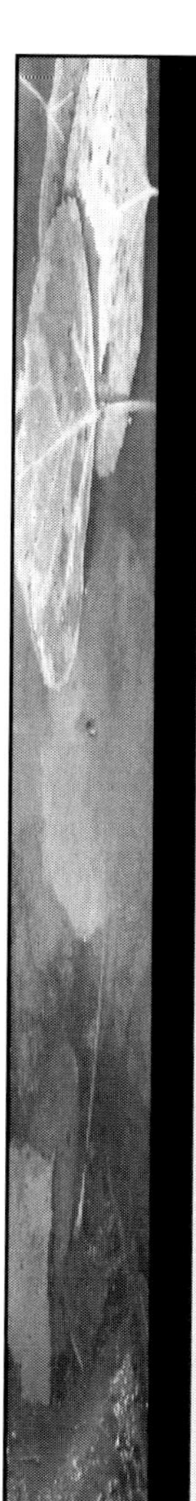

Critical Thinking – Phrenology *(continued)*

While it may seem easy to dismiss bumpy-headed predictions of behavior or intelligence, especially given the magnitude of scientific understanding since the late 1800s, phrenology did made lasting contributions to science. In a way, it set the stage for linking psychology and neurology and sparking a scientific exploration into the possibility of localization of function, or the idea that specific mental functions are located in specific brain areas (Huxford, 2008; van Wyhe, 2004). Today, sophisticated techniques/machines (such as the PET and MRI) reveal much of the brain's activity and provide several new ideas about the relationship of the brain's region to behavior, aptitude, and/or personality.

What are some pseudosciences that exist and persist today? Why is the notion that bumps on the head predict intellectual abilities so appealing to so many people?

Think of a contemporary pseudoscience. Write down what it claims to do in the blank below and answer the subsequent question.

Try it another way, with your own example: Think of something, maybe something that is probably not true, but that some people believe is true. Fill in the blank. Ask others to do so. *Why is the notion that ______________________ appealing to so many people?*

What other examples can you use to complete this question? What answers do you get?

This chapter has provided you with a basic overview of the brain and biopsychology. It is important to remember that we are learning more about the brain every day and advances are being made at a staggering rate. It seems inevitable that psychology and neurology will continue to be linked together in very meaningful ways as both fields of study continue to progress.

REFERENCES

Beyerstein, B. (1999). Whence cometh the myth that we only use 10% of our brains? In S. Della Sala (Ed.), *Mind myths: Exploring popular assumptions about the mind and brain.* Chichster, England: Wiley.

Gazzaniga, M. (2005). Forty-five years of split-brain research and still going strong. *Nature Reviews Neuroscience, 6*, 653–659.

Huxford, M. (2008). Phrenology. In F. Leong, E. Altmaier, & B. Johnson (Eds.),*Encyclopedia of counseling: Changes and challenges for counseling in the 21st Century, (p. 1). Thousand Oaks, CA: Sage.*

Phelps, E. (2006). Emotion and cognition: Insights from studies of the human amygdala. *Annual Review of Psychology, 57*, 27–53.

van Wyhe, J. (2004). Was phrenology a reform science? Towards a new generalization for phrenology. *History of Science, 42*(3), 313.

NAME ____________________ DATE ____________________

WORKSHEET CHAPTER FIVE

CHAPTER 6

CONSCIOUSNESS

Consciousness refers to our level of awareness of what is happening around us. How much we are conscious of at any given time can wane depending on how alert we are and how much mental energy it might require to complete a given task we might be engaged in. It is the hope of the authors of the book that you are consciously aware you are reading the words on this page at this very moment. However, how conscious you are as you read this is a more interesting question.

Think about it – Have you ever found yourself reading a book for one of your classes for a period of minutes and then become aware that although you have been reading the words, you have not really been comprehending what you were reading? In fact, you might realize after the fact that as you were reading the words you were actually thinking about something else like what you were going to eat for lunch or a date you were planning to go on later that night.

This can be explained in terms of levels of consciousness. Although you were reading the book, you were doing so in an automatic or almost auto-pilot fashion using a relatively low level of awareness. To really comprehend what you are reading, it takes a concentrated and higher level of awareness.

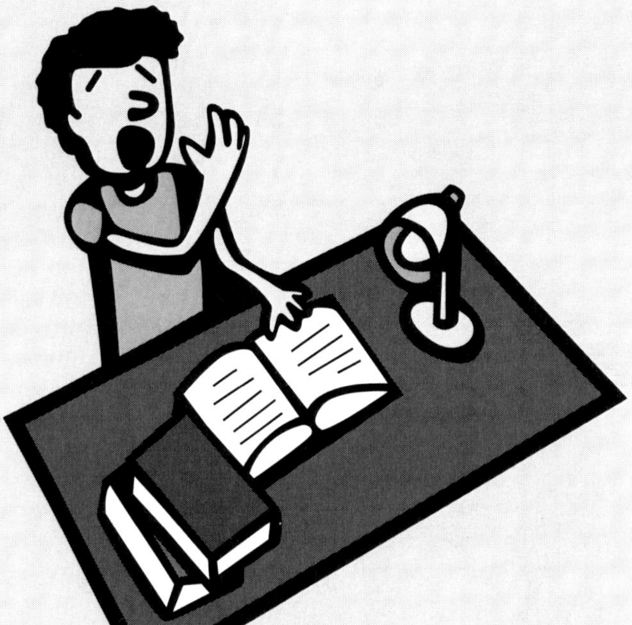

© Miguel Angel Salinas Salinas, 2011. Used under license of Shutterstock, Inc.

THE CONSCIOUSNESS CONTINUUM

© Lisa F. Young, 2011. Used under license of Shutterstock, Inc.

It is important to think of consciousness as existing on a continuum as opposed to believing that we are either conscious or unconscious. In this chapter we will touch on all aspects of the consciousness continuum, including important altered states of consciousness such as sleeping and drug use.

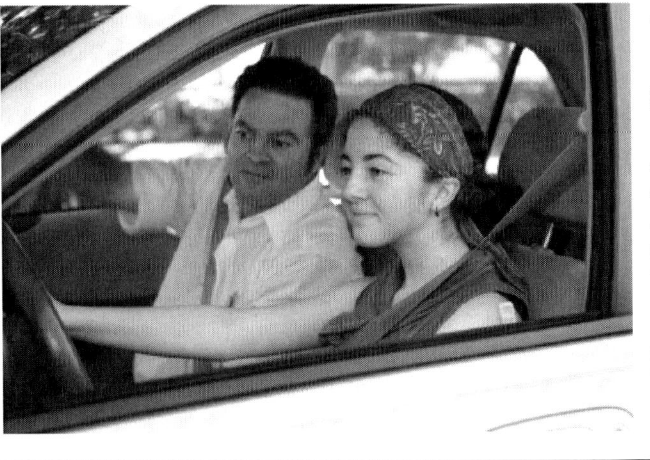

At the top of the consciousness continuum is what is often referred to as *controlled processes*. These are processes that require intense focus to complete. For example, think about how much you had to think about every move you were making the first time you learned how to drive (especially if you were learning how to drive a stick shift). Another example would be studying hard for a test on material you have not been exposed to in the past.

Near the middle of the conscious continuum reside *automatic processes.* These are processes that require minimal conscious effort. Some examples might include riding a bike, brushing your teeth, or typing on a computer.

Think about it – When you first learned to drive a car, it was likely a very controlled process, requiring all of your attention just to stay safe. However, with practice, what was once controlled can become automatic. We know driving becomes an automatic process when we see people adjusting the radio, talking on the phone, eating a burrito, etc., while also driving.

Of course, engaging in such activities at the same time as driving increases the risk of an accident! Just because a process becomes automatic does not mean you are immune from making mistakes.

Near the lower end of the conscious continuum you find processes that lie beneath conscious awareness. You might see these referred to as unconscious or subconscious processes. This includes behaviors like sleeping and subliminal perception (or perceiving stimuli we are not consciously aware of perceiving).

The lowest level of awareness would be when one is not aware or literally has no awareness. This could occur when one is knocked biologically unconsciousness. No awareness also occurs when one is under anesthesia during a surgical procedure.

© Diego Cervo, 2011. Used under license of Shutterstock, Inc.

ALTERED STATES OF CONSCIOUSNESS

In addition to normal waking consciousness, we also experience altered states of consciousness. Some of these altered states happen naturally (sleep) and others can be synthetically created (drugs, meditation, etc.). A variety of altered states of consciousness will be discussed in space that follows.

Sleep

Sleep is an altered state of consciousness shared by all mammals and imperative for survival. Before answering questions such as why do we sleep and dream and how do we progress through the sleep cycle, it is important to understand our body's circadian rhythms. Circadian rhythms function as our body's internal clock and regulate our level of alertness throughout the day as well as our daily sleep cycle.

© Anelina, 2011. Used under license of Shutterstock, Inc.

Generally, we begin becoming more alert as the sun rises and begin to wind down as the sun sets. It is worth noting, however, that not everyone's circadian rhythms are exactly the same. Some people have their optimal level of arousal earlier in the day while others might experience optimal arousal later in the evening. Hence, terms like "morning person" and "night owl" are often used to describe individuals at opposite ends of this arousal spectrum.

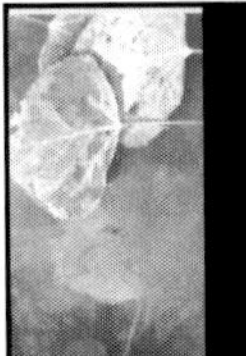

Did You Know? – Disrupted circadian rhythms can cause a number of unwanted side effects such as problems concentrating, fatigue, mood disruptions such as depression, sleep disorders, and other general health problems.

(continued)

Did You Know? *(continued)*

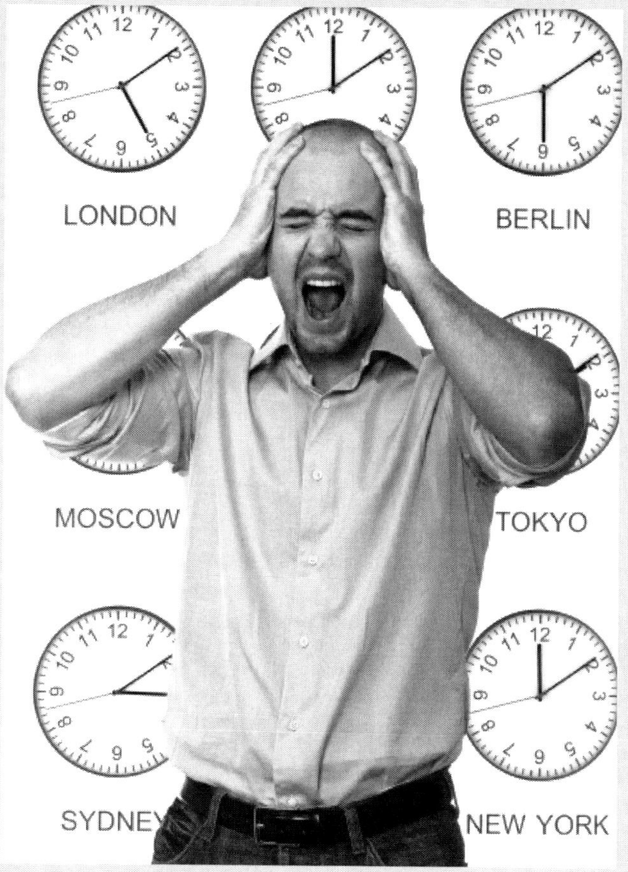

Can you think of activities or life events that have the potential to disrupt circadian rhythms?

Remember the part of the brain called the hypothalamus discussed in Chapter 5, which is important for regulating many of the body's basic drives and functions? As you might have guessed, the hypothalamus is responsible for regulating our circadian rhythms. More specifically, the superchiasmatic nucleus in the hypothalamus receives information from the eyes with regard to the amount of daylight, which then leads to the release of melatonin, an important hormone implicated in sleep.

Perhaps the most important product of our circadian rhythms is the sleep cycle, which occupies on average about a third of each 24-hour cycle. The cycle progresses through five distinct stages throughout the course of the night, but not in a sequential order. There are Non-Rapid Eye Movement (NREM) and Rapid Eye Movement (REM) stages of sleep. Stages 1 through 4 are considered NREM.

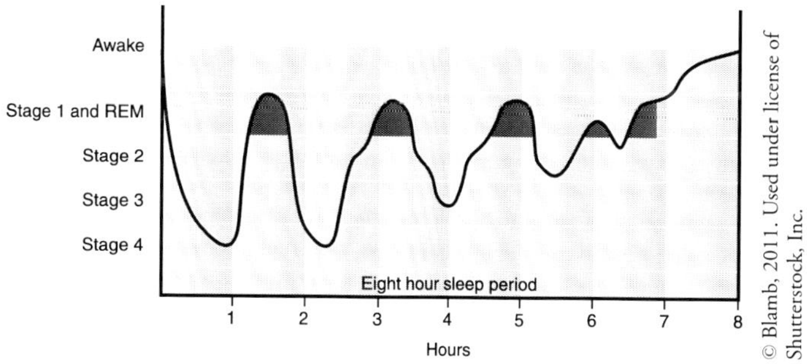

Figure 6.1

The first stage of the sleep cycle is technically being awake. During this stage beta brain waves are present. As the person shuts his eyes, he falls into calm wakefulness, which is also sometimes referred to as awake and drowsy. During this stage alpha brain waves are present. This stage lasts for a short period of time that usually doesn't exceed 10–15 minutes. During calm wakefulness, people often experience feelings of floating or falling, flashing lights and colors, and jerking movements. These experiences are often referred to as hypnagogic activity.

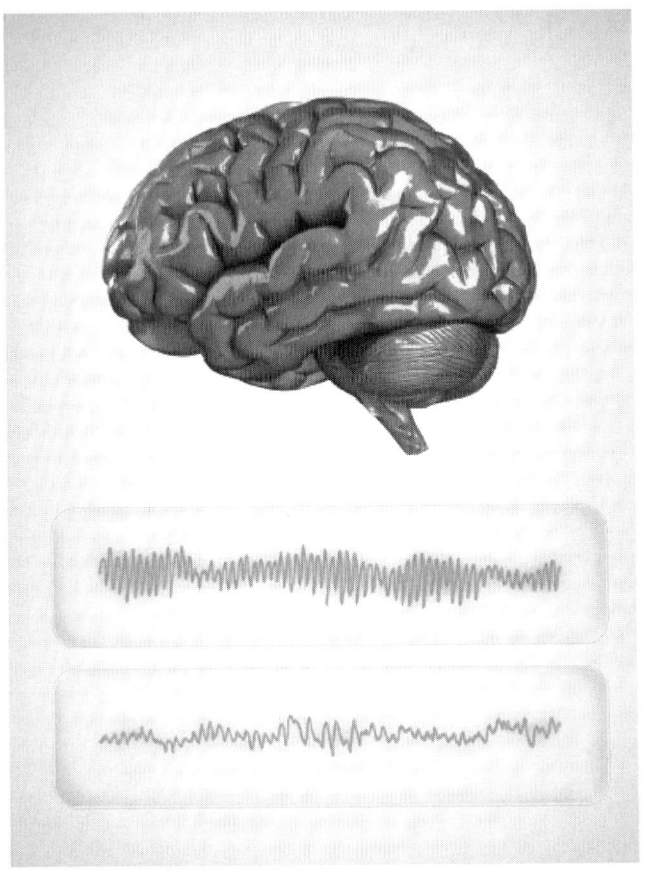

After calm wakefulness, we enter the first stage of NREM sleep, which is referred to as Stage 1. Stages 1 and 2 together are often referred to as light sleep. In Stage 1 theta brain waves are present and bodily functions such as heart rate, breathing, and blood pressure begin to decrease. In Stage 2 the body continues to relax, and both sleep spindles and K-complex brain wave patterns are present. Sleep spindles are indicative of the brain's calming down, whereas K-complexes appear when a noise in the room is registered but does not wake the person up. A loud or potentially dangerous noise could still wake the person up in this stage, but this stage is crucial in making sure good sleep can be achieved and that the person transitions into deep sleep, which is Stages 3 and 4. Recent research also indicates that K-complexes play a role in memory consolidation (Cash et al., 2009).

During Stages 3 and 4, delta brain waves can be observed. As noted previously, these two stages of NREM are considered deep sleep. Stages 3 and 4 serve a biological need in that they ensure we wake up feeling rested and rejuvenated. It is quite difficult to wake someone up when she is in deep sleep. People in these stages of sleep can often sleep through loud noises such as sirens that would easily wake a person up had she been at other stages in the cycle.

Remember, the sleep cycle does not progress sequentially. As noted on the sleep cycle chart in Figure 6.1, after Stage 4 the person cycles back up to Stage 3, then Stage 2 and then arrives at the first REM cycle. At this point, the person has been asleep for about 90 minutes and has completed one full cycle of sleep. Most people progress through four to five full cycles per night.

REM cycles increase in duration as the sleep cycle progresses. Dreaming occurs during REM sleep. REM sleep is also often referred to as paradoxical sleep because brain wave patterns are indicative of the person being awakened and aroused with bodily functions increasing, while the major muscle groups of the body are paralyzed. It is believed REM sleep plays a role in consolidating new memories and experiences as well as learning. This is due in part to the fact that time in REM sleep increases after we experience intense novel experiences or learning (Massicotte-Marquez et al., 2008). Furthermore, infants spend more time in REM sleep (around 40 percent) than do adults (around 20 percent).

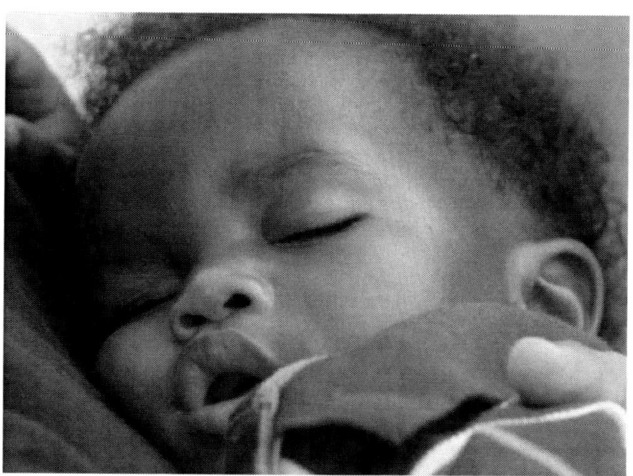

Think about it – As noted earlier, dreaming occurs during REM sleep. Our bodies are also paralyzed during REM sleep. What adaptive function might this serve to help keep us safe? We can't act out our dreams because that would be extremely dangerous.

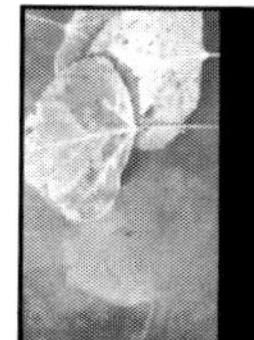

What if I don't dream? – Some people believe they do not dream. All of the research evidence says otherwise. In fact, all mammals show a pattern of random neural firing during REM sleep. People that remember their dreams more frequently wake up at the tail end of a REM cycle.

Why Do We Dream?

As you just learned in the previous section, dreaming occurs during REM sleep. However, the bigger question most people have is, Why do we dream? Many contemporary neuroscientists argue that dreaming is nothing more than random neural firing (Hobson, 1999). The way that neural firing is interpreted during REM sleep is influenced by a person's subjective experience, but the neural firing itself is simply random.

Cognitive theorists have offered another explanation for why we dream. They believe dreaming is actually a process our brain uses to help us learn and consolidate information. As noted earlier, REM sleep does increase after exposure to novel stimuli, which would seem to provide supportive evidence for the cognitive theory. Studies have also found similarities to fears or anxieties we have during a waking state and those that manifest in dreams, indicating we may be sorting through and trying to process the day's events (Domhoff, 2007).

One of the most classic, and also highly controversial, theories of dreaming came out of the psychoanalytic school of thought. Sigmund Freud was the father of this paradigm of psychological thinking, but others such as Carl Jung also made substantial contributions. Freud referred to dreams as "the royal road to the unconscious." He believed that dreams offered insight into repressed desires that were hidden deep in our unconscious minds. Often the content of dreams is expressed symbolically so that the person is not overwhelmed by anxiety. As a result, Freud indicated that we must understand both the manifest and latent content of dreams. Manifest content is essentially the play-by-play of the dream, whereas latent content is the underlying, unconscious, and true meaning of the dream.

d
r
e
a
m

ACTIVITY

So which theory of dreaming is correct? As is often the case in a field as complex as psychology, there are a number of theories to describe the same phenomenon. Your job as a critical thinker and active learner is to weigh all of the evidence (while trying not to engage in confirmation bias as discussed in Chapter 3) and decide for yourself.

Try keeping a dream journal for the next few weeks. Every time you wake up, write down anything you can remember from your dreams. As you progress in the journal, begin to think about which theory of dreaming makes the most sense to you and why.

Sleep Disorders

Millions of people across the world suffer from sleep disorders. These disorders adversely impact both physical and psychological health. Sleep disorders are generally divided into two categories call parasomnias and dyssomnias. *Parasomnias* involve abnormal disturbances, behaviors, or emotions during sleep, while *dyssomnias* involve persistent trouble going to and/or staying asleep that impact the duration and quality of sleep.

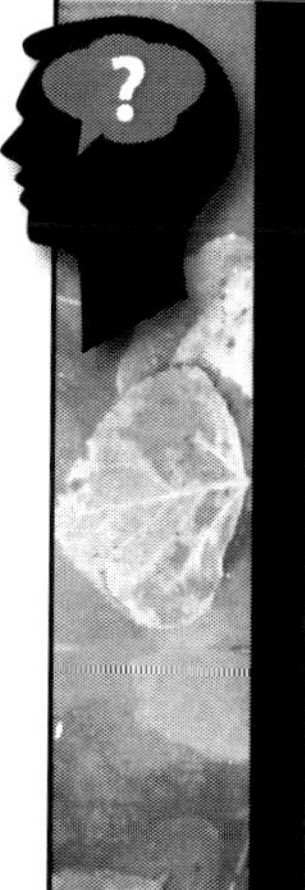

Think about it – Many of us throw around diagnostic terms without realizing it. For example, you might have heard someone say, "I'm suffering from insomnia" when he has trouble going to sleep. While we usually understand what the person is trying to communicate, it is important to note that he likely is not suffering from clinically diagnosable insomnia. In order for someone to be diagnosed with a sleep disorder, he or she has to exhibit the symptoms over a persistent period of time.

We have likely all experienced a feeling of nervousness before the first day of classes or prior to starting of a new job such that it impacts our ability to sleep. However, since this can be traced back to a specific stressor and is not persistent over time, it would not be a diagnosable sleep disorder.

Four Common Parasomnias

- Nightmares: Nightmares are exactly as they sound, bad dreams. These occur during REM sleep and often happen near the end of the sleep cycle. It is believed by neuroscientists that these often occur when random stimulation of the brain cells in the amygdala (fear center of the brain) is taking place. Nightmares can also become more likely for some people during periods of high stress and anxiety.

- Night Terrors: Night terrors are a NREM event and often occur during deep sleep (Stages 3 and 4). Abrupt awakening, intense fear, and physiological arousal characterize these episodes. Since these often occur in deep sleep, individuals will often wake up disoriented to their surroundings. Night terrors are most common in children and often dissipate with age. However, stress can be a precursor to many parasomnias that manifest in adulthood.

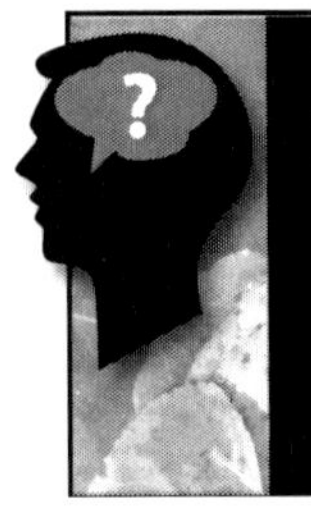

Think about it – How can I tell if my child is having a nightmare or experiencing night terrors? One quick test is to try and talk to the child. If she can articulate why she is afraid and recount some of the dream, it is likely she has experienced a nightmare. If, on the other hand, she appears disoriented and is experiencing fear with no apparent cause, night terrors may be more likely. If these problems are recurrent, talking to a doctor is always recommended.

- Sleep Walking: This is a NREM event that most often happens in deep sleep. It is usually preceded by stressful life events and is often more common in children. Since sleep walking happens most often during deep sleep, sleep walkers are often difficult to wake up. If they are awakened, this can cause fear and confusion. It is recommended that people who live with a sleep walker simply ask him to go back to sleep and guide him back to bed to avoid causing the sleep walker any unneeded anxiety or fear.

- Sleep Talking: Also sometimes referred to as somniloquy, sleep talking can happen in both NREM and REM sleep. What causes it to happen in NREM is when the transition from one NREM stage to another is temporarily stalled. In REM, temporary speech breakthroughs can happen where people may utter words or gibberish. It is sometimes even possible to engage a sleep talker in a short conversation, although the longer you talk with a sleep talker, the more apparent it becomes that he or she is in an altered state of consciousness.

Three Common Dyssomnias

- Insomnia: Some people suffering from insomnia might have trouble going to sleep and lie awake in bed tossing and turning. Others might fall asleep with no problem initially but then cannot stay asleep for an extended period of time. However the condition manifests, the consequences can be very severe. People with this condition often suffer from chronic fatigue, irritability, and have trouble concentrating and focusing on important tasks. Insomnia is often co-occurring with other mental and physical health problems.

- Sleep Apnea: This condition is characterized by prolonged interruptions of breathing during sleep due to obstruction of the airway. These prolonged interruptions of breathing can last for 60 seconds or more, which makes sleep apnea a very serious and potentially fatal condition. A sign that someone is suffering from sleep apnea is often loud snoring followed by a gasping sound as if the person is trying to catch his or her breath. Due to the fact that people suffering from sleep apnea stop breathing for potentially extended periods of time, there is a risk that neurons in the brain can be damaged or killed (Billiard, 2007).

  Treatment for sleep apnea can vary depending on what is believed to be causing the problem. People who are overweight are at a higher risk for sleep apnea. For these individuals, sometimes losing weight alleviates the problem of the airway obstruction during sleep. Having people sleep on their sides instead of their backs can also be helpful. Sleep apnea machines run by ventilators are also sometimes used. While effective for some people, these machines are often bulky and uncomfortable to wear. For some with sleep apnea, the problem is the anatomical structure of the airway. For these individuals, surgery (with no guarantee of success) may be the most viable option.

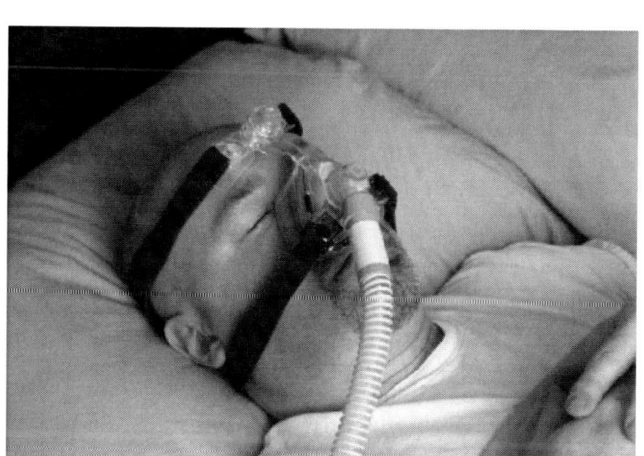

- Narcolepsy: This is a potentially dangerous sleep disorder that causes sudden onset of sleep during waking hours. The sleep attacks mimic REM sleep, which means muscle paralysis is often observed. While the precise cause of narcolepsy is not yet known, recent advances in medication have made the condition far more treatable than it was in the past.

Think about it – How might a diagnosis of narcolepsy change one's life? What common activities that we might take for granted on a day-to-day basis might be impacted by the threat of a narcoleptic attack?

How Are Sleep Disorders Treated?

Despite the common use of drugs to treat sleep disorders in today's society, the best frontline treatment for most sleep disorders remains good sleep hygiene. What follows are some tips that help foster healthy sleep habits. You are encouraged to try these over the next several months and see if you notice a difference in the quality of your sleep.

- Maintain a set sleep cycle. Try to go to bed at the same time every night and wake up at the same time every morning. You will know you have achieved a consistent sleep cycle when you routinely wake up just before your alarm is about to ring.
- The bed is for the two "Ss" only: sleep and sex. Do not read in bed. If you have a TV in your bedroom, get rid of it. No writing on your laptop for work or school. Note: Obviously this tip would be revised for children and exclude the sex component. But the same basic message still applies.
- Make sure your bedroom is cool and dark.
- Do not have a clock you can see from your bed. The clock is a mechanism that can create anxiety. People often look at the clock and calculate how much time they have left to sleep! Is this really a helpful endeavor to encourage a relaxed state of being that will induce good sleep? Many people need an alarm clock (for obvious reasons), but if you have one simply turn it away from you so you cannot see it.
- Avoid drinking caffeine after 3 pm.
- Avoid heavy consumption of alcohol and consumption of alcohol too close to bedtime.
- Exercise at least five times a week. This will encourage healthy sleep. But do not exercise within three hours of your bedtime. Exercising too close to bedtime will speed your body up and actually make it harder to go to sleep.
- Try to minimize stress. If you are a person who thinks about what you have to do tomorrow as you are trying to go to sleep, try writing that information down and putting it in a box in another room. This symbolic exercise can help remind you that whatever is so important that you are carrying it with you to sleep will still be there for you in the morning when you wake up. Give yourself permission to let it go now and come back to it the next day.

Drugs

While sleep is a naturally occurring altered state of consciousness, there are synthetic ways to alter our states of consciousness as well. The most common are psychoactive drugs. Through manipulating our brain's reward center and neurotransmitters, drugs can change how we feel and how we perceive the world around us. More specifically, drugs work by creating either an agonistic or antagonistic effect.

Remember neurotransmission as discussed in Chapter 5 where the sending neuron released chemicals called neurotransmitters into the synaptic gap that bind to receptors on the dendrites of the receiving neuron? Also, do you remember the lock-and-key analogy, which states that neurotransmitters are like keys and the dendrite receptors are like locks?

Well, agonistic drugs work by creating synthetic molecules that can bind to receptor sites and enhance synaptic transmission. So, in other words, agonistic drugs create synthetically created duplicate keys that can bind to receptor sites.

Antagonistic drugs work by blocking the process of neurotransmission. These drugs release molecules that block the dendrite receptor sites so neurotransmitters cannot bind to receptors sides (See Figure 6.2).

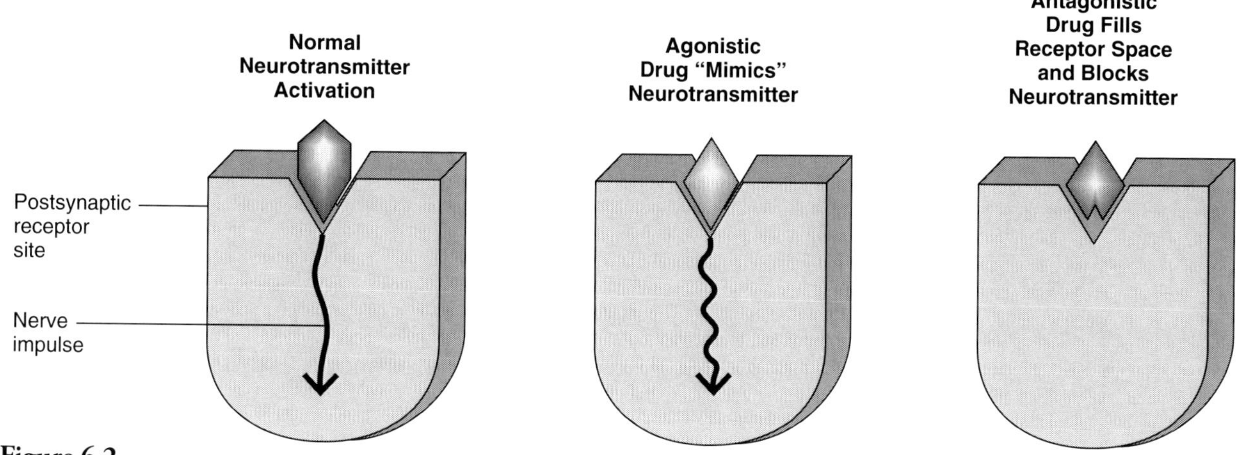

Figure 6.2

ACTIVITY

How does cocaine work?

After a sending neuron releases neurotransmitters into the synaptic gap and communication with the receiving neuron is complete, the sending neuron reabsorbs some of the extra neurotransmitters in the gap. This process is called reuptake. When a person takes cocaine, molecules from the drug will actually block the reuptake pumps, leaving neurotransmitters in the synaptic gap longer then they would have, making a person feel energized and euphoric.

Is cocaine an agonist or antagonistic drug? Explain your answer.

The Process of Addiction

If drugs can alter our perception and potentially make us feel better, you might be asking yourself, What's the big deal? The problem is the potential for addiction and the damage drugs can do to the body and the brain.

There are drugs used by psychiatry, called psychotropic medications, that also have the potential to alter our mood. However, the difference between these drugs and many commonly used street drugs such as cocaine, heroin, methamphetamine, etc. is that psychotropic medications have a low potential for abuse.

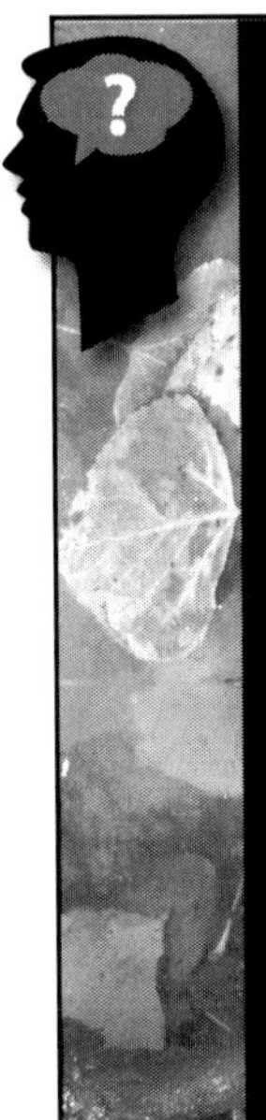

Think about it – What is the stereotypical portrayal of someone struggling with addiction? The dominant image is often a homeless man drinking from a paper bag. The problem with this image is that most people battling addiction look nothing like this and it creates a tool for people to rationalize away potentially serious problems. In truth, addiction does not discriminate. People of all races, religions, and socioeconomic classes struggle with addiction. The first step to understanding addiction is to make sure we are aware and willing to challenge our own biases and assumptions.

Addiction expert Dr. Harvey Milkman, author of *Craving for Ecstasy and Natural Highs* (Milkman & Sunderworth, 2010), defines addiction as "Behavior characterized by compulsion, loss of control, and continuation despite harmful consequences." As the addictive process begins to take hold, people will eventually experience a physical dependence on the drug. This means that they will not be able to physically function even at a minimal level without the drug. Once a person has reached this level of addiction, not having access to the drug on a routine basis will lead to what is referred to as withdrawal. These symptoms can include severe pain, sickness, and overwhelming cravings for the drug. These symptoms differ depending on the specific drug, but in the case of some drugs such as heroin, for example, withdrawal can potentially be lethal.

Long-term use of a substance will lead the body to build up tolerance. What this means is that it is going to take more and more of the drug to achieve the same effect. In other words, the body becomes less sensitive to the drug.

ACTIVITY

Imagine that a man who weighs approximately 180 pounds has never before had a glass of alcohol. He sits down and has two beers over the course of an hour. He is given a blood test to measure blood alcohol content (BAC), and the reading comes out to .05 after consuming the two beers. Over the course of the next two years the man drinks more heavily and develops a tolerance. Imagine that the man comes back two years later and has two beers of the same size. Assuming nothing has changed (the man is still male and he still weighs 180 pounds) what is his BAC? .05

Explain how you came to this conclusion.

It's still the same amount of alcohol; he is just more used to it two yrs. later.

Four Categories of Drugs

There are four general classifications of drugs, each grouped by the effects the substances have once they enter the body.

Stimulants: Drugs in this category speed up the body's central nervous system, creating feelings of euphoria, increased sociability, and increased energy and alertness. The drugs in this category do vary quite substantially, and therefore vary in the intensity of the effects they create. For example, both coffee and cocaine are considered stimulants. While coffee does not create the same kind of euphoric feeling that cocaine does, it also does not cause the same kind of damage to the heart and central nervous system. Other drugs that fall into this category include methamphetamine, ecstasy, and one of the most addictive and widely used drugs in our society, nicotine. Some stronger stimulants such as cocaine, meth, and ecstasy can cause very severe changes in the brain's perception, such as paranoia and psychosis, and can even lead to problems such as body convulsions and death.

Depressants: Drugs in this category have the opposite effect of stimulants and seek to slow down or suppress the central nervous system. Effects of depressants include feelings of relaxation, loss of inhibitions, reduced tension, and even drowsiness. The most popular drug in this category is alcohol. Other drugs like Valium, barbiturates, and Ketamine also fall under this category. When taken in excess, these drugs can cause amnesia, decreased respiration, disorientation, extreme anxiety, and even loss of consciousness or death.

Think about it – Have you noticed how we used the word "buzz" to describe someone who has had a little bit to drink? As a result, it might be tempting to think of alcohol as a stimulant. However, while alcohol may give us an initial stimulant feeling, it actually has a depressant effect on the central nervous system (e.g., loss of inhibitions, less self-conscious, increased relaxation).

Opiates: The purpose of this classification of drugs is to numb the body and relieve pain. They work by imitating the body's natural painkillers, which are called endorphins. These drugs provide a euphoric feeling but one that is different than the euphoria created by stimulants. While stimulant users often feel a rush of energy, people who take opiates often report a more calming form of euphoria. They often report feeling warm all over or like they have "escaped" all the pain (mental or physical) that exists in their lives. Some of the most common drugs that fall under this category include heroin, morphine, and codeine. People who become addicted to opiates often experience extremely painful withdrawal symptoms that require medical attention.

Hallucinogens: This classification of drugs is characterized by effects such as heightened sense of novelty to surrounding stimuli, mild euphoria, and distorted perceptual experiences including mild hallucinations and delusions. Some people who use hallucinogens such as LSD will report having "bad trips." These kind of perceptual distortions often involve extreme fear, anxiety, and paranoia. It is worth noting that marijuana is generally classified as a hallucinogen. However, it also has some features of an opiate, can act like a painkiller, and also provide mild depressant effects.

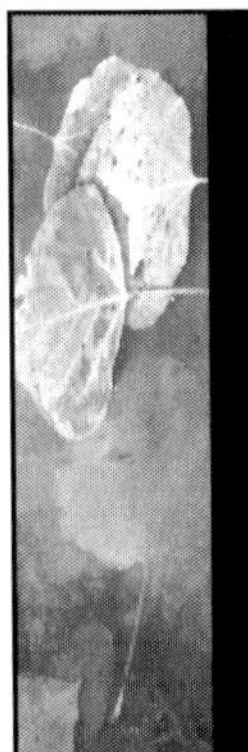

What Do You Think? – After learning about the four major classifications of drugs, why is it that different people become addicted to different drugs? One person might try cocaine and find it to be nothing special but will try heroin and fall in love with it. Give your best hypothesis in the space below: It depends on a person's emotional circumstances as well as how their body will react to it.

Self-Medication Hypothesis: One school of thought in the study of addiction is that people use drugs as a way of self-medicating undesirable feeling states such as depression or anxiety. And, in fact, many of the drugs we talked about above work very well for this . . . initially. The problem is that these drugs are addictive, and many of them are capable of causing severe damage to the brain and the body. Since these drugs work so well, though, people use them as a way to escape undesirable feeling states. This, of course, only serves as a short-term solution to a much bigger psychological problem.

There is an abundance of recent research linking trauma with addiction (Wanberg & Milkman, 2008). This research suggests that many people who experience traumatic events (childhood sexual abuse, natural disasters, war, etc.) are very likely to use drugs as a way to cope with the trauma in the absence of adequate psychological care. Just as was noted in the self-medication hypothesis above, this strategy can work just fine at first. However, once the cycle of addiction is set in motion, it is only a matter of time until the person will need help to stop using. When this happens, it is imperative that both the addiction and the underlying psychological trauma are treated. If just the addiction is treated, there is a much higher rate of relapse back into drug use.

Other Ways to Alter Consciousness

While drugs are capable of producing desirable effects, the risk of addiction and other health problems make them a potentially risky way to alter consciousness. Another way more and more people are experiencing alternate states of consciousness is through *meditation.* Meditation is a purposeful practice designed to completely focus attention and enhance serenity and well being. There are different forms of meditation such as concentrative meditation in which one focuses on something such as each breath or a mantra, and mindfulness meditation in which thoughts are observed but not judged.

Another technique used to induce altered states of consciousness is hypnosis. Hypnosis is a state in which one experiences almost totalizing relaxation and focus and is highly susceptible to suggestion. Once a mystery, hypnosis is now fairly well understood scientifically and is used to help offer people pain relief during childbirth and even at the dentist. Hypnosis can also be a good treatment for people who suffer from chronic pain and can also be used as part of a larger treatment plan to help with psychological trauma, anxiety, and phobias. Some individuals are more suggestible to hypnosis than others, and it is worth noting that hypnosis requires a willing and conscious participant. So, in other words, one could not be hypnotized against his or her will.

Having a better understanding of consciousness and its altered states is powerful information. Such information provides you with the ability to make healthier choices that will improve your psychological and physical health. As you now know, just the simple act of understanding your sleep cycle and getting a good night's sleep can make a huge impact on your day-to-day life.

REFERENCES

Billiard, M. (2007). Sleep disorders. In L. Candelise, R. Hughes, A. Liberati, B. Uitdehaag, & C. Warlow (Eds.), *Evidence-based neurology: Management of neurological disorders* (pp. 70–78). Malden, MA: Blackwell Publishing.

Cash, S. S., Halgren, E, Dehghani, N., et al. (2009). Human k-complex represents an isolated cortical down-state. *Science, 324,*1084–1087.

Domhoff, G. W. (2007). Realistic simulation and bizarreness in dream content: Past findings and suggestions for future research. In D. Barrett & P. McNamara (Eds.), *The new science of dreaming: Volume 2. Content, recall, and personality correlates* (pp. 1–27). Westport, CT: Praeger.

Hobson, J. A. (1999). *Dreaming as delirium: How the brain goes out of its mind.* Cambridge, MA: MIT Press.

Massicotte-Marquez, J., Decary, A., Gagnon, J. F., Vendette, M., Mathieu, A., Postuma, R. B., Carrier, J., & Montplaisir, J. (2008). Executive dysfunction and memory impairment in idiopathic REM sleep behavior disorder. *Neurology,* 1250–1277.

Milkman, H., & Sunderworth, S. (2010). *Craving for ecstasy and natural highs: A positive approach to mood alteration.* Thousand Oaks, CA: Sage Publications.

Wanberg, K. W., & Milkman, H. (2008). *Criminal conduct & substance abuse treatment strategies for self-improvement and change pathways to responsible living.* Thousand Oaks, CA: Sage Publications.

NAME ____ DATE ______________________

WORKSHEET CHAPTER SIX

CHAPTER 7

HUMAN DEVELOPMENT

Imagine you are a parent. If you are a parent, imagine your children at different ages past and future. Although it may prove easy to conjure the idea of children at different ages, it may be difficult to understand exactly what they may go through, how they may experience the world or deal with successes, failures, and difficulties. Will they deal with them like you did? Will they deal with them the way you taught them to? Can you see the subtle difference in these two questions? What is it?

The Whole Person – What makes a good basketball player, chess player, teacher, counselor, scientist, child prodigy, artist? Which of the following traits match each example? Are there some traits that fit some of these descriptions better than others? Is there a description here that needs only a single trait?

Is there a tendency to put some of these jobs into a "one-trait" category?

What traits make a "whole person"?

Moral

Cognitive

Social

Emotional

Physical

The development of a human being is an intricate and multifaceted path riddled with barriers, boundaries, and critical periods. The realm of most interest to development psychologists is the period of ongoing adjustments and modifications that take place from time of conception to the time of death. As you can imagine, this is a field of study as complex as they come, involving other fields of study like biology, chemistry, and sociology and weaving distinct patterns of both individuality and commonality.

Developmental psychology grew from the study of child psychology, which essentially studies the development of children's physical being, cognitive abilities, social interactions, and personality. By studying children's development in these ways, it was thought that we could understand problems that many were having with physical growth, motor skills, learning, language, and social relations.

From this came an idea that these very developmental processes, processes thought of as primarily psychological such as thinking and personality, were possibly beginning to develop much earlier than at birth. Development psychologists thus began focusing their lens on the prenatal period as well, estimating that nutrition and environment of an unborn infant could impact his or her personality, intelligence, and future behavior.

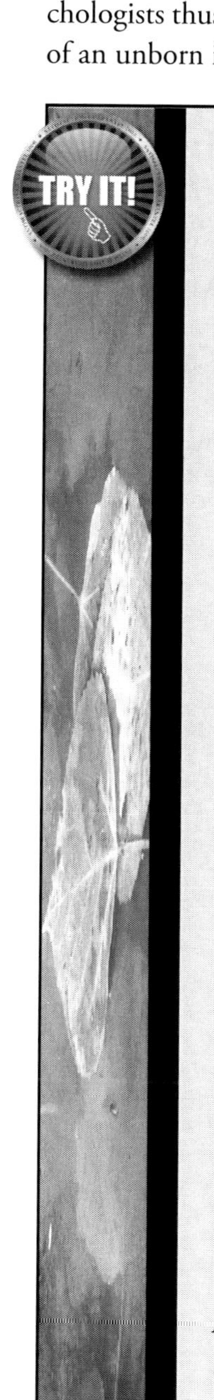

Try It – Rank order

The following is a list of developmental tasks that a healthy child will master. Your task is to rank the various skills from first to last. For example, if you think that the skill of walking comes before the skill of running, you would give walking a 1 and running a 2. Rank the following from 1 to 10.

_____ Walks independently

_____ Runs

_____ Turns head to follow a moving object

_____ Names different toys (ball, doll, truck)

_____ Walks with assistance

_____ Crawls up stairs

_____ Dresses self

_____ Understands that a hidden object is still there

_____ Understands how a kitten and a puppy are different

_____ Links vocalizations to people/things; "da-da" for daddy, "dah" for doll

Which of the skills above are cognitive? Physical? Social? As we learned earlier, it is difficult to tease one category of development apart from the others. For example, it may require strength and muscle coordination (physical) to run, but it takes thought and brain development (cognitive) as well. But in the spirit of good psychology, let's try anyway.

Now, put a C next to the skills you think are *primarily* cognitive, a P next to those you think are *primarily* physical, and an S for social.

Think back to what you know about the nature/nurture problem in psychology. Which of the skills do you think come naturally? Which require teaching?

Finally, imagine you work in a daycare with dozens of children of different ages. You will note some differences in abilities that fall within a range of "normal," which gives you no concern. Some children walk and talk earlier than others, others make friends or relate to others more easily, and some draw, color, or tie their shoes with more facility. But at what point in a child's development is it a concern when he or she doesn't demonstrate these skills so readily? Specifically, you may not have concern that your child is not walking by 12 months, but what if he was not taking steps on his own at 18 months? At what age would you note your concern about the child's development for each of the skills in this exercise?

PSYCHOLOGICAL DEVELOPMENT

From the moment a human sperm joins with an egg, the development of a biological form takes a fragile path toward birth. At the time of birth, babies, although vulnerable and in need of constant care, are indeed able to meet the world with instincts that allow them to perceive and act in ways that help in their survival. A human being develops emotionally, physically, sexually, morally, cognitively, socially, and psychologically. To make it more elaborate, it appears that these human processes are all very much intertwined and quite inseparable.

So, if developmental psychology is such a diverse field, looking into the development of everything from language to depth perception, from hearing to extraversion, you may wonder: What *exactly* does a developmental psychologist study? In short, anything related to the scientific study of mental processes and behavior.

To put it another way, developmental psychologists are the most interested in how factors, both genetic and environmental (remember nature/nurture?), affect how human beings progress on the path of life along with all the commonalities and differences in between. Now let us explore the specific developmental categories and the theories these developmental specialists have put forward.

COGNITIVE DEVELOPMENT

Cognitive psychology is branch of psychology concerned with the study of thought and internal mental processes. It is through these processes that humans remember, process information, understand, communicate, reason, discriminate, learn, judge, and otherwise become aware.

In the early 1920s, Jean Piaget was working to understand children's intelligence by administering many skill-based tasks and verbal questions aimed at problem solving. Some children were able to perform the tasks and answer the questions correctly and some were not. Piaget looked closely at the children's correct and incorrect responses and noticed something common to both: the process of thinking. He discovered that children are not different from adults in that they don't reason or in that they lack intelligence but in that they reason *differently* and have intelligence appropriate to their age. Even when they were thinking *illogically,* children were doing so in a process of becoming more *logical.*

Piaget proposed the cognitive ability of children develops through a series of stages each different from the other. These stages begin at the most basic of cognitive abilities (such as tracking a moving object or imitating a sound) and progress to the very complex (such as symbolic recreation). Because he thought these stages to be separate from each other, the children who have progressed through this stage have skills and abilities that children who have not yet progressed through this stage lack. For instance, a child who has learned *object permanence* (an understanding that objects continue to exist even when they cannot be seen, which develops as early as 3 ½ months but usually around 6 to 8 months) will look for a hidden ball, whereas a child who has not progressed to this stage of development will not look for the ball. The child who has mastered object permanence will not "forget" or otherwise become unskilled in this ability, except perhaps because of some process of disease, but rather progress on through higher stages of cognitive development.

The developing brain is an active brain, and children are using theirs all the time. Piaget offered that children's brains are active in that they are building schemas. A *schema* is a mental structure used to make sense of the world through the organization of ideas, concepts, and actions. By the time we have moved through adolescence into adulthood, we have built numerous schemas informing us about colors, styles, food, gender, animals, mathematics, music, and even love, hate, prejudice, and empathy. Piaget offered that, through the process of assimilation and accommodation, we build these schemas and make sense of the world in which we live. *Assimilation* is a process by which we interpret new experiences based on a given schema. For example, if a child has a schema for dog, the child may call any animal that resembles a dog (those that walk on four legs and have a similar size) a dog. Although a *mistake* in thinking, Piaget noted that it is through these mistakes that children adjust their schemas to make room for the new information, a process called *accommodation.* In the dog example, the child will eventually learn that there are other animals that, while perhaps similar in size and shape to dogs, are indeed not dogs and go by another name. So accommodation involves altering an already existing schema or sometimes creating a new schema altogether.

To gain a better understanding of the development of a child's thinking, let's look at the four stages of cognitive development as Piaget conceived them.

Sensorimotor

From birth to near 2 years of age children identify and interact with their environment with their motor skills and five senses. It is in this stage that children develop object permanence (about 6 to 8 months) and what is known as *stranger anxiety* or an apprehension that children have when exposed to unfamiliar people. During this stage children will grasp at objects, watch them move through real space, and seem to put anything and everything into their mouths.

Preoperational

From around 2 years to near age 7 children begin to learn to use language and understand the link between speech, whether their own or other's, and action. They also learn that pictures or drawings can act as symbols for something else not necessarily present. For example, a child may look at a picture of her father and recognize it as "daddy" or a drawing of a dog as a "doggy." This stage is marked by a development of logical mental operations such as the concept of *conservation* or the idea that a quantity of something remains the same despite changes in its shape. This stage is evident by the presence of *egocentrism,* the inability for child to see another person's point of view and the assumption that others have the same perceptions and points of reference as he or she does.

Concrete Operational

From age of 7 until roughly 12 children begin to use logic effectively to solve problems. They develop the ability to sort objects in an order according to size or shape, lose their egocentrism by developing the capacity to view ideas from the perspective of another, and develop the ability to understand mathematical conversions such as 2+3= 5 and 5−3=2. Children in this stage can now solve conversation tasks, but still have trouble thinking hypothetically.

Formal Operational

From the age of 12 and beyond children develop abstract reasoning, or the ability to conceptualize concrete examples and experiences in larger, broader principles. These young people are able to perform highly sophisticated activities of the mind such as creating an expected reality and solving theoretical problems with their imagination. Teenagers in this stage frequently demonstrate their own form of egocentrism often referred to as adolescent egocentrism. This type of egocentrism comes in two forms: personal fable and imaginary audience. Personal fable involves a teenager's feeling as though his or her difficulties or success are specifically unique to him or her and that others cannot identify with what he or she is going through. Imaginary audience is the adolescent's belief that he or she is the focus of everyone else's attention. This can help explain why many adolescents tend to exhibit an excessive level of self-consciousness.

ACTIVITY

For each example, describe the stage of cognitive development and give a rationale by which you arrived at your answer.

1) A boy stands in front of the television while other members of his family are intently watching a show. His father asks him to move and says, "Don't you understand that we can't see the television with you standing there?" The child shakes his head no and appears confused.

2) A girl learns that her boyfriend is breaking up with her. She is devastated. When her mother attempts to comfort her, she replies: "You don't understand. No one has ever felt as much pain as I am and experienced a breakup this bad." When her mother begins discussing her first breakup years ago, this only makes the girl angrier.

(continued)

ACTIVITY (*continued*)

3) A boy wakes up in the morning. While brushing his teeth he looks in the mirror and sees a new zit bigger than he has ever had. He is nervous all morning about going to school. When he walks into his first period class, he fears that everyone in the classroom is staring at him.

I maginary audience because he thinks he is the focus of everyone's attention.

LANGUAGE DEVELOPMENT

Underlying the major perspectives of development are varying assumptions about its causes and the changes that occur in its path. The cognitive theory covered earlier emphasizes the role of maturation over time, whereas learning theorists see development as the consequence of environment and experience. The most prominent theorists in each camp (cognitive and learning) are B.F. Skinner and Noam Chomsky, respectively.

Skinner used his theory of learning to explain the development and acquisition of language claiming that children are reinforced (see Chapter 3) for making, combining, and using appropriate language in social situations. Chomsky disagreed, often sparking exciting and public debates with Skinner, claiming that children learn language so quickly that it is clearly not a product of learning but rather an inborn, instinctual ability. He vehemently disagreed with Skinner's behaviorist approach, concluding that humans develop language in a fashion similar to the development of progressive coordinated muscle movement, like walking to running. In other words, Chomsky said that we no more learn to speak than we learn to walk and that it is an inborn predisposition. While it may be an easy way to conceptualize this process, Skinner's idea of reinforced behaviors was rendered inadequate as a full explanation for development of language.

And, although the cases of Chomsky and Skinner have developed themselves over the years since their famous debates, most psychologists agree that although language is a developed, natural ability as are most instincts, its most healthy development relies on appropriate environmental stimuli, social cues, and reinforcements. It is clear that babies *develop* their language first in the form of babbling and cooing, then move to first words, to basic partial sentences, and to a final, life-long refinement of grammatical structure and use.

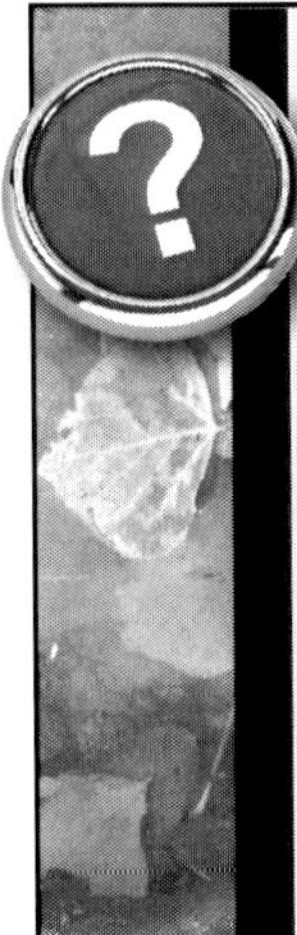

Ask yourself – What is the difference between the terms "develop" and "learn"? We often use the term "learn" to describe the development of a behavior when it may be the case that the behavior develops genetically.

Remember Chapter 3 on learning. Does a goose *learn* to fly south for the winter, requiring systematic reinforcements for appropriate behavior or does it *develop* this behavior from an inborn, genetic tendency? Does a baby human (or any animal for that matter!) need to *learn* to suckle or does this ability *develop*?

What other examples can you think of? How is it that some people think of personality or sexual orientation as mostly *learned* and other similar human traits, like strength or height, as a *developed* process of genetics?

SOCIAL DEVELOPMENT

Much in the way that humans develop the ability to walk, talk, and think, they also progress through a series of steps in their ability to recognize, instigate, maintain, and participate in meaningful relationships. In other words, personality and social behavior also develop. Even in the first months of their lives, babies show patterns of reactions to objects and to people and develop what is known as temperament. Erik Erikson (1963) developed one of the most widely referenced and utilized theories of psychosocial development spanning the entire human lifespan, from birth to death. He hypothesized that humans develop socially through a stage of dilemmas and tasks where the individual learns to construct his or her identity in the context of others through either a healthy or unhealthy outcome. In each stage a conflict surfaces, representing a newly forming personality and its balance with a slew of social pressures. The result is a crisis representing a unique challenge for the individual where he negotiates his relationship with the social world. Erikson's dilemmas are shown in Table 7.1.

Table 7.1 Erikson's Dilemmas

Crisis	Age	Dilemma: Resolution
Trust vs. Mistrust	0–1 years	Environment and caregivers: Consistent or insecure?

Autonomy vs. Shame and Doubt	2–3 years	Self-control: Competence or inability?
Initiative vs. Guilt	3–5 years	Solving problems: Proficient or incompetent?

Industry vs. Inferiority © Morgan Lane Photography, 2011. Used under license of Shutterstock, Inc.	6–12 years	Ability to produce: Useful or inadequate?
Identity vs. Role Confusion © EML, 2011. Used under license of Shutterstock, Inc.	12–18 years	Role in society: Meaningful or vague?
Intimacy vs. Isolation © oliveromg, 2011. Used under license of Shuttestock, Inc.	Young adult	Intimacy/Love: Adequacy or separation?

Generativity vs. Stagnation © Suzanne Tucker, 2011. Used under license of Shutterstock, Inc.	Middle adult	Meaning in life: Creation or inactivity?
Integrity vs. Despair © Orange Line Media, 2011. Used under license of Shutterstock, Inc.	Late adult	Review of a life lived: Peace or regret?

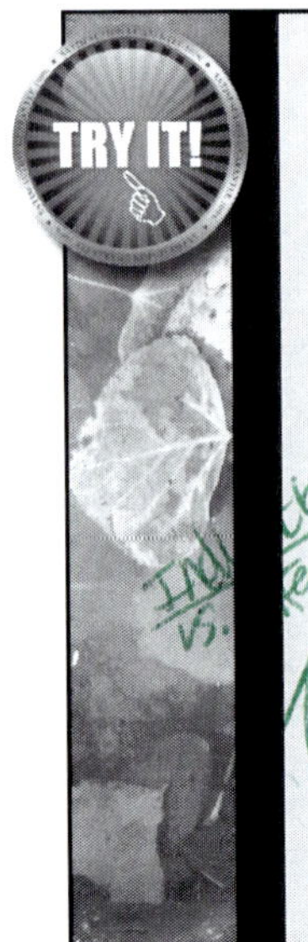

Try it– List and describe with which developmental dilemma each of the following individuals is dealing. On which side of the dilemma do you see each resolving?

- At the start of ninth grade Maggie decides to hang out with a new crowd of friends. She dyes her hair blue and begins listening to different music.
- Inspired by his love for cheeseburgers, french fries, and his mother's frequent serving of casseroles for dinner, John makes cheeseburger casserole for his parents. He stirs in all his favorite ingredients including pickles, mayonnaise, french fries, mustard, and hamburger buns. Smiling, John's parents sit down and eat their entire meal, all the while praising his hard work.
- While fishing off a beach with her family, Pam notices that some rocks are flatter than others. She has an idea and begins finding the flattest rocks, pushing them out on the surface of the water in an attempt to see whether they will float. Witnessing this, her older cousin immediately begins teasing her, exclaiming to all that Pam is stupid and wrongfully trying to make rocks float.

(continued)

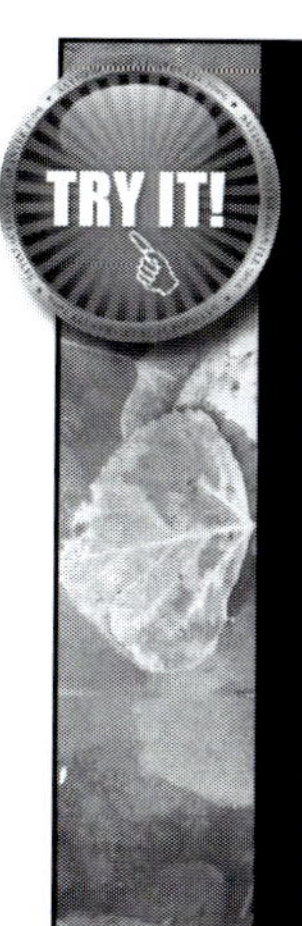

Try It (*continued*)

- Jose, a 45-year-old man, has acquired a lot of wealth working diligently at his corporate job. He has two kids, a wife whom he loves, a house, and a boat. Recently, his oldest son returned home from school with a negative report card. As a result, Jose has begun to feel like his life is without purpose.
- Cedric, a 23-year-old recent college graduate, has recently started dating an attractive woman for whom he is developing strong feelings. After numerous dates, she admits to him her feelings of love. Upon hearing this proclamation, his thoughts drift immediately to the potential large pool of women he will not be able to date as a result of the commitment of admitted love. He begins to distance himself from her.

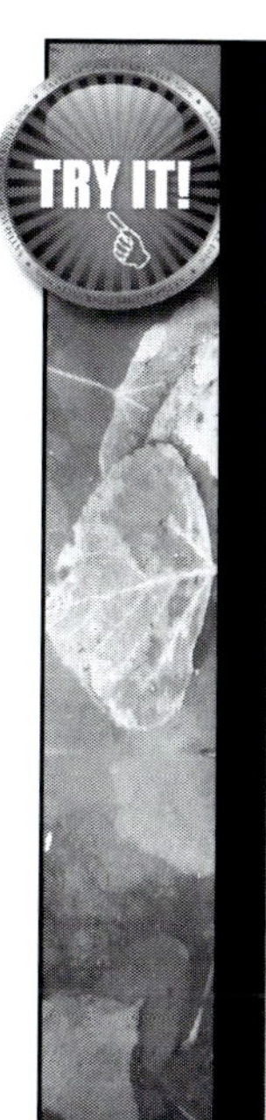

Now try it – Consider the following statements from Ochse and Plug's (1986) personality questionnaire based on Erikson's stages. Which of Erikson's dilemmas do you think was at play and at what end of the dilemma did this person likely fall? In other words, did the person making the statement resolve the dilemma in a healthy or unhealthy way?

- I am prepared to take a risk to get what I want.
- I avoid doing something difficult because I feel I would fail.
- I feel it is better to remain free than to become committed to marriage for life.
- I wonder what sort of person I really am.
- I feel the world's major problems can be solved.
- I feel that I have done nothing that will survive after I die.
- I have a feeling of complete "togetherness" with someone.
- I am unnecessarily apologetic.
- When people try to persuade me to do something I don't want to, I refuse.
- I feel too incompetent to do what I would really like to do in life.

What was it about each statement that led you to your conclusion?

PERSONALITY DEVELOPMENT

While Erikson's stages of development are largely conceptualized as changes in social functioning, it is also clear that his stages are describing the development of a personality. The personality is a collection of traits all existing on a spectrum, which also develop. Some people are extraverted or socially outgoing while others are more introverted and keep to themselves. Some are open to experience and others are more cautious about trying new things. While each trait is different, healthy personalities seem to be created equal. Sigmund Freud was another scholar of a personality development arguably both the first and most recognized theory of personality development to date. There are many theories of how humans develop what seems to be unique to our species, a collection of traits that defines better our identity than any other feature, a personality. For more detailed information on personality theorists and their ideas please participate in Chapter 11.

MORAL DEVELOPMENT

Theories of the development of language and thinking regard humans as cognitive beings. Humans are also social creatures with an ability to relate to and connect with others immediately following birth. To further understand development is to consider how the development of social interactions and cognitions lead to the growth of a moral sense.

© Lightspring, 2011. Used under license of Shutterstock, Inc.

Moral development is the process by which children acquire a perception of which behaviors and attitudes are right and which are wrong. While different schools of thought conceptualize moral development differently, the behaviorists claiming it involves a reinforced system of moral and/or immoral behaviors and a cognitive theorist espousing the importance of thinking and comprehension of increasingly complex concepts, all seem to agree that morality grows and develops parallel to thinking and language.

Specifically, Piaget thought that his theory of cognitive development could be used to understand our moral development as well postulating that there are age-based consistencies in moral judgments. Piaget's contemporary, Lawrence Kohlberg (1981), suggested a model explaining humans' development as moral beings, capable of understanding the dimensions of right and wrong. Kohlberg suggested that all humans progress through a sequence of moral stages that are linked not only to stages of cognitive development but also to social experiences and interactions with other people. In his research into the realm of moral development, Kohlberg asked many people across most age groups (children, adolescents, and adults) to think through different moral dilemmas and decide if the actions posed in the dilemma were right or wrong. What he found led him to conclude that humans develop through three levels of moral reasoning. Kohlberg's stages of moral development are shown in Table 7.2.

Table 7.2 Kohlberg's Stages of Moral Development

Stage	Age	Process
Preconventional Morality	By age 9	Focus is on self-interest and avoidance of punishment.
Conventional Morality	By adolescence	Caring for others emerges. Law and rules are upheld for their own sake.
Postconventional Morality	Adulthood	Universal, human ethics and rights are recognized.

Try it at home – Kohlberg posed different moral dilemmas to many different groups of people across many different age groups. Although he was fascinated with children's responses to different problems involving ideas of right and wrong, it was children's rationale for their decisions that led Kohlberg to believe that morality is a developed concept, like thinking.

(continued)

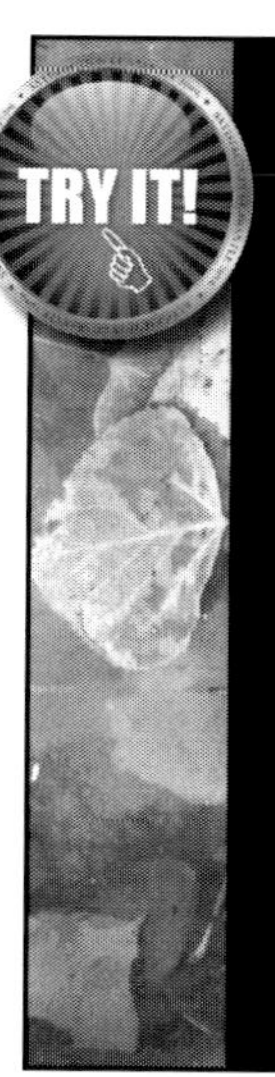

Try it at home *(continued)*

Pose a problem similar to Kohlberg's dilemmas to a child under the age of 9 and ask her if the character's actions were right or wrong.

Mr. Brown has three children, and they are all hungry because they have not eaten in many days. While there is a baker down the street with plenty of bread for all the children to eat and not be hungry, Mr. Brown does not have enough money to pay for the bread. Late at night, when the baker's shop is closed, Mr. Brown breaks in and steals enough bread for his family to eat for a week. Was it right for Mr. Brown to steal the bread? Explain.

What sort of answers do you get from younger children? What sort of answers would you expect from older children or from adolescents? From adults? What do you notice about their reasoning for their answers? Is there an answer to this dilemma that is *more* right than the other? Why?

SOCIAL-EMOTIONAL DEVELOPMENT

There are many factors that influence a healthy development, whether that development is cognitive, physical, emotional, social, or moral. There are some factors that are so center-stage that they are indispensible to a healthy development and, if not present in a healthy manner, will affect literally every other facet. The two that are most primary are *attachment* and *parenting.*

During the first years of life, the emotional bond that forms between infant and parent (or primary caregiver) is called *attachment.* Theorized and studied initially by John Bowlby (1969) and furthered by Mary Salter Ainsworth (1979), relationships demonstrating healthy attachment serve humans throughout their entire lifespan. When the attachment is secure, the infant feels a safe and trusting environment in which he or she is safe to explore and learn about the world and later can establish and maintain intimate and connected relationships. An infant's capacity to flourish in her new world is based almost exclusively on quality of attachments to primary and secondary caregivers.

Based on the interaction with the caregiver, an infant will develop either a secure or insecure attachment. When parents are consistently responsive to and nurturing of the infant's needs, that infant will develop a *secure* attachment. A securely attached infant comes to understand that his needs will be met in a prompt manner and that discomfort, when it is felt, will soon be addressed. If, on the other hand, an infant's parents are neglectful, ambivalent, or inconsistent in their attention to the infant's needs, the infant will likely develop an *insecure* attachment.

There are two common types of insecure attachment: *avoidant* and *anxious/ambivalent.* Avoidant infants tend not to seek closeness or contact with their caregivers. Anxious/ambivalent infants are very anxious when caregivers are not around and happy to see them when they return. However, while they are happy when their caregivers return, they also appear almost angry that they had left in the first place.

Securely attached infants are better adjusted and have higher levels of social involvement as well as better cognitive and language development. Researchers have also found that childhood attachment styles have a tendency to carry over into adult romantic relationships (Clulow, 2007; Lele, 2008).

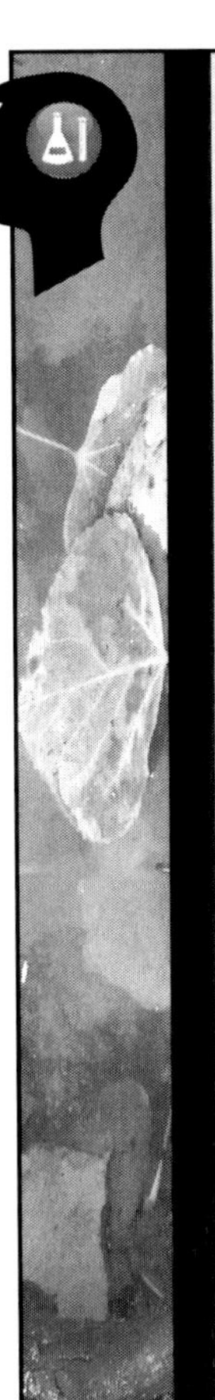

A Thought Experiment – Imagine raising a puppy. From the moment of its birth, you love this puppy. You feed it, pet it, walk it, and wash it when it needs it. You even sleep on the floor with it the first weeks in its new home with you so to help it adjust and to calm its nervous shaking. Now, as difficult as it may seem, imagine having this same new puppy and ignoring its needs, locking it out of sight as well as earshot, allowing it to cry and nervously shake through the night, either because you don't have the time to care for it or because your attitude suggests other methods. Finally, imagine the adult personality, behavior, and temperament of this animal as a result of each of the described puppy experiences. What are the differences?

Can your bridge the gap between this scenario and a human experience? How might an adolescent act if he was neglected as a baby? How might his ability to formulate affectionate and intimate relationships as a young adult be affected?

PARENTING STYLES

Raising psychologically healthy children can be a difficult endeavor offering no guarantees or instructions. However, psychological research does shed some light on what it means to be a psychologically healthy human and what sorts of parents raised such an individual. Some guidelines have emerged over the years and primarily discuss basic *parenting styles* and their effects on children. Psychologist Diana Baumrind (1971) outlined three parenting styles as a result of her many years of observing of parents: *authoritarian, authoritative,* and *permissive.* The main variables at play in each are the control and responsiveness of each parent to their child's wishes. Let's break these down.

- **Authoritarian parenting:** These parents are demanding of their children, often outlining very strict expectations and consequences for not performing. In addition to their demanding style, these parents are also unresponsive to their children's needs or desires. They believe that they need to control the child's behavior so that it adheres to a set of predetermined standards. They expect their children to obey the rules without question and are mostly closed to any input from them.

© Monkey Business Images, 2011. Used under license of Shutterstock, Inc.

- **Authoritative parenting:** These parents are warm, nurturing, and involved with their children's experiences. Like authoritarian parents, they are demanding of their children; however, they feel a need to consider their children's point of view and wishes. There is more of a democratic process in this style of parenting and, although the demands are high and rules are clear, they are discussed with the children, and the children know they are safe and that they have a voice in the family.

© Elena Kouptsova-Vasic, 2011. Used under license of Shutterstock, Inc.

- **Permissive indifferent parenting:** These parents, like authoritative parents, are warm and nurturing; however, they lack rules, structure, or clear expectations of their children's behavior. They are not unresponsive to their children's basic needs; however, they are lacking in responsiveness to their behavior and lack consistency in their reinforcements and punishments.

- **Permissive neglectful parenting:** These parents, like permissive indifferent parents, lack clear rules and structure, but in addition, they lack warmth and nurturance. Children who grow up with parents like this are often left to their own devices with regard to navigating the world around them.

© Cheryl Casey, 2011. Used under license of Shutterstock, Inc.

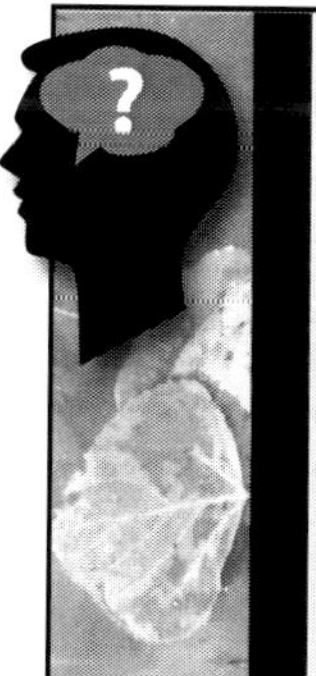

Think about it – How do you think these parenting styles affect young children?

There is a slew of research on this topic. What does this literature suggest about children with parents of different parenting styles?

(*continued*)

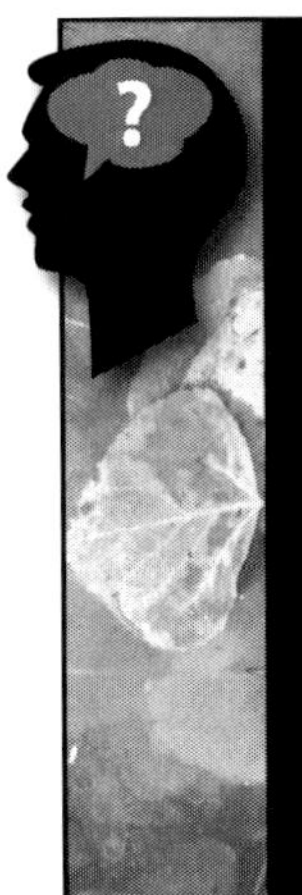

Think about it (*continued*)

Imagine you are hired by a psychologist to write a book on how to be the best parent possible. What would your chapters be titled? What would your advice be? What cautions would you give?

What type of parent are you *or* what type of parent do you hope to be?

DEATH AND DYING

When we started this chapter, we discussed the whole person, which is the individual as made up of many different "parts" with varying traits distinguishing them from others with their own individual sets of traits. When you discussed how people are all different, you likely alluded to differences in personality, varying degrees of temperament, and diversity of people's behavior. We discussed the development of language, thinking, and of morals. In this final section, we will discuss the end of these traits in the death of the individual but also, and perhaps more importantly, the changing and diminishment of these traits.

Although it is nice to think of only the elderly dying and while it is obviously the case that all people die, there is also a large level of protection from the harsher elements of death built into our society. It is also nice to think that older adults are prepared for their demise and that they are at peace. What appears to be more the case is that all humans at all ages die, that they all have some anxiety, whether significant or miniscule, about the prospect of dying and that not everyone, whether elderly or youthful, has a peaceful, wisdom-filled exit.

Elisabeth Kübler-Ross (1969) is the most widely recognized person associated with the psychological study of grief, death, and dying. Her research with hundreds of terminally ill patients led her to her stage theory of death. In short, she believed that people come to terms with their own death the same way that they come to terms with the death of others. She outlined five stages of dying: *denial* ("It's not true"), anger ("Why me?!"), *bargaining* ("I'll do anything to reverse this"*), depression* ("I've lost everything"), and *acceptance* ("I accept my time is near"). While her theory is continually criticized in many social and academic circles, it survives as a template for human movement within the knowledge of death.

Think about it – There are many protective factors against death. Each culture seems to have its own stories of life and death, the process of dying, and all have ceremonies or ritualized behaviors that honor, celebrate and even keep at bay the dead.

(*continued*)

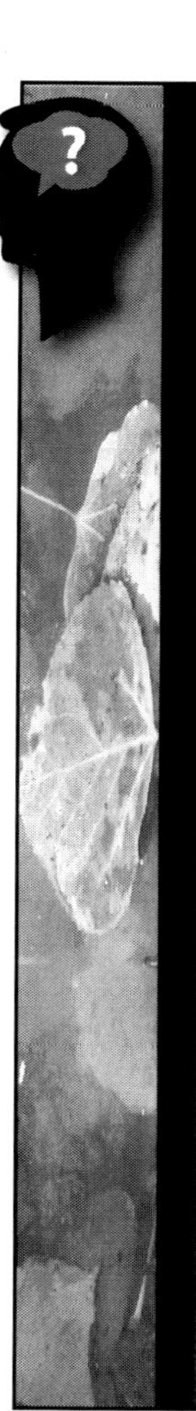

Think about it (*continued*)

What is your cultural experience with death? What times in your life have you come into contact with a person who has beliefs about life and death that are completely different than your own? What were your reactions?

© Ashley Whitworth, 2011. Used under license of Shutterstock, Inc.

Finally, religion seems to be a common cultural component that weighs in on the ideas of life and death perhaps more than any other subject. What are different ideas that different religions offer about death? Despite their differences, do they have anything in common?

What are your thoughts? Beliefs?

REFERENCES

Ainsworth, M. S. (1979). Attachment as related to mother-infant interaction. In J.G. Rosenblatt, R.A. Hinde, C. Beer, & M. Busnel (Eds.), *Advances in the study of behavior.* New York: Academic Press.

Baumrind, D. (1971). Current patterns of parental authority. *Development Psychology Monographs, 4,* 1–103.

Bowlby, J. (1969). *Attachment and loss: Vol. 1. Attachment* New York: Basic Books.

Clulow, C. (2007). John Bowlby and couple psychotherapy. *Attachment & Human Development, 9,* 343–353.

Erikson, E. (1963). *Childhood and society.* New York: Norton.

Kohlberg, L. (1981). *The philosophy of moral development Essays on moral development Volume 1* San Francisco: Harper & Row.

Lele, D.U. (2008). The influence of individual personality and attachment styles on romantic relationships (partner choice and couples' satisfaction). *Dissertation Abstracts International: Section B: The Sciences and Engineering, 68,* 6316.

Kübler-Ross, E. (1969). *On death and dying.* New York: Macmillan.

Ochse, R., & Plug, C. (1986). Cross-cultural investigation of the validity of Erikson's theory of personality development. *Journal of Personality and Social Psychology, 50,* 1240–1252.

NAME ______________________________ DATE ________________

WORKSHEET CHAPTER SEVEN

CHAPTER 8

MEMORY

"Every man's memory is his private literature."
— Aldous Huxley

You and your friend are having a conversation about movies you like. He brings up the movie *Batman: The Dark Knight*, which he said he hasn't seen yet but wants to.

You quickly reply, "Oh yeah! I love that movie. My favorite character is the Joker played by—oh, man. What's his name again? You know, he died recently in New York City?"

You stop to try and gather your thoughts, but still can't remember. Your friend looks at you with a clueless stare. Getting more frustrated with each passing moment you say to your friend, "You know the guy? He was in *Brokeback Mountain* and *10 Things I Hate About You?*"

Despite your best efforts, you cannot remember the name. Of course, you remembered it an hour later when driving home. Isn't that how it always happens?

"Heath Ledger!" you shout to yourself on the highway.

Ever wondered why something seems firmly entrenched in memory yet for some reason cannot be accessed even though you know it is in there somewhere? Maybe you have wondered how we take a piece of information from the outside world and store it in memory. Or, perhaps you might be curious about how you can improve your memory.

All of these topics and more will be covered in this chapter.

WHAT IS MEMORY?

Memory is our ability to recall, recognize, or bring to conscious awareness a prior experience or piece of learned information. Memory is a constructive process that takes place throughout our lives. Without the ability to remember, we would not have any knowledge of past experiences. We would also lack the ability to perform basic life tasks we learn at various points during our lives such as brushing our teeth or dressing ourselves in the morning. Even more disturbing, we would not be able to remember the names or faces of important people in our lives or the words necessary to communicate with them. Without memory, we would also lack the dynamic ability to adapt to our surroundings and learn from our triumphs as well as the mistakes we have made in the past.

It would be nice if memory were as simple as retrieving information from the hard drive of a computer and whatever document we opened would be displayed on the screen in all of its previous glory. Unfortunately, our memories are often flawed and distorted, especially highly emotional ones.

MODELS OF MEMORY

Psychologists and other great thinkers have devised numerous models of memory over the years. The most popular model is the Three-Stage Memory model, but a number of other models exist.

- ***Information Processing Model:*** People often learn the information-processing model of memory by relating it a computer. This model contends that three basic processes happen that contribute to memory: encoding, storage, and retrieval. Encoding involves inputting information into memory. In the computer analogy, *encoding* would take place at the level of the keyboard. After you type something on the keyboard, the information appears on the screen. If you were to hit save, that information would be sent to the hard drive. The hard drive is considered *storage.* Retrieval occurs when we attempt to remember something and retrieve it from storage or long-term memory. In this way, it can be helpful to think of retrieval as happening on the computer screen.

As noted earlier, our brains are rarely as accurate as a computer when it retrieves a document from storage. The memories we retrieve from storage in our brains are often fragmented and flawed. It would be like accessing a paper you just wrote on your computer and certain words were missing. If only our minds were as efficient at retrieval as our computers!

- ***Three-Stage Memory Model:*** This model has been accepted as the gold standard in memory for nearly five decades and has become more sophisticated over time. According to this model, the process of memory advances through three different stages:

Sensory Memory → Short-Term Memory (STM) → Long-Term Memory (LTM)

Sensory Memory: Any external stimuli we sense and perceive in the world enters our sensory memory. Any information that is not passed on from sensory memory to short-term memory is lost. Believe it or not, our sensory memories have a very large capacity. The problem is that visual information only stays in our sensory memory for up to a half second and auditory information for 2 to 4 seconds. Any information not passed on to STM is lost.

K Z R A

Q B T P

S G N Y

George Sperling (1960) completed research that flashed a card showing the 12 letters above. Participants saw the card for 1/20 of a second. Most participants were able to remember only four to five letters, but when they a heard a high, medium, or low tone corresponding to highest, middle, and bottom rows many participants reported most of the letters correctly. Sperling was able to show that all 12 letters were available in sensory memory for less than a second, but if they are not moved on to short-term memory they are lost.

Short-Term Memory (STM): Information that gets passed on from sensory memory ends up in STM. STM can hold information for up to 30 seconds without any kind of rehearsal. Information that is not passed on to long-term memory is lost. We can extend the life of STM briefly by engaging in what is called maintenance rehearsal. An example of this would be if a friend gave you a phone number but your cell phone was a few blocks away in your car. If you continued to repeat the number to yourself until you got to your phone and could input the number, this would be an example of maintenance rehearsal. This strategy is not an effective way to remember something long-term, because as soon as you stop reciting the information to yourself, it will quickly be lost.

Our STM can hold just five to nine items. In order to increase the capacity of our STM, we will "chunk" items together when possible. Chunking occurs when we group items that are similar. For example, with phone numbers we often chunk area codes together as a single item since they are the same in certain areas (example: 303 in Denver, 310 in Los Angeles).

Information that is deemed as important is passed on or encoded to LTM. From an academic context, this might be information that you believe may appear on an exam at a later date! Remember that information that is not passed on is lost.

It's important to remember that *STM is not a one-way street.* In other words, when we retrieve information from LTM, we pull it back into our STM where we can analyze it and interact with it. This is the reason why STM is often referred to as *working memory.*

Long-Term Memory (LTM): The LTM serves as our permanent filing cabinet for memories. It is believed to have a virtually limitless capacity and will hold information for as long as we are alive Information stays in our LTM until we need to remember it, at which point it is retrieved and sent back to our STM or working memory. However, this process does not always run as smoothly as we would like (specific potential problems in memory will be discussed later).

There are two major types of LTM that are referred to as *explicit* and *implicit* memory. Explicit memories are memories that require conscious recall. There are two subtypes of explicit memories referred to as *semantic* and *episodic.*

Semantic memory includes general facts and bits of knowledge about the world such as the color of an orange, the 42nd president of the United States, etc. Someone with a well-developed semantic memory would likely be very good at a game such as Trivial Pursuit. Episodic memories are memories of past experiences and events in our lives. This could include something as simple as what you did last night after dinner with your friends or something much more profound like the birth of a child.

Implicit memory is memory where conscious recall or awareness is not required. Implicit memory also has two subtypes, which are *procedural*, and *classically conditioned* memory. Procedural memory includes basic skills and processes that we often engage in on a daily basis such as brushing our teeth, getting dressed, tying our shoes, and driving to work. Classically conditioned memories include things we learn but are not consciously aware we are learning such as fears, phobias, and other attitudes.

FORGETTING

It might be discouraging to learn that over 60 percent of what you read or learn today will be forgotten within 24 hours. That number increases to nearly 80 percent one week from today. The first person to study this was Hermann Ebbinghaus in 1885. However, Ebbinghaus' research was done by trying to remember nonsense syllabus such as HTE, RAL, etc. If the material is more meaningful to us, we have a better chance of remembering it, but the odds we remember everything are still not as high as we would like. The good news is, though, relearning takes place much faster than initial learning.

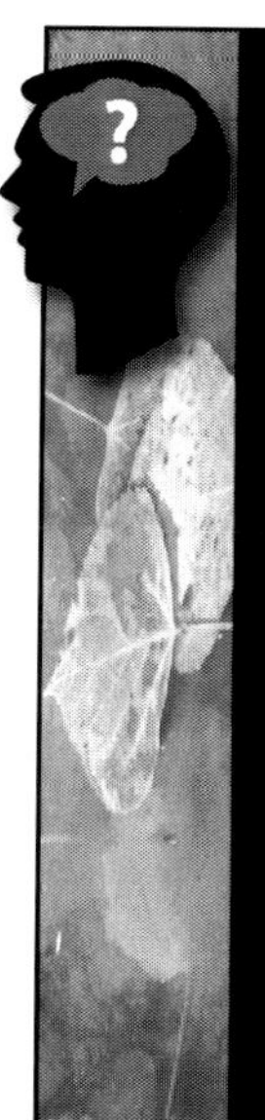

Think about it – Imagine that you have a test coming up in your psychology class. A fellow student decides that since he has the textbook there is really no reason to attend class. Besides, the professor hands out a review sheet, anyway. As a result, he simply waits for the review sheet a week before the test and completes it. Knowing what you know about forgetting and relearning, how would you evaluate this student's approach to studying for the exam? What might you recommend he do differently? Why?

Why Do We Forget?

There are numerous theories that hypothesize why we forget. A few of the most prominent are discussed in the space that follows.

- Decay Theory: Research indicates that memory function declines over time. This decline becomes more rapid if we are not using our brains consistently and exposing ourselves to novel stimuli. It really does seem to be a matter of "use it or lose it." That said, a certain amount of memory decline is inevitable as one progresses into old age.
- Encoding Failure: This happens when our memory system fails to pass on information from STM to LTM. A classic example of encoding failure occurs with the U.S. penny. Few people encode it at such a level that they notice small details of where things are located on the penny. This is due to the fact that we really only have to encode enough information to determine the difference between a penny and other coins we use frequently.
- Retrieval Failure: This occurs when our attempt to retrieve a memory is disrupted in some form. This is often called the tip-of-the tongue phenomenon because the information is in our LTM, but we are temporarily not able to retrieve it. This is the likely explanation for why a person might momentarily forget the name of an actor like the example involving Heath Ledger at the beginning of this chapter.
- Interference: Sometimes two memories get in the way of one another. *Proactive interference* occurs when an old memory gets in the way of a new one. An example of this could occur if your favorite player on a sports team

you root for gets traded away for a new player. When asked to recall the name of the new player, you find that you cannot remember, but you can still remember the name of your favorite player who was traded away. In this example, old information is interfering with your ability to retrieve new information. *Retroactive interference* occurs when new information interferes with your ability to recall old information. For example, let's imagine that the concepts of memory you are reading right now in Chapter 8 were interfering with your ability to remember concepts you already learned about human development in Chapter 7. In this case, new information is interfering with the ability to remember old information.

- Motivated Forgetting: When painful events or experiences occur in our lives, we might wish to forget these experiences. For example, perhaps you have been dreading going to the doctor for your yearly checkup for months, and when the day arrives for you to go, you forget about your appointment. Psychoanalytic thinkers such as Sigmund Freud believed that we purposely forget traumatic or anxiety-provoking experiences because they are too much for our psyches to deal with. This, too, would be an example of motivated forgetting.

Think about it – Tommy just started dating Gina a couple of weeks ago. While they are out on a date, he accidently calls Gina by his ex-girlfriend's name. This is an example of which theory of forgetting? Explain your answer.

Other Factors in Forgetting

- Serial Position Effect: Research has shown that we are more likely to remember items at the beginning or the end of a list than we are items in the middle (Azizian & Polich, 2007).

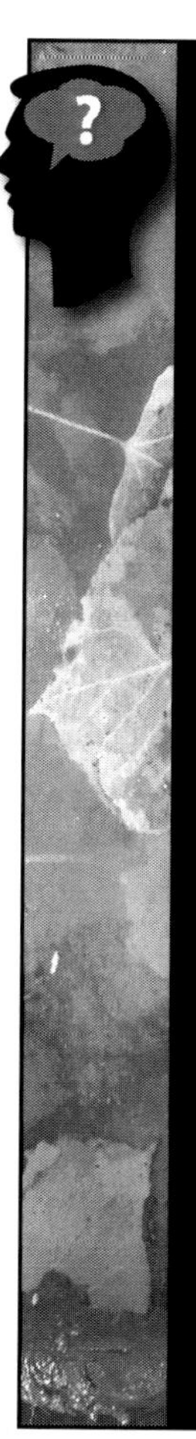

Think about it – If you receive a review sheet for an exam, what strategies could you use to try and avoid the negative effects of serial position effect? Explain your answer.

- Source Amnesia: Source amnesia occurs when we forget the true source of a memory. This often happens simply due to all of the information we take in on a daily basis. It can be easy to forget the context of a message or who actually said what.
- Sleeper Effect: This process is in many ways related to source amnesia. With sleeper effect, a period of months or even years causes us to confuse information we initially labeled as invalid from an unreliable source as later valid because we forgot the true source of the information (Appel & Richter, 2007). For example, imagine that while taking this class you saw a popular national talk show discussing how psychic mediums are scientific and supported by the field of psychology. You initially discounted this idea and laughed it off based on what you learned in class. Now, imagine that two years after this class one of your friends brings up the topic of psychic mediums and says these are scientific and supported by the field of psychology. You think to yourself, "Oh, yeah. I remember my psychology teacher talking about this a couple of years ago." This would be an example of sleeper effect because information that you originally labeled as invalid from an unreliable talk show host was now being deemed valid because you forget the true source of the information and attributed it to your psychology teacher.
- Misinformation Effect: Research has shown that our memories can be shaped after the fact by outside information (Allan & Gabbert, 2008). Perhaps you have noticed this at work in a favorite family story. As the story gets told more and more, certain alterations or exaggerations are added. Over time, it can be hard to remember what actually happened because of the information that was added after the fact. A number of studies have demonstrated that misinformation effect creates false memories (Garry & Gerrie, 2005; Loftus, 1982; Mazzoni & Vannucci, 2007).

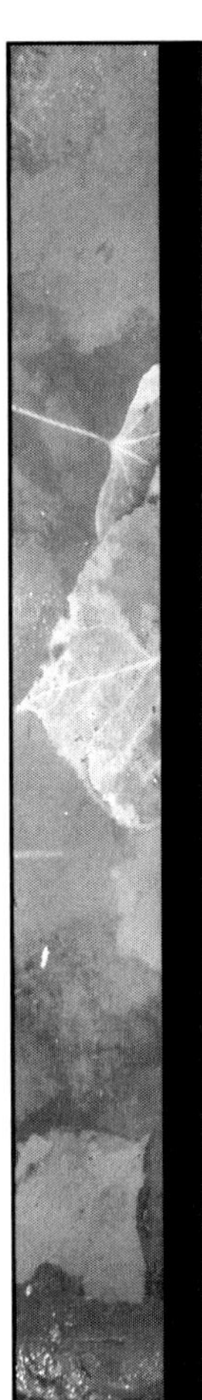

Did you know? – Massed vs. Distributed Practice: As a student, chances are you have come across the term "cramming" with regard to preparing for a test. Did you know there is actually a term in the memory literature to describe this? It is called massed practice. During massed practice, long continuous intervals are utilized to try and learn material. As you might have guessed, massed practice is not nearly as effective as distributed practice, which involves spacing out practice over a longer period of time with smaller intervals.

HOW CAN WE IMPROVE MEMORY

- Elaborative Rehearsal: Remember the term maintenance rehearsal mentioned in the short-term memory section earlier in the chapter? This is a strategy used to momentarily keep information in short-term memory. For obvious reasons, this is not an effective strategy to remember something long term. One of the best ways to make sure a memory is stored securely in long-term memory is to engage in elaborative rehearsal. Finding a way to make the material meaningful to you and create connections between the new information you are attempting to remember and previous information already stored in memory is one great way to accomplish this. This could involve taking a concept talked about in class and relating it to an example you have seen or experienced in your life.

ACTIVITY

Today is exam day in your psychology class. Just minutes before the test is about to begin you notice a student enter the room who appears to be frantically scanning his study sheet. As the tests are distributed, you notice the student reciting concepts to himself. When he receives his test, he quickly scribbles down a few notes on the top of his paper. Is it more likely this student is using maintenance or elaborative rehearsal? Defend you answer.

© Carlos Caetano, 2011. Used under license of Shutterstock, Inc.

- Organization: Creating an organized way to understand concepts can help improve memory. One way to do this often involves creating hierarchies or flow charts to help break down bigger concepts into smaller subcategories. As another example, organization could also take the form of color-coded note cards prior to studying for an exam.
- Retrieval Cues: Certain external cues can improve the chances a memory will be recalled. Below are three of the most important.

© hohojirozame, 2011. Used under license of Shutterstock, Inc.

1) Priming: Have you ever noticed that when you watch a romantic movie, you might begin feeling more of a desire to connect with your significant other? This is likely because of priming. Priming is when a specific event or cue leads to a specific memory. This may also happen when you smell a certain food you enjoyed as a child and it brings back specific childhood memories or when you find yourself scared to go out to the garage after watching a horror flick.

© Diego Cervo, 2011. Used under license of Shutterstock, Inc.

2) Recognition: These are cues that are specific and increase the chance of retrieving a

memory. A good example would be multiple-choice questions on an exam.

3) Recall: In contrast to recognition cues, which are more specific, recall cues are more general. When engaging in recall, you have to search through any potential matches in your LTM. This often proves to be a much more difficult task than recognition. Recall questions on an exam would come in the form of short answer or essay questions where you are not given any responses to choose from or narrow down your search.

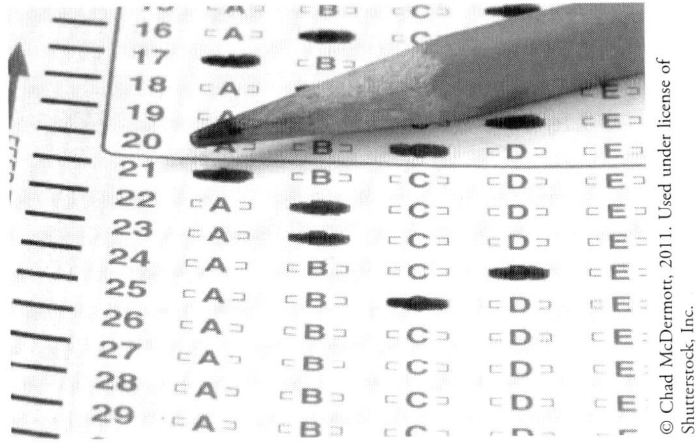

ACTIVITY

Without looking at any outside information, name Snow White's seven dwarfs in the space that follows?

1.
2.
3.
4.
5.
6.
7.

How difficult did you find this task?

Unless you are a big fan of the movie, chances are it was difficult to *recall* correctly all seven. Now, imagine if you were given a list of 12 names, seven of which were the correct names of the dwarfs. Do you think you would have performed better or worse? Why?

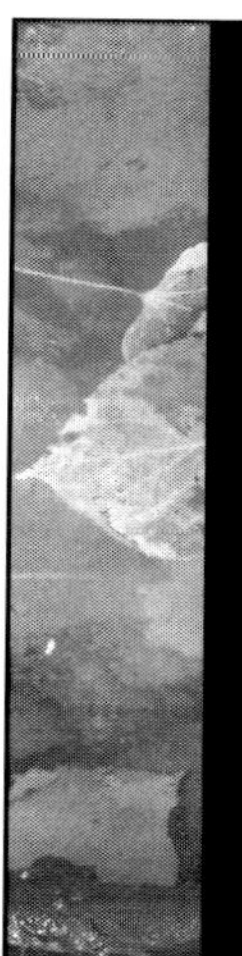

Did you know? – Another classic example of a recognition/recall exercise involves Santa's reindeers. When people who celebrate Christmas are asked to recall the reindeer names, you will often notice them singing. Why are they doing this? Music can serve as a form of elaborative rehearsal and help people with the recall process.

© Martin Hladky, 2011. Used under license of Shutterstock, Inc.

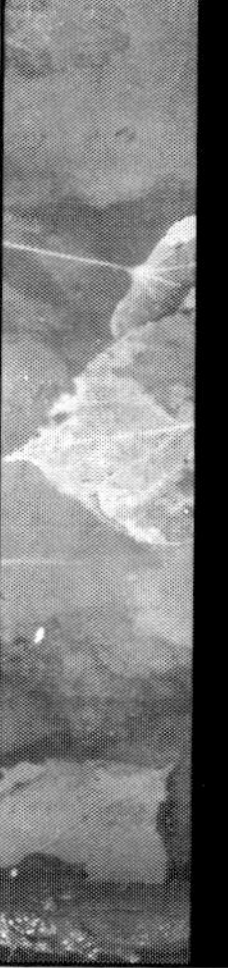

Studying tip – We tend to remember better when we are attempting to recall information in the same environment or context where we learned it. This is called context-dependent memory. As a result, it can actually help to study for an exam in the same room where you learned the material and where you will take the test.

© Dean Mitchell, 2011. Used under license of Shutterstock, Inc.

- Relearn and Teach to Others: Another way you can help improve both memory and learning is through relearning. The more ways you learn a particular piece of information, the more likely you are to remember it. One way to test how much you recall is to teach the topic to others. If you can successfully teach the subject matter to someone else, chances are you have learned it multiple times and will be able to perform better on a test where you are asked to recognize or recall the information.

© Dmitry Shironosov, 2011. Used under license of Shutterstock, Inc.

EMOTIONAL MEMORY

Certain very intense experiences trigger activation of the amygdala in the brain. Recall that the amygdala is in charge of the fight-or-flight response. A certain amount of stress or anxiety often enhances our ability to remember (more on this in Chapter 9), but too much stress can actually hinder memory. When we are exposed to traumatic events (even vicariously), such as the 9/11 attacks, Hurricane Katrina, or the recent earthquake and tsunami in Japan, it activates the amygdala and creates what are called flashbulb memories. While we might assume such emotionally charged memories would be especially accurate, research shows that this is often not the case (Talarico & Rubin, 2007).

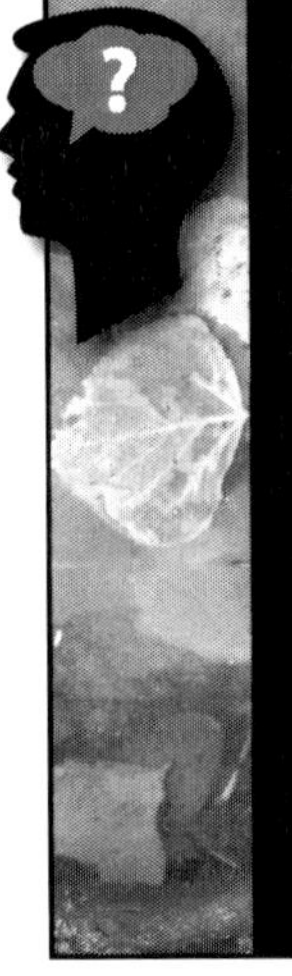

Think about it – Given the fact that our flashbulb memories are not always reliable, what implications might this have on something like eyewitness testimony in a court of law?

DEMENTIA

Traumatic brain injuries or certain diseases can also impact memory. Dementia is one of the most common problems that attacks the human memory system. The most common specific form of dementia is Alzheimer's disease (AD). AD is a progressive disease that begins with simple lapses of memory that many people without AD experience periodically. Over time, though, the disease gets worse and has its most severe impact on explicit memory (Satler et al., 2007), which is memory that requires conscious recall. This means that people with AD often forget life experiences, events, names, and basic facts.

However, implicit memory is not impacted as severely, which means the ability to remember how to perform some basic procedural tasks (tying one's shoe, brushing one's teeth, putting on pants, etc.) remains.

AD has a strong genetic component and usually has an age of first onset of 50 years of age or older. The primary cause of AD is believed to be genetic, but increasing research is indicating that AD can have an earlier onset for those who have experienced recurrent brain trauma such as professional football players (Guskiewicz et al., 2005).

REFERENCES

Allan, K., & Gabbert, F. (2008). I still think it was a banana: Memorable "lies" and forgettable "truths." *Acta Psychologia, 127,* 299–308

Appel, M., & Richter, T. (2007). Persuasive effects of fictional narratives increase over time. *Media Psychology, 10,* 113–134

Azizian, A., & Polich, J. (2007). Evidence for attentional gradient in the serial position memory curve from event-related potential. *Journal of Cognitive Neuroscience, 19,* 2071–2081

Garry, M., & Gerrie, M.P. (2005). When photographs create false memories. *Current Directions in Psychological Science, 14,* 321–324

Guskiewicz, K. M., Marshall, S. W., Bailes, J., McCrea, M., Cantu, R. C., Randolph, C., & Jordan, B. D. (2005). Association between recurrent concussion and late-life cognitive impairment in retired football players. *Neurosurgery, 57(4),* 719–726

Loftus, E. (1982). Memory and its distortions. In A. G. Kraut (Ed.), *The G. Stanley Hall Lecture Series Vol. 2,* (pp. 123–154). Washington, DC: American Psychological Association

Mazzoni, G., & Vannucci, M. (2007). Hindsight bias, the misinformation effect, and false autobiographical memories. *Social Cognition, 25,* 203–220

Satler, C., Garrido, L. M., Sarmiento, E. P., Leme, S., Conde, C., & Tomaz, C. (2007). Emotional arousal enhances declarative memory in patients with Alzheimer's disease. *Acta Neurologica Scandinavica, 116,* 355–360

Sperling, G. (1960). The information available in brief visual presentations. *Psychological Monographs, 74* (Whole No. 498)

Talarico, J. M., & Rubin, D. C. (2007). Flashbulb memories are special after all: In phenomenology, not accuracy. *Applied Cognitive Psychology, 21,* 557–578.

NAME ______________________________ DATE ____________________

WORKSHEET CHAPTER EIGHT

CHAPTER 9

EMOTION AND MOTIVATION

Imagine that you came into this class intensely motivated to succeed in psychology. It is something that interested you all through high school, and your goal was to major in psychology and one day become a practicing psychologist. Your motivation directed toward the pursuit of psychology was at an all-time high. Now imagine that a month later you received an "F" on the first test.

How would this impact your emotional state of being? Would you be angry? Sad? A combination of both?

How would your emotional state in turn impact your subsequent level of motivation? Would this have the same impact on every person?

There is a reciprocal relationship between motivation and emotion. In other words, the way we feel impacts our level of motivation, and our level of motivation can also have an effect on how we feel.

In this chapter we will cover some of the theories and research that underlie both the experience of emotions as well as motivation.

WHAT CAUSES EMOTION?

Think about it – What do you believe drives our emotions? Is it physiological and brain based? Is it because of our thinking patterns? Or, do emotions follow our behavior? Explain and defend your answer.

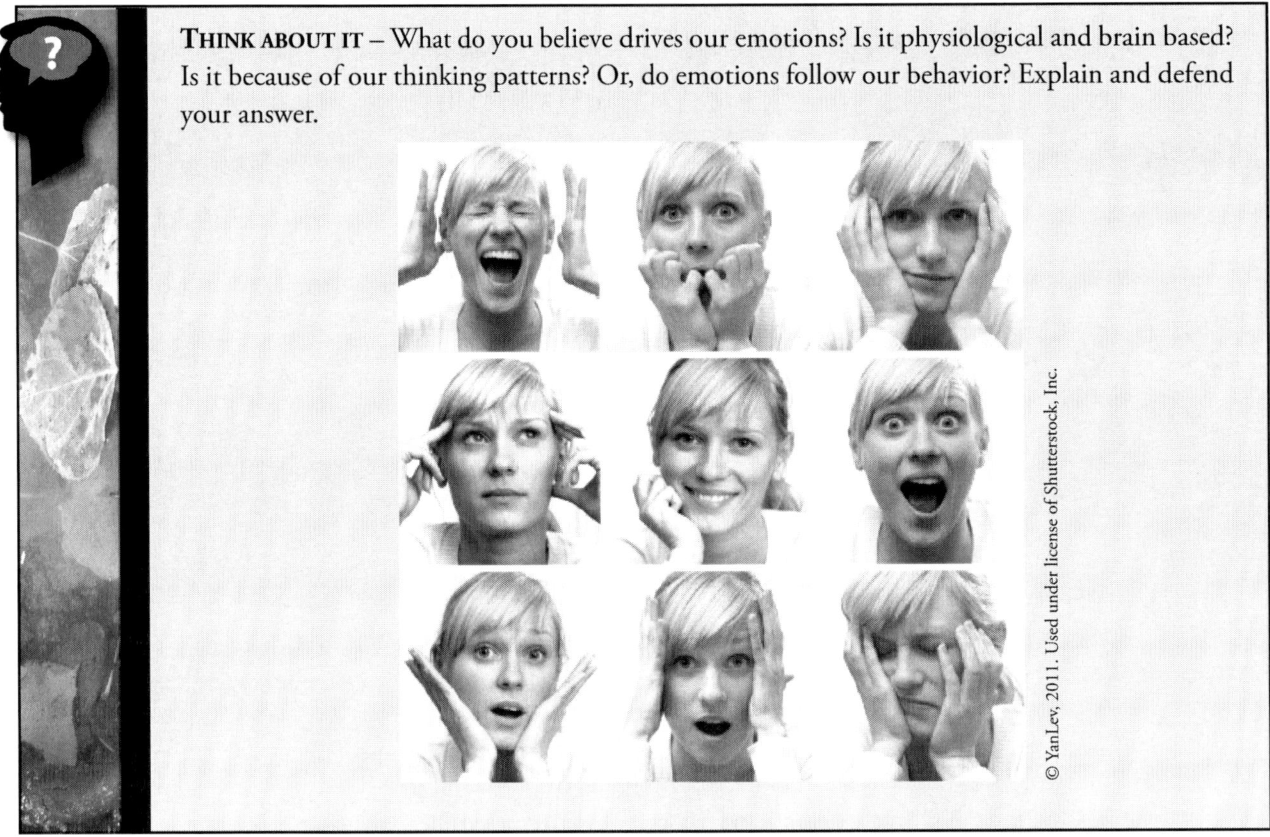

Most scientists believe that physiology, behaviors, and our cognitions all play a role in our experience of various emotional states. All three factors will be discussed in the space that follows.

Physiology and the Brain

Remember the limbic system as discussed in Chapter 5? This is the emotional center of our brain. One specific structure in the limbic system, the amygdala, seems to play a vital role in emotions. The amygdala helps to regulate fear and triggers the "fight-or-flight" response. The cerebral cortex also plays an important role in helping us recognize and regulate our emotions.

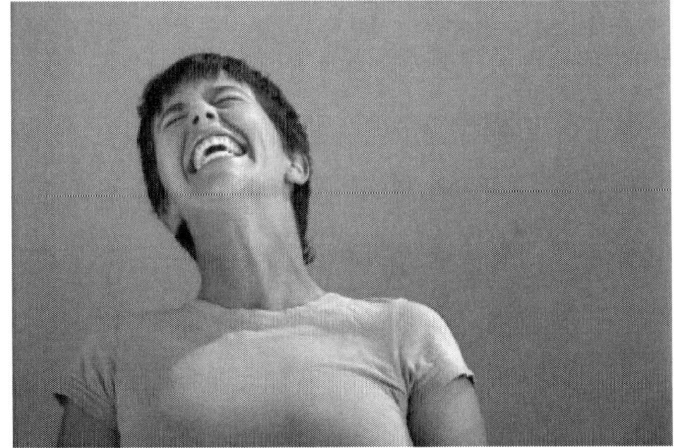

While the brain plays a very important role in emotional experience, our autonomic nervous system (also discussed Chapter 5) is what produces the physiological signs of emotion. As noted in Chapter 5, the ANS has two subsystems called the sympathetic and parasympathetic nervous systems. The parasympathetic system calms the body down while the sympathetic system speeds it up. These two systems combined help your body respond appropriately based on level of arousal and emotional states.

Behavior

While it can be tempting to believe that we express most of our emotional states verbally, we actually express a whole lot more nonverbally through our facial expressions and behavior. Some research has indicated that people who flash genuine smiles (as opposed to the contrived smile you might use when posing for a picture) and laugh more frequently are responded to more positively by strangers and also form better relationships with others (Keltner, Kring, & Bonanno, 1999).

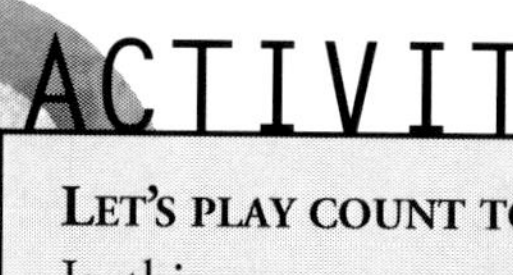

ACTIVITY

Let's play count to 50!
In this game you and a friend are to have a conversation. . . but there's a catch. You cannot use any words. All you can do is count sequentially from 1 to 50. The conversation starts with 1 and ends when you reach 50. Ask people to watch the conversation and see if they can identify how they think you are feeling during the conversation.

Cognitions or Thoughts

Other variables in our experience of emotion include our thoughts and expectations. What we think or expect going into a situation can alter how we feel. Still, some questions remain. Do our thoughts lead to our feeling states, or do our feeling states lead to our thoughts? There are different theories of how this process unfolds; these are discussed in the next section.

THEORIES OF EMOTION

James-Lange Theory

Psychologist William James (1890) created one of the first theories of emotion. Scientist Carl Lange later built on the foundation created by James, leading to the creation of the James-Lange theory of emotion. This theory states that bodily arousal happens *prior* to our emotional feeling states. According to this theory, emotion does not exist in the absence of arousal and expression. Incoming stimuli trigger a physiological state in your brain and autonomic nervous system (ANS), which then leads to actions, and ends with the experience of a subjective feeling state. As an example, let's take the emotion of sadness. Arousal in your brain and ANS leads to changes in facial expressions (frowning), which later produces your subjective experience of sadness. Each singular emotion is viewed as distinct in this theory.

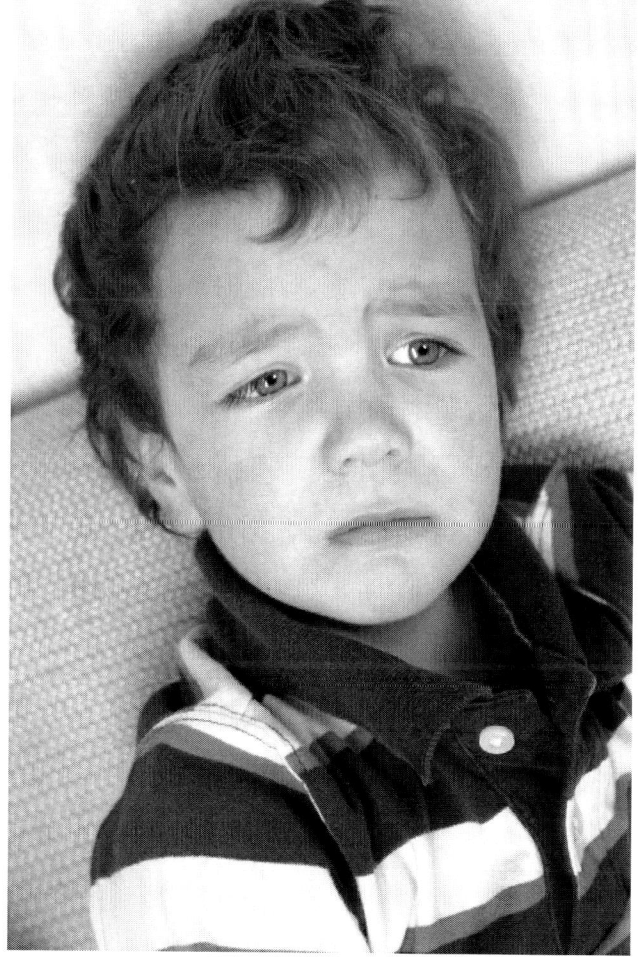

Cannon-Bard Theory

Walter Cannon (1927) and Philip Bard (1934) proposed a different sequence of events leading up to the experience of an emotional state. Unlike the James-Lange theory, which proposed that bodily arousal and actions preceded subjective feelings states, the Cannon-Bard theory believes that arousal, behavioral actions, and subjective emotion all happen at the same time. For example, arousal, a smile, and your subjective experience of happiness are all happening simultaneously. This theory also advanced the idea that in terms of the pattern of physiological arousal, emotions are more similar than they are different.

Schachter's Two-Factor Theory

This theory proposes that a combination of arousal and our ability to cognitively label and interpret that arousal leads to our subjective experience of emotion. For example, crying can mean different things in different contexts. If you have just broken up with a romantic partner, you might be crying because you labeled or interpreted that emotion as sadness. If, on the other hand, a romantic partner just got down on one knee and proposed to you and you are crying, you will likely label or interpret that emotion as happiness.

Facial-Feedback Hypothesis

This model advances the idea that our emotional states are produced, and at the very least, intensified by certain patterns of movement in our facial muscles. The hypothesis is that an external stimulus taken in through our senses is perceived in certain areas of our brain, which then activates patterns of facial movement. Subsequent contractions of certain facial muscles send messages to our brains that help us label or identify the emotions. These patterns can also intensify the subjective experience of certain emotions (Prkachin, 2005; Sigall & Johnson, 2006). In other words, these researchers believe that our facial expressions lead to certain feeling states. So we do not frown because we are sad. Instead, we feel sad because we frown.

ARE EMOTIONS UNIVERSAL ACROSS CULTURES?

Researchers have identified at least six emotions that are believed to be culturally universal given the fact they can be reliably identified by people from both Western and non-Western cultures

(Buck, 1984; Matsumoto, 2000). These emotions include: happiness, surprise, sadness, fear, anger, and disgust. Researchers have also noted that many of these emotions are recognized and also expressed in similar ways across cultures (Ekman, 2004; Matsumoto & Juang, 2008).

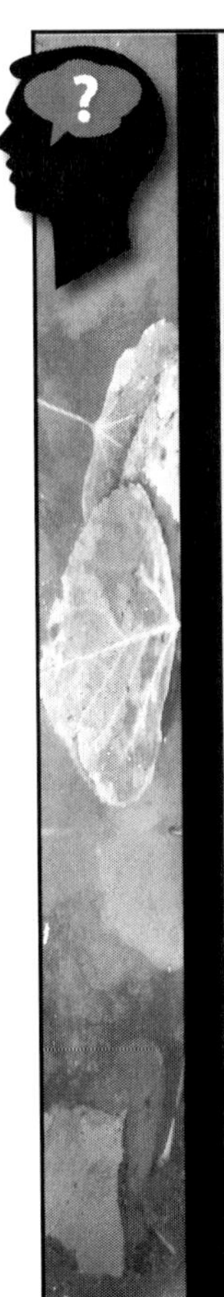

Think about it – Have you ever had a day where you did not know how you were feeling? Perhaps someone started questioning you about it and none of the labels of current emotional states fit. Can an emotional state exist in absence of a label to describe it? Might there be more emotional states than we have language to describe?

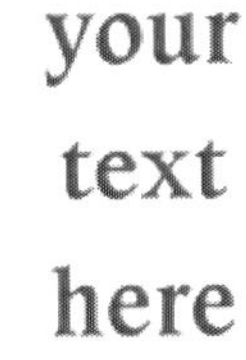

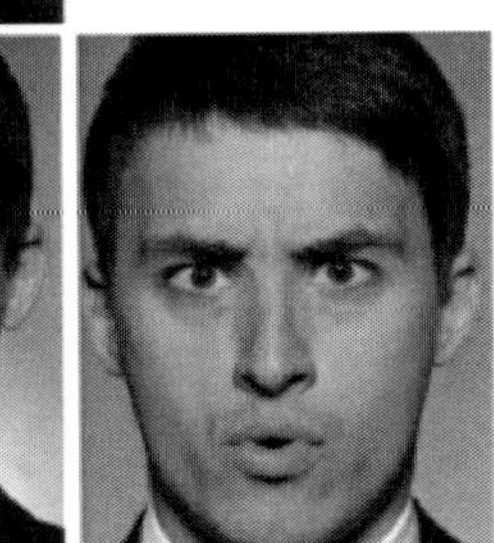

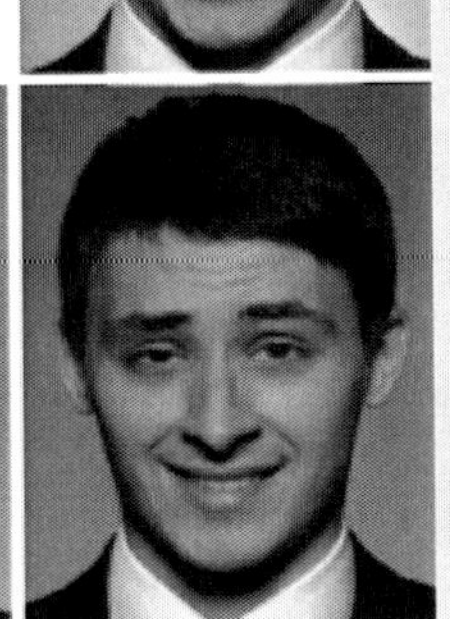

One variable that makes emotions difficult to study is the fact that not all emotions are necessarily expressed or apparent on the surface. In other words, one might feel sad but do her best to mask this emotion externally. What we feel inside and what we actually express can be different. Moreover, cultures have rules for what emotions can be expressed, by whom, and in what situations. These are referred to as cultural *display rules.*

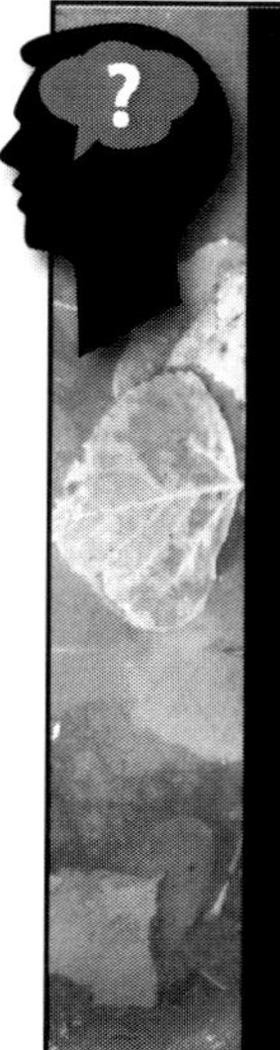

Think about it – Think about the culture you grew up in. Are there certain emotions women are encouraged to express that men are not or perhaps vice versa? In the space that follows, write down some display rules based on gender and the potential cultural consequences a person may face if he or she breaks these rules.

EMOTIONAL INTELLIGENCE

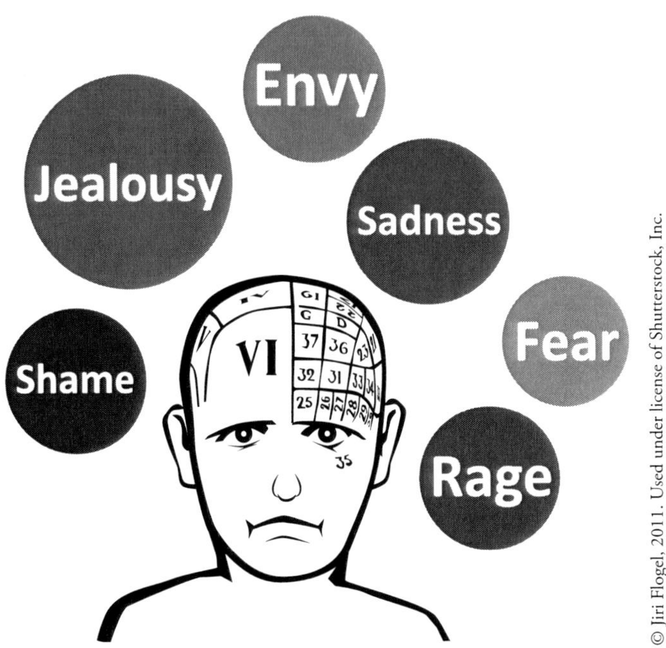

Remember models of intelligence as discussed Chapter 2? Just as some people believe we can measure intellectual ability in the form of an intelligence quotient (IQ), others, such as Daniel Goleman (2000), believe we can do the same for emotional intelligence (EI). In fact, there are some people who believe EI may be a more important measure than IQ in terms of successfully navigating life's challenges.

EI is the ability to recognize the emotions of oneself and others, manage emotions, and form meaningful relationships with others. Goleman believes that criminal behaviors and other forms of interpersonal struggles are often related to low EI scores. This belief led to the creation of training curricula to foster EI in school-aged children so that they can better understand and identify how they are feeling and empathize with the feeling states of others (Casarjian, Phillips, & Wolman, 2007; Reilly, 2005; van Heck & den Oudsten, 2008). Some EI proponents have suggested that EI training should be a part of graduate-level training programs across various disciplines.

One of the most common criticisms of EI is that components of it are hard to identify, operationalize, and measure (Mayer, Roberts, & Barsade, 2008). Moreover, some believe that emotions are highly subjective and that teaching people what emotions are good or bad is dangerous and potentially coercive. While the topic of EI is still controversial, it is an area that is garnering more and more interest in psychology and will likely be the focus of continuing research.

MOTIVATION

Recall the relationship between emotion and level of motivation as outlined at the start of the chapter. The way we feel unquestionably impacts our level of motivation just as our level of motivation can impact how we feel. In this section we will look at different theories of motivation and explore strategies for altering levels of motivation.

ACTIVITY

Imagine that you are working as a manager at the school bookstore and you are responsible for monitoring the effectiveness and performance of a number of employees. Your job is to get the most out of each employee and help him or her achieve an optimal level of motivation. How would you go about trying to motivate your employees?

Would you use the same strategy with each employee? Why or why not?

Theories of Motivation

There are a number of theories that explore what motivates human behavior, including the effects of biology, psychology, and societal factors. We will begin by discussing biological theories of motivation and then move into psychosocial explanations.

Biological Theories

Instincts. The notion of instincts impacting motivation was explored over a century ago and started with a small list of instincts. Over time, scientists expanded the list of instincts to include thousands of behaviors. This led to an unclear description of what an instinct really was. In the last three or four decades a group of scientists provided a more specific description, defining instincts as responses that are inborn and found in virtually every member of a species. Some examples include salmon spawning upstream or bears hibernating in the winter. Some sociobiologists, such as Edward O. Wilson (1975), believe human beings have instincts, too, and that these instincts are genetically inherited. He specifically mentions competition and aggression as two of these instincts (1978).

© Raj Krish, 2011. Used under license of Shutterstock, Inc.

Drive Reduction. This theory states that we all have biological drives that need to be satisfied (Hull, 1952). These drives include basic needs for food and water. Failure to satisfy these drives will over time result in death of the organism. This theory proposes that we all have what is called a state of homeostasis, which is when the body's internal state is stable and balanced.

When a drive such as hunger arises, homeostasis is disturbed. When this happens, a need arises, which can often be felt in the form of tension. The organism must then take some kind of action to return the body to homeostasis. In the case of hunger, the action would involve eating. When the organism eats, the drive of hunger is reduced and the body returns to homeostasis.

© 3445128471, 2011. Used under license of Shutterstock, Inc.

The theory of drive reduction has also been applied to the study of personality and learning (Dollard & Miller, 1950).

Arousal. Our level of arousal can impact our performance. Not enough arousal can lead to our not performing at our best. However, too much arousal can lead to the same result. Arousal theory holds the belief that each of us need to achieve an optimal level of arousal to perform at our best (See Figure 9.1).

Think about this in terms of studying for an exam. If you have no anxiety for an upcoming exam and therefore low levels of arousal, you will likely not perform at your best. You will be more prone to making careless errors and not paying enough attention. If you have too much arousal, you will likely also not perform at your best, but for other reasons. Excessive arousal can lead to problems retrieving

© greenland, 2011. Used under license of Shutterstock, Inc.

items from long-term memory as well as the feeling of test anxiety or "blanking out." In order to perform at your best, a moderate level of arousal is ideal.

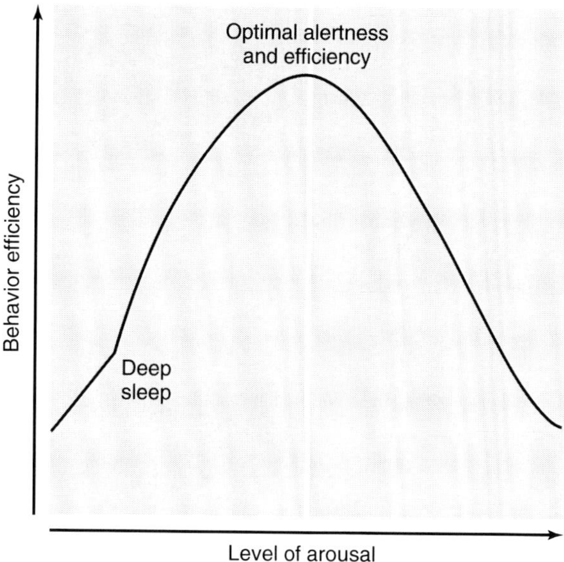

Figure 9.1

Psychology in Action, 9th Edition by Karen Huffman. Copyright © 2010 by John Wiley & Sons, Inc. Reproduced with permission of John Wiley & Sons, Inc.

ACTIVITY

People have different idle speeds of arousal or anxiety. In other words, some people have a higher natural level of arousal.

Think about this in terms of the activity you were asked to complete at the beginning of this section where you were managing employees at the campus bookstore. Imagine that you have several people with high natural levels of arousal whom you are in charge of getting the most from. For these people, what might happen if you yell at them when they make a mistake or if you ride them too hard?

(*continued*)

ACTIVITY (*continued*)

What strategy might work best for employees with high natural levels of arousal? Defend your answer.

Now, imagine that you also have several employees with naturally low levels of arousal who always seem to be "going through the motions" at work. What strategy might you use to get the most out of these employees?

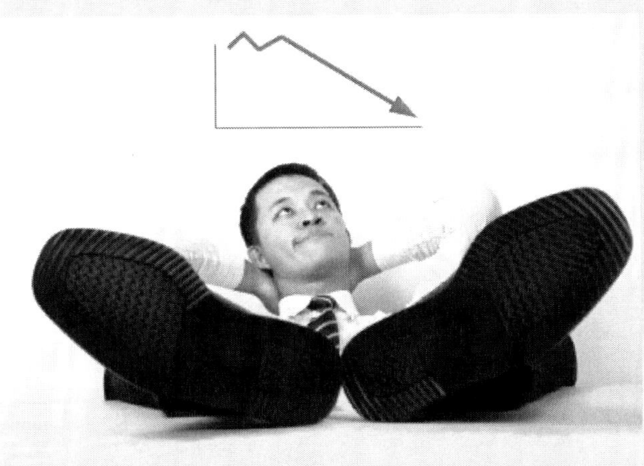

How might this strategy differ from the strategy you would use with people who have higher levels of natural arousal?

Psychosocial Theories

Cognitive Theories. Cognitive theorists believe that the expectancies we have prior to engaging in an event as well as the attributions we make afterward impact our level of motivation (Haugen, Ommundsen, & Lund, 2004). Expectancies are simply what we expect to happen when we engage in a certain behavior. Attributions are the conclusions we draw or how we explain an event after it has occurred. Research has shown that people who attribute their success to the effort they demonstrated as well as their level of ability often work harder when trying to achieve a goal as compared to those who attribute success to simply luck (Houtz et al., 2007; Meltzer, 2004).

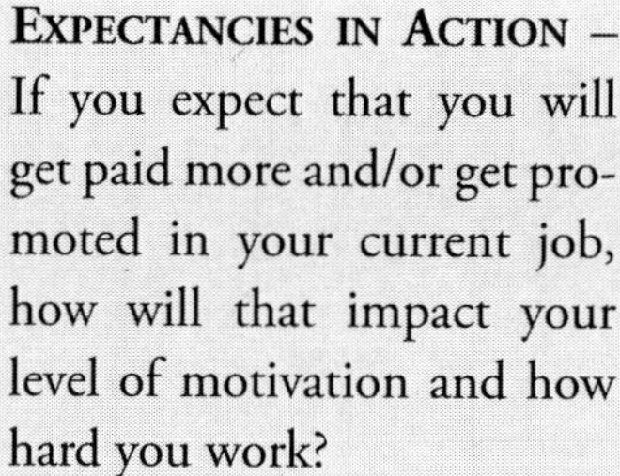

Expectancies in Action – If you expect that you will get paid more and/or get promoted in your current job, how will that impact your level of motivation and how hard you work?

© Dmitriy Shironosov, 2011. Used under license of Shutterstock, Inc.

Conversely, if you expect that you won't get a raise and won't be treated fairly, how will this impact your level of motivation and the amount of effort your put into your work?

© Jaimie Duplass, 2011. Used under license of Shutterstock, Inc.

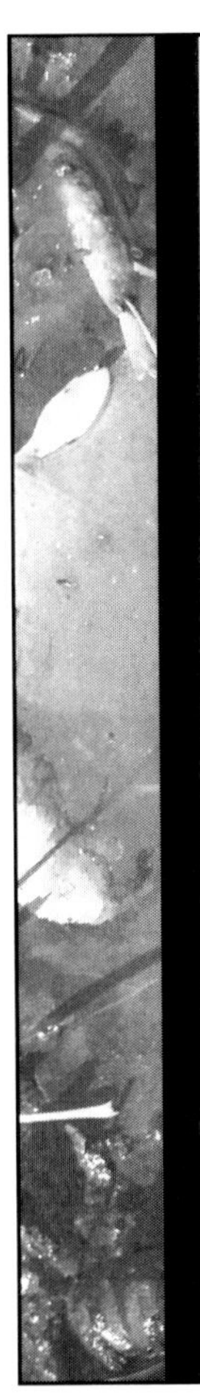

Attributions in Action – Imagine that you have received a grade of "A" on your first psychology test. Upon receiving this grade, you could make several attributions. One attribution might be that all of those hours of coming to class, reading, and studying really paid off. Another might involve saying something like, "The sun even shines on a dog's backside some days," of course, the implication being that you simply got lucky.

Based on the research discussed in the previous section, which attribution will most likely increase your level of future motivation in your psychology class and why?

Incentive Theory. Do you remember the concept of operant condition as discussed in Chapter 3? This is when voluntary behavior is shaped by consequences. Incentive theory is similar to a specific type of operant conditioning called positive reinforcement in that it proposes that people are motivated by the pull of desirable external goals. This does not mean we always get pulled in healthy directions (think eating too much dessert or sacrificing time with family to earn extra money), but motivation to get pulled in that direction can remain nonetheless.

Biopsychosocial Theories

Maslow's Hierarchy of Needs. Humanist scholar Abraham Maslow created a model of motivation that took into account biological, psychological, and social factors (biopsychosocial). Maslow recognized that humans have many needs to be satisfied. However, he did not believe that each of these needs was of equal importance. Thus, he created a pyramid or hierarchy of needs. The basic idea is that lower-level basic needs such as access to food and water *must* be met before a person will attempt to meet higher-level needs such as love or self-esteem.

Maslow believed that physiological needs must be met before any other needs. These are basic needs such as food and water. The second level included safety and security needs. These needs include seeking shelter, as well as a basic drive to seek pleasure and avoid pain. The third level is love and belonging, where Maslow believed people tried to form meaningful relationships with others and experience a sense of community. The fourth level is often referred to as esteem needs. Here, the person attempts to obtain competence in meaningful life activities, achieve, excel, and gain approval from others. The apex of the pyramid is self-actualization. As a humanist, Maslow believed that we were born with an innate drive to fulfill our potential. Self-actualization is a state of inner fulfillment and a realization of one's true potential.

Maslow in Practice – A high school has developed a program to try and help decrease gang activity. The targeted students live in poverty and in a constant state of physical danger. The major aim of the program is to "increase the self-esteem" of gang members, which will then help them feel better about themselves and give up the gang lifestyle.

According to Maslow's hierarchy of needs, do you believe he would agree with the approach of this program? Why or why not?

Maslow's theory is not without its critics. One common criticism is that Maslow's ideas are only applicable to more Western cultures. Others point out examples of people who have not met lower-level needs but have still attempted to move up the hierarchy (Hanley & Abell, 2002; Neher, 1991). How does one explain how people who exist in a war zone on a day-to-day basis still form tight bonds and a sense of community? How do people who live in countries in a perpetual state of starvation still manage to form loving relationships with others?

Perhaps the most appropriate way to interpret Maslow's model in a contemporary context is to say that most often humans are driven to seek at least partial fulfillment of lower-level needs first. That doesn't mean, however, that under a certain set of circumstances that people won't attempt, and perhaps be successful at, achieving higher-level needs without first fulfilling lower-level needs.

Motivation and Achievement

There is often a correlation between motivation and achievement. Moreover, there are certain people who have a high need for achievement (nAch). Psychologist Henry Murray (1938) was one of the first to study this. In the years since, many psychologists have studied achievement and developed assessments to help measure one's need for achievement. This research has led to the formation of six key characteristics that often differentiate those with a high need for achievement from those with a low need (McClelland, 1993; Senko, Durik, & Harackiewicz, 2008).

1. Competitive: People with a high nAch often enjoy the opportunity to compete with others and prove that they can excel. The process of attempting to demonstrate they are proficient is enjoyable.

2. Persistent: People with a high nAch do not give up easily. In fact, they often embrace having to go through adversity to arrive at their desired end goal.

© Lane V. Erickson, 2011. Used under license of Shutterstock, Inc.

3. Responsible: If involved in a group project, you will likely see high achievers take the lead role. They are willing to take the credit or the blame for what takes place and find a sense of satisfaction in this.

© Yuri Arcurs, 2011. Used under license of Shutterstock, Inc.

4. Clear Goals and Feedback: People with a high nAch like a roadmap to success. They like to know what the end goals are and how they can get there. Furthermore, they want competent feedback along the way to that goal so they can revise their strategy if necessary. Competent feedback from a knowledgeable evaluator is preferred regardless of how the feedback is delivered. In other words, direct and less compassionate feedback from a knowledgeable evaluator would be preferred as opposed to warmer but less helpful feedback from a less knowledgeable evaluator.

© Michael D. Brown, 2011. Used under license of Shutterstock, Inc.

5. Tasks of Moderate Difficulty: People with a high nAch like a task to be difficult enough that it presents a challenge but not so difficult that it cannot be completed. This allows for a feeling of completing something worthwhile but avoids the frustration that accompanies being unable to complete a task.

6. More Accomplished: People with a high nAch tend to achieve higher levels of success when compared to their peers.

Think about it – Given what you have learned about people with a high nAch, evaluate the following:

- Jane gets a term paper back with a grade of "A." While she is generally happy with the grade, she notices that there is no feedback on the paper. She finds this to be frustrating and wishes she could see what the professor thought of her work. Is it likely Jane has a high or low nAch? Defend your answer.

- Joey's high school basketball coach wants to give him a little rest before the big game and has him scrimmage with the junior varsity squad so he stays fit but doesn't have to expend as much energy. Joey resists and begs his coach to let him practice full speed against his varsity teammates. Is it likely Joey has a high or low nAch? Defend you answer.

Do you have a high nAch? Put one "X" on each of the six lines where you think you fall. You might fall somewhere in the middle. Answer as honestly as you can.

Very Competitive	Prefer Not to Compete
Persistent	Give Up Easy
Prefer Responsibility	Prefer to Delegate to Others
Prefer Frequent Evaluation	Don't Like Any Feedback
Love a Challenge	Prefer Quick and Easy Tasks
Usually Perform Better Than Others	Rarely Perform Better than Others

It might be easy to assume that a high nAch is always desirable. However, there are times when one's need for achievement becomes too high and creates a sense of perfectionism. This can result in unhealthy patterns of living that contribute to poor physical and psychological health.

It should also be noted that one's need to achieve is heavily influenced by the environment. Much of what we learn about achievement takes place during childhood. Children who develop a high nAch often have parents who reward successful endeavors and encourage autonomy and independence (Maehr & Urdan, 2000). Culture also plays a substantial role. Western culture often encourages more individualistic goals, which can even be seen in cartoons and books aimed at young children (Lubinski & Benbow, 2000). These messages are often subtle and unintended, but still impact young people nonetheless.

REFERENCES

Bard, C. (1934). On emotional expression after decortication with some remarks on certain theoretical views. *Psychological Review, 41,* 309–329.

Buck, R. (1984). *The communication of emotion.* New York: Guilford Press.

Cannon, W. B. (1927). The James-Lange theory of emotions: A critical examination and an alternative theory. *American Journal of Psychology, 39,* 106–124.

Casarjian, R., Phillips, J., & Wolman, R. (2007). An emotional literacy intervention with incarcerated individuals. *American Journal of Forensic Psychology, 25,* 43–63.

Dollard, J., & Miller, N. E. (1950). *Personality and psychotherapy: An analysis in terms of learning, thinking, and culture.* New York: McGraw-Hill.

Ekman, P. (2004). *Emotions revealed: Recognizing faces and feelings to improve communication and emotional life.* Thousand Oaks, CA: Owl Books.

Goleman, D. (2000). *Working with emotional intelligence.* New York: Bantam.

Hanley, S. J., & Abell, S. C. (2002). Maslow and relatedness: Creating an interpersonal model of self-actualization. *Journal of Humanistic Psychology, 42*(4), 37–56.

Haugen, R., Ommundsen, Y., & Lund, T. (2004). The concept of expectancy: A central factor in various personality dispositions. *Educational Psychology, 24*(1), 43–55.

Houtz, J. C., Matos, H., Park, M-K. S., Scheinholtz, J., & Selby, E. (2007). Problem-solving style and motivational attributions. *Psychological Reports, 101,* 823–830.

Hull, C. (1952). *A behavior system.* New Haven, CT: Yale University Press.

James, W. (1890). *The principles of psychology* (Vol.2). New York: Holt.

Keltner, D., Kring, A. M., & Bonanno, G. A. (1999). Fleeting signs of the course of life: Facial expressions and personal adjustment. *Current Directions in Psychological Science, 8*(1), 18–22.

Lubinski, D., & Benbow, C. P. (2000). States of excellence. *American Psychologist, 55*(1), 137–150.

Maehr, M. L., & Urdan, T. C. (2000). *Advances in motivation and achievement: The role of context.* Greenwich, CT: JAI Press.

Matsumoto, D. (2000). *Culture and psychology: People around the world.* Belmont, CA: Wadsworth.

Matsumoto, D., & Juang, L. (2008). *Culture and psychology* (4th ed.). Belmont, CA: Cengage.

Mayer, J. D., Roberts, R. D., & Barsade, S. G. (2008). Human abilities: Emotional intelligence. *American Review of Psychology, 59,* 507–536.

McClelland, D. C. (1993). Intelligence is not the best predictor of job performance. *Current Directions in Psychological Science, 2,* 5–6.

Meltzer, L. (2004). Resilience and learning disabilities: Research on internal and external protective dynamics. *Learning Disabilities Research & Practice, 19*(1), 1–2.

Murray, H. A. (1938). *Explorations in personality.* New York: Oxford University Press.

Neher, A. (1991). Maslow's theory of motivation: A critique. *Journal of Humanistic Psychology, 31,* 89–112.

Prkachin, K. M. (2005). Effects of deliberate control on verbal and facial expressions of pain. *Pain, 114,* 328–338.

Reilly, P. (2005). Teaching law students how to feel: Using negotiations training to increase emotional intelligence. *Negotiation Journal, 21(2),* 301–314.

Senko, C., Durik, A. M., & Harackiewicz, J. M. (2008). Historical perspectives and new directions in achievement goal theory: Understanding the effects of mastery and performance-approach goals. In J. Y. Shah & W. L. Gardner (Eds.), *Handbook of motivation science* (pp. 100–113), New York: Guilford Press.

Sigall, H., & Johnson, M. (2006). The relationship between facial contact with a pillow and mood. *Journal of Applied Social Psychology, 36,* 505–526.

van Heck, G. L., & den Oudsten, B. L. (2008). Emotional intelligence: Relationships to stress, health, and well-being. In A. Vingerhoets & I. Nyklicek (Eds.), *Emotion regulation: Conceptual and clinical issues* (pp. 97–121). New York: Springer Science + Business Media.

Wilson, E. O. (1975). *Sociobiology: The new synthesis.* Cambridge, MA: Harvard University Press.

Wilson, E. O. (1978). *On human nature.* Cambridge, MA: Harvard University Press.

NAME ______________________________ DATE ________________

WORKSHEET CHAPTER NINE

CHAPTER 10

SEX AND GENDER

Imagine you are paging through your local university or college's list of courses. Your eye catches the word "sex" and you stop to read exactly what your eyes have just glanced. What you find is a listing of a 3-credit course on human sexuality encompassing topics that range from researching people having sex, gender issues, prostitution, deviant sexual behaviors, and sexual development. What other topics would you expect to be covered?

The various dimensions of sexuality affect all humans throughout their lives. While there are many topics in the vast field of psychology, few generate as much attention as the study of human sexuality. The same is true for the many topics covered in the media. Sexuality is a commanding topic evoking emotions and powerful beliefs on many levels and across a spectrum of gender, age, and culture.

You might further expect such a sexuality course to explore the sexual attitudes and behaviors of people, not just in your own country but also from countries around the world. You may expect it to cover a history of sexuality and research, giving a summary of how people came to understand the intricacies of sexual behavior. You would be wise to expect such a course to cover a bit on the biology of reproductive processes and may want to set some time aside to study anatomy and physiology. You would also anticipate a lecture on sexual deviance, prostitution, the legality and governance of sexuality, and sex in the media.

It is often said that, when meeting new people, making new friends, or spending holidays with family, the three topics of conversations to avoid are *sex*, *politics*, and *religion*. This chapter will take the opposite approach and ask you to think about and discuss each and their interactions. Psychology takes a unique approach to sexuality. If psychology is defined as the *scientific study of behavior and mental processes* one could imagine that its practioners would be interested in nearly every aspect of human sexuality. Covering even a range of these topics will certainly be impossible for an intro text such as the one you are now reading, but it is our hope that the *Interactive* title provides some extra push and pull and that your activities and discussions as a result of interacting with such a chapter are sufficiently lively.

Discussion – Whether by yourself or with others, make a list of as many sources from which you got your information about sex. This list may include friends, family, news, movies, teachers, etc. Now, rank these sources in order of their influence on your beliefs (1 should be the highest).

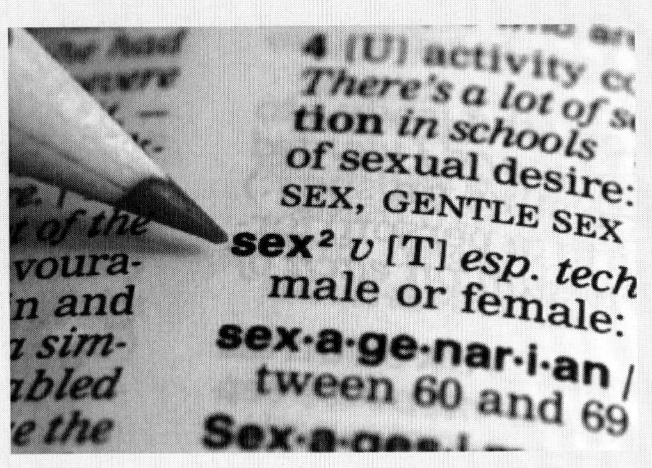

What do you think of these sources? Are they good sources? Is the information objective and unbiased? That is, is their credibility tarnished in any way by their own interests?

What sources of information would you have *liked* to have had? What sources will you provide your own children? Will they be similar? Different? Why? What sources do you imagine your own parents had to inform them about sex and sexuality?

Do you think there is a "best" source for information about sexuality? What is it and what is this source like? Going forward in your own life, what sources will you begin to use to inform your ideas and knowledge of sexuality? Which will you abandon?

Finally, why do you think all the sources you listed have such a heavy interest regarding informing others about sexuality? Put another way, why does sexuality have such gravity?

SEX AND GENDER

While it may seem that the terms sex and gender are interchangeable, it is important in the field of psychology to understand their specific meanings. *Sex* refers to our biological makeup. Male or female, from this biological perspective, is genetic (chromosomes XY and XX respectively) and anatomical (physical differences such as genitalia). *Gender* is a term that includes behaviors and socially constructed roles. Male or female, from this psychological perspective, is influenced by social structures such as family, religion, laws, and culture.

Gender refers to each individual's personal sense of being male or female. While most people's sex and gender line up, it is not always the case. Gender also refers to a collection of behaviors and preferences that are deemed appropriate by the society in which the person lives. What is masculine in some societies, families, or cultures would not appear to be so in others.

These *gender roles* can have an impact on the health of the developing individual, whether child or adult. It is important to understand the difference between sex and gender in order to better grasp the effects of these socially constructed norms on those who don't necessarily fit these standards.

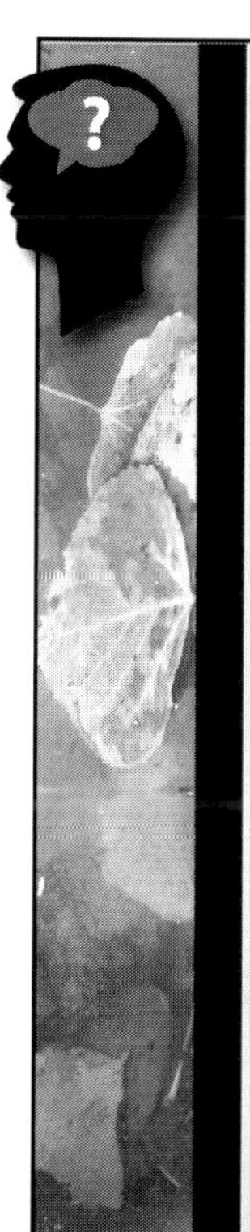

Think about it – Children who differ from socially accepted gender roles are often teased by their peers. In a western culture a young boy who enjoys playing with dolls or a girl who likes to play with trucks and guns does not necessarily fit in to social gender roles. Can you think of examples such as this that affect adults? Try and discuss the following:

A man who drinks __________ at a bar is manlier than a man who drinks __________.

A woman who works as a __________ is less feminine than one who works as a __________.

A man who participates in __________ for fun is less manly.

A woman who participates in __________ for fun is more feminine.

(*continued*)

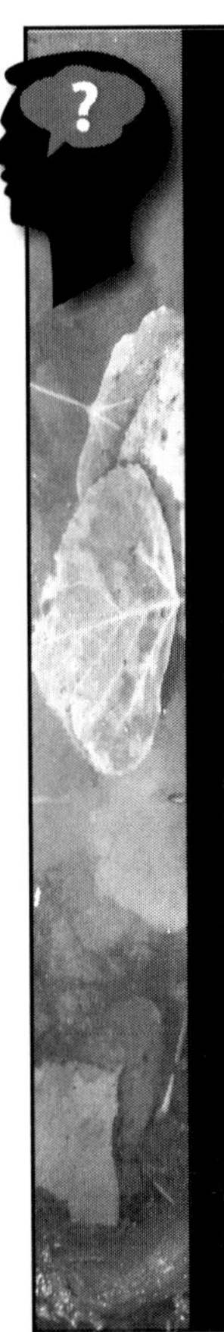

Think about it (*continued*)

A boy who is good at ________ is likely to grow up to be more ________________.

A girl who is good at ________ is likely to grow up to be more ________________.

Certainly kids are chastised for not conforming to socialized gender roles, and this teasing takes many forms (verbal, emotional, physical). However, the degree of teasing as well as the form it takes does seem to vary. Adults are not immune. Men and women are also judged by how well they conform to these traditional stereotypes. Consider the scenarios below.

For which of the following are socialized gender roles more forgiving? For which may a person be teased less or even rewarded? Why?

Imagine a man in a woman's wedding dress, standing up next to the bride. Imagine a woman in a tuxedo.

Imagine a man drinking a pink drink in a tall martini glass. Now imagine a woman drinking a shot of whisky.

Imagine a woman, freshly showered, wearing nothing but a man's button-down shirt. Now imagine a man, freshly showered, wearing nothing but a woman's blouse.

Which examples stand out for you? Which produce more a discrepancy in your mind? Where did you get these ideas?

A leading figure in the early study of sex and gender was John Money. Of worldwide notoriety, Money was known for his scientific approach to the development of sex and gender, or *sexology.* It was in this up-and-coming field that Money first defined the concept of gender role and identity (1955). He argued that gender is not as dichotomous, black and white, or as simple as many had historically assumed and that variations can occur across many variables, which he listed as:

1. Chromosomal (XX, female; XY, male)
2. Gonadal (ovaries, female; testes, male)
3. Prenatal hormonal (testosterone, male)
4. Internal accessory organs (uterus, female; prostate, male)
5. Genitalia (clitoris, female; penis, male)
6. Pubertal hormonal (estrogen/progesterone, female; testosterone, male)
7. Assigned gender
8. Gender identity

Money posited that each of these developmental variables has its own probabilities of error with some overlapping from one to another. This overlap can cause many conditions, such as hermaphroditism and other conditions, often referred to as *intersex*, meaning a person having both male and female sexual characteristics and/or organs. Other times genetic or biological variables (1 through 6 listed above) point to one gender and psychological or social variables (7 and 8) point to another. This is referred to as *transgender*. Transgendered people are those whose gender expression or gender identity differs from social expectations based largely on the sex into which they were born. Many live a life of partial or even a full reversal of gender.

Keep in mind that *gender* and *gender roles* are social constructs and are thus subject to social change. In contrast, *sex* is a biological trait and is generally considered to be static and dictated by genetics (nature) rather than cultivated by society (nurture). Contemplating and researching the difference and occasionally disparate nature of sex and gender can be enlightening as well as helpful for individuals who may, in one way or another, not fit in the box offered to them by society.

THE MAJOR SEX RESEARCH PROJECTS

While sexuality has been a hot topic for many decades now, scientific exploration into the intricacies of sex, that is to say the information that is often taken for granted in more modern times, was at one point a frontier yet to be explored. Some early research focused on a survey of sexual behavior and sought to understand the types of practices in which different people engaged. Other research sought to understand the physiology of sexual response or what specific changes the body goes through from the initial stages of excitement to the final stages of orgasm and beyond.

Currently, the study of human sexuality from a scientific lens includes many goals from understanding the physiological response to understanding behaviors. However, since the days of the early researchers like Alfred Kinsey and Masters and Johnson and with the increased social acceptance of such investigations, the goals have become more specific. The goals of studying sexuality revolve around understanding, predicting, and controlling sexual behavior. Although many have made enormous contributions to the field, we will cover only four in this chapter: Havelock Ellis, the Kinsey Reports, the National Health and Social Life Survey, and the laboratory work of Masters and Johnson.

Havelock Ellis

During the nineteenth century, there were many misconceptions about sex that were taken as absolute truth mostly due to the fact that accurate sex research was never encouraged, and powerful cultural gatekeepers controlled and limited access to such information. This led to medical experts of the time believing that masturbation could cause acne, blindness, and even insanity (Allen, 2000). It was also believed during this time period that nocturnal emissions (wet dreams) could cause brain damage and even death. As a result, men of the time period were encouraged to wear spiked rings around their penises at night to avoid the potential for wet dreams.

It might be easy to laugh at such assumptions over a century removed from when they were first made, but had it not been for the work of people like physician Havelock Ellis (1858–1939), doctors and researchers may not have initiated an honest scientific dialogue about sexual behavior. Like many great discoveries, Ellis's came about accidentally. During his adult life, he noticed he was suffering from nocturnal emissions. Given the prevailing information of the time period, Ellis was terrified and even gave thought to killing himself. After Ellis came to terms with his diagnosis, he formulated a different course of action that he believed could benefit society in the future. As a physician, Ellis decided to document his own demise so that one day doctors could gain a better understanding and perhaps even a cure for nocturnal emissions.

As weeks turned into months, a funny thing happened—not only did Ellis not die, he did not even get sick. Ellis was understandably incensed that the medical establishment of the time had been propagating such mistruths. As a result of his experience, Ellis spent most of the rest of his career researching sex and trying to ensure that the public was receiving accurate sex information.

The Kinsey Reports

Alfred Kinsey and his colleagues conducted the first widespread survey of sexual behavior, seeking to understand the diversity of behavior that was occurring in men and woman of all different ages. They published two volumes, the first a report on the sexual behavior of the human male in 1948; the second on the sexual behavior of the human female in 1953. They surveyed over 11,000 people and attempted to include a vast collection of participants across age, marital status, education, religion, occupations, and sexual orientation. While they sought to achieve a good representative sample of the American population, their sample lacked inclusion of most racial minorities, and thus the results really cannot be seen as a relevant representation of the public. However, this did not completely erode the credibility of Kinsey's findings.

Kinsey's survey methods and ethical considerations, in updated form, remain a good standard for measuring such a sensitive topic. In addition, Kinsey suggested a radical idea about sexual orientation that still holds today: that one's sexual orientation is not as "black and white" as once thought. He suggested that one is not simply "gay" or "straight" but has a sexual orientation that exists on a continuum with varying degrees of attraction to each sex. Kinsey and his team issued two reports that, almost certainly because it followed the end of the World War II, were compared to the atom bomb. The Kinsey reports truly had an explosive effect on an America that would seem very conservative by today's standards.

The National Health and Social Life Survey

Motivated by the increasingly devastating effects of the AIDS epidemic in the 1980s, the United States Department of Health and Human Services sought to complete a survey of the sexual practices and attitudes of adults across the country. The hope was that this information could be used to prevent the spread of AIDS. In 1988 a team of researchers from the University of Chicago headed by Edward Laumann aimed at surveying 20,000 people across the United States, but due to conservative congressional pushback and the resulting cut in their budget, they were limited to a sample of just over 4,000. Interestingly, most people responded, yielding a final group of over 3,400. Unlike Kinsey's research, Laumann and his team emphasized the behavior and attitudes of ethnic minorities, weighing heavily those of African Americans and Latinos.

This study's results, even in diminished form (relative to the study's original design), presented the U.S. government with the most comprehensive information about sexual behavior and sexual attitudes since Kinsey's publications over 40 years earlier (Laumann et al., 1994).

Think about it – While the extensive sex surveys discussed above made incredibly valuable contributions to our understanding of human sexual behavior, what are some of the potential problems researchers might face when employing using self-report surveys in an attempt to gain accurate sex information?

Masters and Johnson

The research teams headed by both Kinsey and Laumann employed a survey and interview method to understand sexual practices. Masters and Johnson took a less subtle method. Kinsey and Laumann's work had mainly investigated the frequency with which sexual behaviors occurred in the population and was based on personal interviews.

In contrast, Masters and Johnson set about studying the structure and physiology of sexual behavior through observing and measuring masturbation and sexual intercourse directly in a laboratory.

Masters and Johnson used direct observation in their research and pioneered a new set of methods for quantifying sexuality. Seeking an ultimate understanding of the human sexual response, Masters and Johnson's research involved teams of trained researchers using devices to measure a variety of physical responses during the progression of a sexual encounter (excitation, plateau, orgasm, resolution). They used devices aimed at measuring even the slightest changes in penis size, vaginal blood flow, volume of blood collected in the clitoris, muscular activity in the rectum, to name just a few.

Using a laboratory and a large research team, Masters and Johnson accounted for the measurement of over 10,000 completed sexual response cycles using 382 women and 312 men. They published two main texts, *Human Sexual Response* (1966) and *Human Sexual Inadequacy* (1970).

Critical Thinking – Whether in the 1940s, 1950s (Kinsey), 1960s, 1970s (Masters and Johnson), or 1980s and 1990s (Laumann), research of any kind into sexual attitudes and practices has come under fire like no other field of research and by many organized groups. The characteristic these groups seem to share is a powerful base in conservative, Christian fundamentalism. These barriers to research into sexual practices persist even into the second decade of the twenty-first century.

Clearly, the pioneering researchers outlined in this chapter were motivated in their own way, in their own cultural context, by the need of their time. Kinsey was motivated, in part, by a frustration with a lack of sexual knowledge among young married couples after seeing examples of how such a lack of knowledge was impacting their relationships and health, Laumann and his team were responding to a need to do something about the rapidly growing AIDS problem in the United States, and Masters and Johnson were trying to understand the actual biological process of human sexual behavior as it had not yet (even through the 1960s!) been studied.

First, what are the benefits of an understanding (or the pursuit of such) of human sexual behaviors and attitudes? What myths about sexuality did the research of Kinsey, Laumann, and Masters and Johnson dispel? Put another way, what harm can come from *not* having the data that these studies produce?

Second, what do you think is motivating sex researchers in *today's* culture?

Now, locate, outline, and discuss the main arguments of a fundamental Christian perspective against such research, past and present. How have these arguments changed? How have they stayed the same?

Why do these arguments persist and even thrive? Why are these arguments centered so strongly on sex research and less so on other fields of study?

SEXUAL ORIENTATION

Still an open question in the scientific community is, what are the factors that cause and/or influence the development of sexual orientation? Kinsey's research was landmark for many reasons; however, his major contribution, as mentioned earlier, was the idea that an individual's *sexual orientation,* or to which of the sexes one has an erotic attachment, exists not as exclusively heterosexual or homosexual but rather with tendencies of each. Kinsey also provided initial estimates of the population's sexual orientation, indicating that nearly 2 percent of women and 4 percent of men reported themselves homosexual. Laumann's team followed up with a similar self-report survey and found the numbers to be slightly less than Kinsey's—1.4 percent for women and 2.8 percent for men (Laumann et al., 1994).

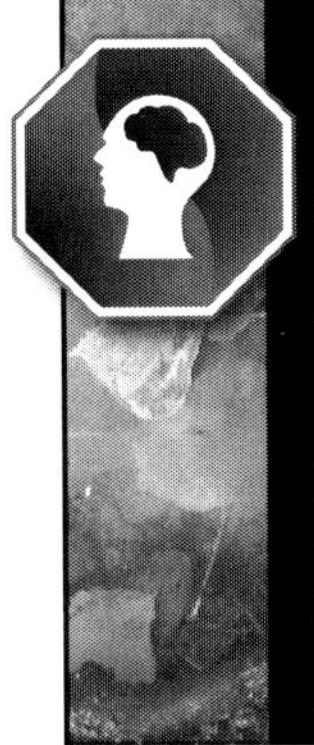

Stop and Think – There continues to be a strong moral component attached to sex and sexual orientation even in the most open societies like the United States. That is, there is a tendency to assign a moral value ("right" and "wrong") to a behavior that exists, whether straight or gay, between consenting adults, a scenario that seems to not merit such a moral label.

Think back to the first discussion in this chapter. You were asked to include a list of sources that inform your ideas and knowledge about sexuality. Do this again.

What sources inform your views on homosexuality? Rank them like you did in the first discussion. Are there differences? What are they?

No one knows what causes sexual orientation, whether heterosexual, homosexual, or bisexual. Assumptions that homosexuality is caused by sexual abuse or misguided parental behaviors are now acknowledged as based in prejudice and even seem as silly as assuming a straight sexual orientation a product of intentional parental effort. What is clear is that sexual orientation is more complex than mere gay or straight.

Historically thought of as a behavior in which people occasionally engaged, homosexuality is now considered a sexual orientation and a developed part of one's identity, much like heterosexuality. There have been many conjectures in the various fields of genetics, medicine, and psychology as to the development of sexual orientation. Although he thought homosexuality a variance from a basic bisexual state within which all humans reside and not necessarily a psychopathology, Sigmund Freud conceptualized sexual orientation as a direct result of experiences with parents and with others involved in a person's upbringing, espousing arguably a nurture-based theory (1905). At one time, the medical community, specifically the American Psychiatric Association, thought of homosexuality as a mental disorder (1973). It wasn't until 1973, in the midst of controversy, that homosexuality was removed from its *Diagnostic and Statistic Manual for Mental Disorders.* The American Psychological Association followed suit, issuing a statement in 1975 declaring that homosexuality implies no impairments that lend any support to a diagnosis of a mental disorder (Fox, 1988).

Biological theories, based largely in evolutionary theory have struggled with understanding the causes of homosexuality. If traits in humans evolve in a way that aids in the long-term survival of the species and this survival requires the successful production of offspring, how can homosexuality persist and not diminish? Dr. Rahman (Rahman & Wilson, 2003) and his colleagues pose a plausible explanation that is the focus of much research around the developed world. They suggest that homosexuality may have evolved to promote attachments with members of one's own sex through a mechanism in neurodevelopment, that there are clear differences in the gay and the straight brain, and that homosexuality, like heterosexuality, cannot be attributed to learned effects. Identical twin studies in the last decade have shown that if one twin is gay there is between a 48 to 65 percent chance that the other twin will be gay depending on the specific study that is cited (Hyde, 2005: Kirk et al., 2000). These studies would seem to indicate a strong genetic influence on sexual orientation.

In a historical and contemporary frame of reference, one does not have to stretch the imagination too far to understand how many homosexuals were thought to have a mental health problem. Given societal attitudes, stigma, intolerance, and overt discrimination toward homosexuals, homosexuals' presentation of symptoms of stress, anxiety, and depression, apparent indicators of a psychiatric illness, are understandable (Meyer, 2003). Today homosexuals seek tolerance and acceptance from society and have accomplished significant gains in their fight for equal rights.

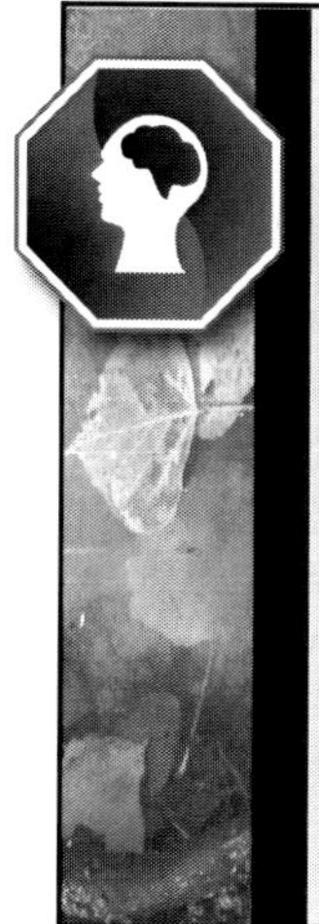

Stop and Think – Many stereotypes about homosexuality and its causes persist today and often are brought forward by inquisitive people in question form. For instance, many straight people may ask a gay man, "*How can you be gay if you've never had sex with a woman?*" or a gay woman, "*How do you know you won't like being with a man?*"

Think of what this question might sound like to a heterosexual person. Try asking:

"*How do you know you are straight if you've never made love with someone of your own sex?*"

"*Do you think what you really need is just a good gay lover to bring you out of being straight?*"

"*Isn't it possible that you being straight is just a phase you're going through and that you'll get over it someday?*"

LOVE

It can be argued that the greatest poets this planet has ever seen have failed miserably at defining the idea of love. The concept of love has tormented the greatest artists and the most confused of teenagers. It takes many forms and exists in the context of many relationships like family, friendships, sexual partners, and even in the workplace. While many artists and scientists have thrown their hats in the ring, we will outline one particular theory of love as it exists in the study of psychology.

Robert Sternberg, president of the American Psychological Association in 1983, provided a theoretical outline for understanding the idea of love and people's experience of it (1986). He thought of love as having three components: passion, commitment, and intimacy. He hypothesized *passion* as the motivational component of love, the part of love that burns the hottest, fades the quickest, and drives people toward each other; *commitment* as the thoughtful process of love involving a decision to exist in a relationship and work to make it better over a period of time; and *intimacy* as the relational bonding that time and hardship offer, leading to empathy and a willingness to sacrifice on the behalf of another.

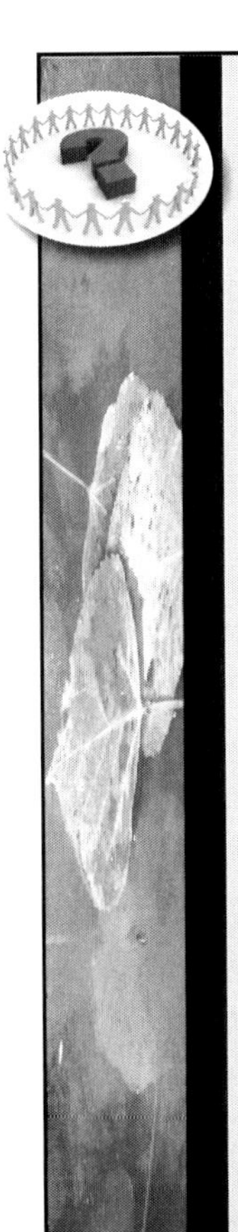

Ask Around – Sternberg's research suggested that most people have experience in relationships that have some of these components but may lack in others. What would Sternberg label a relationship with plenty of passion but no commitment or intimacy? With intimacy but no passion? With commitment but no intimacy?

Ask some family and friends that may have more or different experience in relationships than you what their experiences are with love. When they are telling you a story of a past or current relationship, which of the components of love are they describing?

Using this triangular model of love, what is the difference between how a teenager, young adult, and older adult may experience love? Consider variables like jealousy, gender, and multiple sex partners.

Finally, consider the idea that, in loving relationships, "opposites attract." Now consider what the opposite of you might look like. Imagine a person that speaks only another language, has a different or "opposite" idea of education, religion, and politics than you, is of another ethnicity and from another country than you. Would a relationship between you two be a likely success? Why does the idea of "opposites attract" survive?

Sexual Scripts

The society and culture we are a part of often give us very strong messages about how a sexual encounter is supposed to progress. That is to say, society teaches us what to do, how and when to do it, and with whom (Kimmel, 2007). These sexual scripts often change over time and are disseminated through various forms of mass media. For example, it was rare to see a married couple in the same bed together in television shows or movies in the 1950s. However, today sex scenes in movies are very common and involve people having sex in various different settings.

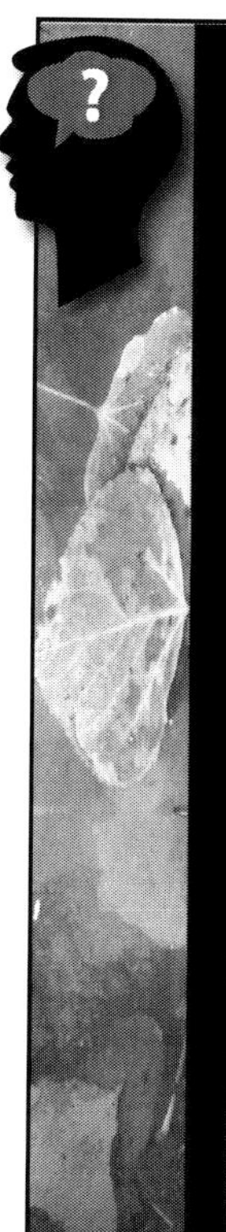

Think about it – Sexual scripts are not necessarily good or bad, but they can set up unrealistic and sometimes unachievable expectations. Think about many contemporary sex scenes in movies. Assuming the scene was not devised for comedic effect, you will notice that the encounter almost always goes perfectly. There is no communication about the encounter ahead of time, yet both people receive pleasure and often achieve orgasm at precisely the same moment. It is as if the encounter is magical and chemistry just takes over.

Do you think this is realistic? Do most couples have perfect sex with no communication?

What do you believe is a more realistic sexual script for most couples in the twenty-first century?

"DEVIANT" SEXUAL BEHAVIOR

Looking back at Chapter 1, we recall that in order to understand something, we must first seek to understand what it is *not*. This question is relevant to this section as well. When we seek to understand what is an "abnormal" sexual behavior, we are faced with the unique task of not only defining *how* the behavior is abnormal but with understanding first what *is* normal. These tasks are intertwined and subject of a worthy and long-standing debate in the field of psychology. The debate and its context will be discussed further in the final chapter, Doing Psychology.

The word *deviant* is used loosely in this chapter and is in quotes to draw special attention to how it may be viewed in a negative light. *Deviant sexual behavior* is a behavior that is not typically exhibited by most people compared to their peers within their specific culture and society. The American Psychiatric Association has defined many uncommon types of sexual behaviors as *paraphilias* and has sought to understand them as they influence people's mental and behavioral health (2000).

Discussion – The main consideration when looking at the impact of deviant or atypical sexual behaviors seems to be one of an ethical nature. The center of any question of whether a behavior is or is not harmful to a person or persons is informed consent. That is, are all parties fully informed of the behavior and willing, consenting adults?

When considering the following definitions of some paraphilias, ask yourself, if one were to engage in such a behavior with another, what situational variables would define the behavior as ethical or unethical? Put another way, under what circumstances would the behavior be of no potential harm or of potential damage to the well-being of another living being (human or animal)? Keep in mind—to be a practicing ethicist, it is important to base your thoughts not on a personal emotional reaction but rather around the question of full, informed consent and potential for harm.

Fetishism is an erotic feeling associated with focus on an inanimate object or body part. Common examples are shoes, leather, rubber, or undergarments.

Transvestic fetishism is an erotic feeling associated with wearing the clothing of the other sex.

Exhibitionism is the erotic sensation associated with exposure of one's genitalia to an unwilling observer.

Voyeurism is the sexual arousal that comes with observing others' sexual behaviors without their consent.

Frotteurism is the erotic sense one obtains by rubbing his genitalia against another person in a crowded space.

Zoophilia is sexual contact between a human and an animal.

Sadism is the erotic connection of sexual pleasure with giving pain.

Masochism is the erotic connection of sexual pleasure with receiving pain.

Finally, can you think of some paraphilias in the United States that might not be considered such in other cultures? Conversely, could some "normal" sexual practices in the United States be considered paraphilias in other countries?

REFERENCES

Allen, P. L. (2000). *The wages of sin: Sex and disease, past and present.* Chicago: University of Chicago Press.

American Psychiatric Association. (1973). Position Statement on Homosexuality and Civil Rights. *American Journal of Psychiatry, 131* (4), 497.

American Psychiatric Association. (2000). *Diagnostic and statistical manual of mental disorders* (4th ed., Text Revision). Washington, DC: American Psychiatric Association.

Freud, S. (1905). Three essays on the theory of sexuality. In J. Strachey (Ed. and Trans.), *The standard edition of the complete psychological works of Sigmund Freud.* Vol. 7, pp. 126–245. London: Hogarth Press.

Fox, R. E. (1988). Proceedings of the American Psychological Association, Incorporated, for the year 1987: Minutes of the annual meeting of the Council of Representatives. *American Psychologist, 43,* 508–531.

Hyde, J. S. (2005). The genetics of sexual orientation. In J. S. Hyde (Ed.), *Biological substrates of human sexuality.* Washington, DC: American Psychological Association.

Kimmel, M. (2007). *The sexual self: The construction of sexual scripts.* Nashville, TN: Vanderbilt University Press.

Kinsey, A., Pomeroy, W., & Martin, C. (1948). *Sexual behavior in the human male.* Philadelphia: Saunders.

Kinsey, A., Pomeroy, W., Martin, C., & Gebhard, P. (1953). *Sexual behavior in the human female.* Philadelphia: Saunders.

Kirk, K. M., Bailey, J. M., Dunne, M. P., & Martin, N. G. (2000). Measurement models for sexual orientation in a community sample. *Behavior Genetics 30*(4), 345–356.

Laumann, E. O., Gagnon, J., Michael, R., & Michaels, S. (1994). *The social organization of sexuality in the United States.* Chicago: University of Chicago Press.

Masters, W., & Johnson, V. (1966). *Human sexual response.* Boston: Little, Brown.

Masters, W., & Johnson, V. (1970). *Human sexual inadequacy.* Boston: Little, Brown.

Meyer, I. H. (2003). Prejudice, social stress, and mental health in lesbian, gay, and bisexual populations: Conceptual issues and research evidence. *Psychological Bulletin, 129,* 674–697.

Money, J. (1955). Hermaphroditism, gender and precocity in hyperadrenocorticism: Psychologic findings. *Bulletin of the Johns Hopkins Hospital, 96,* 253–264.

Rahman, Q., & Wilson, G. (2003). Born gay? The psychobiology of human sexual orientation. *Personality and Individual Differences, 34*(8), 1337–1382.

Sternberg, R. (1986). A triangular theory of love. *Psychological Review, 93,* 119–135.

NAME ______________________________ DATE ______________

WORKSHEET CHAPTER TEN

CHAPTER 11

PERSONALITY

"I hold a beast, an angel and a madman in me, and my enquiry is as to their working, and my problem is their subjugation and victory, downthrow and upheaval, and my effort is their self-expression."
— Dylan Thomas

ACTIVITY

Answer the question, "Who are you?" Make sure to be as descriptive as possible.

Who are we? What causes us to act the way we do? These are questions that human beings have wrestled with for eternity. These are also questions that have been underlying themes of virtually every chapter in this book.

In short, there is no easy answer to the question of why we each act the way we do. In fact, there is often not consensus on how we should go about even studying personality. Some psychologists believe that personality is a construct that can be measured and thus understood empirically, while others believe that to attempt to quantify a human being's personality causes us to lose the true essence of what makes that person uniquely human in the first place.

In addition, some theorists believe we can best understand personality by looking at each individual in a case study format driven by the belief that it is hard to formulate general descriptions of personality that can be applied to large numbers of people. This is referred to as an *idiographic* approach to studying personality. Other theorists believe that the best way to understand personality involves comparing an individual's score on a personality test to a normative data set (a large group of other people who have taken the test) to see if that person scores higher or lower than average. This is often referred to as a *nomothetic* approach to studying personality.

ACTIVITY

Activity– After thinking about idiographic and nomothetic approaches to studying personality, which one do you believe would be more effective and why?

Now that you have completed the previous activity, it is worth noting that both idiographic and nomothetic approaches have made important contributions to our understanding of personality (Hermans, 1988).

There are many factors we must consider when trying to conceptualize personality. One is the influence of biology and genetics versus that of experience and learning. Do we inherit personality from our parents and ancestors, or is personality gained through experience? Most contemporary theorists believe that both genetics and environment play important roles in personality formation.

One particular aspect of experience or environment that many theorists focus on is the importance of childhood experience on the formation of adulthood personality. Many personality theorists argue that there is a disproportional impact of childhood experience, especially childhood trauma, on the impact of adult personality. Conversely, there are other theorists who argue that behaviors we exhibit as adults are independent of their developmental or childhood origins. This leads us to the question of whether personality is consistent over time. For example, Sigmund Freud believed that personality was basically formed by about age 5 or 6 and was relatively stable over time. Other theorists believe that personality is more fluid and constantly changing as we age.

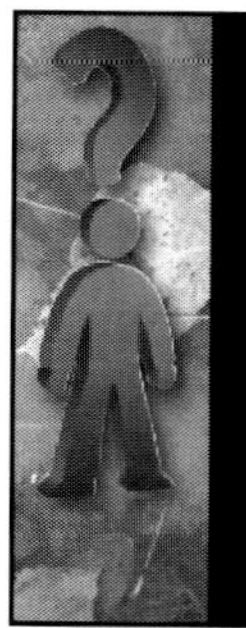

What Do You Think? – Is personality consistent over time or does it change as we get older? What evidence do you have to support your answer?

Another important factor to consider when discussing personality is conscious versus unconscious processes. Psychoanalytic theorists, for example, are especially interested in how experiences we are not aware of, or unconscious experiences, impact our personality and behavior whereas other theories are much more focused on the here-and-now and information that exists within our conscious experience.

One final consideration that can play a crucial role in personality formation is the culture we are a part of. Our culture often provides powerful templates for how people should behave. These templates often dictate what behaviors can be exhibited by whom and in what context. For example, people in the United States tend to score as more assertive, independent, and extraverted on personality tests when compared to other more collectivist cultures where some of these qualities can be discouraged (Triandis, 2001).

THEORIES OF PERSONALITY

Over the years there have been many giants in the study of personality whose shoulders we still stand on today. While the theories created by these individuals undoubtedly have weaknesses (some of which may be more apparent than others 100 years removed from their creation), it is important to try and understand each theory within the context of the time it was created.

Theories are systematically organized conceptualizations that consist of well-organized ideas and constructs with the goal of helping us gain a better understanding of phenomena in the world around us. In traditional science, theories often help us to make predictions. While this is the aim of certain theories of personality, there is probably no more difficult task than predicting how complex beings such as humans will behave and to try and decipher why we think, feel, or behave as we do.

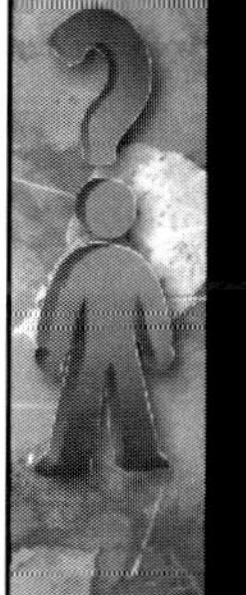

What Do You Think? – What makes a theory a good theory? How can we decide which theory is the "right" theory?

Generally speaking, good theories should be *verifiable.* This means there should be some way to test the theory such that we can confirm or disconfirm its assertions. It is relatively easy to find some level of anecdotal support for virtually any theory, especially those that are vaguely defined. To simply say that you cannot disconfirm a theory is not sufficient evidence for that theory's existence. As such, good theories use specific language to define terms such that these terms can be measured or observed in some way and therefore be either validated or refuted.

Most theories also strive for a certain level of comprehensiveness. Personality theories that can describe multiple developmental stages (childhood, adolescence, adulthood, etc.) as well as different contributing factors to personality (biology, environment, cognitions, adaptation, culture, etc.) are generally considered to be more helpful. That said, sometimes theories that attempt to explain too much actually lose some of their potential impact since they may scratch the surface of many variables but fail to provide true clarity and depth to any one.

Psychoanalytic Theories

Psychoanalytic theories emphasize the unconscious part of the human psyche. That is, items in our psyche that we are not aware of have the greatest impact on personality formation and behavior. While all psychoanalytic theorists generally agree that the unconscious is paramount, different theorists have proposed different models for how exactly the unconscious manifests. Some of the most important psychoanalytic thinkers will be discussed in the space that follows.

Sigmund Freud

Uncle "Siggy," as he is sometimes affectionately referred to by the authors, made undeniably important contributions to the field of psychology. Perhaps none was more important than his conceptualization of the conscious and unconscious mind.

Freud thought of the human psyche as an iceberg. Only the tip of the iceberg is above the surface. This can be thought of as the *conscious.* What resides in our conscious are processes or experiences we are currently aware of. If you are truly paying attention to what you are reading, one item in your realm of conscious awareness at this very moment is the sentence you are reading.

Just a few feet below the water level we find the *preconscious.* Here lies content that is just below the level of conscious awareness but can be easily brought to conscious awareness.

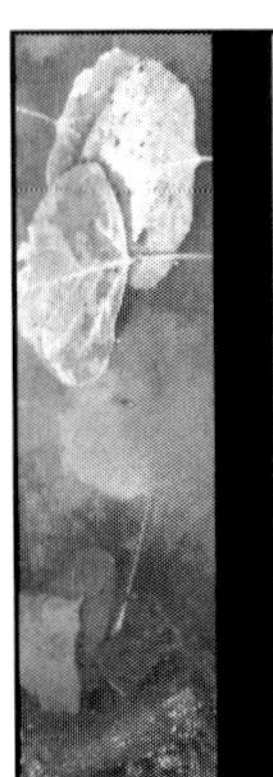

The Preconscious in Action –

What is your phone number? ______________________

What is your address?

____

Chances are you were not thinking of these items before you were asked about them. However, when asked, you were easily able to take these items from your preconscious into conscious awareness.

Freud believed that most of our psyche was composed of the *unconscious.* Look at the diagram of the iceberg again. Notice that the vast majority of that iceberg is well below the surface of the water. Freud believed that this was the portion of our psyche that was most influential. In addition, he believed that many items that were stored deep in our unconscious were kept there because allowing them to reach conscious awareness would cause too much anxiety. Thus, the material is kept there using a defense mechanism referred to as repression. Freud believed that traumatic events, especially those experienced in childhood, are the kind of items that reside in one's unconscious.

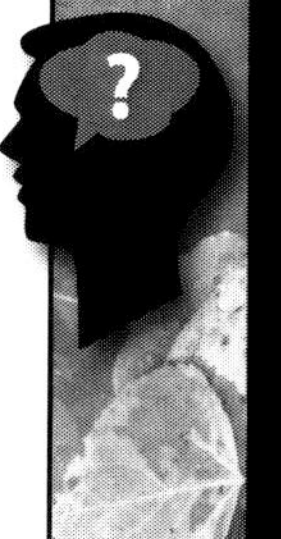

Think About It – What is the difference between Freud's theory of unconscious mind and a state of biological unconsciousness as discussed in Chapter 6?

Freud believed there were three structures of personality referred to as the id, ego and superego. The *id* is the most primitive of these structures and operates on a totally unconscious level. The id seeks to attain pleasure and avoid pain. Our libido or psychic energy is contained by our id. The *superego* is the voice of morality often formed by our parents and broader societal forces. This is the internal voice telling us what is "right" and "wrong" and what we "should" be doing. A small part of the superego is conscious, but most of it remains unconscious. The third structure of personality is referred to as the *ego.* The ego is the most conscious of all three structures but not completely conscious. It is also the most well developed and mature of the three structures. The ego is tasked with dealing with the external reality of the world and must attempt to mediate between the desires of the id and rules and restrictions of the superego. In this way, the ego often serves as the great mediator of personality.

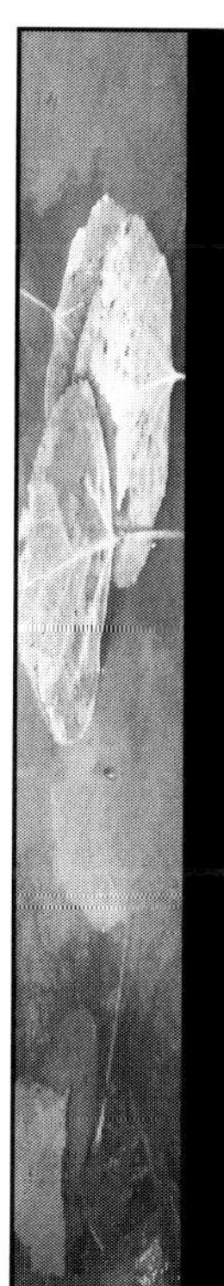

Freud's Structures of Personality in Action – It is likely that all of you have seen a picture with an angel on one shoulder and a devil on the other representing tension within a person's inner dialogue. In Freud's model, the id can be thought of as sitting on one shoulder and the superego on the other. This is not meant to judge one as good or evil, but rather, a model to show that the id and the superego sometimes have competing agendas. It is then the ego's job to mediate between these two agendas.

© Jef Thompson, 2011. Used under license of Shutterstock, Inc.

For example, imagine that an attractive person is walking down the street. The unconscious id would likely communicate a

(*continued*)

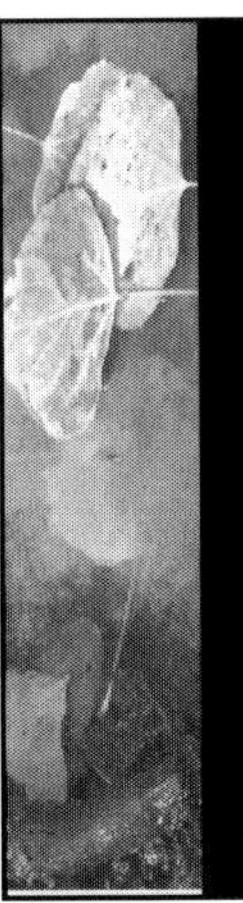

Freud's Structures of Personality in Action (*continued*)

message like: "Have sex with that person immediately." The mostly unconscious superego would interject thoughts such as: "You can't have sex with someone you are not married to," or "You could get a sexually transmitted infection or there might even be an unwanted pregnancy." These statements could, of course, vary based on the moral code you have formed through the teachings of your parents or exposure to various societal institutions. It is now the ego's job to mediate between these conflicting messages. Perhaps the ego would propose a solution such as asking the person to have a cup of coffee. While this would not lead to the ultimate pleasure the id was seeking, it could lead to the fulfillment of such pleasure at a later time. This would likely also satisfy the superego since no major "rules" or "morals" would be violated.

Defense Mechanisms In the previous example, the ego was able to formulate a reality-based solution that satisfied both the id and the superego. As you might have already been speculating, sometimes such an amenable solution is not immediately available. In fact, there are times when the ego has to distort reality to make sure an individual's psyche does not become overwhelmed by anxiety. When the ego does this, it is employing what Freud referred to as a *defense mechanism.*

Some of the most common defense mechanisms are outlined in Table 11.1.

Table 11.1 Freudian Defense Mechanisms

Defense Mechanism	Summary	Example
Denial 	Not perceiving or denying the existence of reality because it is too painful to perceive.	Failure to acknowledge one has cancer even though one's doctor has diagnosed it and even shown visual evidence of the tumor.

(*continued*)

Table 11.1 (*continued*)

Regression  © photobank.ch, 2011. Used under license of Shutterstock, Inc.	Reverting back to an earlier stage of development to cope with an unpleasant situation.	An adult begins sucking his thumb when anxiety in his life becomes overwhelming.
Repression  © Mark Carrel, 2011. Used under license of Shutterstock, Inc.	Stuffing painful or otherwise unacceptable thoughts into the unconscious because they would be too overwhelming to experience in conscious awareness.	Forgetting the details of an early childhood traumatic experience such as physical or sexual abuse.

(*continued*)

Table 11.1 *(continued)*

Defense Mechanism	Summary	Example
Rationalization 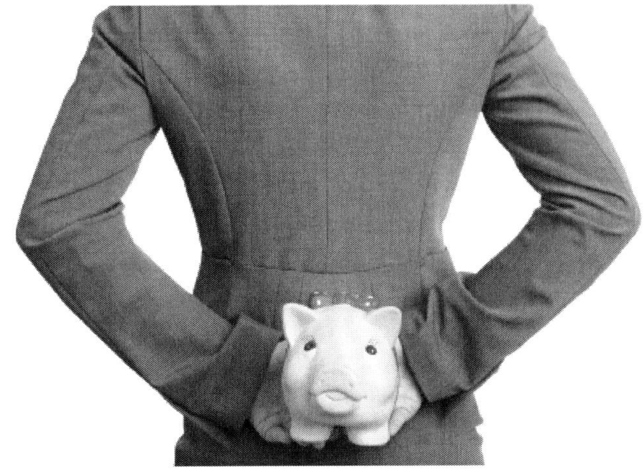 	Conscious and more socially acceptable reasons for a behavior are offered as opposed to the true unconscious and less acceptable reasons.	Cheating on income taxes and justifying it by saying that everyone cheats on taxes at some point.
Intellectualization 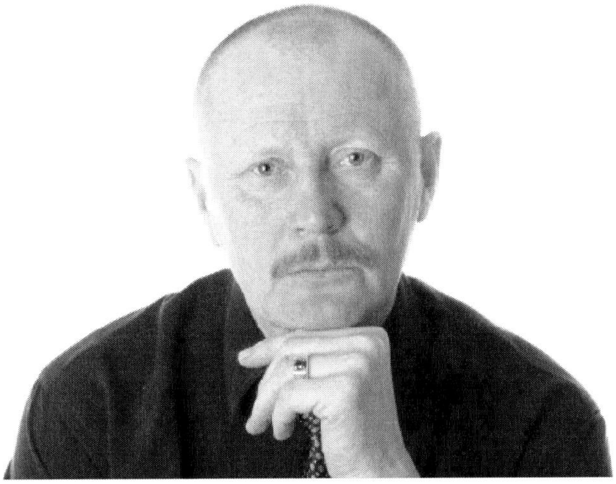 	Focusing on thoughts and details and ignoring feelings and emotional experiences.	Discussing the medical progression of a disease that killed a loved one while ignoring the intense feelings that accompany that loved one's death.

(continued)

Table 11.1 (*continued*)

Reaction Formation  © onime, 2011. Used under license of Shutterstock, Inc.	Behaving in a manner that is inconsistent or opposite of one's unacceptable unconscious impulses.	Preaching to everyone who will listen that homosexuality is wrong while one is privately engaging in the very behavior he or she is condemning.
Displacement  © Peter Polak, 2011. Used under license of Shutterstock, Inc.	The reassignment of an aggressive impulse to a safer target.	A student is furious at a professor after receiving an "F" on an exam and yells at his roommate after returning to the dorm.

(*continued*)

Table 11.1 *(continued)*

Defense Mechanism	**Summary**	**Example**
Projection © Fluffy2008, 2011. Used under license of Shutterstock, Inc.	Taking one's own unacceptable feeling or impulse and ascribing it to someone else.	Accusing your significant other of cheating when you are the one who is actually thinking of cheating.
Sublimation © Sergey Prygov, 2011. Used under license of Shutterstock, Inc.	Unacceptable desires or feelings are expressed in socially acceptable ways.	Someone with aggressive impulses in the world channels those impulses constructively by playing football.

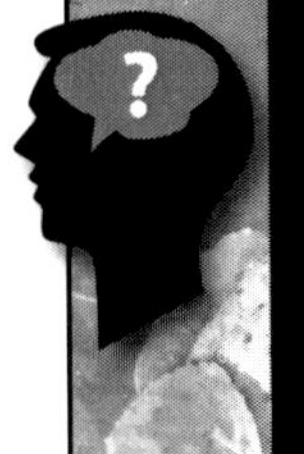

Think About It – Have you used any of these defense mechanisms? If so, which ones?

It is important to note that Freud did not believe that all defense mechanisms were created equal. That is, some defense mechanisms are more sophisticated than others. If an adult is consistently engaging in a very primitive defense mechanism such as denial, Freud believed that was a sign of poor mental health. In contrast, he believed that a defense mechanism like sublimation was more sophisticated and a sign of good mental health. Moreover, engaging in defense mechanisms at appropriate times can serve an adaptive and healthy function (Marshall & Brown, 2008).

Psychosexual Stages Freud proposed a five-stage model of personality development referred to as the *psychosexual stages* of development. In this model he suggested that biological drives contained in the id pushed each child through five distinct stages. Freud believed that if a child's needs were not met, or conversely, if the child was pampered or overindulged in any particular stage that could result in *fixation.* Fixation causes impulses to be repressed, which can lead to individuals regressing to earlier developmental stages during times of anxiety or stress.

Table 11.2 Freudian Psychosexual Stages

Stage	Age	Conflict	Outcomes
Oral	Birth – 12 months	Weaning from nipple or bottle	Fixation in this stage can lead people to pathological behaviors happening near the mouth (smoking, drinking too much alcohol, etc.). Underindulgence in this stage (passively swallowing anything) can lead to passivity and dependence while overindulgence can lead to sadism, aggressiveness, and manipulative personality characteristics.
Anal	1–3 years	Toilet training	Fixation in this stage can result in people being compulsively neat and controlled (anal-retentive) or excessively disorganized, messy, and rebellious (anal-expulsive).
Phallic	3–5 years	Genitals (overcoming Oedipus/Electra complex by identifying with same-sex parent)	Freud believed that during this period children were attracted to the opposite sex parent (Oedipus complex for boys and Electra complex for girls) and that this had to be adequately resolved for optimal development to occur. He proposed this was resolved by identifying with the same sex parent. In addition, he proposed that most girls could never completely resolve this conflict because they would still have hostile feelings toward their mothers since they lacked a penis (penis envy). Freud believed the inability for girls to solve this conflict led to moral inferiority in adulthood.

(continued)

Table 11.2 *(continued)*

Stage	Age	Conflict	Outcomes
Latency	5 years-puberty	Interacting with same-sex peers	This is a "calm" stage according to Freud with no major conflicts. During this time children focus on forming relationships and interacting with same-sex peers.
Genital	Puberty -adulthood	Genitals (forming intimate relationships with others)	Successful resolution of this stage leads to the ability to form meaningful romantic relationships with others while failure results in relationships based on lust that often lack commitment and mutual respect.

What Do You Think? – What are your thoughts about Freud's psychosexual stages? Are there certain things you believe he got right? What criticisms do you have?

Unlike Freud's theory of defense mechanisms, which has endured and is still taken seriously today, his psychosexual stages are widely criticized and rarely advanced as a contemporary theory of personality development. He is often criticized for his use of sexist language and overemphasis on sexual and aggressive drives. That said, his stages laid the foundation for other theories such as Erik Erikson's theory of development, which was discussed in detail in Chapter 7. Erikson, of course, focused less on sexual drives and expanded the stages through middle and late adulthood.

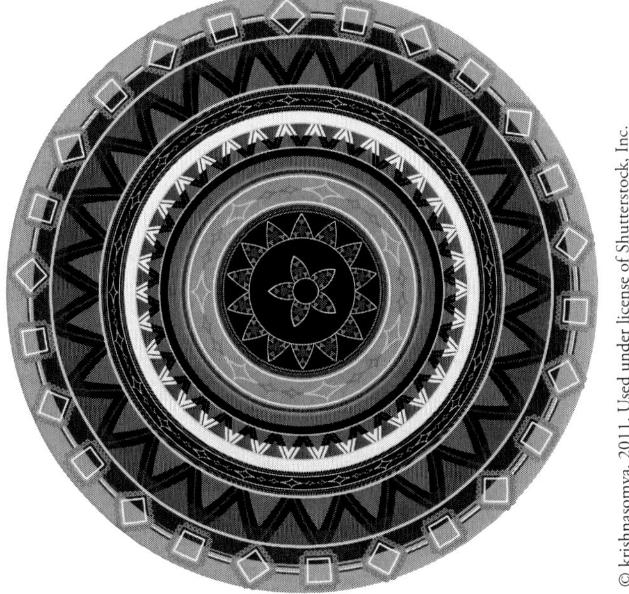

*Carl Jung**

During his professional career, Jung became associated with Sigmund Freud and the two maintained a very intimate, intellectual relationship for years. However, Jung began to question whether sex was the primary driving force of all psychic energy in the psyche as Freud theorized. This led to an eventual split between the two men and saw Jung retreat into a period

*Contributor on Jungian Psychology: Paulo Arroyo, Metropolitan State College of Denver.

of creative illness where he painted his first mandala, recognized the Self as the goal for psychic development, published his book entitled *Psychological Types,* and ultimately confronted his unconscious.

Regarded as mystical, Carl Jung's body of work is well respected as well as disregarded. His theory of a collective unconscious remains particularly controversial. The following quote from Jung really captures his view of personality as well as some of his distrust for overly scientific methods of trying to understand personality.

> My life is a story of the self-realization of the unconscious. Everything in the unconscious seeks outward manifestation, and the personality too desires to evolve out of its unconscious conditions and to experience itself as a whole. I cannot employ the language of science to trace this process of growth in myself, for I cannot experience myself as a scientific problem. (Jung, 1963, p. 3)

Ego and Persona Jung described the psyche as possessing all mental functions such as thought, feeling, and behavior. These functions operate on both a conscious and unconscious level. Jung believed that the psyche had three major components, much like Freud's theory, only Jung used different language. In order for a person to recognize the *Self,* which is a working balance between unconscious and consciousness, one must draw from these three levels of the psyche (conscious, personal unconscious, and collective unconscious) to reach what Jung called individuation, which is the process of becoming a whole person.

The *ego* is regarded as the gatekeeper to consciousness, and, like Freud's concept of the ego, Jung suggested that the ego is the most conscious aspect of the psyche. It is the part of the psyche that allows external stimuli passage to conscious thought. If a person identifies too much with her ego, she will overestimate the role the ego actually plays in the psyche, thus falling into ego inflation. While the objective, empirical world is what we deal with every waking second, Jung stressed that being too caught up in "reality" is unhealthy for the inner, subjective part of our mind.

Along with the ego, the *persona* is a social mask every person puts on to show to the world. It is the aspect of the psyche that adjusts and accommodates itself to the world. Given any situation, humans change their persona to fit the circumstances of the moment. For example, we all have a work persona meaning we have a certain way of being at our jobs. We also have a persona we use when we are with friends and family. As you read this line, you are using your student persona (hopefully).

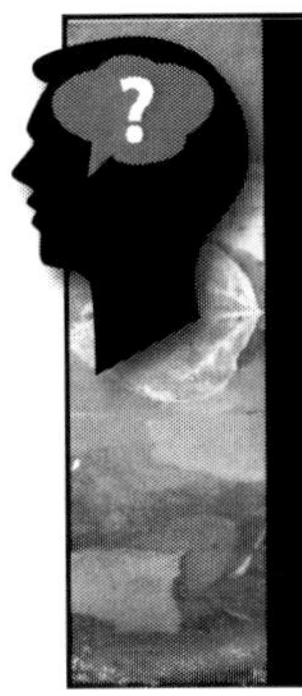

Think About It – Can you give some examples of your persona, or the social masks you wear in different situations in your life?

Why might a persona be adaptive for survival in any given society?

Personal Unconscious Much like Freud's theory of an unconscious, Jung's personal unconscious works in a similar way. This is the level of the psyche that develops through a person's unique experience, much like consciousness. Just as it is the ego's job to mediate what will be brought to conscious awareness, it is the shadow's job to receive everything the ego rejects. The *shadow* is the unconscious contrast to an individual's conscious identity. The shadow is given all the things we do not like about ourselves. Things that rival our conscious identity and traumatic events also reside in the personal unconscious. A key difference between the theories of Freud and Jung is where Freud thought the unconscious is developed solely on a person's interactions with the empirical world, Jung proposed that consciousness is an offspring of the unconscious. Similar to the ego, the shadow is referred to as the gatekeeper to the unconscious.

Along with the shadow, the personal unconscious has two more elements to consider. The first is the *anima,* which is the feminine aspect in every man that is kept unconscious. The second is the *animus.* This is the masculine aspect in every woman that is kept unconscious. A reason as to why both the anima and animus are rejected from consciousness by the ego is because these qualities are considered to be contradictory to socialized gender roles.

Collective Unconscious and Archetypes A deeper layer of the unconscious is what Jung named the collective unconscious. Unlike the personal unconscious, Jung believed this layer is inherited through our ancestors and brain structures that existed before the human brain evolved and developed a neocortex. Many who believe that Jung had no basis for making the claim that the collective unconscious had any sort of genetic component commonly challenge this assertion.

Jung believed the collective unconscious was independent of personal experience. It may also be suggested that because of our collective unconscious, all humans are primed to respond to certain themes in life, which is why literature and movies can have a profound impact on us.

Archetypes are primordial images in our inherited unconscious that influence the way we experience the world in a similar, human way. Jung referred to this function as "psychic instincts" much like animals rely on their instincts when interacting with the world. Although the shadow, anima, and animus are regarded as archetypes of the unconscious, they differ from other archetypes because these three have an impact on conscious experience.

According to Jung, archetypes are theorized to exist in the deepest level of our collective unconscious and are often experienced in our dreams. Stories and myths are also home to these archetypes.

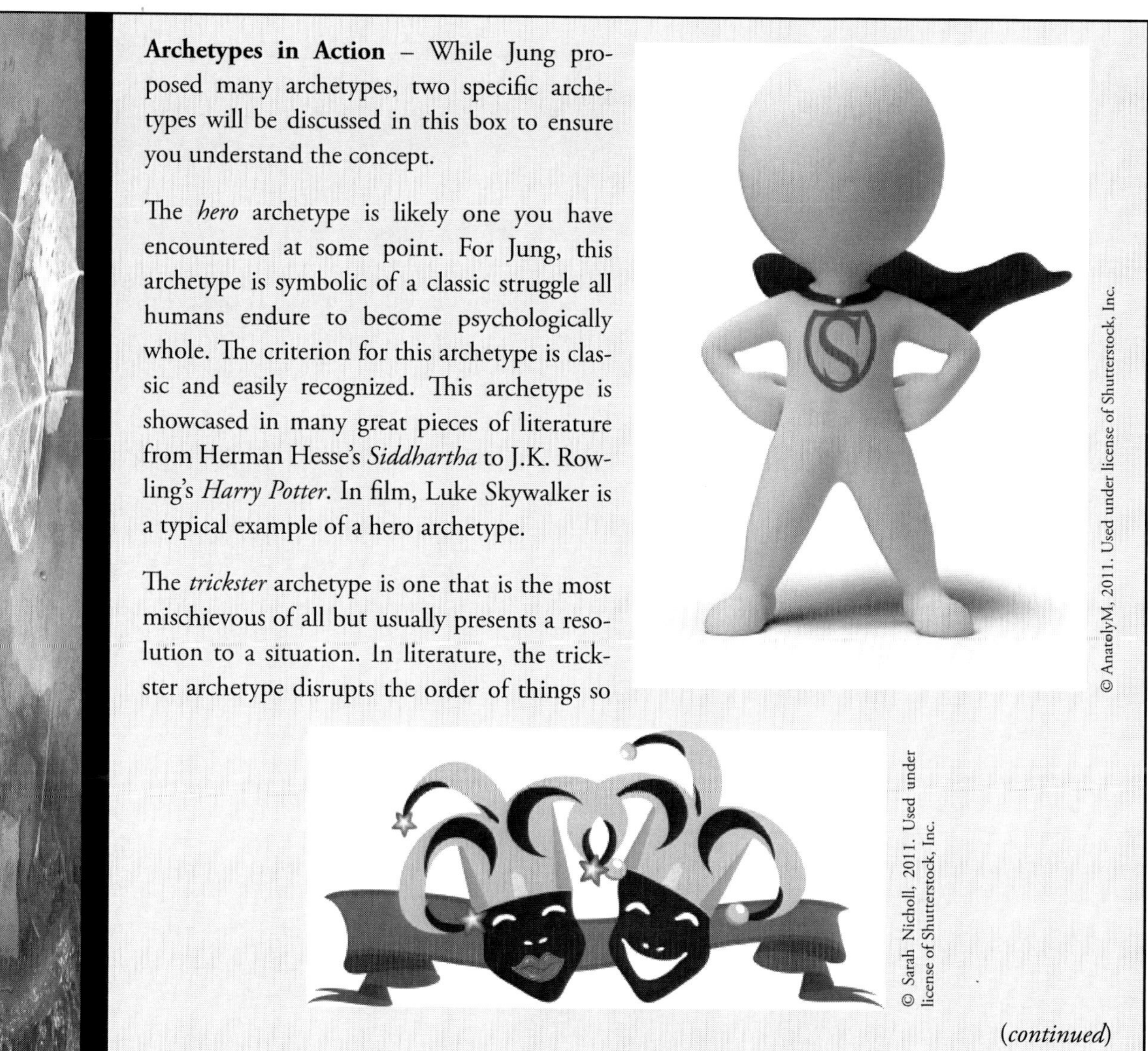

Archetypes in Action – While Jung proposed many archetypes, two specific archetypes will be discussed in this box to ensure you understand the concept.

The *hero* archetype is likely one you have encountered at some point. For Jung, this archetype is symbolic of a classic struggle all humans endure to become psychologically whole. The criterion for this archetype is classic and easily recognized. This archetype is showcased in many great pieces of literature from Herman Hesse's *Siddhartha* to J.K. Rowling's *Harry Potter*. In film, Luke Skywalker is a typical example of a hero archetype.

The *trickster* archetype is one that is the most mischievous of all but usually presents a resolution to a situation. In literature, the trickster archetype disrupts the order of things so

(*continued*)

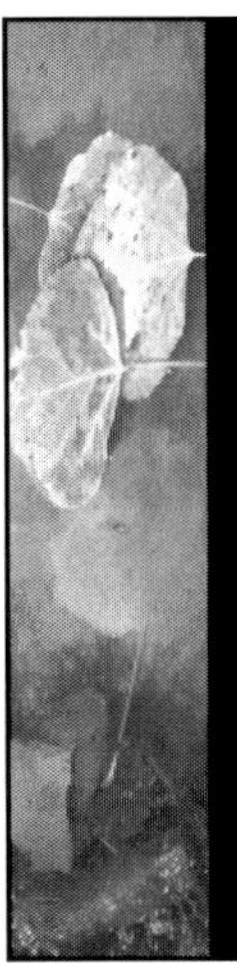

Archetypes in Action (*continued*)

change may occur. You can see this archetype in characters like Chuck Palahniuk's Tyler Durden from *Fight Club*, the character Cipher in the *Matrix Trilogy*, and William Shakespeare's character Puck from a *Midsummer Night's Dream.*

Can you think of any other classic archetypes from movies and literature that fit either of two archetypes just discussed?

Jung's theory remains very controversial in contemporary psychology. Even some of his contemporaries such as Sigmund Freud accused Jung of being too "mystical." Critics often argue that Jung ignored science and lacked empirical backing for his assertions.

Alfred Adler

Much like Jung, Adler was initially influenced by Freud's ideas early in his career. However, over time Adler created his own approach to both therapy and understanding personality.

During his childhood Adler was accident prone and suffered from many physical illnesses. In fact, his first memory involved lying in a hospital bed as a 2-year old with rickets. When he was 5 years of age Adler caught pneumonia and recalled hearing a conversation between his father and a doctor in which the doctor indicated that it was so serious he might die. In addition, Adler remembered being very competitive with his older brother but always seemed to come up short. Adler learned to compensate for his physical problems and found great academic success, even being described as a mathematical prodigy (Bottome, 1947).

It was almost certainly out of these formative experiences that the basis of Adler's theory emerged (Adler, 1929). He believed that all individuals experienced some sort of *inferiority.* If this inferiority was not dealt with in a healthy fashion, he believed it could develop into one of two complexes. An *inferiority complex* occurs when a person feels as though he or she will never be good enough and does not have the strength to overcome life's basic difficulties. A person could also overcompensate in the other direction and develop what Adler called a *superiority complex,* which occurs when people believe they are better than others in almost every aspect. In reality, a superiority complex is masking one's true, unconscious feelings of inferiority.

Adler believed a healthy outcome was achieved through *striving* toward growth and one's personal best. He emphasized that this process required the person to call on the courage within him or her self. In therapy, Adler attempted to identify mistaken styles of life and encouraged people to strive toward what he called a socially useful style of life that involved love, work, and social interaction.

Adler also made famous the idea of the *family constellation.* The family constellation pays special attention to the birth order of children in a family. Adler believed that birth order, along with other factors such as the sex of the child, substantially influenced personality development. Adler also emphasized parent-training programs in which he attempted to help parents avoid either pampering or neglecting their children.

Birth Order in Action – Adler identified certain personality characteristics that he believed most people possessed based on their birth order within their family of origin. This idea remains very popular, despite inconsistent findings, and many current research studies are done with birth order as an important consideration.

Adler believed the following about birth order:

Firstborn Children – Alder viewed firstborn children as problem children. They come into the world as the only child and therefore reap the benefits of all their parents' attention. However, when the second child is born they experience what Adler described as "dethronement." As a result of this, these children may become burned out later in life by trying too hard to regain the throne taken from them by the new child.

(*continued*)

Birth Order in Action (*continued*)

Second-Born Children – Alder believed these children had the most favorable position. Due to the fact that the firstborn child has already carved out a path for him- or herself, second-born children often go against the grain, so to speak, and discover unique ways of viewing and interacting with the world. Furthermore, this child has always had to share parental love and attention, and thus, is rarely spoiled.

Youngest Children – Adler believed that youngest children grew up at extreme risk of being pampered by their parents, which can lead to the child's being spoiled. This can lead to these children having trouble developing independence as they get older.

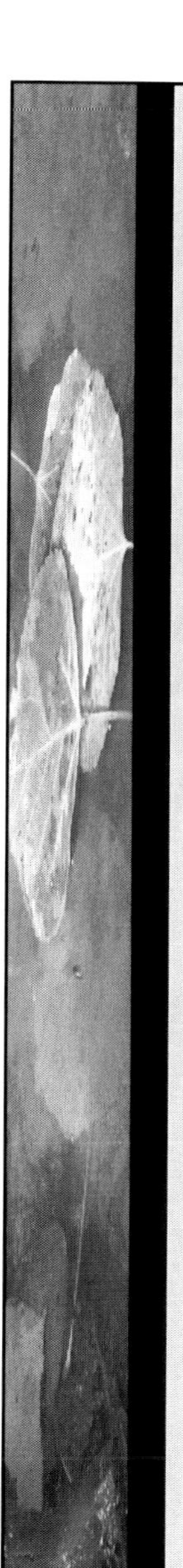

Birth Order in Action *(continued)*

Only Children – Alder believed these children were often spoiled due to the fact that they have no competition for their parents' attention. Alder also believed these children were at risk for developing a dependent relationship with their mothers and also an inflated sense of self-worth in the world since their needs tend to be met whenever they want them met due to lack of sibling competition.

After reading Adler's descriptions of birth order, do you believe these categories are accurate?

Are they accurate descriptions of you?

Do they fit for a current or former romantic partner?

What would you change and why?

Karen Horney (pronounced HORN-eye)

You have probably noticed this is the first woman who has been discussed in this chapter. Like many academic disciplines nearly a century ago, white men dominated the field of psychology. To put things in perspective, Horney was one of just 58 women at the University of Freiburg when she enrolled in 1906 in a class that included nearly 2,300 men. Horney was able to break through the male-dominated field of psychology at the time with her unique combination of intellect, feistiness, and willingness to speak her mind. Like many other influential psychoanalytic thinkers of her time period, Horney initially indentified with many of Freud's ideas only to later distance herself from some of his core concepts. The end result was a theory of personality that integrated ideas proposed by Freud, Jung, and Adler.

Horney's theory focused on the relationship between a child and his or her parents (Horney, 1945). She believed that inadequate parenting early in life led to the development of *basic anxiety,* which is the feeling of loneliness and insecurity in a potentially hostile world. A feeling of *basic hostility* accompanies this feeling of basic anxiety but is repressed by the child because the consequences of expressing it could result in being rejected or punished by the parents. The way in which a child reacts to these feelings is the primary influence on psychological functioning.

Horney identified three ways in which people seek to connect with the world around them: moving towards, moving against, and moving away. The *moving toward* orientation involves seeking love and acceptance from others, *moving against* involves trying to assert authority and control, and *moving away* is characterized by seeking autonomy and independence from others. Horney believed that mentally healthy individuals had a balance of all three styles and understood in what contexts each of the three styles served an adaptive function. In contrast, she noted that people who experienced inadequate parenting early in life tended to rely too heavily on one style thus resulting in poor mental health.

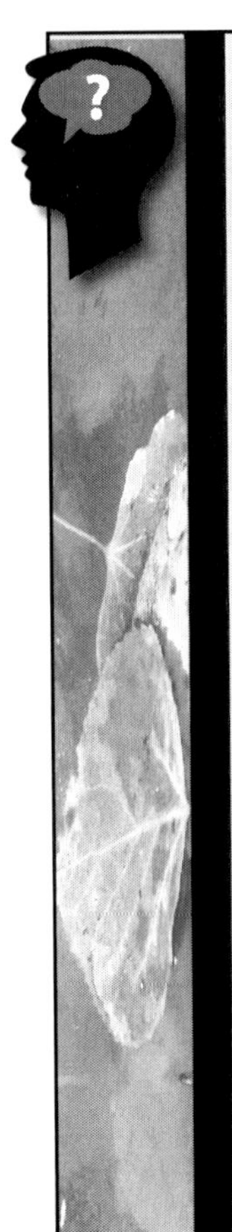

Think About It – It might be easy to dismiss theories such as the ones created by Freud or Jung approximately a century after their creation. And while certain aspects of their theories may be obsolete, these theories laid the groundwork for modern psychology.

It is also important to be humble about our current interpretations of personality (some of which we will discuss later on in the chapter). How do you think people will view what we believe to be true about the world 100 years from now?

Trait Theories

Trait theorists hold the belief that behavior can be described and measured by a basic unit referred to as a trait. This was a stark contrast to the psychoanalytic thinkers of the time whose constructs could not readily be measured. Trait theorists proposed that traits could be inferred from language, observation, and behavior. Traits are theoretical constructs that have allowed for expanded research in the field of personality. Some researchers attempted to further refine this approach by finding more global personality factors that could be applied to many people.

Gordon Allport

Unlike some of the theorists who came before him, Allport was not particularly interested in mental illness and what was wrong with people. He also believed, unlike the psychoanalysts, that the statements of people could most often be taken at face value. In other words, there was no need to dig deeper into some sort of unconscious structure. Allport is widely credited as teaching the first personality course in the United States at Harvard University in 1937.

Allport focused most of his efforts on attempting to understand what he referred to as unique traits. He believed that it might appear on the surface that two people had the same trait, but if one was to dig deeper, he would discover that "no two persons ever have precisely the same trait" (Allport, 1937, p. 297). Allport famously inferred traits from Webster's Dictionary in which he found nearly 18,000 traits. He also inferred traits from documents such as letters, behavior, and personality measures.

Generally speaking, Allport was skeptical with regard to the use statistics and methodology as a tool to attempt to understand personality traits. As you might have guessed, given his affinity for unique traits, Allport favored a more idiographic approach (individual case studies). His biggest fear was that the uniqueness of the individual would get lost in methodological excess (Allport, 1940). He believed the best way to understand the unique traits of individuals was to engage them in direct conversation.

Raymond Cattell

In contrast to Allport, Cattell was a strong proponent for the use of statistics and research methods as a means to understanding personality traits. He pioneered the use of a complicated statistical procedure called factor analysis in personality study. This procedure allowed Cattell to take the tens of thousands of traits like the ones identified by Allport and condense them into a smaller number of more general factors that could be applied to the masses in an effort to help predict behavior. Cattell (1957) called factor analysis "a research tool as important to psychology as the microscope was to biology" (p. 4).

Through factor analysis, Cattell was able to create his famous personality test called the 16-PF (16 Personality Factors). This test measured 16 underlying traits of personality using 16 multiple-choice scales. The 16 factors measured were warmth, reasoning, emotional stability, dominance, liveliness, rule-consciousness, social boldness, sensitivity, vigilance, abstractness, privateness, apprehension, openness to change, self-reliance, perfectionism, and tension. This was a revolutionary step in the study of personality because it allowed for a form of empirical measurement in a way that had not previously been accomplished.

What Do You Think?– Although Allport and Cattell taught together for a short time at Harvard University, Cattell remarked that he believed it was often tough on students because when it came to understanding personality, they "spoke two different languages." Allport emphasized unique traits and was skeptical of the use of statistics and research, whereas Cattell believed empirical understanding of personality was imperative.

After considering both positions, which one do you most agree with and why?

The Big Five Factors of Personality

Personality researchers Paul Costa and Robert McCrae (1992) followed in Cattell's footsteps and used factor analysis to create the Big Five Factors of Personality. The Big Five are referred to by many in the field as the gold standard for contemporary trait measurement.

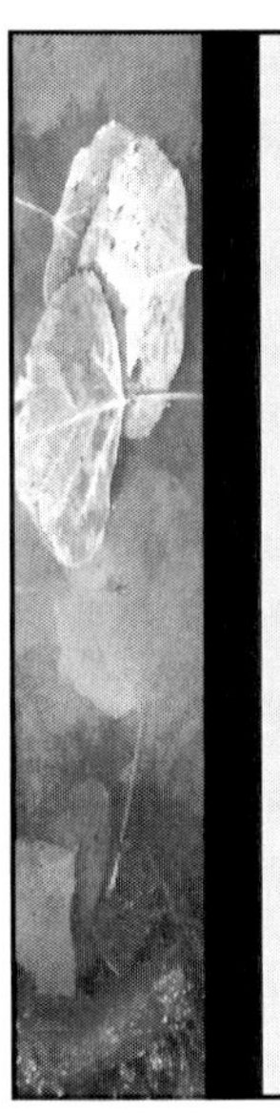

Study Tip – An easy way to remember the Big Five Factors is to remember the word **OCEAN** as noted below.

Openness

Conscientiousness

Extraversion

Agreeableness

Neuroticism

It is important to think of each of these five factors as existing on a continuum. In other words, with regard to openness, for example, one is not simply open or closed to experience. Instead, there is a large degree in between where most people fall.

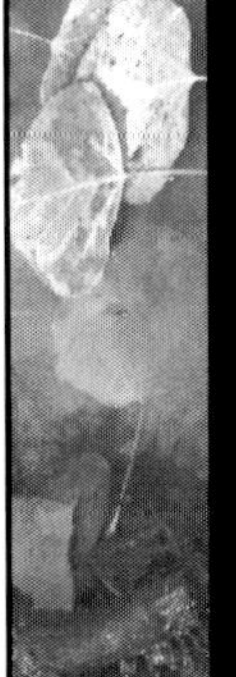

The Big Five in Action

For each of the Big Five listed below, put an X on the line where you believe you fall on the continuum. After you complete this, go back and put an O on the line where you believe your "ex" or a former romantic partner falls. Each continuum moves from low score to high score with some examples of traits of high and low scorers within each factor listed below. *Try and be an honest and objective evaluator!*

(*continued*)

The Big Five in Action (*continued*)

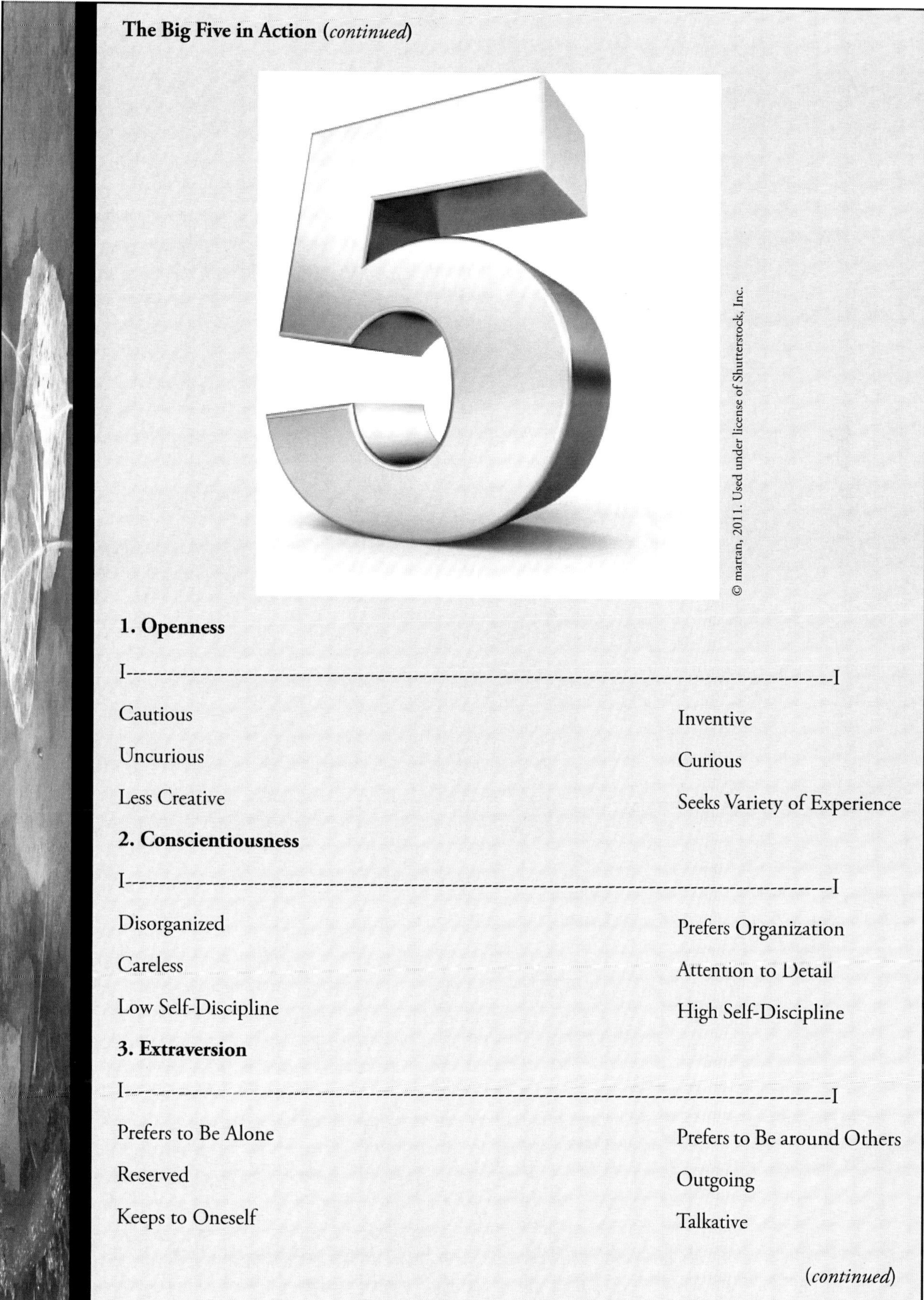

1. Openness

I--I

Cautious	Inventive
Uncurious	Curious
Less Creative	Seeks Variety of Experience

2. Conscientiousness

I--I

Disorganized	Prefers Organization
Careless	Attention to Detail
Low Self-Discipline	High Self-Discipline

3. Extraversion

I--I

Prefers to Be Alone	Prefers to Be around Others
Reserved	Outgoing
Keeps to Oneself	Talkative

(*continued*)

The Big Five in Action (*continued*)

4. Agreeableness

I--I

Cold/Detached	Friendly
Suspicious	Trusting
Antagonistic	Cooperative

5. Neuroticism

I--I

Calm	Nervous
Secure	Self-Conscious
Less Emotional	More Emotional

Now that you have completed this activity, look at where you believe both you and your "ex" fell on each continuum. Speculate as to why this relationship was unsuccessful and write down your hypotheses below:

Humanistic Theories

Humanists believe that every person comes into the world with an innate inner drive to realize her or his full potential. Moreover, they believe that human beings are basically good. In other words, people are not born evil. They are at worst neutral.

Unlike the theorists who came before them, humanists paid special attention to feelings. They believed personality developed based not on our reaction to unconscious childhood trauma or measurable personality traits, but instead developed as a result of our internal feeling states and basic feelings of self-worth. Subjective internal states help guide us toward our "true" or "authentic" selves.

Carl Rogers and Abraham Maslow are widely credited as making the most substantial contributions to humanistic psychology.

Carl Rogers

While Rogers did not consider biological impacts on personality as overly important, his theory is based on a biological metaphor. Rogers created a term called the *actualizing tendency*, which is the force for positive growth that is innate in all living things (Rogers, 1961). This tendency is what guides us toward reaching our full potential and achieving self-fulfillment. Rogers also described the importance of trusting our inner feelings or impulses (gut feelings). He referred to this as the *organismic valuing process* and believed that these inner feelings guided us in the direction of growth and good mental health (Rogers, 1964).

Rogers also spent a great deal of time investigating the "self." He described both the *real self* and the *ideal self.* Rogers described the ideal self as the self we felt we "should" be. The ideal self is often influenced by society and those around us as well as by our need for approval. The ideal self is something that is always out of reach, so to speak, and is a standard we simply cannot meet.

Rogers believed the real self was the self that contained the actualizing tendency, or our innate tendency for growth. This self is authentic and contains our real or authentic qualities. The real self leads to good health while over identification with the ideal self can lead to poor mental health.

A person experiences what Rogers referred to as *incongruence* when there is a conflict between the real and ideal self. In other words, incongruence occurs when there is a difference between whom one actually is (real self) and whom one thinks one should be (ideal self). Rogers believed this led to neuroses or poor mental health. To achieve good mental health Rogers posited people must experience *congruence,* which is when a relative degree of consistency exists between the ideal and real self.

When congruence occurs there is substantial overlap between the way we see ourselves (self-image) and what we are actually experiencing in the world (experience) as noted in Figure 11.1.

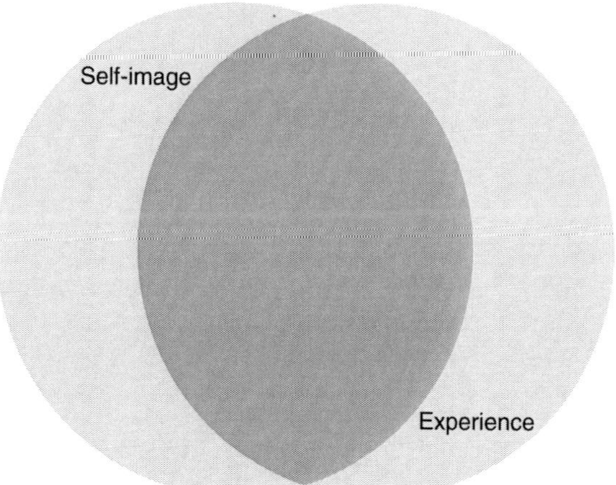

Figure 11.1 Rogers' concept of congruence.

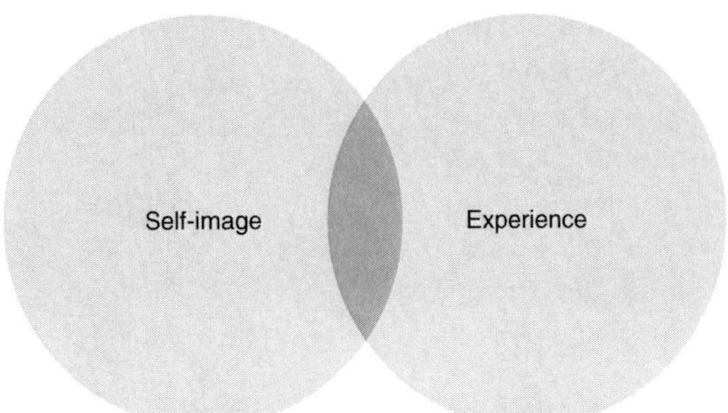

Figure 11.2 Rogers' concept of incongruence.

On the other hand, incongruence occurs when there is very little overlap between our self-image and our experience in the world (see Figure 11.2).

Perhaps Rogers' most important contribution to psychology was his client-centered approach to therapy. This will be discussed in detail in Chapter 12 when approaches to therapy are covered.

Abraham Maslow

Remember Maslow's theory as discussed in Chapter 9?

In terms of personality, Maslow believed, like Rogers, that human beings are basically good and have an innate drive toward growth and self-fulfillment. Maslow spent much of his time researching the process of self-actualization, or the way in which people attempt to reach their full potential. He found that self-actualized people were able to reach their potential through a complex blend of forming meaningful relationships while also maintaining uniqueness and individuality within the culture they are a part of (Maslow, 1968). He thought of self-actualization as an ongoing journey that one experienced throughout life as opposed to a final destination or goal that one simply arrived at. In fact, Maslow believed very few people ever attained self-actualization in its purest form.

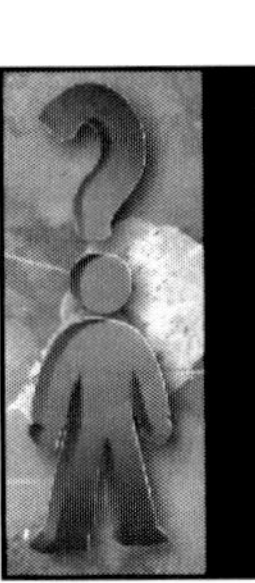

What Do You Think? – Both Rogers and Maslow believed that people were basically good and at worst neutral. What do you think? Is this a naïve assumption? Make sure to support your answers.

They also believed that people had a natural tendency toward growth. What do you think about this assumption?

Social-Cognitive Theory

Social-cognitive theorists pay specific attention to the external environment around a person and the way the environment shapes the person as well as the way the person shapes the environment. The environment, along with what we think about the world around us, helps to form personality. So, in other words, the way we think about people and the world around us is key to understanding personality similarities and differences.

Albert Bandura

When most people think of Bandura, they think of his famous Bobo doll study as discussed in Chapter 3. However, Bandura himself has stated that he believes his most important contribution is that of self-efficacy. *Self-efficacy* can be thought of as someone's belief about whether he or she expects to be successful. Bandura (1980) defined an individual with high self-efficacy as one who could "organize and execute given courses of action required to deal with prospective situations." Furthermore, if an individual believes he or she will be successful, it will impact the amount of effort he or she exerts and the goals he or she sets.

ACTIVITY

Take out a piece of notebook paper and crumble it up. Now find a trashcan. Stand approximately 10 feet from the trashcan. Now shoot the paper as if it were a basketball. Once you make the shot, move back 5 feet. Once you make that shot, move back another 5 feet.

What did you notice about this activity? Chances are if you made the shot on your first several tries, it made you more confident. You might have also noticed your level of motivation for participating increase as well as the amount of effort and thinking/strategy you put into the activity.

If, on the other hand, you missed your first several shots, you probably noticed a contradictory effect. Your confidence likely decreased, as did your motivation and effort level. This is self-efficacy in action!

Bandura also discussed what he called *reciprocal determinism,* which is the concept that behavior, cognitions, and environment all interact to help form personality (see Figure 11.3). That is, what we think and how we act influences the environment around us just as the environment influences how we think and act.

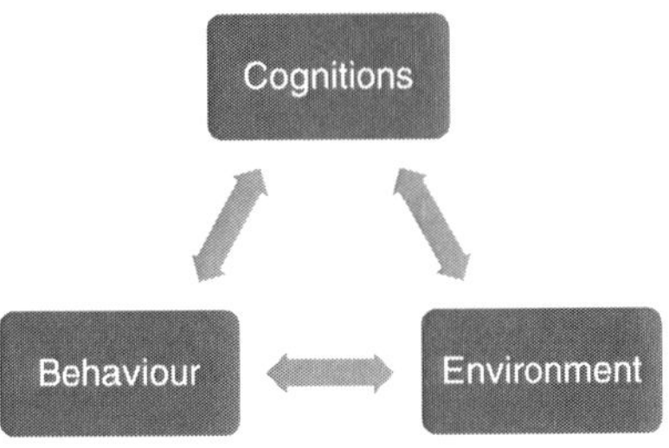

Figure 11.3 Bandura's reciprocal determinism.

CAN WE MEASURE PERSONALITY?

Over time psychologists have made substantial efforts to quantify or measure personality. Theorists such as Raymond Cattell were very much in favor of this. As Cattell (1957) once noted, "I have always felt justifiably suspicious of theory built too much ahead of data" (p. 50). On the other hand, theorists such as Carl Jung, Gordon Allport, and Abraham Maslow were skeptical of traditional science and attempts to quantify human personality. Maslow (1968) once famously proclaimed, "Science is the only way we have of shoving truth down the reluctant throat" (p. viii).

It seems there will always exist a certain tension between those who wish to understand personality through subjective experience and those who wish to obtain a more objective and scientific understanding. Perhaps the study of personality is better as a result of this ongoing tension. Whatever the case, it is important to understand some of the basic tools psychologists use to try and measure personality.

Observations

One way psychologists can gather data about someone's personality is by observing that person's behavior and expressive traits. This is done systematically, and ideally, in multiple contexts. Such observations can provide valuable insights into how a person behaves and what external variables may be informing that behavior.

Stop and Think – While observations may sound like an easy way to gather data, they are often time consuming. Moreover, it is quite possible that two people could view the same person engaging in the very same behavior and describe and interpret that event differently. Also, people often behave differently when they know they are being watched, which could adversely impact the results.

Clinical Interviews

A clinical interview is a tool that has been used by psychologists and personality theorists of many different orientations for over a century. These interviews can take a very structured form where psychologists follow a pre-established format and sequence of questions or a semi-structured form where a person's answer to any particular question can lead to a spontaneous question formulated by the psychologist based on answers to previous queries. Certain structured interview formats can include numerical rating scales that help to get a more objective picture of the participant and allow for the ability to compare her or his responses with others.

© Ambrophoto, 2011. Used under license of Shutterstock, Inc.

While interviews can provide valuable insights into personality, this method is not without its flaws. People can, of course, lie to an interviewer and may wish to represent themselves as better or worse than they actually are depending on the circumstances. Interviewers might also make different interpretations of the same self-report data.

Projective Tests

Many of you have probably seen the famous "inkblot" tests in popular culture portrayals.

The goal of these tests is to get participants to "project" parts of their personality onto ambiguous stimuli like a card from the *Rorschach Inkblot Test.* Psychoanalytic practitioners such as Freud believed that projective tests provided insight into unconscious elements of personality (parts of personality one is not aware of) that patients would not disclose if asked directly. Other tests such as the *Thematic Apperception Test (TAT)* attempt to do the same thing by showing participants black-and-white pictures of people and then asking the participant to tell a story about what is happening.

© ker toh, 2011. Used under license of Shutterstock, Inc.

Despite their long history and continued use, projective tests remain controversial. Critics argue that projective tests traditionally lack statistical validity (measuring what they purport to measure) and reliability (consistency of the results). More specifically, there can be problems with what is called interrater reliability, which is the degree of agreement between two or more people observing and interpreting the same response. In other words, two psychologists could interpret the same response on a projective test differently, thus making these test results too subjective in the eyes of some.

Objective Tests

This type of assessment often uses self-report inventories or questionnaires. These kinds of tests utilize the nomothetic approach to studying personality as noted at the outset of the chapter. These tests must demonstrate statisti-

© Jirsak, 2011. Used under license of Shutterstock, Inc.

cal validity and reliability as well as meet important empirical standards before they are accepted as useful tools in the field.

One clear advantage of objective tests is that they can be administered to a large number of people in a relatively short period of time. They also allow for a certain amount of generalizability. These are just several of the reasons why objective tests are generally the most frequently used tool in personality assessment.

The most commonly used and empirically validated objective personality test is the *Minnesota Multiphasic Personality Inventory (MMPI)*. The MMPI is currently in its second edition. The test consists of 567 items and can take, on average, between one to two hours to complete. Participants are asked to respond "True," "False," or "Cannot say" to statements such as:

My sleep is fitful and disturbed

My soul sometimes leaves my body

I like mechanics magazines

No one seems to understand me

The MMPI is designed to help psychologists understand personality as well as help them diagnose what may be troubling an individual seeking therapy or other psychological services. To meet this end, there are 10 clinical subscales. For example, people who are experiencing symptoms of depression are likely to score higher on certain questions while people with symptoms of schizophrenia are likely to score higher on a separate set of questions. There are also four validity scales that research has shown are quite effective at identifying people who are lying, answering randomly, or trying to act either more or less psychologically healthy than they actually are (Weiner, 2008).

While objective tests are widely used, it does not mean they are exempt from criticism or have no weaknesses. Many other assessments are not as comprehensive and thorough as the MMPI, and thus are more susceptible to participants lying and either "faking good" or "faking bad." Cultural bias can be a problem, too. Critics point to research that indicates participants from Mexico, Central America, and South America consistently score higher on some of the clinical scales of the MMPI, which raises questions about whether the test is biased toward a more Western notion of what is healthy and unhealthy (Lucio et al., 2001).

What Do You Think? – After completing this chapter, what do you believe is the best way to understand personality? Science? Philosophy? Mysticism? Some other mechanism of construing reality? Make sure to defend your position.

REFERENCES

Adler, A. (1929). *The practice and theory of individual psychology* (P. Radin, Trans.) (2nd ed.). London: Routledge & Kegan Paul.

Allport, G. W. (1937). *Personality: A psychological interpretation.* New York: Henry Holt.

Allport, G. W. (1940). The psychologist's frame of reference. *Psychological Bulletin, 37,* 1–28.

Bandura, A. (1980). Gauging the relationship between self-efficacy, judgment, and action. *Cognitive Therapy and Research, 4,* 263–268.

Bottome, P. (1947). *Alfred Adler: Apostle of freedom* (J. Linton & R. Vaughn, Trans.). London: Faber & Faber.

Cattell, R. B. (1957). *Personality and motivation structure of measurement.* Yonkers, NY: World.

Costa, P. T., Jr., & McCrae, R. R. (1992). Four ways five factors are basic. *Personality and Individual Differences, 13, 653-665.*

Hermans, H. J. M. (1988). On the integration of nomothetic and idiographic research methods in the study of personal meaning. *Journal of Personality, 56,* 785–812.

Horney, K. (1945). *Our inner conflicts: A constructive theory of neurosis.* New York: Norton.

Jung, C. G., (1963). *Memories, dreams, reflections.* New York: Random House.

Lucio, E., Ampudia, A., Duran, C., Leon, I., & Butcher, J. N. (2001). Comparison of the Mexican and American norms of the MMPI-2. *Journal of Clinical Psychology, 57,* 1459–1468.

Marshall, M., & Brown, J. D. (2008). *On the psychological benefits of self-enhancement: Theory, research, and clinical implications* (pp. 19–35). Washington, DC: American Psychological Association.

Maslow, A. H. (1968). *Toward a psychology of being* (2nd ed.). New York: Van Nostrand.

Rogers, C. R. (1961). *On becoming a person: A therapist's view of psychotherapy.* Boston: Houghton Mifflin.

Rogers, C. R. (1964). Toward a modern approach to values: The valuing process in the mature person. *Journal of Abnormal and Social Psychology, 68,* 160–167.

Triandis, H. C. (2001). Individualism-collectivism and personality. *Journal of Personality, 69,* 907–924.

Weiner, G. (2008). *Handbook of personality assessment.* Hoboken, NJ: Wiley.

NAME ____ DATE ______________________

WORKSHEET CHAPTER ELEVEN

CHAPTER 12

INTRODUCTION TO CLINICAL AND COUNSELING PSYCHOLOGY

"I cannot forget what one of my patients once answered when I asked him, 'What do you believe was the reason that I could succeed to cure you after all these years of misery?' He answered, "'I became sick because I had lost all hope. And you gave me hope.'"
— Alfred Adler

In this chapter we will explore both the history and current interpretations of "mental illness," including contemporary psychological diagnosis. In order to do so effectively, we will have to attempt to distinguish so-called "normal" behavior from behavior considered to be "abnormal," which can be a very tricky exercise (as you will soon find out). After defining the general criteria for abnormal behavior, we will then explore the primary tool used for diagnosis in psychology as well as more specific diagnostic categories and patterns.

After gaining an understanding of some of the most common symptoms and behaviors clinicians are likely to see in therapy, the second half of the chapter will focus on psychological treatment approaches, of which there are many. The focus will be on some of the most widely used and important approaches both historically and in modern therapeutic practice. Current research about treatment effectiveness and what clients find most helpful in therapy will also be discussed.

PSYCHOLOGICAL DISORDERS AND DIAGNOSIS

History

The idea of what is normal or abnormal behavior has been something present in virtually all cultures since the beginning of time. However, the way in which various civilizations have attempted to *explain* and *treat* this behavior over the course of history has varied quite substantially.

During the Neolithic Era, the consensus was that people who demonstrated the same sort of patterns that would meet the criteria for modern psychological diagnosis were under control of evil spirits. The accepted treatment of the time involved engaging in a process referred to as *trephining,* which was exercised by drilling a hole in the front of the skull to allow the evil spirit to leave the body (Millon, 2004).

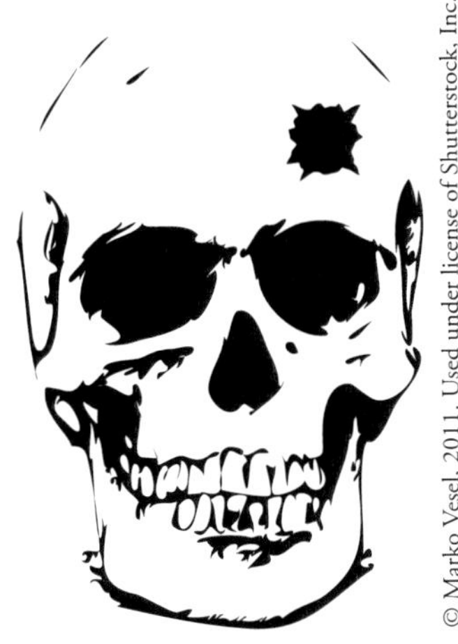

© Marko Vesel, 2011. Used under license of Shutterstock, Inc.

In Europe during the Middle Ages it was common to believe that people demonstrating abnormal behavior were possessed by the devil. A method of choice for attempting to cure the person was the process of *exorcism,* which involved using loud noises, prayer, potions, and physical violence to chase away the evil spirit. Toward the latter end of this time period, people were being locked up in asylums where inhumane treatment was unfortunately all too common (Millon, 2004).

In the late 1700s, a French physician named Philippe Pinel began questioning the ethics of locking people up in asylums, which he believed were essentially prisons. The conditions were so bad at this time that many inmates had no lighting or heat in their cells. Pinel noticed that not all of these individuals were the same and that there were many subtleties and nuances in their conditions. He began having conversations with people and noticed an improvement in their conditions, some so much that they could be released and function in the world again. He advocated that psychological treatments always be tried before more severe methods such as medication or involuntary confinement were used. Pinel's work was in many ways the first step toward formulating what is now referred to as the use of the medical model in psychology.

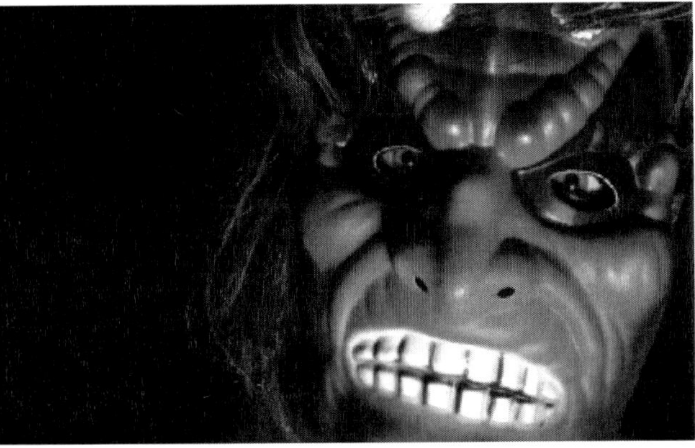

© Diego Cervo, 2011. Used under license of Shutterstock, Inc.

During the 1940s in the United States, the events of World War II created a previously unmatched need for psychological services. Pepinsky, Hill-Frederick, and Epperson (1978) indicated that a need for psychological services was created by the large number of veterans returning from combat and their subsequent need to be re-assimilated into everyday life. This led to a marriage of sorts between the scientific method, medicine, and psychology. Hill and Corbett (1993) elaborated on two specific "White/Western-European cultural values" (p. 4), including individuals' quests for self-fulfillment and the positivist belief in science and its ability to provide answers to complex questions that laid the groundwork for the emergence of a type of psychological counseling that would be critically examined using the scientific method.

© Unholy Vault Designs, 2011. Used under license of Shutterstock, Inc.

Schwebel (1984) noted that a strong commitment to the scientific method was upheld after World War II because the federal government had increased their financial support for the completion of research projects guided by the scientific method and the aforementioned cultural values of the time. Hill and Corbett also noted that the fields of clinical and counseling psychology started to gain momentum in this same timeframe, essentially meaning that the field of counseling and the use of the scientific method to study counseling came of age simultaneously.

What Do You Think? – After taking a brief look at the history of understanding psychological impairment, do you think science and the medical model represent the best ways to understand abnormal behavior? Make sure to defend your answer.

What's Normal, Anyway?

Normal or Abnormal: That Is the Question – Answer the following questions and make sure to defend your answers and state why you believe what you believe:

(continued)

Normal or Abnormal: That Is the Question *(continued)*

How does a mentally healthy person act?

How do we determine if a thought or behavior is unhealthy?

Who gets to define what is normal?

Did the culture you grew up in impact the way you answered the first three questions?

When trying to determine if a behavior is worthy of psychological treatment, psychologists typically consider four factors, all of which will be discussed in the space that follows. It is important to note that all four of these factors must be considered holistically (Hansell & Damour, 2008). Furthermore, it can be helpful to think of each one of these categories as existing on a continuum from low to high:

I--I

Low High

Statistical Infrequency

If a behavior occurs that is not frequent in the culture, this *could* be one factor that is considered when judging a behavior as abnormal. However, meeting this criterion alone is not sufficient for psychological diagnosis. Some behaviors may be statistically infrequent but not destructive in any way. In fact, some statistically infrequent behaviors may be exceptional and help advance society in important ways.

Violation of Cultural Norms or Rules

All cultures have some basic norms or rules that give recommendations or directives as to the way people should behave in given situations. Again, this criterion alone is not enough to label a behavior as unhealthy, but it is one factor worthy of consideration. There are also times when people may violate laws or norms for the greater public good. For example, think of civil rights activist Rosa Parks who refused to give up her seat on a public bus. While she broke a rule of her culture at the time, it certainly dud not mean she met the criteria for any diagnosis.

Personal Distress

This criterion focuses on how the person subjectively views his or her experience. If a person's behaviors, thoughts, or feelings cause him or her significant discomfort such that it interrupts the quality of life, he or she will likely score high on this criterion. This can sometimes be a good judge of whether someone needs psychological assistance. However, it is not a perfect indicator. Some people struggle with psychological disturbances that are egodystonic, which means they know they need help. For these people, reports of personal distress might be particularly helpful. In contrast, some people struggle with psychological disturbances that are egosyntonic, which means they do not realize they need help (addiction, antisocial personality disorder, etc.). For these individuals, this measure may be far less reliable.

Impairment or Disability

If a behavior or feeling state contributes to a person's not being able to function on a day-to-day basis (i.e.,

cannot work, does not perform basic self-care tasks such as showering and eating, has trouble forming meaningful relationships with others, etc.), he or she would likely score high on this criterion. People who score relatively high on this criterion may also may also have irrational thought patterns that could potentially lead to them engaging in high-risk behavior.

Think about it – After reading the four criteria above, it has hopefully become clear that labeling a behavior as abnormal is a difficult task. Moreover, just because a behavior is rare or runs counter to the culture does not necessarily mean it meets the criteria for a psychological diagnosis. As a general rule, if the behavior is statistically infrequent, breaks cultural rules or laws, and causes harm to self or others, it is at least worth investigating further.

Modern Day Psychological Diagnosis

Modern psychology uses a classification system of mental disorders referred to as the *Diagnostic and Statistical Manual of Mental Disorders (DSM-IV-TR)*. This is a manual that contains nearly 1000 pages and attempts to use the best available scientific research to clearly describe and classify over 200 diagnoses in 17 major categories. The first iteration of the DSM was released in 1952. The fourth version was released in 1994, with a text revision (TR) to the fourth edition released in 2000. The DSM-V is scheduled for release in May 2013, which will lead to some changes based on the latest scientific research (American Psychiatric Association, 2011). Our discussion will focus primarily on the DSM-IV-TR, which is still in use at the present time.

The DSM-IV-TR uses a five-axis approach to diagnosis as noted in Figure 12.1.

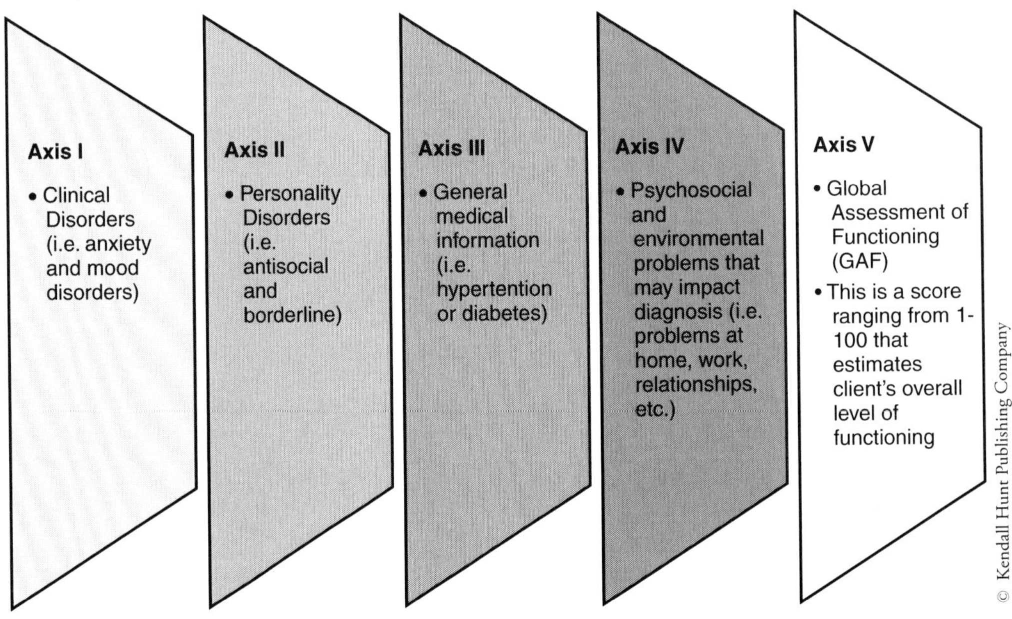

Figure 12.1 Five axes used in the DSM-IV-TR.

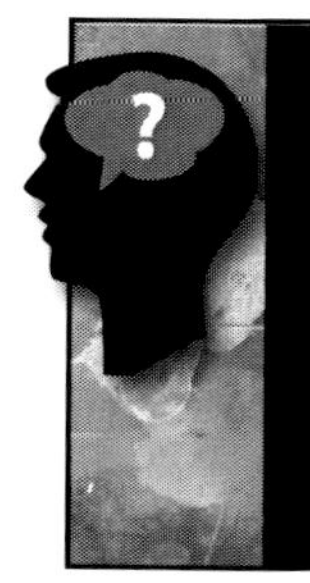

Think about it – After reading about the five-axis system of diagnosis, it might be tempting to conclude that anyone could read the DSM-IV-TR and begin diagnosing him- or herself or others. It is important to note that DSM-IV-TR was designed to be used by trained professionals in the fields of psychiatry and psychology. Thus, even as tempting as it may be, this manual was not designed for students or others without formal training to diagnosis their friends and family members.

Major Categories of Mental Disorders

As noted earlier, the DSM-IV-TR contains 17 major categories of mental disorders and over 200 diagnoses. Those 17 major categories include (1) anxiety disorders; (2) mood disorders; (3) schizophrenia and other psychotic disorders; (4) dissociative disorders; (5) personality disorders; (6) substance-related disorders; (7) somatoform disorders; (8) factitious disorders; (9) sexual and gender identity disorders; (10) eating disorders; (11) sleep disorders; (12) impulse control disorders; (13) adjustment disorders; (14) disorders usually first diagnosed in infancy, childhood, or adolescence; (15) delirium, dementia, amnestic, and other cognitive disorders; (16) mental disorders due to a general medical condition (not elsewhere classified); and (17) other conditions that may be a focus of clinical attention.

In an introductory text such at this one, it would simply be impossible to cover each one of these major categories in detail. Instead, we will cover five of the most common categories that students are often curious about.

Anxiety Disorders

Anxiety is an important natural response to stress that helps to alert the body to potential threats. It also helps provide the motivation necessary to study for a test or overcome certain obstacles in our lives. However, when an individual becomes overwhelmed by anxiety such that he or she cannot function and it disturbs his or her quality of life, he or she very well may qualify for a specific anxiety disorder. Genetics, brain chemistry, and environment are all believed to play a role in the development of anxiety disorders. Five major types of anxiety disorders will be considered.

Generalized Anxiety Disorder. People who meet the criteria for this disorder experience persistent, free-flowing anxiety that lasts for a duration of at least six months and cannot be traced to a particular event or stimulus. In other words, they often feel a sense of fear or anxiety but cannot identify what is causing it. Physical symptoms such as fatigue, headaches, body pain, trouble sleeping, excessive sweating, involuntary muscles twitches, and heart palpitations can be observed.

Post-Traumatic Stress Disorder (PTSD). In order to meet the criteria for PTSD, one must have first been exposed to a traumatic event that is characterized as being outside the realm of everyday experience. The person must then persistently re-experience the event. This often takes the form of flashbacks, nightmares, or intense physiological reactions to some outside trigger that reminds the person of the traumatic event. People must also demonstrate persistent avoidance of stimuli associated with the trauma as well as a kind of emotional numbing that involves an inability to experience certain emotions. These symptoms must be present for at least 30 days. If it has been less than 30 days and similar symptoms are present, the person is diagnosed with what is called acute stress disorder. People who have experienced combat, some kind of physical or sexual assault, or have lived through a natural disaster are particularly susceptible to developing either PTSD or acute stress disorder.

Panic Disorder. People who have reoccurring panic attacks qualify for this diagnosis. However, experiencing an isolated panic attack does not mean one has a panic disorder, as many people have at least one panic attack during their lifetime. A panic attack is a quickly occurring physiological experience in which a person experiences a sudden intense fear followed by intense physical symptoms such as trouble breathing, chest pain, heart palpitations, body weakness, and sometimes abdominal distress. Again, one does not qualify for panic disorder until several spontaneous attacks occur.

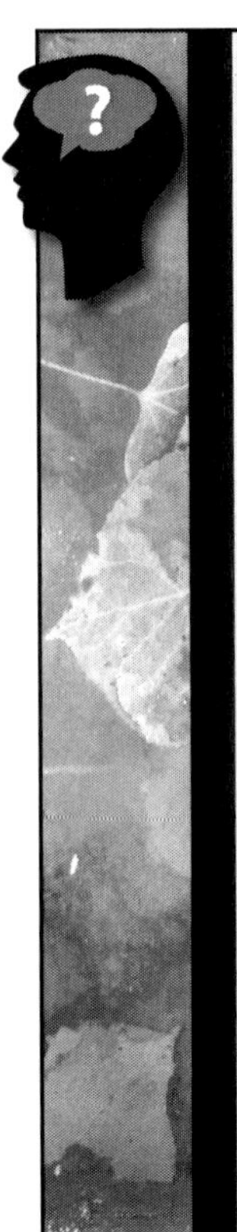

Think about it – Many people who experience a panic attack initially believe they are having a heart attack. Why do you think that is?

Phobias. Remember the story of "Little Albert" as discussed in Chapter 3? Through classical conditioning John Watson was able to create a phobia of rats in a young child. A phobia is an intense, irrational fear of a certain object or situation. The DSM-IV-TR recognizes three specific categories of phobias: specific phobias, social phobias, and agoraphobia. A *specific phobia* is a fear of a specific object or situation. These could include a specific fear of an animal, insect, heights, or being trapped in a small, enclosed space (claustrophobia). *Social phobias* often take the form of people being afraid of publicly embarrassing themselves. This could include a fear of public speaking or some other kind of performance. A fear of eating in public is also a common social phobia. *Agoraphobia* occurs when people are afraid of having a panic attack in a crowded area with no possibility of escape. For some people who qualify for the diagnosis of agoraphobia, the fear becomes so pervasive that they will not leave their homes. It is important to note that people with phobias often recognize the fear as being irrational, but the experience is still one that occurs and severely impacts their quality of life.

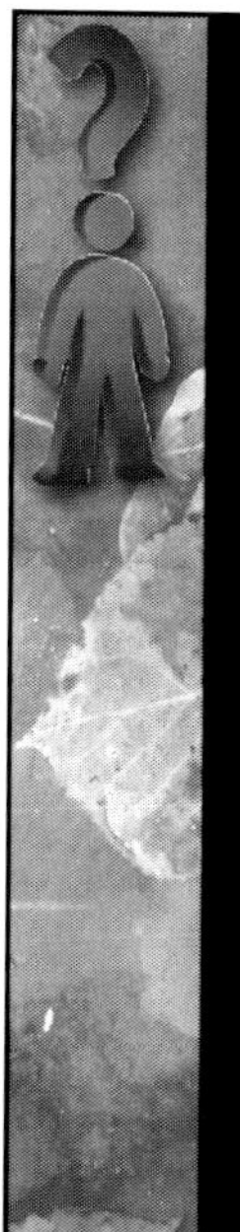

What Do You Think? – Imagine yourself being the person in the photo looking down at your feet. If you have an intense, irrational fear of this situation, in which of the three categories would your phobia likely fall? Make sure to justify your answer.

Obsessive-Compulsive Disorder (OCD). OCD is characterized by the presence of *either* unwanted obsessions or compulsions. *Obsessions* are defined as unwanted or intrusive thoughts. Common obsessions include a fear of death (oneself or a loved one), contamination, troubling sexual thoughts, or the fear they will be harmed by others. *Compulsions* are behaviors. These behaviors are usually ritualistic in nature and help to temporarily relieve an individual's anxiety. Typical compulsions include excessive hand washing, repeatedly double-checking, counting, and the need to put items is a specific order. While these compulsions may temporarily reduce anxiety, they are not an effective long-term solution. In

fact, people with OCD may spend hours everyday engaging in compulsive behaviors. This can make it difficult to maintain a normal social life or hold down a steady job. OCD is egodystonic, which means that people who meet the criteria for this diagnosis are aware their behavior is problematic and often want to change. However, the overwhelming anxiety that surfaces when they attempt to stop feeds back into the pattern of engaging in compulsions for temporary relief of anxiety.

It is worth noting that OCD will likely no longer be considered as an anxiety disorder when the DSM-V is released. The primary reason for this is the emergence of new research that demonstrates specific neural pathways in the brain associated with the presentation of OCD that differ from the other anxiety disorders (American Psychiatric Association, 2011).

Mood Disorders

You may not have heard the term "mood disorder" before. Chances are, though, you have heard the term depression. All of the diagnoses in this category have some kind of depressive component. Moreover, they represent a pattern of dramatic fluctuation in mood away from one's "normal" or baseline feeling state. Much like anxiety disorders, a combination of genetics, brain chemistry, and environment are believed to lead to mood disorders.

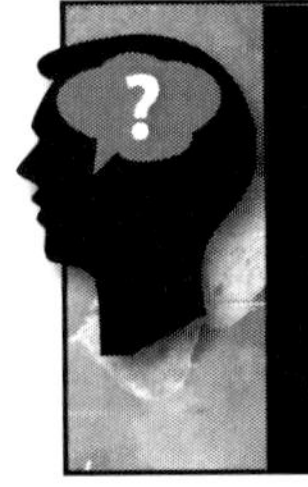

Think about it – As we begin exploring mood disorders, it is important to understand just how significant the disturbance is for people who meet the diagnostic criteria. This is not simply a "case of the blahs" or having "the blues" as all human beings experience at various times throughout their lives. Instead, these are huge fluctuations in mood that dramatically interfere with a person's quality of life and, in some cases, their safety and well being.

Major Depressive Disorder. Symptoms of major depressive disorder take the form of persistent sadness, the inability to feel pleasure, loss of interest in once pleasureable activities, significant weight loss, and a change in social, educational, or occupational functioning. The symptoms must be consistently present for at least a two-week period and not be better accounted for by another diagnosis. People struggling with major depressive disorder often cannot trace the depressive episode back to a specific situation or event, and the depression is usually so severe that people stop taking care of themselves, cannot go to work or school, and have sleep distrubances. In some cases a major depressive episode can be accompanied by psychosis (being detached from reality) and sucicidal ideation. In addition, cognitive problems are often present where a person has trouble engaging in problem solving and thinking rationally (Swartz, 2004).

Most major depressive episodes, if left untreated, will last for about six months. However, some cases can last for years.

What Do You Think? – When do you believe a person suffering from a major depressive episode is most likely to attempt suicide and why?

Dysthymic Disorder. This is a disorder characterized by a low-grade depression that is present more days than not for at least two years. The symptoms are similar but less severe (sleep disruption, low self-esteem, eating too much or too little, trouble concetraiting, feelings of hopelessness, etc.) than what is seen in major depressive disorder. However, about half of all people who are diagnosed with dysthymic disorder will have at least one episode of major depression at some point in their lives.

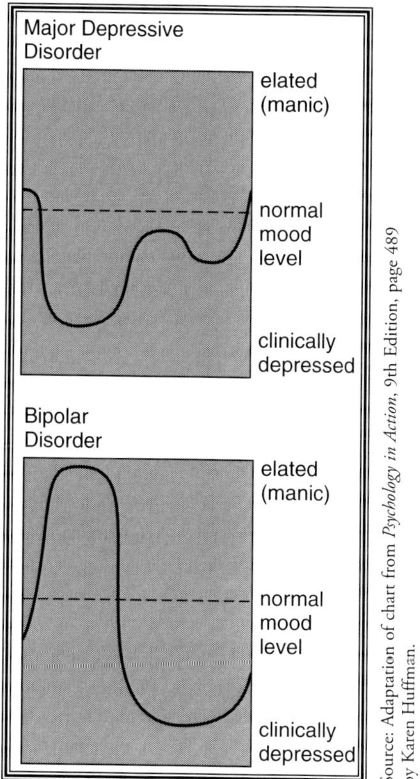

Source: Adaptation of chart from *Psychology in Action*, 9th Edition, page 489 by Karen Huffman.

Figure 12.2

Bipolar Depression. This diagnosis is characterized by extreme highs and lows in mood. The lows are similar to what a person experiences during a major depressive episode. However, instead of simply returning to baseline mood after a period of time, people struggling with bipolar disorder fluctuate to an overexcited state of being well above baseline mood. These highs are referred to as *mania.* When a person is experiencing a manic episode, he or she tends to have incredibly high amounts of energy, talk very quickly, move fast from one thought to another, not sleep for days for days at a time, have an inflated sense of self, and may have delusions of grandeur (feeling as though they are someone very important or even famous). During a manic episode, people may devise seemingly unrealistic schemes to get rich and engage in other risky forms of behavior. There is often a sense of detachment from reality. Manic episodes can last anywhere from a few days to months at a time, whereas the depressive episode of the biplar cycle typically lasts much longer. People struggling with bipolar disorder are at a substantially higher risk for substance abuse and dependence. Moreover, bipolar depression has a suicide risk significantly above the rate of many other DSM-IV-TR diagnoses as well as that of the general population (Hawton et al., 2005).

It should be noted that there are actually two types of bipolar disorder. What was just descripted above is Bipolar I Disorder. Bipolar II Disorder consists of what is called hypomania, which is a less severe form of mania. So in other words, the high is not quite so high and typically does not carry with it a sense of detachment from reality.

Cyclothymic Disorder. Just as dysthymic disorder is a sort of low-grade depression, cyclothymic disorder can be thought of as a low-grade form of bipolar disorder. The highs are periods of hypomania, whereas the lows are dysthymic as opposed to major depressive level lows.

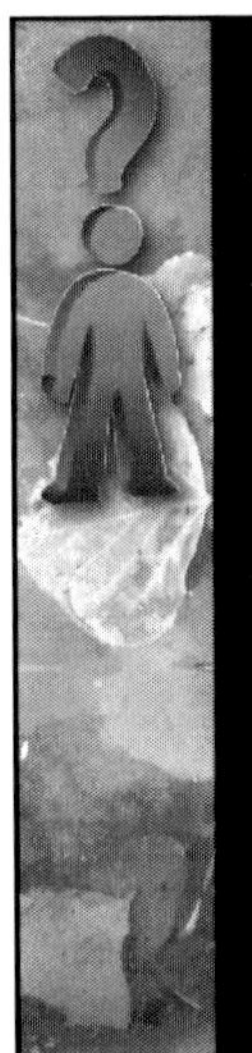

What Do You Think? – It is interesting to note that mood disorders are diagnosed at a rate two to three times higher in women than men. Why do believe this is? Make sure to defend your response.

Schizophrenia. Schizophrenia is a chronic and severe brain-based disorder with a strong genetic component (people who share genes with someone who has schizophrenia are at an elevated risk of developing the disorder themselves) that causes people to become detached from reality.

The *diathesis-stress model* contends that stress is likely to trigger a schizophrenic episode in people who are genetically predisposed to schizophrenia (Jones & Fernyhough, 2007). Other research has pointed to brain abnormalities such as larger cerebral ventricles in people diagnosed with schizophrenia (Galderisi et al., 2008) and too much of the neurotransmitter dopamine (Ikemoto, 2004). Other research has shown that prenatal exposure to teratogens and the mother's contracting various viral infections could be correlated with the future development of schizophrenia (Ellman & Canon, 2008).

In summary, most of what we know about schizophrenia is correlational and not causal. Thus, we do not yet know what *causes* schizophrenia.

The presentation of schizophrenia consists of both positive and negative symptoms. *Positive symptoms* are exaggerations of normal thoughts and behaviors. Two of the most common are hallucinations and delusions. *Hallucinations* occur when someone perceives something that is not really there. This could include any of the major senses (seeing, hearing, smelling, and feeling). A common hallucination involves hearing voices. It can mimic the sound of TVs or radios playing in the background. In very rare instances, voices may instruct a person to hurt themselves or someone around them. These cases are quite rare, but may seem more frequent due to their portrayal in popular film and media. *Delusions* are severely distorted thinking patterns. Delusions of grandeur are common in people struggling with schizophrenia and often take the form of a person believing he or she is very important. Believing one is Jesus Christ is a common presentation. Delusions of persecution are common and involve the belief that someone is following them or out to get them. Delusions of reference are commonly observed as well. This often takes the form of the person believing a news reporter or newspaper article is delivering a secret message just to him or her. Other positive symptoms can include *thought disturbances.* This can cause people to engage in disorganized thinking patterns that make both verbal and written communication very difficult. This pattern of communicating is often referred to as a "word salad." Another common presentation is the use of neologisms, which is creating words that do not exist. This often involves combining existing words like taking the word snake and shark and saying "snark." A final positive symptom one might observe is *movement disturbances.* These can take the form of a person's repeating the same motions for long periods of time. In some subtypes of schizophrenia people experience catatonia where they do not move or respond to people around them in the world. They are in a catatonic state. Advances in medication and treatment have made this symptom less common.

Negative symptoms occur when a normal behavior or thought process is removed or lost. These symptoms are often more subtle and difficult to recognize. They may also be mistaken for other disorders. Some negative symptoms include lacking pleasure in everyday life activities, speaking very little in social situations even when pressured to interact, and flat affect (person shows no emotion on his or her face and speaks in monotone voice). Cognitive symptoms can also be present. These involve having trouble maintaining focus, problems evaluating information and using it to make rational decisions (executive functioning), and problems using information immediately after learning it (working memory).

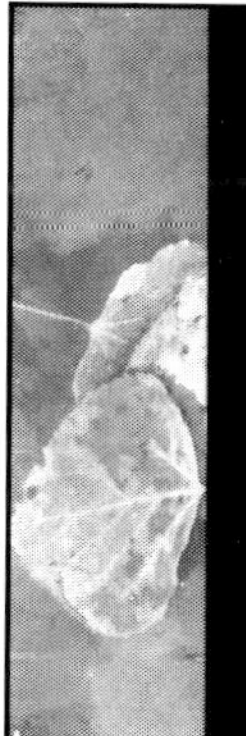

Have You Ever Noticed? – People in television, film, and the news media often use the term schizophrenia incorrectly. For example, a sports announcer recently said that a basketball team was "schizophrenic" due to the fact that it would play really well one game and really poorly the next. Does this sound anything like the positive and negative symptoms of schizophrenia described above?

What the sports announcer was likely intending to reference was a dissociative disorder. These disorders involve "splitting" of the personality, often in response to trauma. More specifically, had he known, he might have been referring to a controversial diagnosis know as dissociative identity disorder (DID), which involves the development of multiple personalities.

It is worth noting that positive symptoms of schizophrenia are more common in what is referred to as rapidly developing schizophrenia, whereas negative symptoms tend to be more prevalent in slower developing schizophrenia. Also, the DSM-IV-TR classifies five specific subtypes of schizophrenia: paranoid, catatonic, disorganized, undifferentiated, and residual. However, these subtypes have been criticized because they do not help predict the course of the illness or differentiate in terms of either prognosis or treatment. As such, identification of positive and negative symptoms has become more important since positive symptoms in rapidly developing or *acute* schizophrenia are correlated with better adjustment and recovery. DSM-V is proposing a model of viewing schizophrenia as existing on a spectrum with other disorders in an effort to make differential diagnosis between disorders more clear and accessible (American Psychiatric Association, 2011).

ACTIVITY

Imagine for a moment that you enter your psychology class today just as you had been doing all semester. Now imagine that you begin talking with a classmate who sits directly to your right. You make a comment about the professor to which this student replies, "What are you talking about? There is no one up there." You explain to the student, in an attempt to clarify your initial statement in case of any confusion, that you are referring to the person who has been teaching the class to her and everyone else this semester at which point she states, "That person doesn't exist! You're crazy!" Now imagine that you have a similar conversation with several other students who are sitting near you and they all insist the person you are speaking of does not exist. However, you know that you have perceived a person teaching the class every day this semester.

© ARENA Creative, 2011. Used under license of Shutterstock, Inc.

What would it feel like to have everyone telling you what you perceived was not reality?

What is the one thing you *would not* want someone close to you to do in this situation?

(continued)

ACTIVITY (*continued*)

What is one thing someone close to you could do to help you feel comfort in this situation?

Personality Disorders. In the five-axis system of diagnosis, personality disorders are placed on Axis II. This category of diagnoses is controversial with some pushing for it to be removed from the DSM-V due to lack of evidence while others offer their unwavering support. In the end, there will almost certainly be some kind of reformulation of personality disorders. Two personality disorders that are likely to remain largely intact include antisocial and borderline.

Antisocial personality disorder describes an individual who has a profound disregard for the rights of others. A cardinal feature of this disorder is that the person lacks a conscience or the ability to empathize with others. These individuals tend to be impulsive (act without thinking) and exhibit egocentric (feeling the world revolves around them) attitudes and behaviors. They also have a superficial charisma and charm that initially draws people to them. While there are certainly famous serial killers or other people in the criminal justice system for whom diagnosis of this disorder would be appropriate, there are many more people in the world who qualify for this diagnosis who cause harm in different ways. One example could include white-collar criminals such as Bernie Madoff or executives at Enron such as Kenneth Lay and Jeffrey Skilling who caused great financial and psychological damage to employees who trusted them with no sense of empathy or responsibility for the life-altering damage they caused to thousands.

Antisocial personality disorder tends to be especially problematic because individuals with this diagnosis do not feel bad about their behavior and do not recognize it as being a problem. Research indicates that both genetics (Raine & Yang, 2006) and environment play a role in the development of the disorder. More specifically, environmental factors such as parental abuse and neglect are correlated with future development of antisocial personality disorder (Ansell & Grillo, 2007).

Borderline personality disorder is marked by impulsivity and instability in mood, self-image, and relationships. Relationships with others can fluctuate very quickly from "I love you" to "I hate you." The person can also have internal feelings about him- or herself that fluctuate in much the same fashion. There is often a constant need for approval and reassurance. It is not uncommon to see people who fit the criteria for this diagnosis engage

in high-risk sexual behavior as well as the use of drugs. Suicidal ideation and self-injurious behavior are also common (Chapman, Leung, & Lynch, 2008).

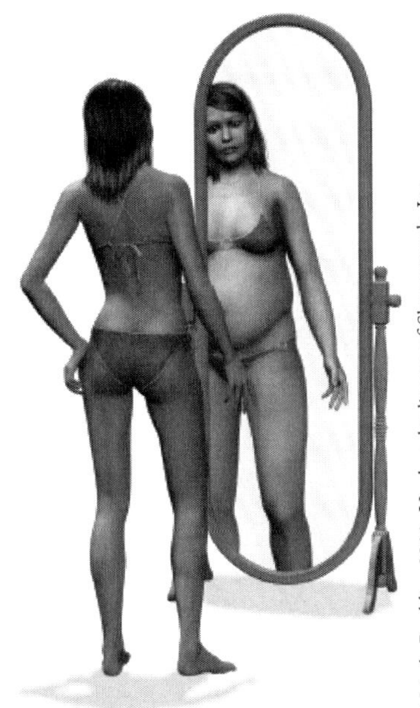

A history of both childhood abuse and neglect are common in people diagnosed with borderline personality disorder (Minzenberg, Poole, & Vinogradov, 2008). There is also emerging research that points to structural changes in the brain (Mizenberg et al., 2008).

Eating Disorders. This group of disorders is marked by a severe disturbance in the amount of food one consumes (either over- or under-eating) along with body weight, size, or shape unduly influencing how one feels about oneself. Over time, the person begins to lose control over her behavior. In this way, eating disorders can mimic patterns of behavior seen in addiction. Despite a great deal of research, there is no consensus as to what causes eating disorders. Like with the other disorders discussed in this chapter, environmental and biological influences are both believed to play important roles (Behar, 2007; Kaye, 2008).

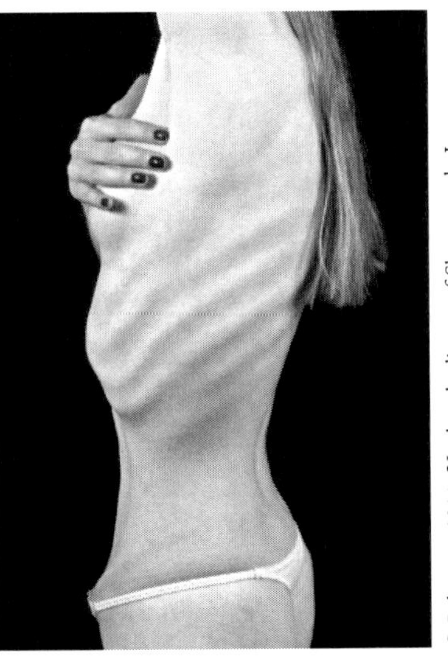

Eating disorders primarily impact women, although the number of men reporting eating disorder symptoms has increased over the course of the last few years (Greenberg & Schoen, 2008; Weltzin et al, 2005). While it is estimated that over 50 percent of women from Western cultures experience at least some symptoms of eating disorders, it is believed that no more than about 2 percent of women actually meet the full criteria for either anorexia nervosa or bulimia nervosa, both of which will be discussed in the space that follows.

Anorexia nervosa is marked by a significant fear of becoming overweight that results in obsessive and dangerous attempts to lose weight. To assist in the weight loss process, people struggling with anorexia may starve themselves or engage in excessive exercise. As the disorder progresses, physical symptoms such as thinning of the hair, discolored skin, brittle nails, fatigue, absence of menstruation, and a drop in body temperature can all occur. Death rates are quite high as compared to other

DSM-IV-TR diagnoses, and it is estimated, depending on what study is referenced, that somewhere between 5 and 20 percent of all people who are diagnosed with anorexia will die as a result of the disorder. While on the surface it may appear that anorexia is about food, the underlying causes are often rooted in trying to regulate emotions and gain a sense of control over one's surroundings (Kaye, 2008).

Think about it – If a woman in Western culture begins to lose weight, what kind of feedback is she often met with? Is it possible this feedback could act as a form of operant conditioning referred to as positive reinforcement (Chapter 3) for disordered eating?

Bulimia nervosa also falls under into the category of eating disorders, but its presentation differs from that of anorexia. Bulimia is a cycle of binge eating followed by the act of purging. Typical methods of purging include inducing vomiting with one's finger or the use of laxatives. After purging, people often report feeling ashamed or disgusted. The cycle often repeats itself again with people binging and eating large quantities of food to help regulate their emotions followed by shame that leads to purging.

Unlike anorexia, where over time it becomes physically obvious that something is wrong, people struggling with bulimia usually fluctuate between average to slightly above average weight. Severe physical problems can result from bulimia. For people who induce vomiting, stomach acid can cause damage to the esophagus and tooth decay. Over time the vomiting response can become almost reflexive or automatic.

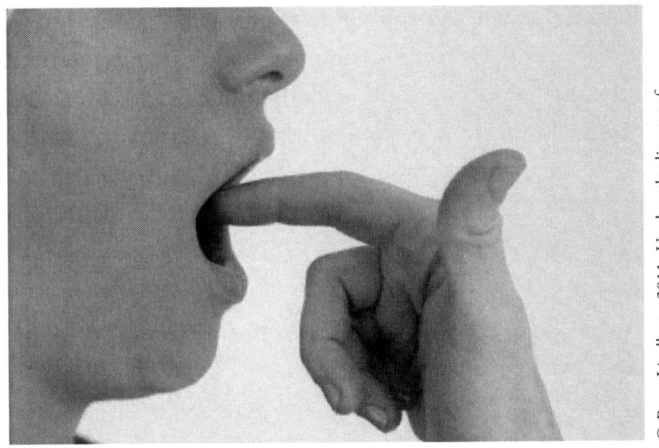

This can lead to heart problems and also severe damage to the stomach. For individuals who use laxatives as a means to purge, long-term damage to the digestive system can occur with some people even being forced to have parts of their colons removed.

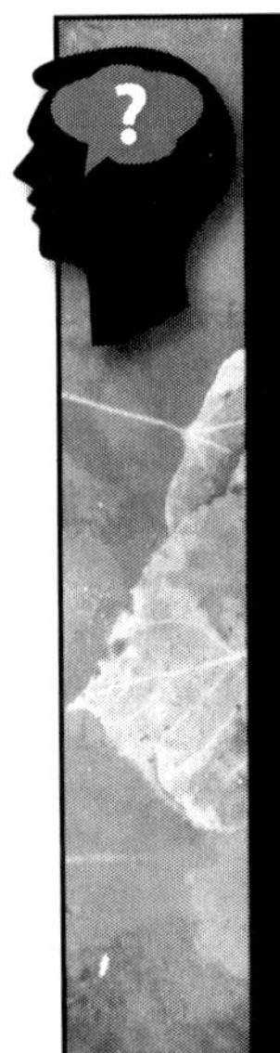

Think about it – A study done by Harvard professor Dr. Anne Becker (2002) looked at the attitudes of women on the island of Fiji after the introduction of Western television in 1995. She discovered that nearly 74 percent of the 63 young women who participated in the study considered themselves to be "too fat" after exposure to American television for approximately three years while showing no such symptoms prior to the introduction of American TV.

What implications do you believe a study like this has on our understanding of body image and eating disorders?

Do People Fit Just One Diagnosis?

You have now been introduced to a few of the major diagnostic categories in the DSM-IV-TR, and it all seems so easy, right? Just pinpoint the correct diagnosis and off we go with treatment. Unfortunately, real-life presentations are rarely so simple. Some people may not fit the criteria completely for any single disorder but still need assistance. Other people meet the criteria for more than one disorder. This is called *comorbidity.*

Substance abuse, for example, is comorbid with many of the disorders already discussed in the chapter. This makes a great deal of sense in that drugs work really well to help alter undesirable feelings states. However, the addictive process that can ensue complicates both diagnosis and treatment.

Let's consider an example concerning a specific diagnosis. PTSD, as discussed earlier in the chapter, as well as other forms of trauma that may not fit into a diagnostic category are often comorbid with substance abuse. What this means is that both conditions have to be identified correctly and then treated.

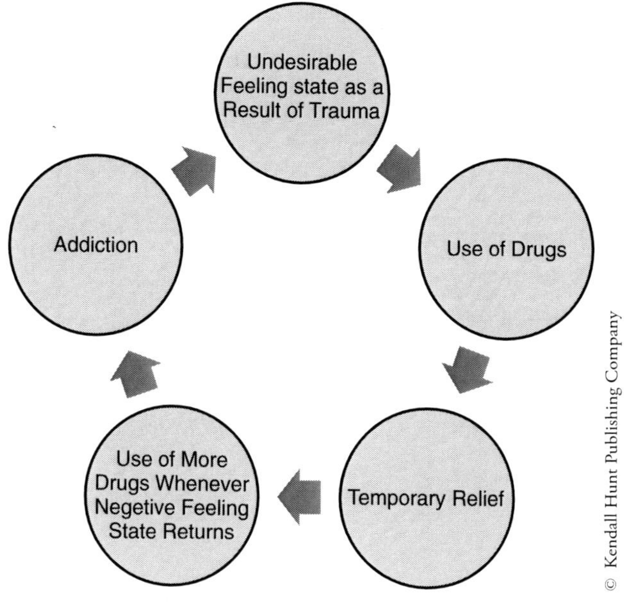

Figure 12.3

In Figure 12.3, it is imperative that both the addiction and the trauma get treated. If just the addiction to drugs is treated and the underlying trauma is not, the chance a person will relapse and begin using drugs again is substantially higher.

Strengths and Weaknesses of The DSM-IV-TR

It is important to note that the DSM-IV-TR is not perfect, nor has it been over time. The hope is that with each new revision, the manual will become more refined and provide better guidance to psychologists and other clinicians.

A strength of the DSM is that is it has created a common language to help clinicians communicate quickly and with a relatively high degree of accuracy with regard to symptoms that people may be experiencing. Substantial effort has been made to thoroughly describe the diagnostic categories such that it helps to standardize diagnosis and treatment.

However, not everyone believes the DSM is the best tool for conceptualizing the field of mental health. Some critics insist that psychology does not work like medicine and therefore should not work within the confines of the medical model. Wampold, Ahn, and Coleman (2001) wrote: "The empirical support for a medical model of psychotherapy is nonexistent. We contend that it will neither scientifically explain results nor further the field" (p. 272).

One of the most vocal critics of the DSM and the medical model has been psychiatrist and professor Thomas Szasz. He contends that mental illness is a myth and that the medical model discourages people from taking responsibility for happenings in their lives. Szasz (1960, 2004) believes that labels like the ones in the DSM can become a sort of self-fulfilling prophecy that boxes people into a prescribed way of feeling and behaving. Or, as narrative therapist Stephen Madigan (2000) so eloquently put it, "The person becomes the problem."

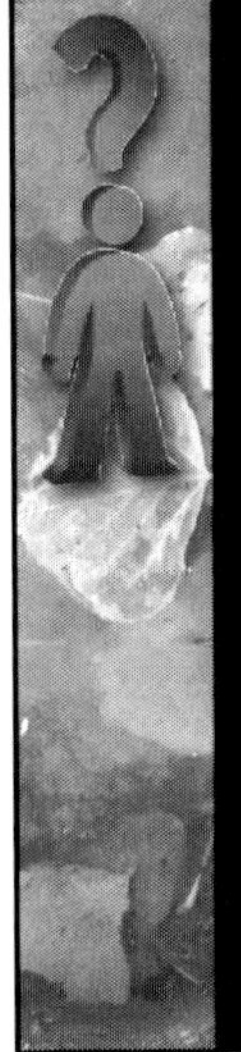

What Do You Think? – As you just read, some people in the broad fields of psychology and psychiatry believe that labels do more harm than good and can actually be counterproductive to people getting better. Others, however, believe that labels can have a normalizing effect. That is, when people discover they are not the only ones struggling with a mood disorder or schizophrenia, it actually makes them feel like there is hope and that they are not alone.

After weighing both perspectives, where do you stand on this issue and why?

PSYCHOTHERAPY

Now that we have covered some of the major diagnostic categories present in the DSM-IV-TR, you might be asking yourself how one would go about treating these. This section of the chapter will cover some of the major approaches to psychotherapy. *Psychotherapy* is the term most often used in the research literature to describe various different approaches or techniques used in talk therapy with the hope of improving functioning, increasing self-awareness, and alleviating symptoms. Terms like counseling and therapy are often used interchangeably with the term psychotherapy.

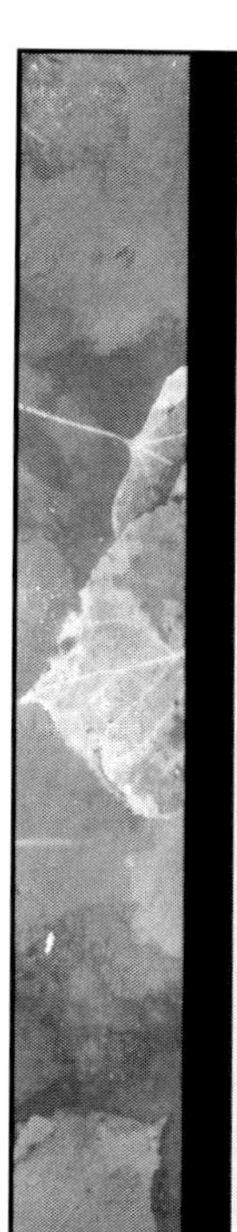

What Have You Seen? – How is therapy often portrayed in the movies or in other forms of popular media? Be as specific and descriptive as you can.

© Phase4Photography, 2011. Used under license of Shutterstock, Inc.

When you have finished this chapter return to this activity and evaluate whether you believe therapy is represented fairly and accurately in popular media.

Common Factors Research

Before moving on to specific models of therapy, it is important to understand that there are many different approaches. Depending on what models are combined or not combined it is estimated that there are anywhere from 60 to 250 different approaches to therapy.

Research has clearly indicated that psychotherapy works, meaning that many studies through the years have demonstrated psychotherapy to be superior to placebo or no treatment (Barker, Funk, & Houston, 1988; Dush, 1986; Lambert & Ogles, 2004; Lipsey & Wilson, 1993; Prioleau, Murdock, & Brody, 1983; Seligman, 1995; Shadish, 2000). However, despite all of the different approaches clinicians have developed for working with clients, results over the past five decades have consistently indicated that no one model or philosophy of psychotherapy works better than any other (Asay & Lambert, 1999; Lambert & Ogles, 2004, Miller, Duncan, & Hubble, 1997, 2004; Wampold, 2001). Furthermore, the data across a number of studies showed that all of the techniques utilized in marriage and family therapy as well as individual counseling were all about equally effective when client outcome was measured (Doherty & Simmons, 1995, 1996; Lambert & Ogles, 2004; Shadish et al., 1993).

© Morphart, 2011. Used under license of Shutterstock, Inc.

This phenomenon of all the models of psychotherapy being about the same with regard to their level of efficacy (how well they work) is sometimes referred to as the "Dodo-bird" effect in reference to the classic story *Alice's Adventure in Wonderland* (Duncan, Miller, & Sparks, 2004). Recall from the story that Alice stages a chaotic and disorganized race among creatures. When the races ends, all of the other creatures turn to the Dodo bird and ask who won the race, to which the Dodo bird replies, "All have won and all must have prizes."

This research prompted the creation of the common factors model, which is sometimes also referred to as the contextual mode. This model holds the assumption there are four factors common to successful therapy, regardless of the model of therapy employed. The four common factors that are generally identified throughout the literature that affect client outcomes include extratherapeutic factors (resources outside of therapy the client brings with him or her), relationship factors (the therapeutic relationship between client and therapist), expectancy factors (client's sense of hope and whether he or she believes therapy will be successful), and therapeutic models or techniques (Duncan & Moynihan, 1994; Frank & Frank, 1991; Hubble, Duncan, & Miller 1999; Lambert, 1992; Miller et al., 1997; Roszenweig, 1936; Wampold, 2001). The vast majority of the research indicates approximately 40 percent of the variance in client outcome can be attributed to extratherapeutic factors, 30 percent to relationship factors, 15 percent to expectancy factors, and 15 percent to the use of specific models or techniques (Duncan & Moynihan, 1994; Lambert, 1992; Lambert & Barley, 2001; Miller et al., 1997).

What this means is that therapy is but one variable in a complicated equation of change. Moreover, it demonstrates that outside resources the client brings with him or her as well as the ability for a therapist to form an effective therapeutic relationship with a client account for 70 percent of the change process, while the specific techniques used account for only about 15 percent.

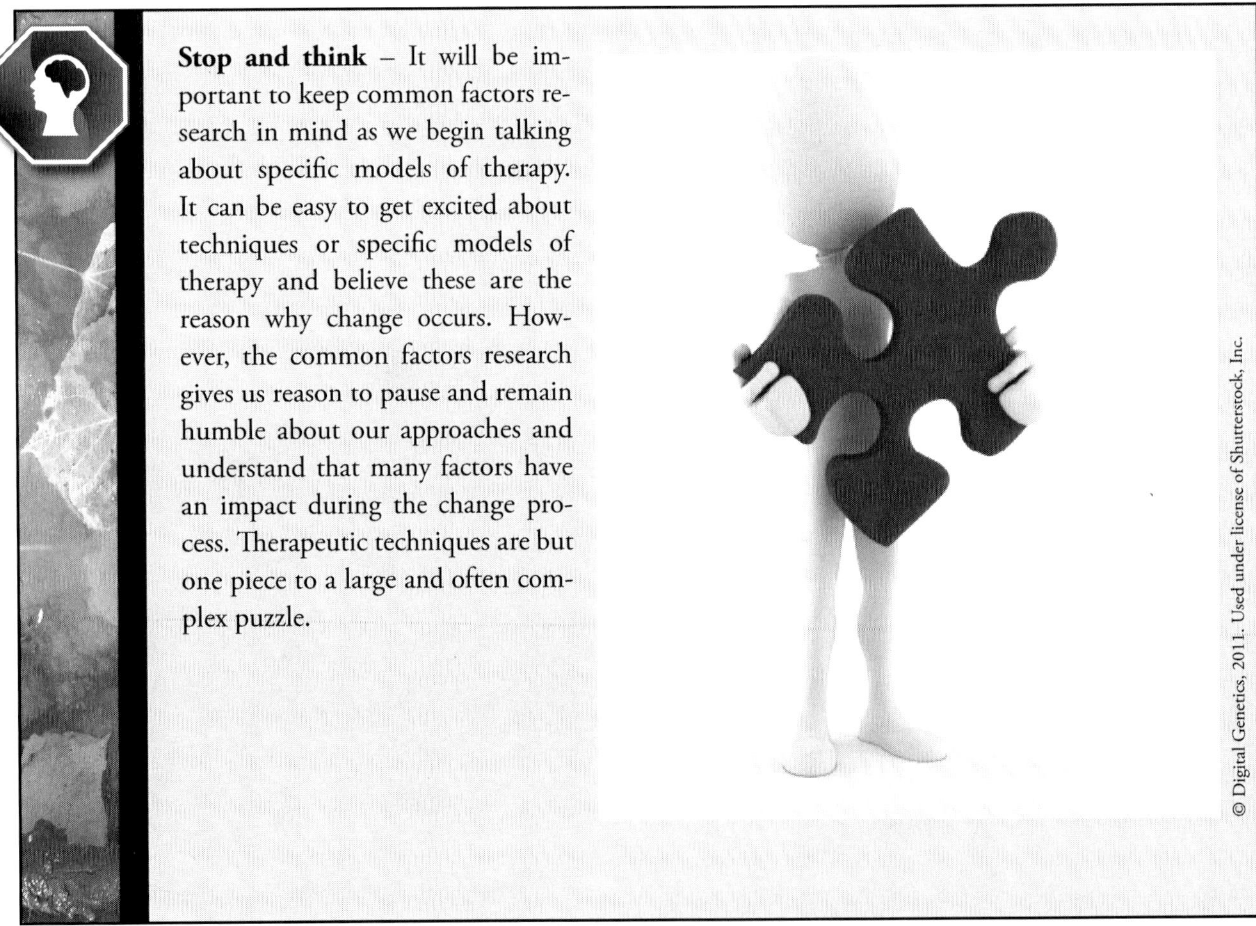

Stop and think – It will be important to keep common factors research in mind as we begin talking about specific models of therapy. It can be easy to get excited about techniques or specific models of therapy and believe these are the reason why change occurs. However, the common factors research gives us reason to pause and remain humble about our approaches and understand that many factors have an impact during the change process. Therapeutic techniques are but one piece to a large and often complex puzzle.

Approaches to Psychotherapy

There are generally three "waves" that are referred to when tracing the historical roots of psychology: psychoanalysis, behaviorism, and humanism. The idea is that later waves were created as a reaction to earlier ones. We will cover the approaches to therapy following this pattern of evolution and also add postmodern approaches to therapy, which some people are calling "fourth-wave" psychology.

First Wave – Psychoanalysis

Sigmund Freud was the founder of psychoanalysis. The goal of psychoanalysis is to bring unconscious material to conscious awareness where it can be processed in the here and now. Freud was especially concerned with repressed childhood trauma. Freud proposed an energy hypothesis, which stated that the more energy that was used dealing with the unconscious conflict, the less energy that would be available for dealing the person's current reality. Freud designed specific techniques that he believed would help relax the person's defenses and allow the space for unconscious material to surface.

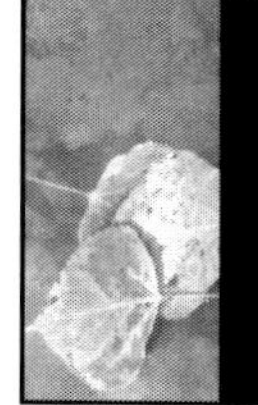

Think Back – If you do not remember, make sure to take a look back at Chapter 11 where Freud's defensive mechanisms, one of which is repression, are discussed. It might also be helpful to remind yourself about the id, ego, and superego, and the ways in which the ego uses defense mechanisms when it becomes overwhelmed.

Freud proposed that dreams were "the royal road" to our unconscious. As such, he believed that *dream analysis* was an important technique for tapping into a person's unconscious. He believed it was the job of the analyst to help interpret the dream. This was accomplished by the analyst's examining the actual content of the dream (manifest contest) and then looking for the symbolic, underlying meaning (latent content).

Free association was a central technique used by Freud in psychoanalysis in which a person says whatever comes to his or her mind without censoring the content. Freud believed that items that immediately surfaced held significant value with regard to what the unconscious might be trying to conceal. Over time as the person became more comfortable and began to let his or her guard down, Freud believed unconscious content would gradually emerge. Just as in dream analysis, it was the analyst's job to listen closely and tie together consistent themes and interpret what might be troubling the patient.

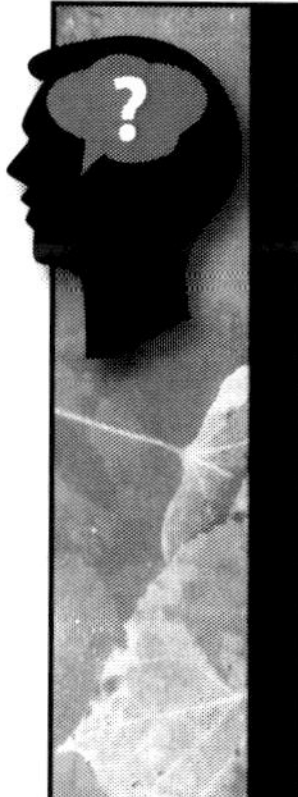

Think about it – We all have that little voice in our head, or internal dialogue, that we rarely share with others. In most instances, it is healthy to have this kind of filter. But imagine what it would be like to let go of that and have a conversation with someone without censoring what we say as Freud advocated with the use of free association.

While it might have therapeutic benefit, how difficult would it be for you to do this?

(*continued*)

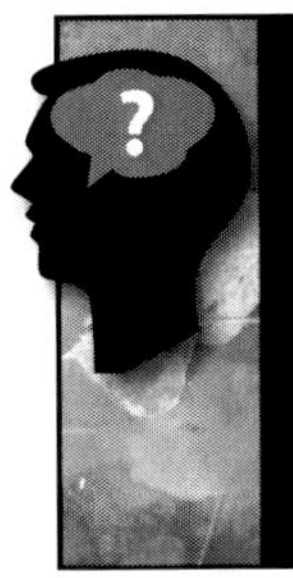

Think about it *(continued)*

How comfortable do you believe you would have to feel with the psychoanalyst?

During the process of psychoanalysis analysts are constantly scanning for *resistance,* which is when a person hesitates or is unwilling to discuss certain content. This could come in the form of a client's changing the subject or reporting that he forgot what he was trying to say. Freud believed it was the job of the analyst to be immediate about this and challenge the patient to confront what he was avoiding.

Psychoanalysts are also on the lookout for transference and countertransference. *Transference* occurs when a patient transfers or displaces feelings she has toward another person in her life onto the therapist. This might take the form of a patient's transferring angry feelings she has toward her father onto a male psychoanalyst. If the analyst is aware of the transference, he can respond accordingly and help the client work through the previously unresolved issue. However, for this process to resolve in a healthy fashion, the analyst has to avoid what is called countertransference. *Countertransference* occurs when the analyst reacts emotionally to the patient because of the analyst's own unresolved psychological issues.

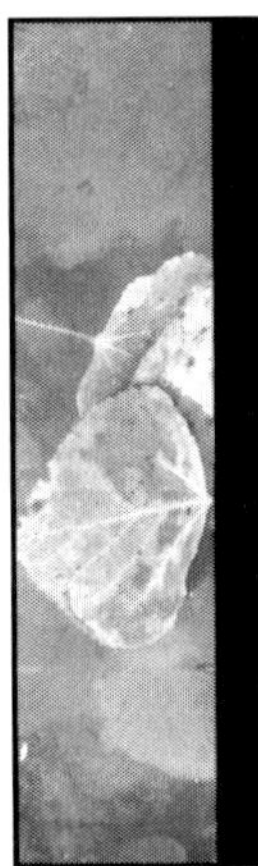

The Couch – In many popular Hollywood portrayals clients in therapy are lying down on a couch. This is actually very rare in modern therapeutic practice. However, Freud believed this setup allowed for the patient to become more relaxed, therefore making it more likely unconscious material would find its way to the surface.

While many people over the years have reported psychoanalysis as being helpful and it is still used today, its use is limited for a number of reasons. First, it is often quite expensive and sessions take place multiple times per week for months or even years. Given the fact most insurance companies do not cover this kind of treatment, it is just not practical for most people. Second, it is limited in what it can be applied to. It is often not effective for very acute problems such as suicidality or other major forms of mental illness such as schizophrenia or bipolar disorder. Finally, it is very difficult to measure concepts like the unconscious mind scientifically. As noted earlier, though, there is evidence that patients find psychoanalysis as being helpful (Wachtel, 2008).

Psychodynamic therapy is a briefer and more contemporary form of therapy that embraces some of the core tenets of psychoanalysis. Self-psychology, object relations, and ego psychology are all examples of psychodynamic approaches to therapy. These approaches are more contemporary in the sense that the client does not lie down on a couch, and the approach is more directive with the therapist asking questions and reflecting what the client says as opposed to simply waiting for elements of the unconscious to emerge. While past experiences are still processed in psychodynamic work, there is more of a focus on current experiences. There is also usually a more specific goal, which means psychodynamic approaches can be used more effectively to treat specific DSM diagnoses (Lerner, 2008).

Second Wave – Behaviorism

Remember the work of B.F. Skinner, John Watson, and Ivan Pavlov as discussed in Chapter 3? These men were all behaviorists and believed that if we could not observe something, we should not study it. This was in large part a reaction to psychoanalytic thinkers who came before them who based their theories on constructs that were not observable (i.e., the unconscious mind). A number of techniques still used in therapy today emerged out of this second wave of psychology.

Systematic desensitization is a process of helping people relax while being confronted with stimuli they are fearful of. The hope is that the fear response triggered by the amygdala in the brain will eventually be replaced by a relaxed or calm response. This approach has been used with good success to treat phobias.

Imagine that someone has a specific phobia of snakes. The client would first be taught relaxation techniques. Next, a hierarchy of fears is created that the client will gradually be exposed to. For example, the process might start with the client just saying the word snake. Next, a picture of a snake is introduced. That is followed by watching a video of a snake. By the end of treatment the client would be exposed to a real snake and confront what she is afraid of. If the client begins to feel anxiety, she is reminded to use her coping mechanisms and attempt to achieve a state of relaxation. When deep relaxation occurs, the body is parasympathetic dominant, making a fear response impossible. When successful, the fear response is extinguished at the conclusion of treatment.

Forms of *operant conditioning* as outlined by Skinner can also be used as behavioral forms of therapy. These techniques are frequently used in an attempt to shape good and bad behavior in children. Therapists often teach parents how to reward or reinforce desirable behaviors they would like to see more of while withdrawing attention to extinguish behaviors they wish to avoid. Reinforcements can be implemented using a *token economy*, which is when children are immediately rewarded for desirable behavior in the form of a token. These tokens can later be redeemed for desirable rewards such as treats, computer time, etc.

Another technique that can be helpful is called *shaping*. This occurs when approximations of a desired behavior are rewarded in hopes of the child's eventually achieving the desired behavior in its totality. Skinner used this technique to reward rats that he wanted to push a lever when they raised their paw. While raising of the paw was not the desired behavior, he found that if he rewarded this approximation of the desired behavior, it would eventually lead to the rat's pushing the lever. This same sort of shaping can be done with children to help them progress toward a desired behavior.

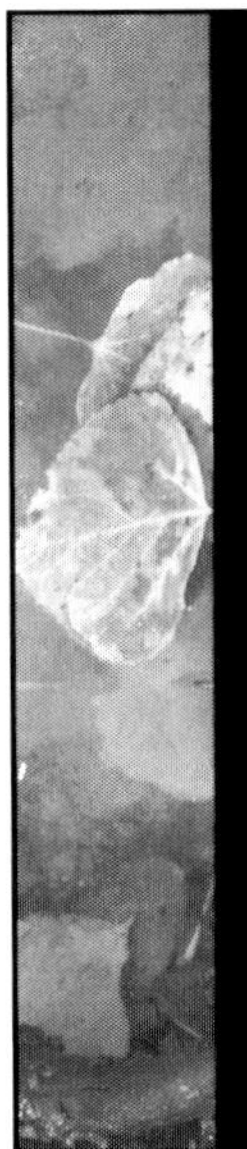

Did You Know? – Techniques like shaping and role-playing have been used successfully in working with children diagnosed with autism, a disorder in which children display marked difficulties in social interactions and communication. Initially, children are rewarded for any utterances with the desired goal of eventually communicating with another person. Later in the process, children are rewarded for actual words or attempts made to communicate with others.

While many people are attracted to behavioral methods of therapy because they are extremely concrete, this approach is not without its weaknesses. Operant conditioning does not always transfer from one context to another. For example, if a desired behavior is shaped in the therapist's office, that same behavior may not carry over to the home or school settings. Other critics question the ethics of shaping the behavior of children and who has the authority to decide what behaviors are good or bad in society.

Cognitive-Behavioral Therapy (CBT)

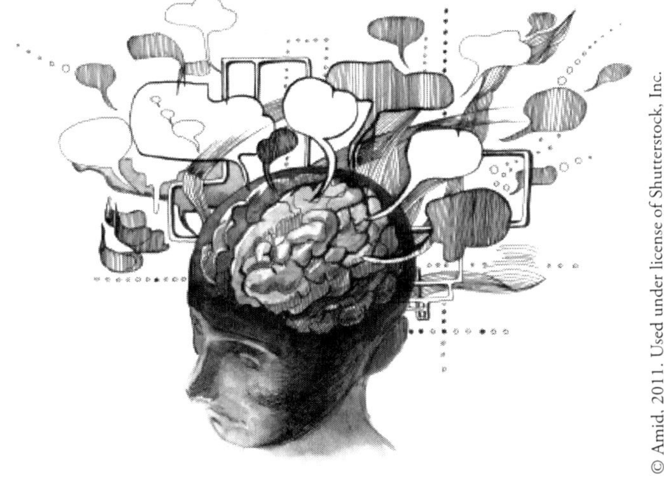

As the name implies, cognitive-behavioral therapy (CBT) looks not only at behavior but also at thought processes. The assumption is that faulty ways of thinking can negatively impact mood and behavior. CBT therapists are especially interested in the self-talk of clients and helping to restructure their thought processes. Two of the most important names in CBT are Albert Ellis and Aaron Beck.

Albert Ellis had an undeniable impact on the conceptualization and practice of CBT. His focus was on irrational beliefs and how those beliefs lead to negative emotions and behaviors. His specific approach was called *rational-emotive behavior therapy (REBT).* Within REBT, Ellis created the A-B-C-D approach. "A" is the activating event that occurs when a person is blocked from achieving a meaningful or desirable goal. "B" refers to the irrational belief that is often arrived at out of frustration as a result of being blocked from a desirable goal. "C" refers to the consequence that

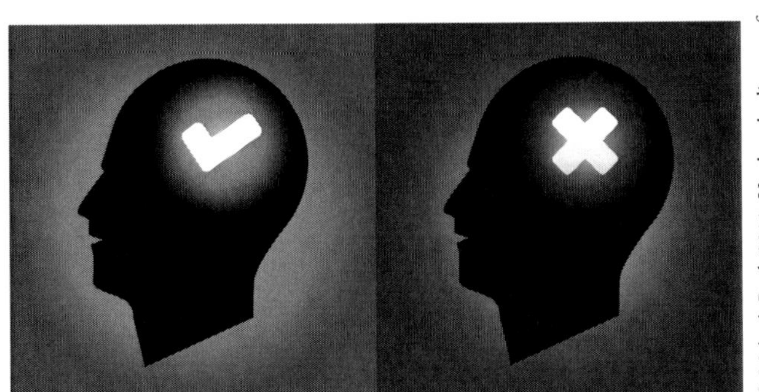

comes about as a result of the irrational belief. This consequence is most often a negative feeling state, which helps to strengthen the irrational belief. "D" is the process of disputing the irrational belief, which is what is learned in therapy (see Figure 12.4).

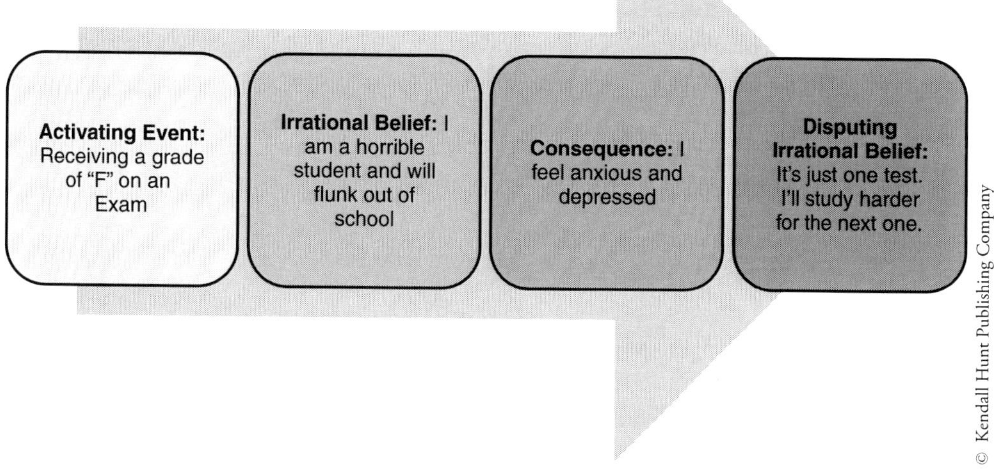

© Kendall Hunt Publishing Company

Figure 12.4 Albert Elllis's rational-emotive-behavior therapy A-B-C-Ds.

Ellis had a direct and sometimes confrontational style in therapy. He was famous for coining the phrase "don't should on yourself." He was interested in peoples' use of language and words like "must" or '"should" and how these absolute ways of thinking can negatively impact emotions and behaviors. The goal of therapy is for the client to recognize his or her irrational thoughts and, over time, dispute them without the assistance of the therapist. Clients are encouraged to test out new ways of thinking in the world and see how this impacts their emotions and behaviors (Ellis, 2004).

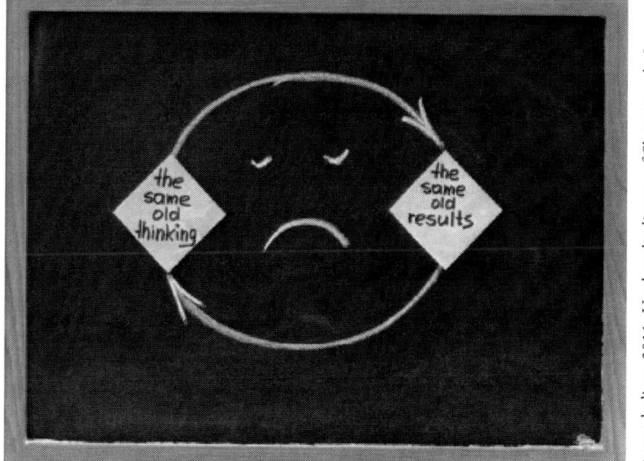

© marekuliasz, 2011. Used under license of Shutterstock, Inc.

Aaron Beck is another important name to remember when thinking about CBT approaches to change. Beck (1976) focuses specifically on maladaptive patterns of thinking that lead to depressive feeling states. A few of the most common are discussed in the space that follows.

© Rynio Productions, 2011. Used under license of Shutterstock, Inc.

- All-or-Nothing Thinking. This is a right-or-wrong, black-or-white approach to seeing the world. For example, a student who says if I don't get an "A" on a test, I am failing.
- Overgeneralization. This occurs when a person believes a single negative event will turn into

a continuous pattern of failure. For example, a student performs poorly on one exam and then believes he will fail out of school and is just generally a worthless human being.

- Disqualifying the Positive. This involves a person's ignoring positive events and rejecting them as not valid experiences. It is as if these positive events do not really count. This way of thinking allows negative beliefs to persist even in the face of contradictory evidence.
- Jumping to Conclusions. In this style of thinking, a person makes a hard-and-fast conclusion before gathering any evidence that could support or refute the conclusion. It typically takes two forms: the fortune-teller error and mind reading. The fortune-teller error involves predicting a negative outcome prior to an event and treating that prediction as though it is set in stone and nothing will change it. Mind reading occurs when people assume others are thinking negatively about them without any evidence and without checking in with the person to see whether this assumption is true.
- Magnification. Perhaps you have heard someone tell you or someone you know she is "making a mountain out of a molehill." This would be a good example of magnification, which occurs when people exaggerate the importance of a relatively minor negative event.

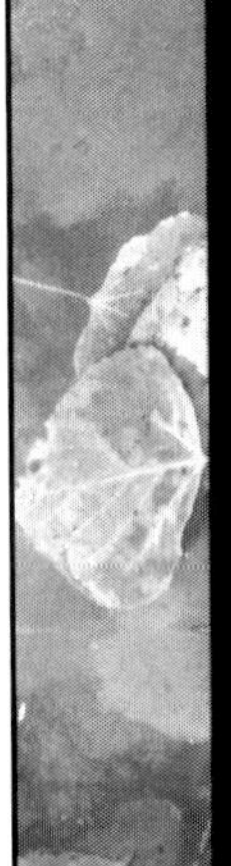

How's Your Thinking? – Do you engage in any of the maladaptive thinking patterns Beck described? How specifically?

What are some ways you can change your thinking to be less self-defeating and healthier?

Beck's goal in therapy is to help people recognize their specific negative thinking patterns. Once these thought patterns are identified, the client can be taught how to "reality test" these beliefs in the world around them in such a way that the negative beliefs can be disconfirmed. This process can initially be done in the room with the therapist serving as a "reality tester." The ultimate goal is to help the client understand how his or her negative thinking patterns are leading to his or her feelings of depression. The therapist also simultaneously makes an effort to help clients reconnect with healthy activities that bring them pleasure.

There is an abundance of research that demonstrates CBT's effectiveness in working with a variety of presenting problems (Kellogg & Young, 2008). However, critics often contend that CBT largely ignores the unconscious, ignores the client's past, and holds a faulty belief that changing thoughts always leads to a change in emotions. Critics also note that CBT is no more effective than any other model of therapy but simply lends itself better to empirical research (Wampold, 2001).

Third Wave – Humanism

Carl Rogers was a pioneer of applying humanistic ideas in therapy. His specific approach is called *client-centered therapy.* At the time, this term was revolutionary in that Rogers was referring to the people he saw in therapy as clients as opposed to patients. Rogers believed this helped to create a more egalitarian therapeutic relationship, which he noted as being crucial to the change process (Rogers, 1951). As the name "client-centered" implies, the client is the one who drives the process of therapy. The therapist's job is to act more as a facilitator of change. Rogers believed that if a therapist could create the proper conditions in therapy, the client would find his or her own answer to the question or problem of living that brought him or her to seek counseling in the first place. What this means is that you likely won't see a Rogerian therapist giving advice or engaging in interpretation of what the client's experience "really means."

The following are the three core conditions Rogers believed must be in place for change to occur in therapy:

1. Unconditional Positive Regard (Prizing): This is when a therapist values and respects the client as a person. The therapist must convey this sense of warmth and acceptance to the client. This does not mean, however, that the therapist accepts all of the behaviors the client engages in. For example, imagine working with a man who was in prison with a label of sex offender. Rogers believed a therapist could still accept and value the person as a human being while also disagreeing with the behavior that led to him being incarcerated.

© Kuzma, 2011. Used under license of Shutterstock, Inc.

2. Congruence (Genuineness): The therapist must behave in a way where his or her behavior matches his or her inner experience. Another way of saying this is that the therapist must be genuine or real. This concept may seem easy to apply for positive inner feeling states the therapist has toward the client, but Rogers also believed that if the therapist had a negative view of the client or even disliked him or her, it was better to communicate that directly.

Think about it – What does it mean to be real? In today's society some people have taken a more hostile view of being real, which takes the form of "I'm going to act however I want to act and don't care what impact it has on others." This is not what Rogers was advocating for.

© FuzzBones, 2011. Used under license of Shutterstock, Inc.

As a client of one of the author's once said, "There are different ways to deliver a present. You can drive by someone's house and throw it through the window. Or, you can wrap it up, put a bow on it, and hand it to the person. It's the same message inside."

© TTPhoto, 2011. Used under license of Shutterstock, Inc.

(continued)

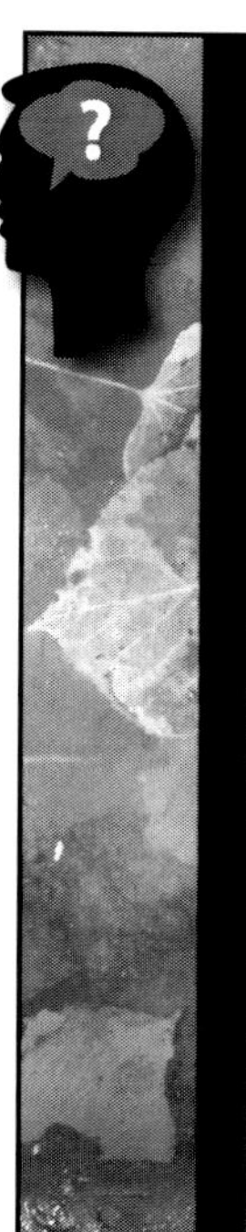

Think about it (*continued*)
This was perhaps Rogers' greatest strength. He could communicate a message that might be very hard to hear in a way the client could receive it and really listen to it while simultaneously not watering down the message.

© Christos Georghiou, 2011. Used under license of Shutterstock, Inc.

3. Empathic Understanding: Empathy, as Rogers described it, is really a two-part process. First, the therapist must achieve a deep understanding of what it feels like to be the client. In essence, this is an attempt to try and enter the client's inner experience. Once that is achieved, the therapist must then communicate or reflect back to the client what was said so the client knows the therapist has an understanding of his or her subjective experience.

© Lisa F. Young, 2011. Used under license of Shutterstock, Inc.

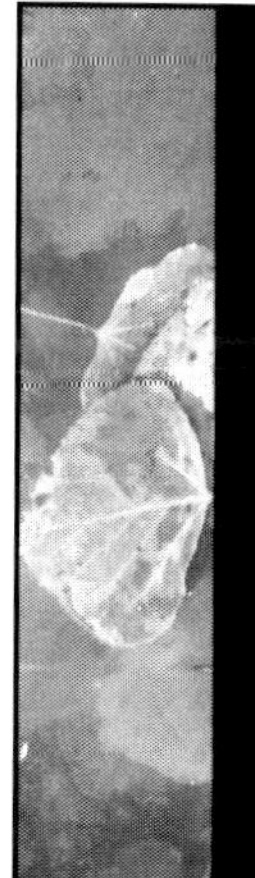

How Good a Listener Are You? – Rogers believed in active listening. This does not involve the therapist passively sitting and nodding his or her head as is often portrayed on television or in the movies. Instead, it involves paraphrasing, clarifying, and reflecting what the client said. This is done to help ensure that the client knows he or she is being heard, and hopefully, understood.

While it might sound easy to simply listen to someone, we are usually not as good at it as we think.

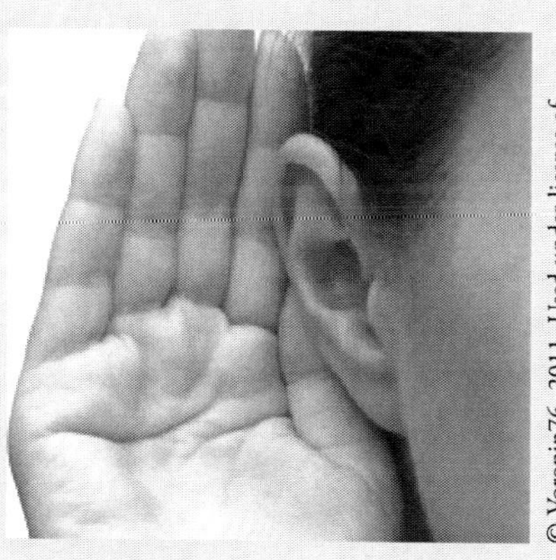
© Voronin76, 2011. Used under license of Shutterstock, Inc.

(*continued*)

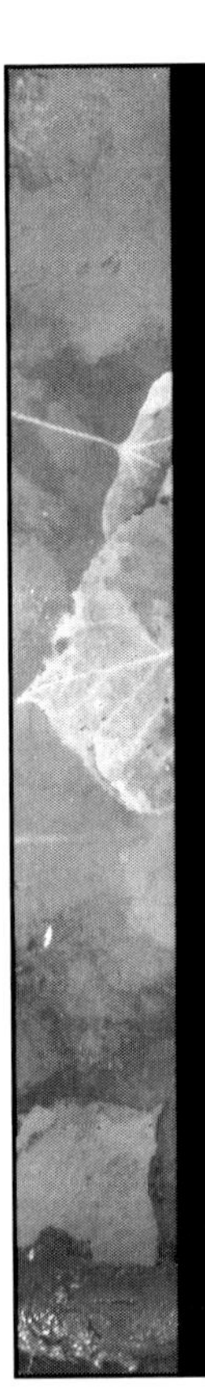

How Good a Listener Are You? *(continued)*

Often, people are thinking of what they are going to say next instead of truly focusing on listening and understanding another's inner experience.

Sometime in the next 24 hours engage in active listening with someone you care about, perhaps a family member or a romantic partner. In addition to using active listening, try and create the three core conditions that Rogers noted.

When you are finished, write down how you felt, how the person responded to you, and what you found to be easy and also more difficult about the process.

Rogers believed that the core conditions were both *necessary and sufficient* for change to occur in therapy, and he tirelessly conducted research to show the effectiveness of the person-centered approach. Rogers was one of the pioneers in his time with regard to using new technology such as audio recordings as ways to further deconstruct therapy sessions (Rogers, 1942). Modern researchers have continued to find support for Rogers' core conditions (Kirschenbaum & Jourdan, 2005).

While most therapists believe that Rogers' core conditions are necessary, not everyone believes them to be sufficient. That is, many people believe that Rogers' core conditions are imperative but not sufficient by themselves for change to occur. A common criticism is that Rogers' conditions simply do not provide enough direction for clients who have experienced trauma or may be struggling with more severe forms of mental illness.

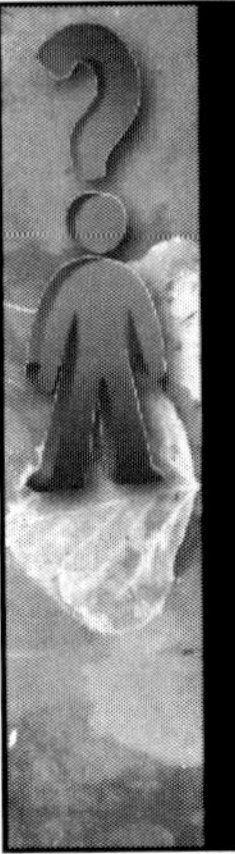

What Do You Think? – Is it possible to combine Rogers' core conditions with some of the other models we have talked about such as psychoanalysis or CBT? Defend your response.

Existentialism

Existentialism is not an easy concept to define. As a philosophy, it is a set of systems concerned with free will, personal choices, and responsibility. As a method of psychotherapy, it is a course centralized on the belief that an individual's inner conflict is due to inevitable confrontations with (and avoidances of) the givens of human existence. Irvin Yalom (1980) labeled the four inescapable givens of human existence as *death, freedom, meaninglessness,* and *isolation.* While it may seem a gloomy prospect to ruminate on these concepts (and at a therapist's insistence at that!), the lasting effect is quite the opposite.

© Vladimir Nikulin, 2011. Used under license of Shutterstock, Inc.

An existential therapist seeks to help a client understand his or her choices as individual choices. The therapist helps the client confront the idea of his or her own mortality and to overcome the terror associated with death. The therapist helps the client understand the scope of his or her power and importance, accept his or her own free will, and seek to think and behave in ways that emphasize realness and authenticity. Because individuals must ultimately make their own choices, they are free. But because individuals choose freely, they are ultimately responsible for their choices.

© Frederick R. Matzen, 2011. Used under license of Shutterstock, Inc.

Think about it – Remember the introduction to Chapter 5 and the activity that asked you to image your mind as if in the movie, *The Matrix?* Try this again. Imagine you are the main character, Neo.

(*continued*)

Think about it (*continued*)

You are confronted with two choices:

Ignorance of the responsibilities that could be yours

or

A wider, newer, and more painfully real view of the world for how it really is.

With these choices come complications. If you choose a full view of the world for how it really is, you will get the added pressure of having to live as a hunted rebel, in hiding, and against the dominant population. If you choose ignorance to your responsibilities, you will have a pleasant life relatively immune from pain and discomfort.

Which do you choose? Why?

Keep in mind: This is probably more of a question to live with than it is one you can answer today and move on.

For an existential psychotherapist, responsibility is the element of freedom many people wish to avoid and to which they give very little thought. They see a chronic denial and avoidance of responsibility as major contributing factors to mental health concerns like depression, anxiety, and neurosis as well as at the core of addictions, family strife, and problems at work. When their clients realize that they are in every respect responsible for their decisions, actions, and beliefs, they often experience an increase in the very symptoms (depression, anxiety) they came to therapy to conquer! This can lead to many outcomes. The existential therapists' job is to help the client understand that authentic, human change comes only in claiming responsibility and facing up to the realities of existence. Only then can clients exact purposeful power and choose, to the fullest outcome possible, their future. They steer their clients away from more comfortable ways of coping with the realities of the world (such as denial, ignorance, and avoidance) and help them in their struggle to accept their history of self-deception as well as their future of increased (albeit painful) accountability to themselves, others, and even the world at large.

As a form of psychotherapy, existentialism is usually lumped into the camp of humanism. Many existentialists resist this compartmentalization and continue to source their techniques of analysis and therapy from the storehouse of the psychoanalysts and theoretical orientation from the philosophers of existentialism such as Heidegger, Buber, Sartre, de Beauvoir, and Camus. However, some have found humanistic, relationship-driven techniques more effective at guiding clients toward change and more palatable for therapeutic use and adopted the principles set forth by Irv Yalom, Rollo May, and James Bugental.

Fourth Wave – Postmodern Approaches to Therapy

There are those who believe we are experiencing a fourth wave of psychotherapy right now with the recent growth of approaches like narrative therapy and solution-focused brief therapy, both of which are considered postmodern approaches to therapy. Modernists believe that reality is objective and can be validated through the scientific method and empirical measurement. Postmodernism holds the philosophical belief that no absolute truth exists. Everyone's reality is different, and reality is socially constructed (Freedman & Combs, 1996). In postmodern approaches the therapist is viewed as a collaborator as opposed to an expert. As DeJong and Berg (2008) noted:

> We do not view ourselves as expert at scientifically assessing client problems and then intervening. Instead, we strive to be expert at exploring clients' frames of reference and identifying those perceptions that clients can use to create more satisfying lives (p. 19).

Narrative therapy focuses on the stories of peoples' lives and holds the belief we are all multistoried and our lives can be reauthored at any time. Clients come to therapy with their life stories only partially written. It is like picking up a book and opening it somewhere in the middle. Part of the story has already been written and is affecting what is on the current page, but yet, there are still many pages that have not yet been written. The job of the narrative therapist is to help the client write a more preferred life narrative in the remaining portion of his or her book of life.

Narrative therapists believe that we each make our own meaning, and it is not produced for us. Clients are the utmost experts on their own lives and have local, or what a narrative therapist might call "insider," knowledge that is unique to them (Monk et al., 1997). Narrative therapists are also interested in dominant cultural stories that tell people how they "should" behave and ways in which these stories can be harmful to individuals who do not fit into society's boxes of what is normal.

Perhaps narrative therapist Stephen Madigan (2000) described this approach best when he said, "Be very careful of the stories you tell about yourself and that others tell about you because eventually they will live you."

When clients show up to therapy, a negative story or narrative is often dominant in their lives. The initial job of the therapist is to deconstruct or unpack the problem story. Madigan (2000) indicated that as the story unfolds, the therapist attempts to poke holes in the problematic story. After unpacking the problem story, the primary job of the therapist then becomes to afford space for the client to explore other stories. This is accomplished by utilizing what narrative therapists call externalizing language. People and problems are viewed as being separate (Carey & Russell, 2002). Madigan (2003) indicated that labeling persons with psychological description, or seeing the person and the problem as one in the same, is not beneficial to the therapeutic process and further perpetuates the privilege of dominant knowledge over the client's local knowledge. This also positions the therapist to stand side-by-side with the client and fight against the problem story.

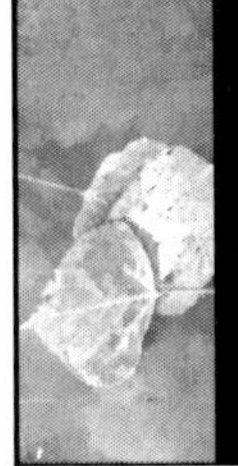

Externalizing Language in Action – Narrative therapists would not likely ask someone how long he has been "depressed." This sort of language tends to blur the line between the person and the problem. Instead, narrative therapists would likely ask a question like, "How long has depression been interrupting your life?" or "How long has depression been following you?" By separating the person from the problem, narrative therapists believe more space is created for change to occur.

As the problem story is told by the client, the therapist is advised to be on the lookout for what are called unique outcomes. Unique outcomes, or as they are sometimes called, sparkling moments, are instances where the person shows signs of resisting the problem story. Using unique outcomes, a new story is created, and this story is then placed next to the problem story. This is referred to as the reauthoring process. Madigan (2000) describes this as "thickening the plot" of the client's life. Therapists are encouraged to listen to, and give more credence to, the client's local knowledge since problems often arise from dominant knowledge. Drawing on the expertise and wisdom of the client is central to narrative therapy.

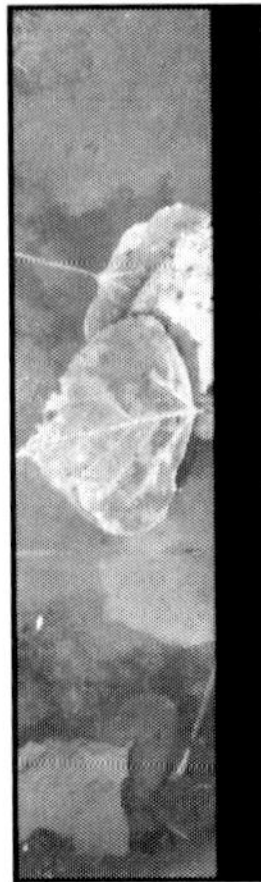

The Power of Problem Stories – Have you ever noticed how negative events and stories seem to have a lot of power in our lives? Perhaps you have been on a nice weekend getaway with a romantic partner for 72 hours. 71 of those hours could have been wonderful with quite literally thousands of positive interactions. However, just one negative interaction can be enough to ruin the entire weekend.

The same process can take place with a story of something like depression in a client's life. That story of depression rears its ugly head and causes the client to forget other narratives that are also present in her life. The client can then come to be defined by depression while ignoring other aspects of her existence. In other words, the problem story is but one piece in a much larger puzzle of who the person really is.

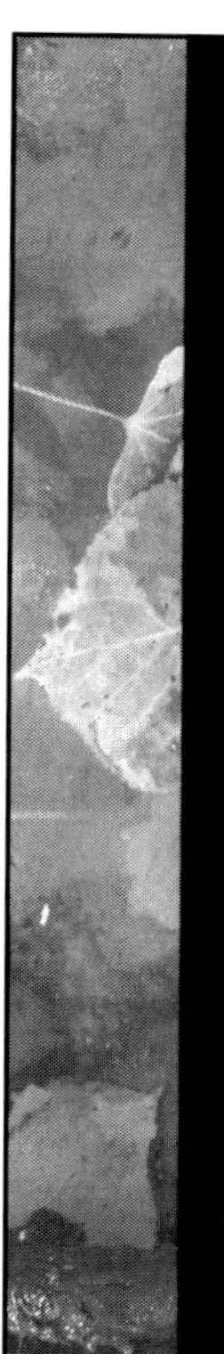

The Power of Problem Stories (*continued*)

Can you think of a time when a dominant life narrative caused you to forget or lose touch with other parts of yourself?

Solution-focused brief therapy (SFBT) is another postmodern approach to therapy. Insoo Kim Berg and Steve De Shazer were both SFBT pioneers. This approach holds the belief that the past is not nearly as important as the future or the present. De Shazer (1991) notes that the past does not have to be understood or explored for a problem to be solved in the present. This approach notes that people are capable of devising their own solutions, and the solutions they choose might not be right for other people struggling with the same problem.

This is generally a very quick approach to therapy that minimizes the importance of psychological diagnosis, detailed clinical histories, and in-depth explorations of the problem (De Shazer & Dolan, 2007). The focus in on finding what is already working in the client's life and trying to apply this to problem that brought him or her into therapy (O'Hanlon, 1999) as well as finding exceptions to the problem (Metcalf, 2001). To this end, clients are encouraged to use solution language as opposed to the problem language they likely brought with them to counseling. Sessions are framed more as consultations, and the therapist provides feedback and notes the progress made at the end of each session as well as clarifying what future steps toward solving the problem might be.

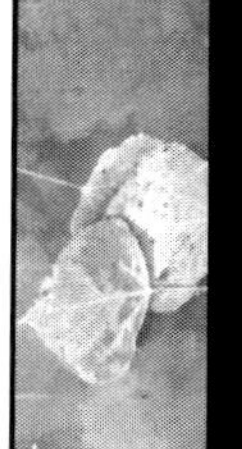

SFBT in Action – Sometimes clients have a very difficult time picturing what the future might look like free of the problems that brought them into counseling. When this happens in SFBT, therapists often used what is called the *Miracle Question* as a way to help client's visualize a new existence.

(*continued*)

SFBT in Action (*continued*)

The Miracle Question can be tweaked a bit by each therapist who uses it, but it essentially goes something like this:

Imagine that you go to bed tonight and when you wake up the next morning a miracle had occurred in your sleep. When you awake, you notice that the problem that brought you here to see me has been solved. As you begin to move around your world, what are some of the things you notice around you that let you know your life had suddenly gotten better?

Now, try this question out for yourself with a problem that has been on your mind. Make your response as specific as possible.

A common criticism of postmodern approaches to therapy is that they rely too heavily on the resources of the client. In other words, what happens if clients do not have an answer and cannot find one? Some people come to counseling seeking answers from an expert, which runs contrary to the theoretical underpinnings of postmodern work. Also, people criticize the brief nature of postmodern approaches to therapy and whether changes made are enduring. Furthermore, narrative therapy specifically can be a complex practice since it does not rely on the linear implementation of techniques and instead relies on a basic philosophical understanding of the underlying tenets of the approach and the creativity of each therapist in practice (Monk et al., 1997).

Eclecticism

In real-world practice, many therapists combine multiple approaches to help clients achieve the change they are searching for. This is referred to as an eclectic approach to therapy. Generally speaking, this can be helpful and allows the therapist to help tailor his or her intervention to individual clients. However, it is important that the therapist knows why she is using the chosen theories or techniques and have a strong foundation and understanding of what she believes drives change.

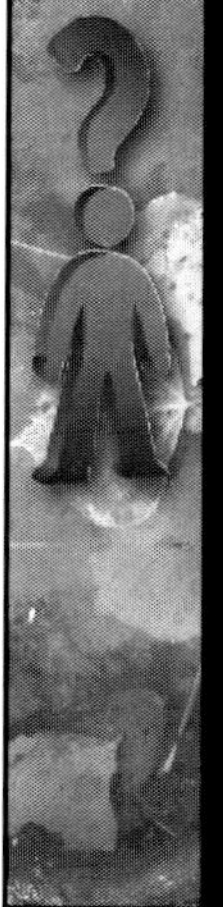

What Do You Think? – It can be tempting to say that all ideas are created equal and that any new approach to counseling should be accepted as valid. What could be some of the potential dangers of adopting this approach?

FUTURE DIRECTIONS

As noted earlier in the chapter, there is an abundance of research that says psychotherapy is effective. Much of this research has been quantitative in nature, meaning the experience of participants in therapy is turned into numbers or statistical data. More recently, scholars in the field have called for qualitative inquiries investigating the outcome and process of psychotherapy. Levitt, Butler, and Hill (2006) noted, " . . . psychotherapy researchers have been calling for qualitative approaches. . . . They argue that these methods allow a focus on subjectivity that is appropriate for understanding therapy and allow clients to articulate and contextualize elements of change that appear to be important in their own experience" (p. 314).

Heath, O'Halloran, and Walters (in press) examined what clients and therapists found to be most helpful in both the process and outcome of psychotherapy. Results indicated that clients' valued egalitarian, genuine, and safe relationships, as well as a client-directed approach to change much like Rogers advocated for many years earlier and that these factors helped clients achieve their desired outcome. In other words, the therapist's way of being and interacting was much more important than the specific tools they were using. Clients also noted the importance of being matched with a therapist who "got them." Having similar worldviews seemed to be of particular importance to clients. Therapists indicated that while they believed it was important to have research to back up the approaches to treatment they were using to ensure they were effective, they were skeptical of "manualized" or "scripted" ways of conducting therapy and said that this made them feel less congruent in counseling.

Understanding *why* and *how* counseling is working through the eyes of the client and not just whether it is working will continue to be a research area of interest in the future. Such research will help therapists better understand the change process and why clients are benefitting from it. Assessing the client's perception of change during the process of therapy where alterations can be made midstream could prove to be especially valuable and invites clients "to become full and equal participants in the treatment process" (Saggese, 2005, p. 562).

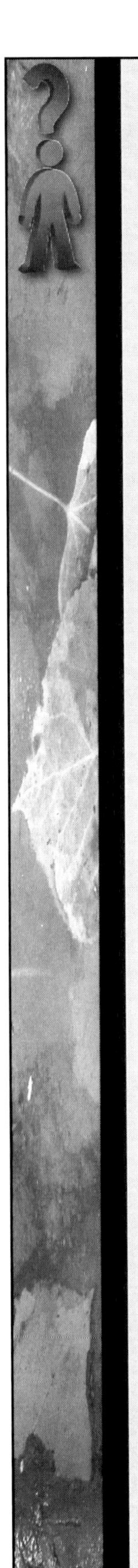

What Do You Think? – Would you feel bad about getting a broken leg treated by a doctor? Chances are, most people would not give it second thought. However, when it comes to seeking counseling for psychological or emotional challenges there is often still a stigma attached to seeking help. In truth, many people who seek counseling do not have a diagnosable mental illness. While therapists are certainly trained to work with diagnosable conditions, many individuals seek assistance around basic problems of living or are simply seeking self-improvement.

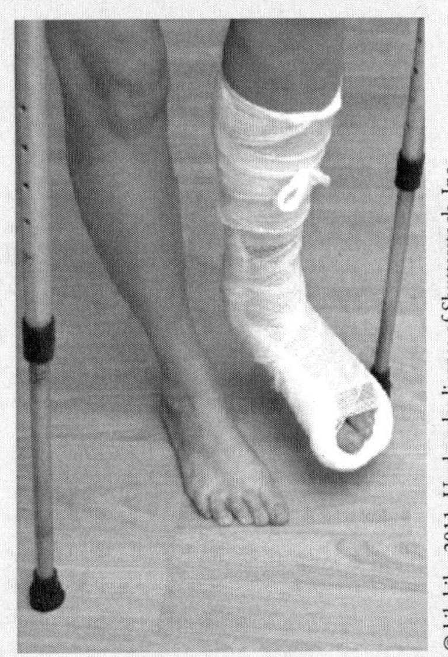

After reading this chapter, would you seek counseling for yourself if you felt you could benefit from it? Why or why not?

What kind of therapist do you believe would be a good match for you? Why?

REFERENCES

American Psychiatric Association. (2011). *New framework proposed for manual of mental disorders: APA revisions a key step in development of DSM-V.* [Online]. Retrived on 6/1/11: www.dsm5.org/Newsroom/Documents/DSM5Structure_050411.pdf

Ansell, E. B., & Grillo, C. M. (2007). Personality disorders. In M. Hersen, S. M. Turner, & D. C. Beidel (Eds.), *Adult psychopathology and diagnosis* (5th ed., pp. 633–678). Hoboken, NJ: Wiley.

Asay, T.P., & Lambert, M.J. (1999). The empirical case for the common factors in therapy. Quantitative findings. In M.A. Hubble, B.L., Duncan, & S.D., Miller (Eds.), *The heart and soul of change: What works in therapy* (pp. 33–56). Washington, DC: American Psychological Association.

Barker, S.L., Funk, S.C., & Houston, B.K. (1988). Psychological treatment versus nonspecific factors: A meta-analysis of conditions that engender comparable expectations for improvement. *Clinical Psychology Review, 8*, 579–594.

Beck, A. T. (1976). *Cognitive therapies and emotional disorders.* New York: New American Library.

Becker, A. E., Burwell, R. A., Gilman, S. E., Herzog, D. B., & Hamburg, P. (2002). Eating behaviours and attitudes following prolonged television exposure among ethnic Fijian adolescent girls. *The British Journal of Psychiatry, 180,* 509–514.

Behar, R. (2007). Gender related aspects of eating disorders: A psychosocial view. In J. S. Rubin (Ed.), *Eating disorders and weight loss research* (pp. 39–65). Hauppauge, NY: Nova Science Publishers.

Carey, M., & Russell, S. (2002). Externalising—commonly asked questions. *The International Journal of Narrative Therapy and Community Work, 2,* 3–18.

Chapman, A. L., Leung, D. W., & Lynch, T. R. (2008). Impulsivity and emotion dysregulation in borderline personality disorder. *Journal of Personality Disorders, 22,* 148–164.

DeJong, P., & Berg, I. K. (2008). *Interviewing for solutions* (3rd ed.). Belmont, CA: Brooks/Cole.

De Shazer, S. (1991). *Putting difference to work.* New York: Norton.

De Shazer, S., & Dolan, Y. M. (with Korman, H., Trepper, T., McCullom, E., and Berg, I. K.) (2007). *More than miracles: The state of the art of solution-focused brief therapy.* New York: Haworth Press.

Doherty, W.J., & Simmons, D.S. (1995, January). Clinical practice patterns of marriage and family therapy: A national survey of therapists and their clients.

Journal of Marital and Family Therapy, 21(1), 3–16.

Doherty, W.J., & Simmons, D.S. (1996, January). Clinical practice patterns of marriage and family therapy: A national survey of therapists and their clients.

Journal of Marital and Family Therapy, 22(1), 9–26.

Duncan, B.L., Miller, S.D., & Sparks, J.A. (2004). *The heroic client: A revolutionary way to improve effectiveness through client-direct outcome-informed therapy.* San Francisco, CA: Jossey-Bass.

Duncan, B. L., & Moynihan, D.W. (1994). Applying outcome research: Intentional utilization of the client's frame of reference. *Psychotherapy, 31*(2), 294–302.

Dush, D.M. (1986). The placebo in psychosocial outcome evaluations. *Evaluation & the Health Professions, 9,* 421–438.

Ellis, A. (2004). Why rational emotive behavior therapy is the most comprehensive and effective form of behavior therapy. *Journal of Rational Emotive & Cognitive Behavior Therapy, 22(2),* 85–92.

Ellman, L. M., & Cannon, T. D. (2008). Environmental pre and perinatal influences in etiology. In K. T. Mueser & D. V. Jeste (Eds.), *Clinical handbook of schizophrenia* (pp. 65–73). New York: Guilford.

Frank, J.D., & Frank, J.B. (1991). *Persuasion and healing: A comparative study of psychotherapy* (3rd ed). Baltimore, MD: John Hopkins University Press.

Freedman, J., & Combs, G. (1996). *Narrative therapy: The social construction of preferred realities.* New York: Norton.

Galderisi, S., Quarantelli, M., Volpe, U., Mucci, A., Cassano, G. B., Invernizzi, G., Rossi, A., Vita, A., Pini, S., Cassano, P., Daneluzzo, E., De Peri, L., Stratta, P., Brunetti, A., & Maj, M. (2008). Patterns of structural MRI abnormalities in deficit and nondeficit schizophrenia. *Schizophrenia Bulletin, 34,* 393–401.

Greenberg, S.T.,& Schoen, E.G. (2008). Males and eating disorders: Gender-based therapy for eating disorder recovery. *Professional Psychology: Research and Practice, 39*(4),464–471.

Hansell, J. H., & Damour, L. K. (2008). *Abnormal psychology* (2nd ed.). Hoboken, NJ: Wiley.

Hawton, K., Sutton, L., Haw, C., Sinclair, J., & Harriss, L. (2005). Suicide and attempted suicide in bipolar disorder: A systematic review of risk factors. *Journal of Clinical Psychiatry, 66*(6), 693–704.

Heath, T., O'Halloran, M. S., & Walters, M. (in press). What works in psychotherapy: Qualitative accounts of psychotherapists and clients. *Journal of Psychotherapy Integration.*

Hill, C.E., & Corbett, M.M. (1993). A perspective on the history of process and outcomeresearch in counseling psychology. *Journal of Counseling Psychology, 40*(1),3–24.

Hubble, M.A., Duncan, B.L., & Miller, S.D. (1999). *The heart and soul of change: What works in therapy.* Washington, DC: American Psychological Association.

Ikemoto, K. (2004). Significance of human striatal D-neurons: Implications in neuropsychiatric functions. *Neuropsychopharmacology, 29*(4),429–434.

Jones, S. R., & Fernyhough, C. (2007). A new look at the neural diathesis-stress model of schizophrenia: The primacy of social-evaluative and uncontrollable situations. *Schizophrenia Bulletin, 33,* 1171–1177.

Kaye, W. (2008) Neurobiology of anorexia and bulimia nervosa. *Physiology & Behavior, 94,* 121–135.

Kellogg, S. H., & Young, J. E. (2008). Cognitive therapy. In J. L. Lebow (Ed.), *Twenty-first century psychotherapies: Contemporary approaches to theory and practice* (pp. 43–79). Hoboken, NJ: Wiley.

Kirschenbaum, H., & Jourdan, A. (2005). The current status of Carl Rogers and the person-centered approach. *Psychotherapy: Theory, Research Practice, Training, 42*(1), 37–51.

Lambert, M.J. (1992). Implications of outcome research for psychotherapy integration.In J.C. Norcross & M.R. Goldfried (Eds.), *Handbook of psychotherapy integration.* New York: Basic.

Lambert, M.J., & Barley, D.E. (2001). Research summary on the therapeutic relationship and psychotherapy outcome. *Psychotherapy, 38*(4),357–361.

Lambert, M.J., & Ogles, B. (2004). The efficacy and effectiveness of psychotherapy. In M.J. Lambert (Ed.), *Bergin and Garfield's handbook of psychotherapy and behavior change* (5th ed., pp. 139–193). New York: Wiley.

Lerner, H. D. (2008). Psychodynamic perspectives. In M. Hersen & A. M. Gross (Eds.), *Handbook of clinical psychology, vol 1: Adults* (pp. 127–160). Hoboken, NJ: Wiley.

Levitt, H., Butler, M., & Hill, T. (2006). What clients find helpful in psychotherapy: Developing principles for facilitating moment-to-moment change.*Journal of Counseling Psychology, 53*(3), 314–324.

Lipsey, M., & Wilson, D. (1993). The efficacy of psychological, educational, and behavioral treatment: Confirmation from meta-analysis.*American Psychologist, 48,* 1181–1209.

Madigan, S. (2000). *Family therapy with the experts: Narrative therapy with Dr. Stephen Madigan* [Video series]. Boston: Allyn & Bacon.

Madigan, S. (2003). *Child therapy with the experts: Narrative therapy with children with Stephen Madigan* [Video series]. Boston: Allyn & Bacon.

Metcalf, L. (2001). Solution focused therapy. In R. J. Corsini (Ed.), *Handbook of innovative therapy* (2nd ed., pp. 647–659). New York: Wiley.

Miller, S.D., Duncan, B.L., & Hubble, M.A. (1997). *Escape from Babel: Toward a unifying language for psychotherapy practice.* New York: Norton.

Miller, S. D., Duncan, B. L., & Hubble, M. A. (2004). Outcome-informed clinical work. In J. Norcross & M. Goldfried (Eds.),*Handbook of psychotherapy integration.* New York: Oxford University Press.

Millon, T. (2004). *Masters of the mind: Exploring the story of mental illness from ancient times to the new millennium.* Hoboken, NJ: Wiley.

Minzenberg, M. J., Fan, J., New, A. S., Tang, C. Y., & Siever, L. J. (2008). Frontolimbic structural changes in borderline personality disorder. *Journal of Psychiatric Research, 42,* 727–733.

Minzenberg, M. J., Poole, J. H., & Vinogradov, S. (2008). A neurocognitive model of borderline personality disorder: Effects of childhood sexual abuse and relationship to adult social attachment disturbance. *Development and Psychopathology, 20,* 341–368.

Monk, G., Winsdale, J., Crocket, K., & Epston, D. (1997). *Narrative therapy in practice: The archaeology of hope.* San Francisco: Jossey-Bass.

O'Hanlon, W. H. (1999). *Do one thing different.* New York: Harper Collins.

Pepinsky, H.B., Hill-Frederick, K., & Epperson, D.L. (1978). *The Journal of Counseling Psychology* as a matter of policies. *Journal of Counseling Psychology, 25*, 483–498.

Prioleau, L., Murdock, M., & Brody, N. (1983). An analysis of psychotherapy versus placebo studies. *The Behavioral and Brain Sciences, 6*, 275–310.

Raine, A., & Yang, Y. (2006). The neuroanatomical bases of psychopathy: A review of brain imaging findings. In C. J. Patrick (Ed.), *Handbook of psychopathy* (pp. 278–295). New York: Guilford Press.

Rogers, C.R. (1942). The use of electrically recorded interviews in improving psychotherapeutic techniques. *American Journal of Orthopsychiatry, 12*,429–434.

Rogers, C.R. (1951). *Client-centered therapy: Its current practice, implications, and theory.* Boston: Houghton Mifflin.

Roszenweig, S. (1936). Some implicit common factors in diverse methods in psychotherapy. *American Journal of Orthopsychiatry, 6*, 412–415.

Saggese, M. L. (2005). Maximizing treatment effectiveness in clinical practice: An outcome-informed, collaborative approach. *Families in Society: The Journal of Contemporary Social Services, 86*(4), 558–564.

Schwebel, M. (1984). From past to present: Counseling psychology's socially prescribed role. In J.M. Whiteley, N. Kagan, L. Harmon, B.R. Fretz, & F. Tanney(Eds.), *The coming decade in counseling psychology* (pp. 283–300). Schenectady, NY: Character Research Press.

Seligman, M.E. (1995). The effectiveness of psychotherapy: The consumer reports study. *American Psychologist, 50*(12), 965–974.

Shadish, W. (2000). The effects of psychological therapies under clinically representative conditions. *Psychological Bulletin, 126*, 512–529.

Shadish, W.R., Montgomery, L.M., Wilson, P., Wilson, M.R., Bright, I., & Okwumabua, T. (1993). Effects of family and marital psychotherapies: A meta-analysis. *Journal of Consulting and Clinical Psyhcology, 61*, 992–1002.

Swartz, K. L. (2004). Depression and anxiety. *Johns Hopkins White Papers.* Baltimore: Johns Hopkins Medical Institutions.

Szasz, T. (1960). The myth of mental illness. *American Psychologist, 15,* 113–118.

Szasz, T. (2004). The psychiatric protection order for the "battered mental patient." *British Medical Journal, 327,* 1449–1451.

Wachtel, P. L. (2008). *Relational theory and the practice of psychotherapy.* New York: Guilford.

Wampold, B.E. (2001). *The great psychotherapy debate: Models, methods, and findings.* Hillsdale, NJ: Erlbaum.

Wampold, B.E., Ahn, H., & Coleman, H. (2001). Medical model as a metaphor: Old habits die hard. *Journal of Counseling Psychology, 48*(3), 268–273.

Weltzin, T.E., Weisensel, N., Franczyk, D., Burnett, K., Klitz, C.,& Bean P. (2005). Eating disorders in men: Update. *Journal of Men's Health & Gender, 2*(2), 186–191.

Yalom, I. (1980). *Existential psychotherapy.* New York: Basic Books.

NAME ______________________________ DATE ____________________

WORKSHEET CHAPTER TWELVE

CHAPTER 13

SOCIAL PSYCHOLOGY*

"Man is a social animal."
– Benedict Spinoza

Nearly every day, humans interact in some way and at some level with others in society. Whether in a close relationship with a friend or family member or with someone more distant such as a teacher or doctor, our thoughts, feelings, and actions are significantly influenced on a daily basis by the presence of others. Think of your favorite foods, activities, and hobbies. Where did these preferences come from? How did they develop? Perhaps a friend or relative introduced you to a new food, or maybe a childhood friend give you an idea about a game that you have made a hobby of as an adult. When you think about it, claiming an idea as uniquely from one's own storehouse of thought can be more than just a bit difficult. It is likely that any thought, feeling, or action has been subject to the thoughts and behaviors of others.

*Chapter Contributor: Jonathan Lussier, Metropolitan State College of Denver.

Compared to the rest of the animal kingdom, human beings have an unparalleled ability to communicate their thoughts and feelings to one another and thus find themselves much more able to influence the thoughts, feelings, and behaviors of others. While these influences can have positive effects and lead to the betterment of human life, they also can create false impressions and biases both about oneself and others. Social psychology is the branch of psychology that investigates these effects and biases as well as social influence, social perception, and social interaction. To study social psychology is to understand that human beings are fundamentally social by nature, that they both shape their society and are shaped by it, and that each person has, as a tool of survival, the tendency to formulate stereotypes.

ACTIVITY

Frequently parents and teachers warn kids of the danger of peer pressure in an attempt to steer them away from dangerous behaviors or arm them with the fortitude to say "no" to potentially harmful activities. "Peer pressure" seems to carry a negative connotation with many parents, teachers and kids of all ages.

Can peer-pressure be positive? How?

Make a list of people who you believe have influenced you the most. Now, using *only one word* written next to this person's name, describe his or her influence.

Look at your list of names and descriptors. Are these *positive* or *negative* descriptions of influence? Did you have a tendency to portray more positive or negative influence? Why do you think this is?

The sphere of social influence varies greatly and can span from the impact of just one individual to the impression of an entire government. Our relationships with individuals, groups, and governments all affect our thoughts, feelings, and behavior. While these influences are involved in nearly every area of our lives, it does seem that their scope and severity can be mediated. Can you imagine what the world would be like if every one of its seven billion individuals did as he or she pleased, completely unaffected by the thoughts and feelings of others?

The previous chapters looked at aspects of psychology that surveyed more the perspective of the individual. In this chapter that focus is widened to include the influence of groups of individuals, their behaviors, and ways that we are all influenced by each other, for better or for worse.

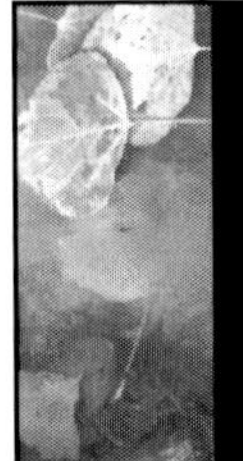

Social Psychology in Action – While it might be difficult at first to see how influences of others can have a tangible impact on our lives, there are some different ways of thinking that can help bring such impacts to awareness.

(*continued*)

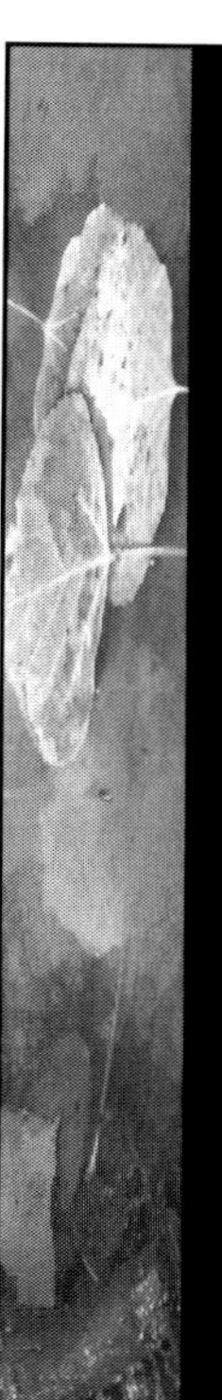

Social Psychology in Action (*continued*)

What are you wearing today? Are your clothes of a fashionable brand? Do they include a logo of a sports team, company, or other group? How do you value these groups in your life?

What about shoes/hats/jewelry/tattoos?

How did you learn to value these things? How were you convinced to select some of the elements of your attire?

How can an increased knowledge of social influences be of benefit to your life?

SOCIAL COGNITION

Social cognition is the process by which we humans encode, store, process, and access information as it relates to relationships with other humans. Put another way, it is the study of human thought in social situations. While a social cognitive process is helpful in navigating everyday relationships and solving nuanced yet simple problems, it can often be riddled with bias, resulting in stereotypes and prejudice. Below are some descriptions of cognitive patterns and biases of the human mind.

Schemas

Schemas are one of the most commonly used tools our brain uses in social situations. They are concepts or mental structures that organize information in our brain and give us a plan for how to navigate simple, complex, or novel social situations and/or think about a new idea, person, or behavior.

Fundamental Attribution Error (FAE)

Think of a time someone else arrived late for a class, meeting, or appointment. Perhaps you made a judgment about why she was late. Perhaps she is a forgetful or lazy person? Chances are you did not think about whether situational circumstances were the root cause of her tardiness. The *fundamental attribution error* is the tendency to value the role of personality or disposition over situational factors when considering the causes of the behavior of others. This cognitive bias is labeled as such because it is *fundamentally* based in how the brain works.

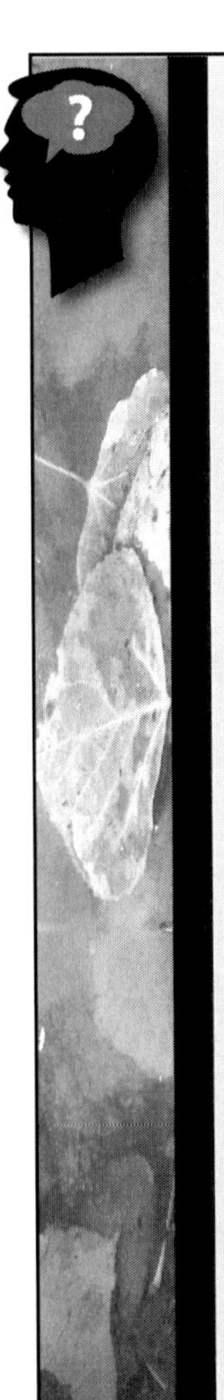

Think about it – Imagine you are driving in a busy city. You look around and see many people who appear to be homeless and pleading to passersby for spare change. What are some possible explanations for these people's unfortunate circumstances? Is it possible that you lump these explanations together in groups that attribute their situation to a certain personality trait? Social circumstance? Mental health problem?

Is it likely that each of these people has *exactly* the same reason for being homeless or in such need?

Think of a time in which you observed someone, yourself included, commit this error.

What are your ideas on why the fundamental attribution error persists? Is there evidence that it is diminishing or expanding in the general population? Explain.

Cognitive biases are variations in normal judgment and involve tendencies toward quick judgments, most likely leading to behavior that historically aided in adaptation and survival. They often lead to distortions in the perception, judgment, and interpretation of reality. Some of these biases are described below.

The *saliency bias* involves the tendency of the person to focus on the most noticeable features of another when attempting to understand the root causes of his or her behavior. Psychologists theorize that this bend in focus toward dispositions is because they are simpler to formulate and that this is a much easier process than seeking to understand more complex, situational factors.

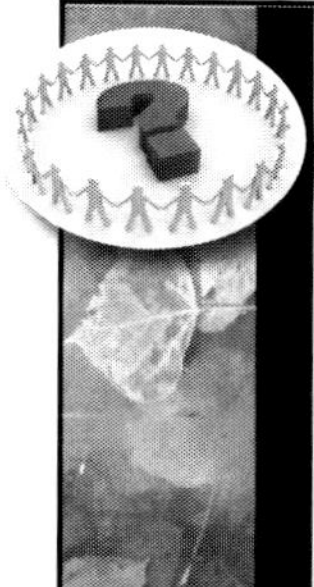

Ask Around – Is it indeed easier to label someone's actions as being part of who he or she is rather than to think about all of the contextual variables that may have contributed?

Give friends and family a quick description of these different types of cognitive bias. Ask them if they have examples or have witnessed these biases first-hand.

What are the differences in their examples and yours?

The *actor-observer bias* involves the tendency to assume the causes of our own behaviors as situational and those of others as dispositional. One explanation is that we are aware of all the situational factors that affect our behaviors because we experience them directly, whereas we are most often ignorant of these same factors as they affect others' behavior.

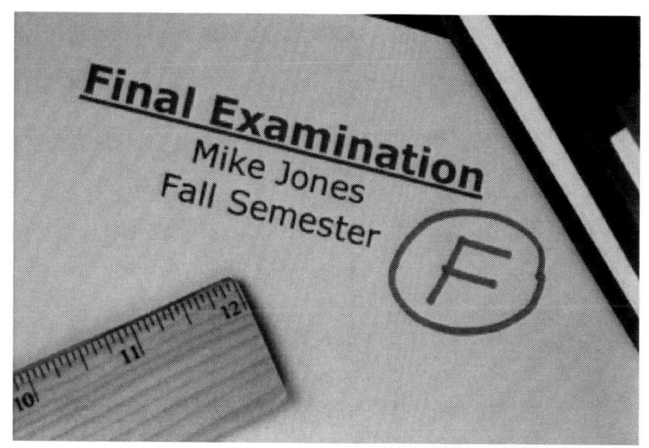

Have you ever noticed a tendency, whether in yourself or in others, to credit successes to internal factors and failures to external ones? This tendency is often referred to as the *self-serving bias*. Great examples can be found in the classroom setting. For example, students who received high marks on an exam may profess them a product of their high intelligence or hard work. On the other hand, students who received low marks may be more likely to cite an illness, the unfairness of the teacher, or trick questions.

ACTIVITY

The self-serving bias can be both helpful and detrimental. It is clearly not conducive to good mental health to constantly blame oneself for everything that may go wrong. Then again, it also would not be healthy to consistently attribute all one's shortcomings to external factors.

Discuss the possibility of a healthy balance between the two. What factors would need to be present for such a balance?

The *hindsight bias* is the impulse to see events that have already occurred as being more foreseeable than they were before they came to pass. Have you ever observed a couple that breaks up and later heard someone say (or perhaps were guilty yourself!), "I knew they would never last"?

The hindsight bias involves the overestimation of one's predictive abilities of the possibility of an event after its outcome. Additional examples include stock market analysts claiming an "expected" sharp rise or fall or sports commentators' claims that a team's improbably victory was unsurprising, or "I knew it all along."

Try it at home – You will need a coin, paper, and pencil for this activity. You are going to flip this coin 51 times. Before each flip record on which side you think the coin will land. Write down the results.

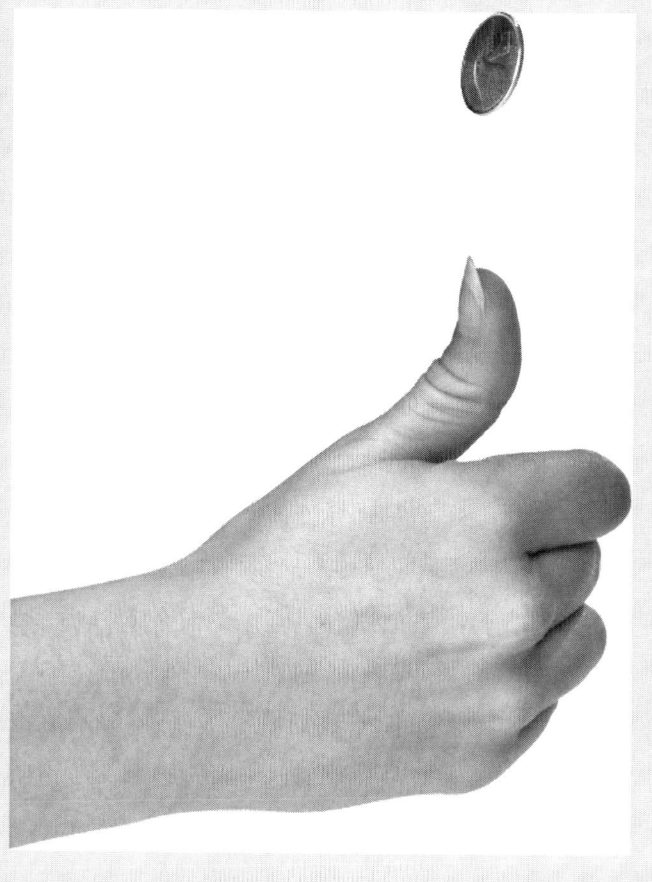

What was your experience like while flipping the coin? Did you experience any "hot streaks" or "cold streaks"? What were your feelings during those streaks? Did these "streaks" influence your behavior or cause you to change your prediction?

What if you were to predict all 51 flips of the coin prior to the exercise and not each individual time? Do you have any cognitive bias that would suggest to you that this would yield less of a predictive value?

Finally, consider what it would ACTUALLY mean if you could predict better in bulk form prior to the exercise versus for each individual flip? If this were true, what would be the implications?

Can you see examples of this in the world around you? What factors make it possible for people to maintain their beliefs in these untruths?

ATTITUDES AND PERSUASION

An *attitude* is an evaluation, positive or negative, that we have toward something or someone, whereas *persuasion* is a form of social influence that involves the process toward the acceptance of an idea, attitude, or behavior. Our attitudes are learned dispositions that reflect how we think, feel, and act. They are formed through experience and observation and are not necessarily permanent. While they undoubtedly change over time, attitudes formed through personal experiences are much more enduring and are good predictors of behavior. When considering how we go about changing our attitudes, psychologists pay special attention to the persuasive role of friends, family, culture, and society at large.

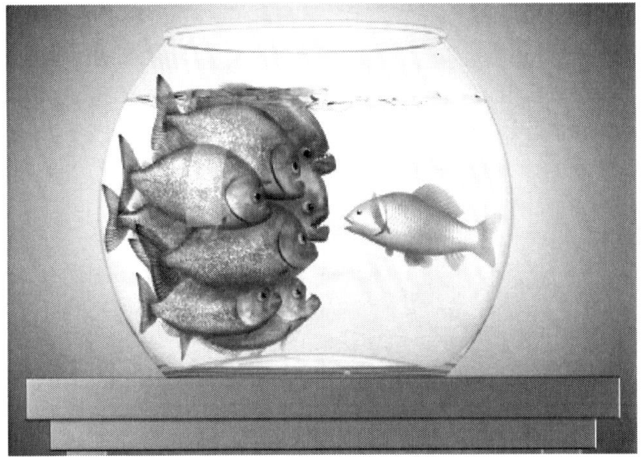

© lexaarts, 2011. Used under license of Shutterstock, Inc.

Think about it – What are some of your strongest attitudes? Do you remember where these attitudes came from? How were they learned?

If attitudes are a good indicator of future behavior, wouldn't it be logical for a company to try to change your attitude on their product? How would changing your attitude affect your behavior?

Can you think of examples of a company's efforts to change people's attitudes?

Can you think of a time when you were persuaded to change your attitude or purchase a product? List some examples you think turned out well and some that perhaps did not turn out so well.

© Junker, 2011. Used under license of Shutterstock, Inc.

Cognitive dissonance is a feeling of discomfort resulting from conflict between one's behavior and one's beliefs. Leon Festinger and J. Merrill Carlsmith (1959) conducted an experiment that illustrates the idea of cognitive dissonance. In their experiment, participants were given extremely mundane and boring tasks to accomplish over a period of one hour. At the conclusion of the hour, the participants were asked to explain their experience of the tasks but were told to frame their descriptions in such a light as to convince an upcoming participant (a confederate of the study) that the tasks were fun and exciting. In one group the participants were offered $1 for telling the other participant how fun the experiment was, while the other group of participants were offered $20. If the participant took the payment and lied to the other participant about how fun the experiment was, then he or she was later asked about his or her true feelings. What do you think happened? Were the participants who were paid $20 more likely to feel good about their participation than those who were paid only $1?

Actually, those who were paid only $1 reported enjoying the boring experiment much more than those who were paid $20! When the participants were asked to lie about enjoying the experiment, they experienced discomfort as a result of conflict between their behavior (telling the participant the experiment was fun) and their attitude (that the experiment was boring and mundane). Those who were paid $20 reported lesser change in attitude toward the experiment because they could easily explain their behavior (lying to the other participant) in terms of the money received. For those who were only paid $1, they found the money an insufficient justification for lying. As a result, their discomfort (cognitive dissonance) caused them to change their attitude toward the experiment.

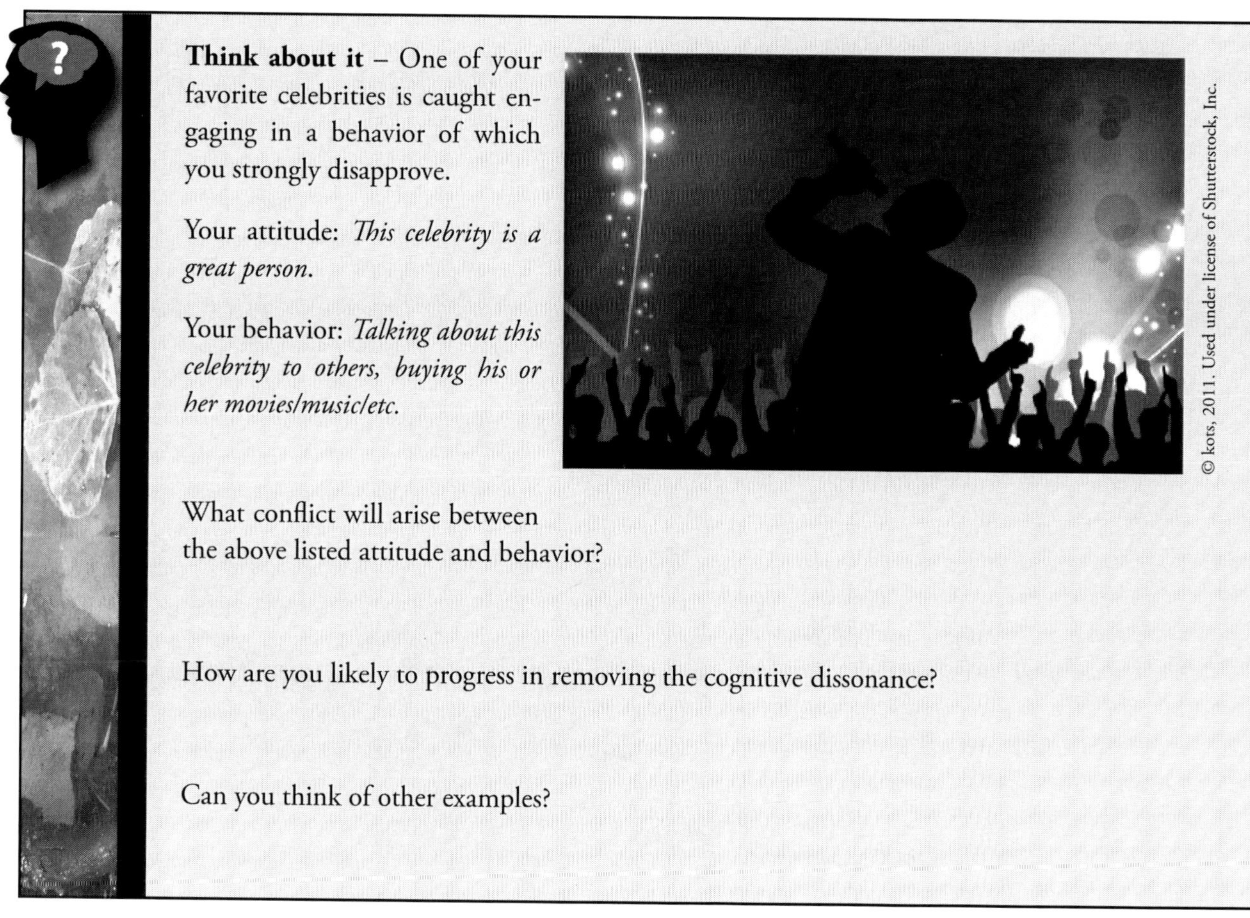

Think about it – One of your favorite celebrities is caught engaging in a behavior of which you strongly disapprove.

Your attitude: *This celebrity is a great person.*

Your behavior: *Talking about this celebrity to others, buying his or her movies/music/etc.*

What conflict will arise between the above listed attitude and behavior?

How are you likely to progress in removing the cognitive dissonance?

Can you think of other examples?

PREJUDICE, STEREOTYPES, AND DISCRIMINATION

Prejudice is an attitude toward an individual based on a real or perceived membership of an identified group. More often than not prejudices are negative, such as, *African Americans are more criminally minded* or *blondes are less intelligent.* It is easy to see the harm negative prejudices cause, yet positive prejudices can cause harmful effects as well. Consider the seemingly positive prejudice that *all Asians are good at math* or *Jewish people are good with business.* What negative effects may arise?

Similar prejudices are made up of different components. The cognitive component of prejudice, also known as the *stereotype*, makes up the thoughts and beliefs toward people based solely on their membership in a group.

The second component, the affective component of prejudice, involves the feelings and emotions we possess toward people of that group. The behavioral component, or *discrimination*, refers to our actions, informed by our stereotypes, toward the members of that group.

© El Greco, 2011. Used under license of Shutterstock, Inc.

In addition to personal experience and observation, prejudice can be a product of our brain trying to simplify the world for us. Prejudice, like any attitude, is learned through personal experience and observation throughout one's life. Like attitudes, prejudices can be learned from friends, family, and from society. In societies with a dominant culture, *ethnocentrism* is often prevalent, exposing beliefs that one's own culture is superior and/or normal, and other cultures, measured in relation to one's own, are inferior.

SOCIAL INFLUENCE

Obviously culture and society shape and influence us in innumerable ways and across our relative lifespan. Observing these influences by examining other cultures is often illuminating, although perhaps more difficult when viewed within the bounds of one's own culture. Growing accustomed to these influences, many often forget they are there and, as a result, underestimate the effects they have. In this section we will discuss conformity and obedience.

Conformity

Social psychologists define *conformity* as changing behaviors to match the opinions and behaviors of others. A social psychologist named Solomon Asch (1951) attempted to measure the influence conformity can have on individuals. In his original experiment, participants were led to believe they had volunteered for a study on perception. The participants were shown a display of three lines and were asked to match the line that was closest in length to a fourth line. The corrected answer to the question was made to look obvious to the participants; one of the three lines clearly matched the fourth while the others obviously did not. Participants were placed in groups of seven; however, six of the participants were confederates (working in collaboration with the experimenter).

© Joerg Hausmann, 2011. Used under license of Shutterstock, Inc.

The experiment began and all the participants chose the correct line (it was that clear which was the correct response). On subsequent trials, however, one participant (confederate) purposely gave the wrong answer. The number of dissenter/confederates increased until all were choosing the wrong line. This left just one (often confused) participant. Asch wanted to find out if the participants would stick with the answer they knew was correct or if they would select the obviously wrong answer, thus conforming to the group.

Asch's experiment resulted in more than a third of participants conforming to the group and selecting the wrong answer. In the control group,the participants were under no peer pressure and gave the correct response nearly 100 percent of the time.

Of important note is that two-thirds of the participants still chose the correct answer and were seemingly uninfluenced by others' behavior. Although the majority chose not to conform in his study, the one-third that did surprised Asch and gave rise to concerns about society as a whole. He widely questioned methods of education and the values promoted within our society. Additional questions remained such as, if people conformed as a result of such small amounts of social pressure, what would happen if these same people were given a direct order?

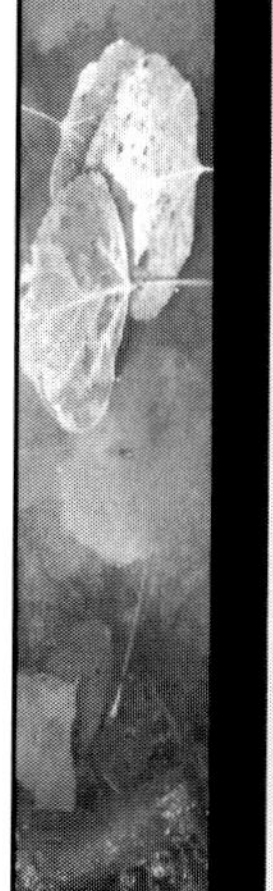

Conformity in Action – Describe an experienced you've had in which you have conformed to others. Did you conform while privately disagreeing, or did you actually come to believe in what you were conforming to?

What might be an "antidote" to or a protective factor against conformity?

Can you think of large-scale example of conformity?

Obedience

As we have read, conformity is altering one's behavior or beliefs to fit in with the group. In a similar vein, in the early 1960s a psychologist named Stanley Milgram (1963), motivated in large part by a flummoxed curiosity regarding the atrocities of Nazi Germany, wanted to measure the extent to which people will follow commands (*obedience to authority*) as well as their willingness to obey an authority figure who, in the case of this famous experiment, ordered them to perform acts that conflicted with their better judgment. Milgram's research resulted in arguably the most famous, landmark, and controversial study in all of psychology.

The study was conducted at Yale University's psychology laboratory and began with participants being told they were engaged in a study on processes of learning and memory. The experimenter, a tall man donned in a full lab coat, informs the two men that the study is specifically attempting to measure the effect of punishment on learning and memory. The experiment involves one of the participants taking on the role of "teacher" and the other taking the role of "learner." The teacher was to read a list of word pairs to the learner, whose job it is to recite them back correctly. The experimenter told the teacher that errors committed by the learner needed to result in a punishment, in this case, electric shocks to be delivered by the teacher. The electric shocks were to increase in intensity for every incorrect response given by the learner.

The two participants are assigned the roles by drawing slips out of a hat. The first draws a slip and proclaims it says "learner." Unbeknownst to the second man, he is actually a confederate (working in collaboration with the experimenter and who received no actual electric shock). The second participant (the only actual participant in the study) is assigned the role of teacher and both are led to an adjacent room where the experimenter straps the learner into a chair and applies electrode paste to conduct the electricity and avoid burns. The experimenter then takes the teacher back to the main room where a machine said to be a shock generator is present. The switches on the shock generator are labeled by voltage ranging from 15 to 450 volts. The switches include labels like "slight shock" and "XXX." The experimenter gives the teacher a slight shock to serve as a reference to what the learner will experience. The experimenter then hands the teacher the lists of word pairs and tells him to begin.

The teacher begins reciting the word pairs to the learner. As per the study's design the learner (confederate) often gets the answer wrong, and the teacher is told to administer the punishment each and every time. For each incorrect answer, the teacher is told to increase the voltage. The teacher begins to hear the groaning of the learner from the adjacent room in response to the shocks. After the teacher administers 150 volts the learner shouts, "Experimenter get me out of here! I refuse to go on!" By 270 volts he begins screaming in pain from the shocks. At 300 volts the learner refuses to answer, to which the experimenter tells the teacher to treat as "wrong answers." After 330 volts, the screams and protests of the learner fall silent and there is no response. The experimenter tells the teacher to continue to administer shocks all the way until the 450 volts, and the experiment ends.

How far do you believe the participants took this experiment? That is, how much "shock" did they administer even in the midst of protesting screams and demands to stop? Do you believe anyone would go all the way to 450 volts? Milgram described his study to groups of peers, students and civilians, and asked them this very question. Nearly all of them believed the participants would stop at a voltage of 150 or when the learner stated his refusal to continue his experiment.

What Milgram's found was much different than these estimates. Out of his original experimental group of 40, 26 of them (65 percent) continued with the experiment all the way to a voltage of 450. Curiously, prior to his study, Milgram polled a group of psychiatrists who reached a consensus that one would have to be sadistic to complete the experiment to such a degree.

Yet the participants in Milgram's study were far from sadistic. All seemed to suffer some distress and internal conflict. Some laughed nervously, sweated, and repeatedly stated they did not want to hurt the learner. When teachers protested their wishes to discontinue the experiment out of fear of injuring the learner, the experimenter would respond by saying either, "the experiment requires that you continue" or "it is absolutely essential that you continue." In most cases this was enough to keep the teachers'cooperation with the experiment.

Understandably, the results of his study disturbed Milgram. Following his original study, he repeated it many times, manipulating variables in an attempt to find out the core factors that could help explain why participants showed such high levels of obedience. After many experimental replications, he came to identify four factors that affected the level of obedience exhibited in his experiments (1974).

Saliency of Authority Figure: When orders came in the form of a voice recording, when the experimenter left the room, or when the experimenter was dressed in ordinary clothes, obedience would drop significantly.

Saliency of Victim: When the learner was in the same room or the experimenter forcibly placed the learner's hand on the shock plate, obedience dropped significantly.

Responsibility: When teacher inquiries regarding the responsibility of learner's health were answered, "I am responsible" by the experimenter, obedience remained high. When responsibility was shifted to the teacher, however, only 3 percent obeyed to 450 volts.

Group Influence: Group influence had a profound effect on obedience. When two other teachers (confederates) chose to disobey, the third teacher only obeyed 10 percent of the time. When the others chose to obey, the third teacher obeyed 70 percent of the time.

Many psychologists questioned Milgram's ethics following the publication of his study. They argued against his treatment of participants, arguing that their distress is not worth the results garnered. Milgram made sure to fully debrief each and every subject in his study. In fact, most reported the experience as helpful and informative. Today, it would be difficult to fully replicate his study because ethical standards have shifted. This shift does not seem to diminish the great amount of insight into human obedience to authority gained from Milgram's work.

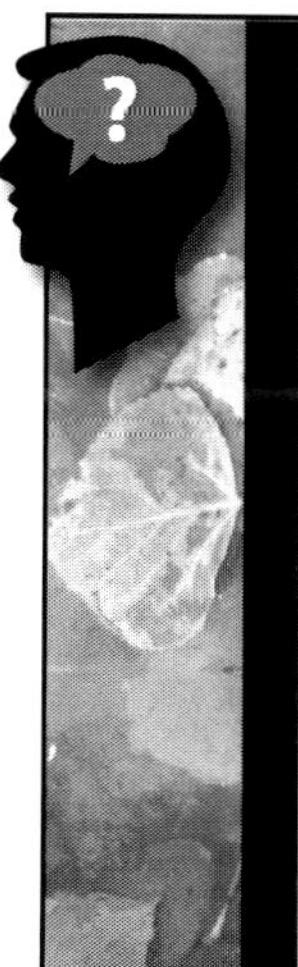

Think about it – Thinking about Milgram's results, do you think that human beings can be coerced into anything given precise circumstances?

Describe a time you were in a situation where an order was given you were uncomfortable with. What were some of the factors that helped contribute to your obedience? To your refusal?

Much of Milgram's motivation for these studies was a curiosity about the atrocities visited on Jewish people, minorities, disabled, and homosexual individuals in Nazi Germany. His primary curiosity revolved around the question of mutual intent. Put another way, he wanted to know

(*continued*)

Think about it (*continued*)

if soldiers carried out orders to kill millions of people in the many death camps around Germany because they had a similar moral standing with those given the orders or if they were simply obeying orders.

What does his study suggest? How can the results of his study be used to understand and prevent such an atrocity?

While the results of the studies performed by Milgram and Asch may raise some concern about obedience and conformity, one must also think about the many advantages of both obedience and conformity. Can you picture the chaos that would ensue if everyone decided to make his or her own rules on driving etiquette and which traffic rules to obey and which to disregard? Conformity and obedience are two important reasons that cities of millions of individuals can coexist in relative harmony. On the other hand, where would the civil rights movement be if world figures such as Martin Luther King, Jr. or Gandhi decided to conform and obey?

GROUP INFLUENCE

Every one of us is part of many different groups. Our membership and participation in these groups varies. How we initiate and maintain status as a member and the value we place on being a member are important considerations when looking at the influence of these groups. When we are a part of a group, we are often assigned *roles*. These roles act as norms and serve to guide individuals' thinking and behavior. Psychologist Philip Zimbardo postulated on these roles and looked compellingly into how groups affect behavior. This question captivated Zimbardo and resulted in him designing and carrying out, in part, the now famous Stanford Prison Study (1972).

Seeking to simulate a prison environment, Zimbardo carefully selected and screened 24 male students attending Stanford University. The participants were paid $15 a day to imitate life in a prison for two weeks. Participants were then randomly placed into either one of two groups, prisoner or guard.The participants were treated in a manner commensurate to their roles. For example, prisoners were arrested and booked into prison where they were given

ID numbers and prison clothes and later locked into prison cells. Guards meanwhile were given uniforms, clubs, whistles, and authority over the prisoners.

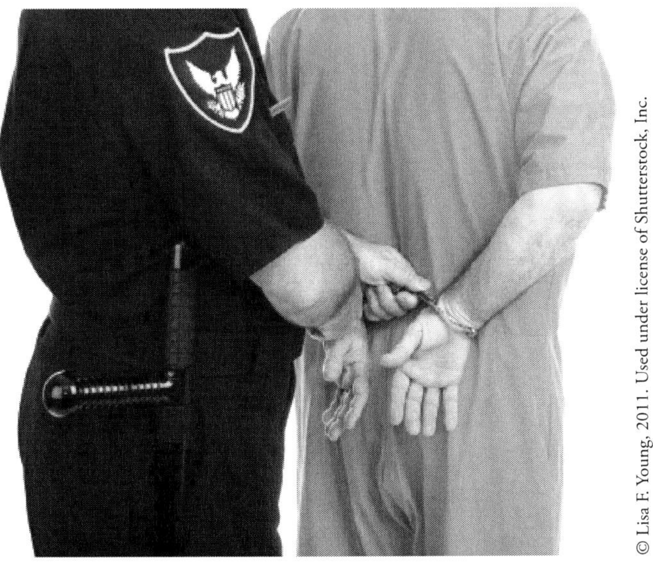
© Lisa F. Young, 2011. Used under license of Shutterstock, Inc.

The results of this study were unexpected. All of the guards took part in some form of what Zimbardo described as abuse of power. Prisoner disobedience was met with retaliation from the guards who in response assigned degrading tasks and removed basic privileges such as eating and sleeping. Over time prisoners became depressed and submissive, and the guards' abusive behavior increased. Just four days into the experiment a third of the prisoners had to be released due to severe psychological reactions to the experience. After only six days, the experiment, originally scheduled for two weeks, was cancelled due mainly to the startling psychological changes being exhibited by all participants.

Like Milgram, Philip Zimbardo was met with criticism and challenges to the ethics of his study. What the study did seem to provide, however, was great insight into the powerful roles groups can have on our behavior. It also serves as an example of a phenomenon known as *deindividuation*, or the loss of individuality that accompanies immersion in a group. Following the conclusion of Zimbardo's experiment, guards and prisoners reported becoming so absorbed by the roles they had been given that they at times forgot they were volunteers. Their roles became their reality.

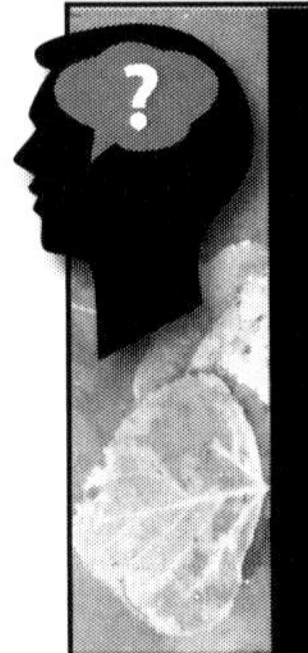

Think about it – Deindividuation has been used to explain violent acts committed by humans. Do you believe this is a sufficient explanation for such behavior?

What other variables need be considered?

REFERENCES

Asch, S. E. (1951). Effects of group pressure upon the modification and distortion of judgment. In H. Guetzkow (Ed.), *Groups, leadership and men*. Pittsburgh: Carnegie Press.

Festinger, L. A., & Carlsmith, L. M. (1959). Cognitive consequences of forced compliance. *Journal of Abnormal and Social Psychology*, 58, 203–210.

Milgram, S. (1963). Behavioral study of obedience. *Journal of Abnormal and Social Psychology*, 67, 371–378.

Milgram, S. (1974). *Obedience to authority: An experimental view*. New York: Harper and Row.

Zimbardo, P. G. (1972). Pathology of imprisonment. *Society*, 9, 4–8.

NAME ______________________________ DATE ____________________

WORKSHEET CHAPTER THIRTEEN

CHAPTER 14

DOING PSYCHOLOGY

"My psychology belongs to everyone."
— Alfred Adler

Having participated in a book of this sort has hopefully brought up many questions for you about psychology, its history and future, as well as its many fields of study. A comprehensive understanding of the field of psychology is expectedly a life-long undertaking. However, assembling a basic idea about psychology is a goal within reach. While subjects are surveyed, activities understood, final exams mastered, and material pored over, students often want more from an introductory psychology course or a book like this.

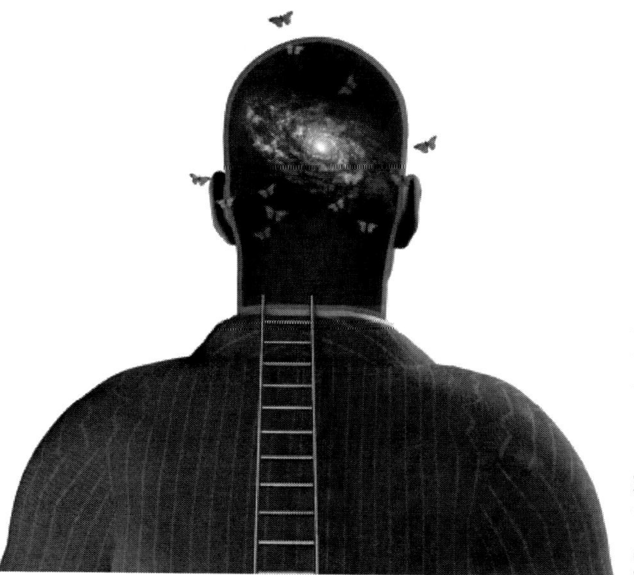

Semester after semester and year after year some students, following the course final and finding themselves sufficiently seduced by the material, have their curiosity so piqued that they are impelled to act. Their first step is again and again a muddled, casual set of questions. These inquiries are by and large based in the student's contemplation of a career in psychology and usually centered on a counseling or clinical path. They have questions about graduate school, career placement, research requirements, clinical internships, specialties, salary, and time commitment to such an occupation.

The authors here, having taught undergraduate psychology courses for many years, have found that fulfilling these inquiring students' curiosity in any constructive way very much requires a more lengthy conversation, clarifications of the reasons behind the questions, a debunking of myths, a description of graduate programs and appropriate undergraduate preparation for such, and a clarification of what psychologists, in a multiplicity of disciplines, *actually do* day in and day out.

Although our responses, reactions, and reflective, clarifying questions are themselves more often a repeat of material covered in the course than not, it is not necessarily a student's misunderstanding or lack of attention but rather a curiosity about the applied, nuanced nature of an actual career in psychology. They want to know what it is *really* like to be a psychologist. An impossible query to address fully, our approach is habitually one of humble referral. We offer this final chapter not to more fully answer these inquiries but to offer ideas about where to look, what questions to ask and to whom, to clarify a bit about what psychology is and what it is not, and what graduate school will look like. Our advice to students concerning their interest in the career of the psychologist, distilled into its most simple form is: *You're off to a great start. Go find out.*

WHAT PSYCHOLOGY IS AND WHAT IT IS NOT

Psychology is a hard term to pin down in its exact reference and intention. Claims that it is the study of behavior and claims that it is the study of the mind are each valid though *behavior* and *mind* are very different notions all together. Think back to Chapter 1. What did you conclude was a good definition of psychology?

In the first volume of the *British Journal of Psychology*, James Ward (1904) offered that psychology is the "science of internal experience as observed through the inner sense, and so is sharply contrasted, though otherwise coordinate, with the sciences of external experience" (p. 15). A more current definition offered by the British Psychological Society contends that psychology is the scientific study of people, the mind and behavior (2011). The American Psychological Association offers a more clinical perspective in that, "Psychology is a doctoral-level profession," and "psychologists study both normal and abnormal functioning and treat patients with mental and emotional problems" (2011). While these organizations do not necessarily disagree with each other's definition of their shared field of study, they do offer such descriptions that could lead a student in many directions.

Whether its purpose is academic or clinical, *psychology* seems best described as the scientific pursuit of understanding the behavior and mental processes of organisms. To study psychology is to understand these divergences and complications. It is to understand that there are many psychologists in numerous disciplines working in various distinctive roles. It is also important to understand some common false impressions about psychology. A variety of these are listed below. Can you think of others?

Psychology and Psychiatry

Psychiatry is a distinctive branch of medicine that deals with the diagnosis and treatment of mental disorders. A *psychiatrist* is the practitioner of psychiatry and has a medical degree such as an MD (doctor of medicine) or DO (doctor of osteopathic medicine). Like a gynecologist is a medical doctor who specializes in diseases of the female reproductive system or an oncologist is a medical doctor who specializes in tumors and malignant diseases like cancer, a psychiatrist is a medical doctor who specializes in mental illness. Like psychiatrists, psychologists can be referred to as a doctor (they likely have a doctorate degree); however, psychologists do not require a medical doctorate but rather a PhD (doctor of philosophy) or PsyD (doctor of psychology). Although the terms psychiatrist and psychologist are often used interchangeably (they do quite often work together to treat a patient), their roles are actually quite distinct. Psychologists do not have a medical degree and are not as tied to the diagnosis and treatment of mental illness as psychiatrists.

Psychology as a Science

While there is an abundance of *pseudoscience* (a belief or practice that claims to be scientific but which does not utilize scientific means), psychology itself has firm roots in proper scientific methodology.

Psychology as Common Sense

Many people, both educated and uneducated, recognize psychology to be something it is not. Even those working in a related field are not immune and have ideas of psychology that are clearly not accurate. In a survey of close to 1,000 members of the American Association of Marriage and Family Therapists, Yapko (1994) found that:

- More than half agreed with the statement *hypnosis can be used to recover memories from as far back as birth.*
- Nearly one third agreed that *the mind is like a computer, accurately recording events that actually occurred.*
- Nearly one in four agreed that *someone's feeling certain about a memory means the memory is likely to be correct.*

Although the statements Yapko used in his survey might seem like widespread "common sense," they are known by psychological science to be unmistakably false. Why then do these ideas persist?

Psychology and the Couch

Although close to 90 percent of psychologists work in the clinical, counseling, and school disciplines, the pervasive social idea of what it means to be a clinical or counseling psychologist often involves lying on the couch and talking about one's problems (U.S. Department of Labor, 2011). Psychologists work in an assortment of disciplines other than clinical and counseling psychology (experimental, cognitive, developmental, education, engineering, forensic, health, sports, neuropsychology, research, industrial/organizational, rehabilitation) and draw on a variety of perspectives (biological, cognitive, behavioral, evolutionary, humanistic).

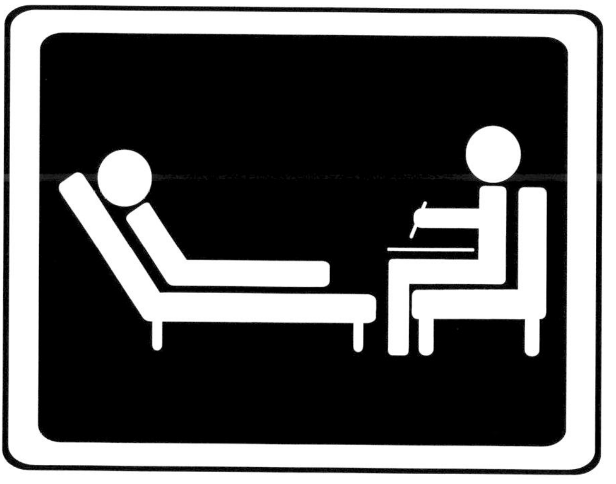

Psychology as Self-Help

While most psychologists, regardless of whether they are in the direct practice of helping people, have a doctoral education emphasizing the scientific method and research toward the betterment of people's lives, self-help books like many found in most large bookstores, while repeatedly using language that suggests otherwise, are very often not rooted in such research and/or scientific methods.

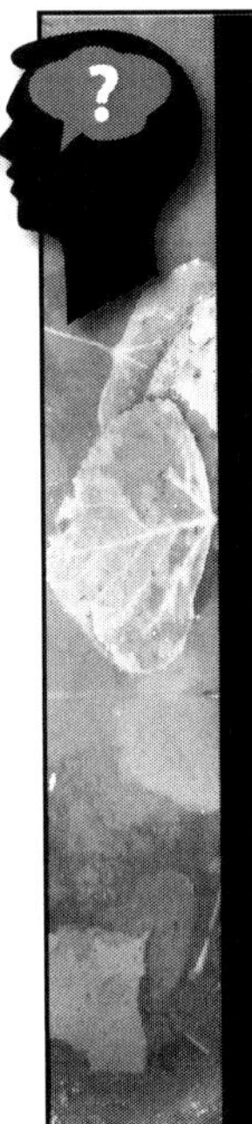

Think about it – Self-help books represent a multimillion-dollar industry and can be found, in some form, in nearly every bookstore and library.

What is the difference between psychology and self-help? Why are they often seen as the same? Why is it easy for many to confuse the two?

What are the possible harmful effects of self-help books that seem to ignore or give no mention of psychological research?

Finally, why do you think self-help books sell much more than psychology books?

TYPES OF PSYCHOLOGY AND PSYCHOLOGISTS

We have skimmed over and labeled different fields of study and practice within the realm of the psychologist. Below is a summary of some different fields and the psychologist's role within.

Clinical/Counseling Psychology. While clinical psychologists have been traditionally employed in medical settings, there has been a movement away from distinguishing between the clinical and the counseling psychologist. Both the clinical and the counseling psychologist work with patients to reduce the suffering they are reporting.

They work to diagnose mental illness, if applicable, and to reduce its impact on the patient's life. They also seek a contextual understanding of patients and their problems, seek to minimize or manage cognitive, emotional, and behavioral problems, and often specialize in supervision and training of other counselors.

Neuropsychology. Neuropsychologists look at the relationship between the brain and behavior. Because behavior is an exceptionally sensitive indicator of the function of the brain, neuropsychologists are educated in the specific measurements of such behavior so to draw conclusions about the function of a patient's brain and further how to help those with damage, injury, or disorders in the brain.

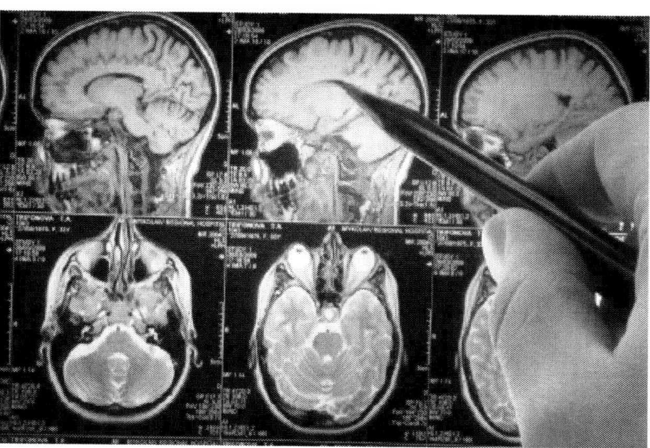

Sports Psychology. Sports psychologists work with athletes to improve their performance and motivation as well as to help them deal with the demands of both competition and extensive training. They can also assist coaches, referees, and trainers to deal with similar demands as well as with health-care workers to effectively disseminate programs to help patients maintain physically healthy behaviors.

Educational/School Psychology. Educational psychologists work mainly with children and adolescents in school-based settings. They employ their skills with these children and/or with their parents and teachers to assess, diagnose, and treat learning difficulties/disabilities, social, and emotional problems.

Comparative Psychology. Comparative psychologists work with non-human animals and attempt to understand their behaviors and mental processes. These psychologists work to understand the complexities of not only animals' behavior but also their development, maturation, learning, and relationships within their own species and among others, especially the human species.

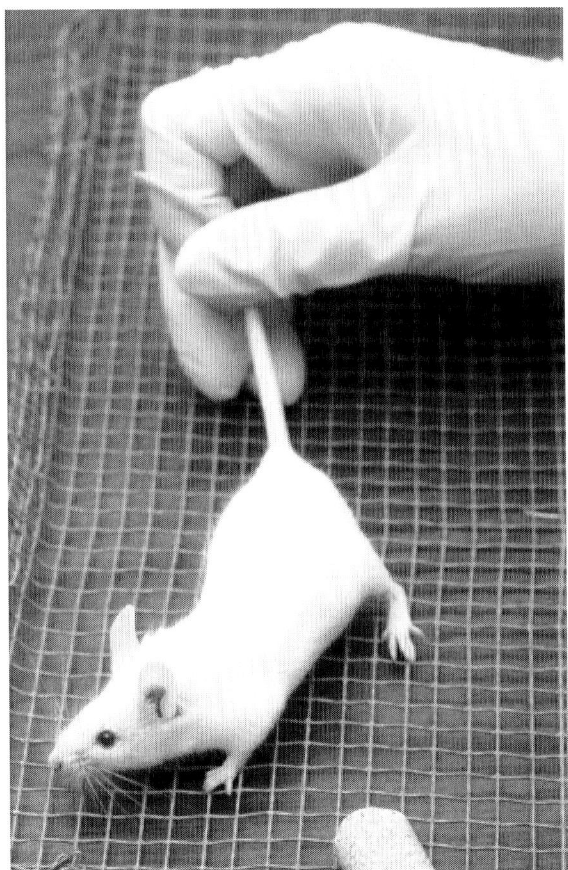

Developmental Psychology. Developmental psychologists work to understand the systematic changes that occur in human beings over the course of their life span. Usually employed with universities, these psychologists employ a variety of research (quantitative and qualitative designs) to build a more accurate framework for appreciating the development of thinking, emotion, sexuality, morals, social relationships, and intelligence over time.

Industrial/Organizational Psychology. Industrial/Ooganizational psychologists apply psychological principles to the work setting. They work with organizations to maximize their growth, profit, worker performance, and human resources. They work heavily with survey methods, training programs, and employ research strategies to help employers in order take full advantage of their resources and avoid waste.

Forensic Psychology. Forensic psychologists apply psychological principles to and within the legal system. They study criminal law extensively and seek to understand criminal behavior. They are heavily versed in psychological research to be able to make recommendations for how to decrease the scope and severity of active criminal behavior. These psychologists are also frequently involved in the evaluation of a witness and/or jury member as well as in evaluations of child custody.

SO YOU WANT TO BE A PSYCHOLOGIST

Psychology degrees have become one of the most popular undergraduate choices at colleges around the world. The U.S. Department of Education indicates that the number of undergraduate psychology degrees awarded by American colleges has increased 242 percent, from 38,187 in 1970 to 92,587 in 2008. To put this in perspective, the average increase for all undergraduate degrees over the same span of time and across all fields of study was around 185 percent (2009). Psychology is on the rise for many reasons.

Whether a desire to learn about one's self or others, a psychology degree can be an enticing topic. Psychology is a newer science relative to the likes of biology and physics and the topics and types of work described in introductory courses are alluring to future job seekers. Psychology can also be a springboard to graduate work in many fields like business, medicine, military studies, social work, and law. Its abundant specialties offer many opportunities for study as well as to make a difference in the lives of others.

A bachelor's degree in psychology usually takes four years of full-time study to complete. Students pursuing a psychology degree take individual, specific courses in developmental, cognitive, abnormal, biological, personality, social, historical, and experimental psychology. At the bachelor's level, graduates work much less in the clinical realms such as counseling or clinical psychology. Their focus is often in legal systems, market research, business, childcare, teaching/education, or working in roles supportive of counselors, psychologists, and psychiatrists.

Again, the job of the psychologist is a doctoral-level position. Many people with a plan to complete a bachelor's degree in psychology will at some point consider a graduate-level education. This involves the pursuit of a master's degree, a doctoral degree, or both. While the decision to go to graduate school is exciting, the wide field of training programs and degrees can be daunting. In these authors' experience, students who plan graduate school after completing a psychology undergraduate degree are looking to expand their career options and potential for advancement in a variety of psychology-related fields. Again, given the variety of fields of psychology study outlined in this text and in this chapter, students can find the selection of training programs and types of degree overwhelming. While graduate study is stressful, expensive, and time consuming, most graduate students we have come across report it as a gratifying experience and well worth their effort.

An excellent text for any aspiring psychologist student is Mayne, Norcoss, and Sayette's *Insider's Guide to Graduate Programs in Clinical and Counseling Psychology* (2011).

MASTER OR DOCTOR?

As we mentioned before, graduate school is expensive and quite a commitment of time and resources. It is also very often competitive and demanding. Students admitted to a graduate program typically have a grade point average of above 3.25, and graduate schools admit a significantly lower number of students than undergraduates. If you are thinking of continuing your study of psychology, thus thinking of graduate school, you should give these circumstances your utmost consideration. The decision that lies ahead of you is which degree to pursue, the master's or the doctorate?

A *master's degree* is a degree that usually involves two to three years of study and should be considered a minimum requirement for an undertaking of psychology as a career. The most common degrees in psychology are the Master of Arts (MA) and the Master of Science (MS). The distinctions are easily understood but are often slight. Each degree is similar in its time commitment and academic standards of performance, the MS emphasizing research and statistics and the MA emphasizing liberal arts. Job opportunities are more abundant at the master's level and also more inclusive of clinical or applied positions with direct patient contact. These graduates find themselves working in mental health, university, or corporate counseling centers, in social services departments alongside social workers, in a corporate setting with a human resources or market research department adjacent business leaders, and in clinics/hospitals alongside physicians, nurses, and psychologists.

Clinical jobs at the master's and doctorate level are almost always regulated by the state and thus require a license to practice. Although the states differ somewhat in their requirements for licensure, most of them require a graduate degree from an accredited institution. These applied, clinical jobs are ordinarily similar to each other but bear some important distinctions. If your goal is to work directly with clients in a clinical sense, you should be looking for training programs with an active accreditation by their respective field and make sure that this accreditation is accepted by the state in which you plan to practice and, for good measure, by most others as well.

A *doctorate degree* is a degree that usually involves three to five years of post-masters education and is the highest degree that can be obtained in psychology and most fields of study. The most common doctoral degrees held by psychologists are the Doctor of Philosophy (PhD) and the Doctor of Psychology (PsyD).

An important distinction to understand here is the one between fields of study/practice. The accrediting organization for psychologists (clinical, counseling, and school) is the American Psychological Association (APA).

While there are many psychology programs in which one can receive a master's degree, take note that the APA considers the role of the psychologist a doctoral level position and thus *does not* accredit master's level programs.

Further, there is an assortment of doctoral programs across the United States offering degrees in counseling, clinical, or general psychology; however, not all are APA accredited. If you're seeking a career as a *licensed* psychologist, it is best to seek a program with an active APA accreditation. In addition, most states protect the term psychologist and forbid its use unless the person is specifically licensed in that state. Having an APA accreditation helps to ensure a minimal level of quality of training. A full list of these criterion can be found at the APA's website (www.apa.org/ed/accreditation).

HOW TO GET GOING

A constructive academic foundation for a beginning psychology student is a complex set of academic and personal ventures wrought with choices. While a favorable undergraduate education in psychology is a great start, there are subtleties worthy of extended consideration.

First, the student should seek to understand logical and scientific processes. Planning a graduate education and/or career in psychology should include courses outside of psychology that help them to think logically and critically as well as scientifically. Courses like biology, statistics, chemistry, physics, and mathematics are particularly helpful for many reasons. These courses help the psychologist to see the world for how it is and give important insight into the causes of and relationships between often quite subtle conditions. They help psychologists to understand the biological, electrical, and chemical characteristics of the brain's functioning. These courses also help the psychologist to think analytically as well as to use the basic statistics and research methods so vital to the field's evolution.

Second, a student should seek an understanding of human motivation. Planning a graduate education and psychology career working with human beings will certainly be more prolific and successful if the student is conscious of human emotion, need, motivation, and spirituality. The student should take courses in history, literature, religion, art, sociology, animal behavior, anthropology, music, and education for a variety of reasons. In many ways, the psychologist seeks to help people move from the role of passive recipient and/or victim of illness or circumstance into that of the full participant, active in the reconstruction of his or her lives. These courses empower psychologists with an immense ability to think critically about the status quo so to make positive changes in the lives of their clients and in their communities. They also seek to aid the psychologist in understanding clients of all ages in their historical and cultural context. Finally, these types of courses help the psychologist comprehend the complex interplay between permanence and change, to make sense of challenging problems that result from such interplay, and to clarify the origin and development of ideas and social discourse that affect the mental health of their patients.

Third, an aspiring student should seek contact and conversation with a professional. Whether the decision is to become a social worker, counselor, family therapist, or psychologist, a student should begin a course of inquiry and request in-person, real-time interviews (be very sure you are prepared!). Students should then hunt for details about the nuances of the job and how other psychologists experienced their own professional development. Ask interesting, central questions:

> *What would you do differently? What is a typical day like for you? What type of psychologist are you? How did you obtain your goals? How do you stay good at what you do? What advice do you have for students of my generation? How would you recommend going about deciding on a field in psychology? What questions should I be asking myself? With the experience and interest I have, which psychology career do you think I would enjoy the most?*

Finally, and arguably most importantly, aspiring psychologists who are interested in direct client care must be emotionally stable and mature. Further, they must be able to deal effectively with people in different phases or disruption of development, disability, emotion, crisis, and thought. Psychologists are intelligent and compassionate with abilities to lead and inspire others. They are compassionate when others are not. Psychologists are both academically and clinically oriented seeking first to improve the lives of others. Finally, psychologists are skilled in the subtle conceptualization, diagnosis, and navigation of mental health and social problems, and independently oriented toward research and ongoing professional development.

© Sychugina, 2011. Used under license of Shutterstock, Inc.

Ask Yourself and Ask Around – In the spirit of your participation in this interactive text as well as our own personal ongoing interest and experience, the authors here urge all students interested in a career in psychology to conduct a thorough self-examination. Take stock of your needs, motivations, desires, expectations, and career aspirations as well as your work ethic, experiences as a student, and academic abilities.

© Bruce Rolff, 2011. Used under license of Shutterstock, Inc.

Never can a perfect or even ample list of appropriate considerations be devised especially given the abundance and multiplicity of students and psychology teachers. However, and again in the spirit of an interactive text, we offer one final activity.

Now that you've participated in this interactive text, you perhaps have a unique perspective given the following questions. Write down your answers and compare them to your fellow student's. Compare your answers to the answers of a student who has never taken a psychology course. Compare your answers with a teacher, a friend, a family member, or colleague. *What do you notice?*

In ten words or less, give your newly educated *opinion* of the following:

- Psychology is ____ ____________________.

(continued)

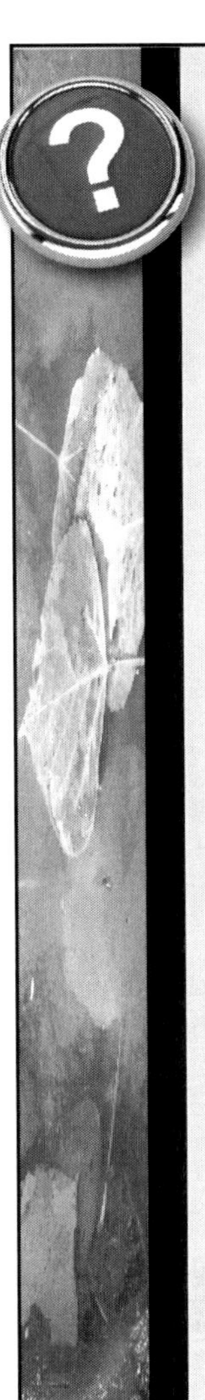

Ask Yourself and Ask Around (*continued*)

- What *does* the ____________________ psychologist do?

- The psychologist/historical figure in psychology I found myself most interested in was ______ ______________________________ because s/he ______________________________.

- What is the *right* reason to become a psychologist? The *wrong* reason?

- If you were to become a psychologist, which career path would you choose? Why?

- What do you think would be your biggest strength as a _______________ psychologist?

- If you could do research and adequately address in your results one significant problem facing psychologists today what would it be?

- On the road to becoming a psychologist, the biggest roadblock in my way will be my ______ ______________________________.

- Working through this interactive text has ______________________________________ ______________________.

REFERENCES

American Psychological Assocation. (2011). *Definition of "psychology."* Retrieved March 2011 from www.apa.org/about/index.aspx

British Psychological Society. (2011). *About psychology and the Society.* Retrieved from www.bps.org.uk/the-society/about-psychology-and-the-society/about-psychology-and-the-society_home.cfm

Mayne, T. J., Norcross, J. C., & Sayette, M. A. (2010). Insider's guide to graduate programs in clinical and counseling psychology (2010-2011 edition). New York: Guilford.

U.S. Department of Education, National Center for Education Statistics. (2009). Higher Education General Information Survey. Retrieved from http://nces.ed.gov/programs/digest/d09/tables/dt09_271.asp

U.S. Department of Labor. (2011) *Bureau of Labor Statistics Occupational Outlook Handbook,* 2010-11, Washington, DC: USDL. Edition.

Ward, J. (1904). On the definition of psychology. *British Journal of Psychology, 1*, 3–25.

Yapko, M. D. (1994). Suggestibility and repressed memories of abuse: A survey of psychotherapists' beliefs. *American Journal of Clinical Hypnosis, 36*(3), 163–171.